ARISTOTLE'S *Nicomachean Ethics*

ARISTOTLE'S
Nicomachean Ethics

⊙ ⊙

TRANSLATED, WITH AN
INTERPRETIVE ESSAY,
NOTES, AND GLOSSARY BY
ROBERT C. BARTLETT AND
SUSAN D. COLLINS

⊙ ⊙ ⊙ ⊙ ⊙ ⊙ ⊙ ⊙ ⊙ ⊙ ⊙ ⊙ ⊙ ⊙

The University of Chicago Press
CHICAGO AND LONDON

The University of Chicago Press, Chicago 60637
The University of Chicago Press, Ltd., London
Paperback edition 2012
Printed in the United States of America

20 19 18 17 16 15 14 13 12   5 6

ISBN-13: 978-0-226-02674-9 (cloth)
ISBN-13: 978-0-226-02675-6 (paper)
ISBN-10: 0-226-02674-4 (cloth)
ISBN-10: 0-226-02675-2 (paper)

Library of Congress Cataloging-in-Publication Data

Aristotle
[Nicomachean ethics. English. 2011]
Aristotle's Nicomachean ethics / translated,
with an interpretive essay, notes, and glossary by
Robert C. Bartlett and Susan D. Collins.
p.   cm.
Includes bibliographical references and index.
ISBN-13: 978-0-226-02674-9 (hardcover : alk.
paper)
ISBN-10: 0-226-02674-4 (hardcover : alk.
paper) I. Ethics—Early works to 1800.
I. Bartlett, Robert C., 1964–   II. Collins,
Susan D., 1960–   III. Title.
B430.A5B37 2011
171'.3—dc22

2010041424

♾ This paper meets the requirements of ANSI/NISO
Z39.48-1992 (Permanence of Paper)

CONTENTS

INTRODUCTION

"Aristotle was born, spent his life in philosophizing, and died."[1] So begins a justly famous lecture on the philosophy of Aristotle. The point of the remark is clear: that Aristotle was a philosopher is the single most important fact about him; all other biographical details, to say nothing of matters of mere happenstance, vanish in comparison. Yet students turning to Aristotle for the first time cannot know what it means to be a philosopher, and so it is probably worthwhile to learn something more about the man — if only as a first step on the long road to discovering for oneself what sort of a human being this "lover of wisdom" is, the "philosopher."

Such knowledge of Aristotle's life as we have stems from sources both numerous and inconsistent, even contradictory. The rough consensus is about as follows. Aristotle was of course a Greek, born in 384 BCE in the northern city of Stagira to Nicomachus and Phaestis, Nicomachus then being court physician to King Amyntas III of Macedon.[2] At the age of seventeen or so, Aristotle traveled to Athens, *the* center of learning in the Greek world — the "school of Greece," as Pericles put it[3] — and there he became a pupil of the philosopher Plato. Indeed, Aristotle was to re-

---

1 · "Many, many years ago, I attended a series of lectures on Aristotle's philosophy. The lecturer began his exposition as follows: 'As regards Aristotle himself, as regards the circumstances and the course of his life, suffice it to say: Aristotle was born, spent his life in philosophizing, and died.'" Jacob Klein, "Aristotle: An Introduction," in *Lectures and Essays*, ed. Robert B. Williamson and Elliott Zuckerman (Annapolis, MD: St. John's College Press, 1985), p. 171.

2 · See, e.g., Diogenes Laertius, *Lives of the Eminent Philosophers* 5.1. The extant biographical sources are collected in Ingemar Düring, *Aristotle in the Ancient Biographical Tradition* (Göteborg: Universitets Arsskrift, 1957).

3 · Thucydides, *The War of the Peloponnesians and Athenians* 2.41.1.

main at Plato's side at the Academy for some twenty years, until 347, when he was prompted to leave either by rising anti-Macedonian sentiment in Athens that made it impossible for the Stagirite to remain or, perhaps, by Plato's death.[4] At all events, it is certain that Aristotle thus forms a link in what must be the most impressive chain of great thinkers the world has ever seen: Aristotle was the student of Plato, who was in turn the student of Socrates. That the constellations were once so aligned as to produce three great philosophers in close succession and in the same locale is astonishing; that written accounts survive of their thoughts and deeds is one of fate's most generous blessings.

Upon leaving Athens, Aristotle eventually made his way to the court of Philip II of Macedon, where, according to a widespread but by no means certain tradition, he became the principal tutor of young Alexander, who had not yet become Great but soon would.[5] Shortly after the death of Philip and the accession of Alexander, Aristotle returned to Athens, in 335–34, enabled to do so (as some accounts have it) because he had persuaded Alexander to treat Athens mildly in the aftermath of the Macedonian conquest of Greece. Once there, Aristotle founded his own school at the Lyceum, a meeting place and gymnasium named in honor of the god Apollo Lyceus. His students came to be known as "Peripatetics," though there is some uncertainty as to the meaning of the name. It is clearly related to the Greek verb *peripatein*, to walk or stroll about, and may therefore allude to Aristotle's reported habit of offering instruction while walking with his students.[6] Or the term may simply refer to the covered courtyard or colonnade (*peripatos*) found among the buildings making up the school. In any case, Aristotle taught and wrote in Athens for about a dozen years, until 323, when he was brought up on charges of impiety,[7] just as his intellectual grandfather Socrates had been some seventy-five years before. Unlike Socrates, however, Aristotle chose to flee Athens and

---

4 · Anton-Hermann Chroust argues that political tensions alone were responsible for Aristotle's departure: see "Aristotle Leaves the Academy," in *Aristotle: New Light on His Life and on Some of His Lost Works* (Notre Dame, IN: University of Notre Dame Press, 1973), 1:117–24.

5 · For arguments debunking the claim that Aristotle was Alexander's teacher, a claim that can be traced to no close contemporary of Aristotle's but only to relatively late sources, see Anton-Hermann Chroust, "Was Aristotle Actually the Chief Preceptor of Alexander the Great?" in *Aristotle*, 1:125–32.

6 · Diogenes Laertius, *Lives* 5.2.

7 · See, e.g., ibid., 5.5–6 and Athenaeus, *The Deipnosophists* 696a–b.

so to prevent it from "erring against philosophy a second time," as he is said to have said.[8] He died in Chalcis, on the island of Euboea, in 322.

Not all of Aristotle's works survive, but those that do run to more than twenty volumes in a standard Greek-English edition. The range of subjects covered by those works is astounding—from logic and rhetoric, to morals and politics, to biology and physics, to "metaphysics," what Aristotle himself referred to as "first philosophy." In brief, Aristotle took as his proper study the whole world, or the world as a whole, from the subhuman (plants and animals), to the human (moral and political life), to the suprahuman (the cosmos), including the nature of being itself.

There are four extant writings attached to Aristotle's name that deal with right action and matters of character, that is, with "ethics": the *Eudemian Ethics, Nicomachean Ethics, Magna Moralia*, and *Virtues and Vices*. It is relatively easy to see that the *Nicomachean Ethics* deserves its privileged place among them. For almost all scholars regard the *Virtues and Vices* as spurious, and a good many doubt the authenticity of the *Magna Moralia*.[9] While this certainly does not mean that one cannot learn from these works, only a long and tendentious argument could hope to establish that they properly form a part of the study of Aristotle. As for the *Eudemian Ethics*, it is widely agreed to be from the hand of Aristotle but seems to be a less polished, perhaps earlier, version of the *Nicomachean Ethics*.[10] The text of the latter as it has come down to us

---

8 · See, e.g., Aelian, *Varia Historia* 3.36 as well as Düring, *Aristotle in the Ancient Biographical Tradition*, 341–42.

9 · For a helpful overview of the scholarly controversies concerning the authenticity and rank of the "four extant Peripatetic ethical treatises," see C. J. Rowe, *The Eudemian and Nicomachean Ethics: A Study in the Development of Aristotle's Thought* (Cambridge: Cambridge University Press, 1971), 9–14. More or less recent attempts to place the *Magna Moralia* in the Aristotelian corpus—as a work of Aristotle's youth or perhaps of his late maturity, or as a posthumously edited treatise—include John Cooper, "The *Magna Moralia* and Aristotle's Moral Philosophy," in *Schriften zur aristotelischen Ethik*, ed. C. Müller-Goldingen (Hidelsheim: G. Olms, 1988), 311–33; and Pierre Pellegrin, "Préliminaires," in *Les Grand Livres d'Éthique*, trans. Catherine Dalimier (Paris: Arlea, 1992), 9–26.

10 · C. J. Rowe, *Eudemian and Nicomachean Ethics*, contends that the "philosophical inferiority" of the *Eudemian* to the *Nicomachean Ethics* is "almost universally accepted" (10n1). Anthony Kenny has argued that the *Nicomachean* is the earlier of the two texts: see *The Aristotelian Ethics: A Study of the Relationship between the Eudemian and Nicomachean Ethics of Aristotle* (Oxford: Oxford University Press, 1978). For similarities and differences between the two works, consult the invaluable commentary of

comprises ten "books," each divided into a number of chapters, though these divisions are presumably the work of later editors. Its title (which Aristotle himself never uses) is derived from the name that both Aristotle's son and father bore, Nicomachus; the title may either refer to the former, perhaps as editor of the text, or pay homage to the latter: no one is certain. But it is certain that the *Nicomachean Ethics* is a carefully organized and cohesive work that Aristotle presents as the first of his two-part "philosophy of human affairs," an inquiry he completes in the *Politics*: each book refers to the other, and so together they form an extended whole, intended to be such by their author.[11]

What part, then, does the *Ethics* play in this "philosophy of human affairs"? As Aristotle himself notes, the question at the heart of his book is of "great weight" for human beings: what is the human good, or—it turns out to be the same question—what is happiness? This concern for the human good that we hope constitutes our happiness will at some point grip every human heart and is always at work in our doings and strivings. For happiness (*eudaimonia*: literally "having a good daimon") signifies more than mere sentiment or feeling, more than the pleasure of the moment or even of a series of satisfied desires. *Eudaimonia*, we can say for now, encompasses the excellence specific to human beings as human beings—what Aristotle famously calls "virtue" (*aretē*). Such virtue, moreover, can be identified only in relation to the activity and hence the way of life that are best for human beings as such, as the kind of beings we are. For Aristotle, then, the question of how to be happy is the question of how to live well as a human being, and living well is inseparable from attaining the virtue or virtues that make possible the best activity. In addition, because human beings are always found in some sort of community with one another, Aristotle's inquiry into the best life requires his dual investigations into human affairs: the *Nicomachean Ethics*, which examines the human good while acknowledging at the outset the claim of the political community, and the *Politics*, which examines the political community while acknowledging in the end the priority of the (suprapolitical) human good.

Michael Woods in his *"Eudemian Ethics" Books I, II, and VIII*, 2nd ed. (Oxford: Clarendon Press, 1992).

11 · See *Nicomachean Ethics* 10.9, especially 1181b12–23; *Politics* 1261a30–31, 1280a16–20, 1295a36–37, 1332a7–10.

In our time, a chorus of voices may here protest, if not in unison then in perfect harmony: there *is* no single greatest human good or best way of life! Everybody now knows that nobody knows what *the* good life is! To undergraduate freshman and sophisticated scholar alike, this view of things is mother's milk, which means that the average freshman is superior, in the most important respect and without lifting a finger, to Aristotle himself. According to the prevailing view, the individual's good is necessarily "subjective"; it is "relative," relative to the tastes and inclinations of this or that individual. And because we can know not the good but only the fact of its "subjectivity" and "relativity," each of us really has no alternative but to pursue happiness according to whichever opinions of it propel us onward, while tolerating or celebrating as much as possible the differing opinions of others. Some such claim of the relative or unknowable character of the good or good life constitutes the orthodoxy of our time; it is for us the chief product of the modern political-philosophic revolt from ancient thought in general and from Aristotle in particular.

So it is that a good many readers who approach the *Ethics* for the first time today understandably bring with them the conviction, or the hunch, that Aristotle's project is impossible. "Interesting," maybe, but impossible. Yet such readers must admit, at least to themselves, that they have not conducted a full inquiry into the question. They must admit that they are guided less by knowledge than by sanctioned opinion, or by inherited prejudice, in a matter whose importance goes well beyond the proper approach to an old book.

To such readers we offer a couple of observations that may encourage in them a new sort of open-mindedness to the inquiry into human happiness that is central to this work. First, the implication that we moderns, or postmoderns, are the first to have glimpsed the truth about "the good," and hence that Aristotle lived in naive obliviousness to "value relativism," is simply untrue. For Aristotle proceeds in full awareness of a version of relativism more radical and perhaps more impressive than our own. The relativism known to Aristotle can be traced at least as far back as the pre-Socratic thinker Heraclitus and is crystallized in a pithy saying of the great Sophist Protagoras: "human being is the measure"—the "measure," that is, "of the things that are, that they are; of the things that are not, that they are not."[12] As this saying can be and indeed was interpreted, our very

12 · Plato, *Theaetetus* 152a2–4.

perception of the beings—the things in the world "out there"—is wholly dependent on, because nothing more than the experience of, the perceiving individual; such perception is in no way a reliable access to the objective world. And what applies to the beings applies equally to what we hold to be just or unjust, good or bad, that is, to all of our deepest moral convictions: they exist, so to speak, only in the element of transitory opinion. At the beginning of the *Ethics*, as it happens, Aristotle states a troubling consequence of just this view: if there is no knowable good or end in accord with which human beings can order their lives, then all human longing is finally "empty and pointless."[13] But even in the shadow of this unsettling thought, which he does not here refute or even quite reject, Aristotle presses on, for the question of our good or happiness is too important to presuppose an answer, any answer, to it. Aristotle's great familiarity with "relativism," then, for some reason did not lead him to abandon his inquiry into the human good. Is it obvious that our relativism grants us the license to forgo such an inquiry for ourselves?

Second, Aristotle's tough-minded determination to get to the bottom of things is connected with another of his opening observations: every political community, he argues, supplies us with an authoritative answer to the question of the human good. The political art is "architectonic" regarding this good: it orders the arts and sciences as well as human action, bringing to bear on all these its considerable educative power and deploying to that end the full array of means at its disposal, persuasive as well as coercive. And since every human being is raised in a particular political community, he or she is fundamentally shaped by that community's view of the good and of good action; our opinions about good and bad, noble and base, just and unjust will, to begin with, reflect that overarching communal view. But here too, even in the face of the political community's impressive power—in the face of the prevailing moral orthodoxy that every thriving community will promote—Aristotle presses on: his own inquiry into the good is "a sort of political inquiry," he notes in passing; but this amounts to saying that he does *not* accept the political community's "authoritative" answer to the question of the good life that is given to or

---

13 · Or to recall the argument of one of Aristotle's liveliest modern critics, Hobbes, "there is no *Finis ultimus* (utmost aim) nor *Summum Bonum* (greatest good) as is spoken of in the books of the old moral philosophers," and hence happiness is but "a continual progress of the desire, from one object to another," a desire after desire, as he also notes, that ceases only in death. Thomas Hobbes, *Leviathan*, ed. Edwin Curley (Indianapolis: Hackett, 1994), chap. 11.1–2. See also *Nicomachean Ethics* 1094b14–19.

imposed on all citizens. To judge by Aristotle's deeds in the *Ethics*, we too must investigate the human good so that we may know, with the greatest possible independence, the truth of the matter—including, of course, whether no truth in the matter is finally available to human beings.

Against the odds, then, Aristotle's *Nicomachean Ethics* can be both compelling and liberating for modern readers. The *Ethics* has at its heart the most important human question, and, to repeat, it acknowledges the power of authoritative political opinion even as it refuses, with all due politic reserve, to bow to it. Its inquiry is complex, beginning from and examining the common opinions about happiness, considering at length those "that are especially prevalent or are held to have a certain reason to them" (1095a29), and culminating in an argument about the simply best life. This investigation must range widely because it encompasses the full scope of human happiness and the various compelling opinions about the matter—opinions about pleasure, honor, and virtue, for example, or about chance, the afterlife, and the gods.

The most celebrated part of the *Ethics* is its investigation of the moral and intellectual virtues that make the most powerful claims to constituting human perfection. Yet the manner of this investigation, as well as much of its substance, will probably strike some readers as perplexing, especially at first. That is as it should be. Why, for example, does a treatise on happiness devote five of its ten books to an examination of moral virtue, in the course of which the very term *happiness* all but disappears? Why in the world are there eleven—not ten and not twelve— moral virtues, and how did Aristotle arrive at these particular ones? And if he wishes us to focus on moral virtue, why does Aristotle devote only one book to justice but two to friendship? How is the problem of happiness connected with intellectual or contemplative virtue, the culminating theme of the *Ethics*, and just how does "prudence" differ from "wisdom"?

These questions rightly demand answers, but the initially perplexed reader can take some solace in the fact that perplexity here may be the product of alertness. And such alertness, together with a sort of toughness, is surely necessary to learn from "the Philosopher." For in the course of his inquiry, Aristotle will challenge some of the guiding opinions, and deepest hopes, of his readers. That the goods at stake are the greatest ones, for anyone who opens the *Nicomachean Ethics* with a desire to learn, is indicated by a characteristic remark concerning friendship: "without friends, no one would wish to live, even if he possessed all other goods" (1155a5). In the pages of the *Ethics*, then, we witness, and gradually become a party to, the hunt for the life that is truly worth living—a life somehow "nobler and more divine" than any we may now know or even conceive of.

The *Nicomachean Ethics* has engaged the interest of serious readers across centuries and civilizations—of peoples ancient and medieval, pagan and Christian, Muslim and Jewish. We remain convinced that it can still engage readers today. For even with the modern assault on ancient thought, the study of Aristotle not only has continued, from his time to our own, but is now even flourishing, as doubts about what has been called the modern "project" continue to deepen. The very great difficulty of Aristotle's work demands of us, it is true, continual study, reflection, and conversation. But—to paraphrase Machiavelli's beautiful praise of the ancient thinkers from whom he learned so much, even as he disagreed with many of their conclusions—readers today who enter the venerable court of Aristotle's Lyceum will find themselves solicitously received there; and if they bring to the *Ethics* the questions they begin to divine are the truly fundamental ones, they will find that Aristotle, in his humanity, will reply.[14]

14 · See Niccolo Machiavelli, letter to Vettori, December 10, 1513, in *Machiavelli and His Friends: Their Personal Correspondence*, ed. James B. Atkinson (Dekalb: Northern Illinois University Press, 2005).

A NOTE ON THE TRANSLATION

This translation of Aristotle's *Nicomachean Ethics* attempts to be as literal as sound English usage permits. We hold that literal translations, while certainly having their limits and even frustrations, nonetheless permit those without a reading knowledge of the original language the best possible access to the text. St. Thomas Aquinas, for example, unable to read a word of Greek, still became a supreme interpreter of Aristotle on the basis of William of Moerbeke's remarkably faithful translations of Greek into Latin, just as Averroes (Ibn Rushd) became "the Commentator" on "the Philosopher" despite having had access to the works of Aristotle only in Arabic translation.

To be sure, we do not claim to have attained such fidelity to the original as did the great medieval translators. What is more, the distance between contemporary English and ancient Greek is often great, and any simple substitution of this English word for that Greek one would result in a largely unintelligible hash, one no longer in Greek but not yet in English either. What, then, do we mean by "literal translation"? We begin from the assumption or prejudice that Aristotle composed the *Ethics* with very great care—whether or not the text we have consists of or is derived from lecture notes—and hence that he chose every word with (as Maimonides would say) "great exactness and exceeding precision." We have attempted to convey that exactness and precision. In practice this means that we have rendered all key terms by what we hold to be the closest English equivalent, resorting to explanatory footnotes when the demands of idiom or intelligibility have made this impossible. Readers may therefore be confident that an appearance of *nature*, for example, is due to the presence of the same Greek word or family of words (*phusis, phuein*) in the original. It hardly needs to be said that the identification of "key terms" and their English counterparts depends finally on the translators' interpretation of Aristotle, on an understanding of his intention. The outlines of that understanding are found in the interpretive essay; the choice of key terms and their equivalents, in the list of Greek terms and the glossary.

Readers will naturally disagree here and there with our choices. But because we have tried to stick to them as consistently as possible, students of the English text can at least observe the contexts in which a given term appears and so begin to determine for themselves its nuances or shades of meaning. We note in this regard that we do not blush to translate *aretē* as "virtue" in all its appearances, despite the fact that it is easy in Greek to speak of the *aretē* of an eye or a horse (1106a17–19) and despite the somewhat stodgy, perhaps even slightly Victorian, sound of *virtue*. *Aretē*, one can say provisionally, "both brings that of which it is the *aretē* into a good condition and causes the work belonging to that thing to be done well" (1106a15–17); it is the chief characteristic of a given type of thing at its peak that also permits or promotes that peak. When Aristotle speaks of the *aretē* of a human being, then, be it in action or in thinking, he does not have in mind the idiosyncratic, let alone relativistic, excellence ("flourishing") peculiar to this or that individual. To the contrary, Aristotle argues that there are eleven and only eleven moral *aretai* characteristic of human beings who act as they ought to act; those human beings with the *aretai* are "serious"; those without them, "base" or "corrupt" or even "wicked." Hence *virtue*.

One exception to strict literalness should be noted in advance. The title of the work contains a form of the word *ēthika*, the plural of the adjective *ēthikon*, which might be rendered as "what pertains to character": *ethics* means the things pertaining to one's character, and it is to these that Aristotle's book is chiefly devoted. In the body of the *Ethics*, however, we have rendered the same adjective, when it modifies *virtue*, not as *ethical* but as *moral*: moral virtue pertains to one's character, itself the product of habit (*ethos*), as distinguished from the virtue of thinking, the product of education and experience (see 2.1, at the beginning). Perfect consistency, then, would demand speaking of either the *Nicomachean Morals* or ethical virtue; but in rendering each as we have, we bowed to the tradition and to more or less ordinary usage.

Aristotle's Greek is notoriously terse or compressed, and where the grammar or meaning of the Greek clearly requires supplying a noun or verb or phrase, we have done so without encumbering the translation with square brackets. We have instead reserved the use of such brackets to indicate the inclusion of words or phrases that in our judgment are required for sense but that are to a greater degree open to interpretation or debate; occasionally, we use square brackets also to note an alternative translation that captures the nuance of a term. In addition to alerting readers to departures from strict consistency or literalness, the notes explain historical and literary allusions and the more important textual difficulties or alternatives; all dates in the notes are BCE.

The translation is based on Ingram Bywater's edition of the Greek text (*Ethica Nicomachea* [Oxford: Clarendon Press, 1894]), although we have frequently consulted and been much aided by the philological studies and textual commentaries cited in the bibliography. The numbers and letters found in the margins of the translation reproduce as closely as possible the standard Bekker pagination, based on his 1831 edition of the works of Aristotle as it appears in Bywater's edition. We refer to books of the *Ethics* and also their chapters by Arabic numerals; these divisions, it should be said, are not due to Aristotle.

Parts of the interpretive essay appeared in earlier versions in Robert C. Bartlett, "Aristotle's Introduction to the Problem of Happiness: On Book I of the *Nicomachean Ethics*," *American Journal of Political Science* 52, no. 3 (July 2008): 677–87; and in the following by Susan D. Collins: "The Moral Virtues in Aristotle's *Nicomachean Ethics*," in *Action and Contemplation: Studies in the Moral and Political Thought of Aristotle*, ed. Robert C. Bartlett and Susan D. Collins, 131–53 (Albany: SUNY Press, 1999); "Moral Virtue and the Limits of the Political Community in Aristotle's *Nicomachean Ethics*," *American Journal of Political Science* 48, no. 1 (January 2004): 47–61; and "Justice as a Virtue," chapter 3 of *Aristotle and the Rediscovery of Citizenship* (New York: Cambridge University Press, 2006), 67–90.

We are grateful to the anonymous reviewers for their invaluable suggestions, as well as to the generous friends who read portions of the translation and suggested many improvements: Wayne Ambler, Christopher Bruell, Eric Buzzetti, Lorna Dawson, Erik Dempsey, Amy Nendza, and Lorraine Pangle. This expression of gratitude does not of course imply their agreement with the choices we ultimately made; still less does it implicate them in the errors and other infelicities that undoubtedly remain. Joshua Bridwell, Matthew Grinney, Jasmine Jenkins, and Robert

Ross aided in the preparation of the manuscript. Thomas Cleveland deserves special thanks for compiling the general index. Robert Bartlett is indebted to the Earhart Foundation and its officers for a summer research grant that permitted him the freedom to complete his contributions to this volume.

BIBLIOGRAPHY

Editions of the Greek Text and English Translations

Apostle, Hippocrates G., ed. and trans. *Nicomachean Ethics*. Dordrecht, Holland: D. Reidel, 1975.

Bekker, Immanuel, ed. *Aristotelis Opera*. 5 vols. Berlin: Walter de Gruyter, 1960 [facsimile of the 1831 ed.].

Broadie, Sarah, and Christopher Rowe. *Nicomachean Ethics*. Oxford: Oxford University Press, 2002.

Burnet, John, ed. *The Ethics of Aristotle*. With an introduction and notes. New York: Arno Press, 1973 [reprint of the 1900 ed.].

Bywater, Ingram. *Ethica Nicomachea*. Oxford: Clarendon Press, 1894.

Crisp, Roger, ed. and trans. *Nicomachean Ethics*. Cambridge: Cambridge University Press, 2000.

Irwin, Terence, ed. and trans. *Nicomachean Ethics*. Indianapolis: Hackett, 1985.

Ostwald, Martin, ed. and trans. *Nicomachean Ethics*. New York: Macmillan / Library of Liberal Arts, 1962.

Pakaluk, Michael, ed. and trans. *"Nicomachean Ethics," Books VIII and IX*. Oxford: Clarendon Press, 1998.

Ross, David, trans. *Nicomachean Ethics*. Revised by J. L. Ackrill and J. O. Urmson. Oxford: Oxford University Press, 1998.

Sachs, Joe, ed. and trans. *Nicomachean Ethics*. Newburyport, MA: Focus Publishing, 2002.

Susemihl, Franz. *Aristotelis Ethica Nicomachea*. Leipzig, 1880.

Taylor, C. C. W., ed. and trans. *"Nicomachean Ethics," Books II–IV*. Oxford: Oxford University Press, 2006.

Telford, Kenneth A., trans. *Aristotle's "Nicomachean Ethics."* Binghamton, NY: Institute of Global Cultural Studies, Binghamton University, 1999.

Thomson, J. A. K., trans. *The "Ethics" of Aristotle*. Revised by Hugh Tredennick. New York: Viking Penguin, 1976.

Commentaries and Philological Studies

Aspasius. *The Earliest Extant Commentary on Aristotle's Ethics*. Edited by Antonina Alberti and R. W. Sharples. Berlin: Walter de Gruyter, 1998.

Aspasius et al. *On Aristotle's "Nicomachean Ethics" 8 and 9.* Edited by David Konstan. Ithaca, NY: Cornell University Press, 2001.

Bywater, Ingram. *Contributions to the Textual Criticism of Aristotle's "Nicomachean Ethics."* New York: Arno Press, 1973 [reprint of the 1892 ed.].

Eterovich, Francis H. *Aristotle's "Nicomachean Ethics": Commentary and Analysis.* Washington, DC: University Press of America, 1980.

Gauthier, René Antoine, and Jean Yves Jolif. *L'Éthique à Nicomaque.* 2nd ed. 2 vols. Louvain: Publications Universitaires; Paris: Béatrice-Nauwelaerts, 1970.

Grant, Sir Alexander. *The Ethics of Aristotle.* 4th ed. 2 vols. New York: Arno Press, 1973.

Greenwood, L. H. G. *Aristotle "Nicomachean Ethics" Book Six.* New York: Arno Press, 1973 [reprint of the 1909 ed.].

Grosseteste, Robert. *The Greek Commentaries on the "Nicomachean Ethics" of Aristotle.* Leiden: E. J. Brill, 1973.

Joachim, H. H. *The Nicomachean Ethics.* Edited by D. A. Rees. Oxford: Clarendon Press, 1951.

Natali, Carlo. *Aristotle's "Nicomachean Ethics" Book VII.* Oxford: Oxford University Press, 2009.

Rassow, Hermann. *Forschungen ueber die Nikomachische Ethik des Aristoteles.* Weimar: Hermann Boehlau, 1874.

Stewart, J. A. *Notes on the "Nicomachean Ethics" of Aristotle.* 2 vols. Oxford: Clarendon Press, 1892.

Thomas Aquinas. *Commentary on Aristotle's "Nicomachean Ethics."* Translated by C. I. Litzinger. Beloit, WI: Dumb Ox Press, 1993.

Other Works Consulted

Athenaeus. *The Deipnosophists.* Edited and translated by Charles Burton Gulick. 7 vols. Cambridge, MA: Harvard University Press, 1927–41.

Die Fragmente der Vorsokratiker. Edited by Hermann Diels and Walther Kranz. 10th ed. 3 vols. Berlin: Weidmann, 1961.

Euripides. *Fabulae.* Edited by J. Diggle. 3 vols. Oxford: Clarendon Press, 1981–84.

Greek-English Lexicon. Edited by Henry George Liddell and Robert Scott. Revised and augmented by Henry Stuart Jones. Oxford: Clarendon Press, 1968. [Cited as LSJ in the notes.]

Greek Lyric Poetry From Alcmaeon to Simonides. Edited by C. W. Bowra. 2nd ed. Oxford: Clarendon Press, 1961.

Hesiod. *Theogonia Opera et Dies Scutum.* Edited by Friedrich Solmsen. 3rd ed. Oxford: Clarendon Press, 1990.

Homer. *Ilias.* Edited by Martin L. West. 2 vols. Stuttgart: B. G. Teubner, 1998.

———. *Odyssea.* Edited by Arthur Ludwich. 2 vols. Stuttgart: B. G. Teubner, 1998.

Sophocles. *Fabulae.* Edited by H. Lloyd-Jones and N. G. Wilson. Oxford: Clarendon Press, 1990.

Theocritus. *Bucolici Graeci*. Edited by A. S. F. Gow. Oxford: Clarendon Press, 1952.

Theognis. *Theognidis et Phocylidis Fragmenta*. Edited by M. L. West. Berlin: Walter de Gruyter, 1978.

Thucydides. *Historiae*. Edited by H. S. Jones and J. E. Powell. 2 vols. Oxford: Clarendon Press, 1942.

OUTLINE

ARISTOTLE'S
Nicomachean Ethics

◎ ◎

Book 1

Every art and every inquiry, and similarly every action as well as choice, is held to aim at some good.[1] Hence people have nobly[2] declared that the good is that at which all things aim. But there appears to be a certain difference among the ends: some ends are activities, others are certain works apart from the activities themselves, and in those cases in which there are certain ends apart from the actions, the works are naturally better than the activities.[3]

1094a

5

1 · Aristotle introduces several central terms here: *technē*, a technical art or craft, such as shoemaking, and the knowledge that goes together with it; *praxis*, action, which issues from the parts of the soul characterized by longing and desiring; and *proairesis*, choice, closely tied to action. See the glossary for these and other key terms. The verb Aristotle uses here for "is held to" (*dokein*) is related to the noun translated as "opinion" (*doxa*); it may mean simply that something "seems" to be the case or that it is "held" to be so by opinion.

2 · *Kalōs*: the adverb related to a central term, *to kalon*, which has a range of meanings for which English requires at least three: "noble," "beautiful," and "fine." It denotes (physical) beauty but also and above all, in the *Ethics*, what is admirable in a moral sense. It will be translated most frequently as "the noble" ("noble," "nobly," "in a noble manner") and, in the rare cases in which it refers unambiguously to physical beauty, as "beautiful." In the present instance, Aristotle may say that the declaration in question is a "noble" one because it expresses a noble sentiment—that all things aim at the good—but not necessarily a true one: the conclusion drawn does not in fact follow from the premises given in the first sentence.

3 · Another set of key terms is introduced here: *telē* (singular, *telos*), the "end" or goal of a thing; see also *teleios*, n. 37 below. *Energeiai* (singular, *energeia*), "activity," means the state of being engaged in an act or the carrying out of a deed (*ergon*); it is thus related to the next term, *erga* (singular, *ergon*). *Ergon* cannot be captured by one English word; it may be translated as "work," "product," "task" or—especially when used in contrast to "speech" (*logos*)—"deed."

Now, since there are many actions, arts, and sciences,[4] the ends too are many: of medicine, the end is health; of shipbuilding, a ship; of generalship, victory; of household management, wealth. And in all things of this sort that fall under some one capacity[5]—for just as bridle making and such other arts as concern equestrian gear fall under horsemanship, while this art and every action related to warfare fall under generalship, so in the same manner, some arts fall under one capacity, others under another—in *all* of them, the ends of the architectonic ones are more choiceworthy than all those that fall under them, for these latter are pursued for the sake of the former. And it makes no difference at all whether the ends of the actions are the activities themselves or something else apart from these, as in the sciences mentioned.

CHAPTER TWO

If, therefore, there is some end of our actions that we wish for on account of itself, the rest being things we wish for on account of this end, and if we do not choose all things on account of something else—for in this way the process will go on infinitely such that the longing[6] involved is empty and pointless—clearly this would be the good, that is, the best.[7] And with a view to our life, then, is not the knowledge of this good of great weight, and would we not, like archers in possession of a target, better hit on what is needed? If this is so, then one must try to grasp, in outline at least, whatever it is and to which of the sciences or capacities it belongs.

But it might be held to belong to the most authoritative and most architectonic one,[8] and such appears to be the political art.[9] For it or-

---

4 · Or, "knowledge" in the strict sense (*epistēmē*, here in the plural). We use "science" or "scientific knowledge" to distinguish *epistēmē* from the other term Aristotle uses for knowledge, *gnōsis*.

5 · Or, "power" (*dunamis*), here and throughout.

6 · This is the first instance of the term *orexis*, which we translate as "longing" and which refers in general to the appetency of the soul, of which *epithumia*, "desire," is a species. The term is related to the verb *oregein*, which we translate as "to long for."

7 · *To ariston*: the superlative of *to agathon*, "the good." Although some translators render this term as the "highest" or "chief" good, we consistently translate it as "the best" to capture the sense that it is indeed a peak but may also be simply the best of the goods available to human beings.

8 · "One" might refer to "science" (*epistēmē*), "art" (*technē*), or "capacity" (*dunamis*).

9 · Aristotle here uses substantively the feminine singular adjective *politikē* (the political), without therefore specifying the noun it is meant to modify, as can be easily done

dains what sciences there must be in cities and what kinds each person
in turn must learn and up to what point. We also see that even the most
honored capacities—for example, generalship, household management,
rhetoric—fall under the political art. Because it makes use of the remaining[10] sciences and, further, because it legislates what one ought to do and   5
what to abstain from, its end would encompass those of the others, with
the result that this would be the human good. For even if this is the same
thing for an individual and a city, to secure and preserve the good of the
city appears to be something greater and more complete: the good of the
individual by himself is certainly desirable enough, but that of a nation   10
and of cities is nobler and more divine.

The inquiry, then, aims at these things, since it is a sort of political inquiry.

CHAPTER THREE

The inquiry would be adequately made if it should attain the clarity that
accords with the subject matter. For one should not seek out precision in
all arguments alike, just as one should not do so in the products of crafts-
manship either. The noble things and the just things, which the politi-   15
cal art examines, admit of much dispute and variability, such that they
are held to exist by law[11] alone and not by nature. And even the good
things admit of some such variability on account of the harm that be-
falls many people as a result of them: it has happened that some have
been destroyed on account of their wealth, others on account of their
courage.

It would certainly be desirable enough, then, if one who speaks about   20
and on the basis of such things demonstrate the truth roughly and in
outline, and if, in speaking about and on the basis of things that are for
the most part so, one draw conclusions of that sort as well. Indeed, in the
same manner one must also accept each of the points being made. For it

---

in Greek. "Science," "art," or "capacity" are all grammatically possible. We will translate the word consistently by (the) "political art"; the ending *-ikē* generally indicates
that an art (*technē*) is involved.

10 · The MSS add at this point the word *practical* (or sciences "related to action": *prak-
tikais*), but Bywater, followed by Stewart and Burnet, deletes it. One MS omits the word
translated as "remaining."

11 · Or, "convention," "custom" (*nomos*); this is the first appearance of this important
term.

belongs to an educated person to seek out precision in each genus to the
extent that the nature of the matter allows: to accept persuasive speech
from a skilled mathematician appears comparable to demanding demonstrations from a skilled rhetorician. Each person judges nobly the things
he knows, and of these he is a good judge. He is a good judge of a particular thing, therefore, if he has been educated with a view to it, but is a good
judge simply if he has been educated about everything. Hence of the political art, a young person is not an appropriate student,[12] for he is inexperienced in the actions pertaining to life, and the arguments[13] are based
on these actions and concern them.

Further, because he is disposed to follow the passions, he will listen
pointlessly and unprofitably, since the end involved is not knowledge
but action. And it makes no difference at all whether he is young in age
or immature in character:[14] the deficiency is not related to time but instead arises on account of living in accord with passion and pursuing each
passion in turn. For to people of that sort, just as to those lacking self-
restraint,[15] knowledge is without benefit. But to those who fashion their
longings in accord with reason and act accordingly, knowing about these
things would be of great profit.

About the student, and how one ought to accept [what is being said],
and what it is that we propose, let these things stand as a prelude.

CHAPTER FOUR

Now, let us pick up again and—since all knowledge and every choice have
some good as the object of their longing—let us state what it is that we say
the political art aims at and what the highest of all the goods related to action is. As for its name, then, it is pretty much agreed on by most people;

12 · *Akroatēs*, literally, "listener" or "auditor," perhaps of spoken lectures, perhaps of
such lessons as are conveyed by listening—to the poets or to one's father, for example
(consider 1.4, end and 1.13, end).

13 · *Logoi* (singular, *logos*). The term will be translated as "argument," "reason," "speech,"
or "definition," depending on the context; see also the glossary.

14 · The first appearance of this important term (*ēthos*), which appears, as a plural adjective, in the title of the work and is there translated as "ethics," but is literally "things
pertaining to character."

15 · That is, those who are unable to do the correct thing, though in some sense they
know what it is. Aristotle will analyze both "self-restraint" and "lack of self-restraint"
(*enkrateia* and *akrasia*) at 7.1–10.

for both the many[16] and the refined say that it is happiness,[17] and they suppose that living well and acting well[18] are the same thing as being happy.   20
But as for what happiness is, they disagree, and the many do not give a response similar to that of the wise. The former respond that it is something
obvious and manifest, such as pleasure or wealth or honor, some saying
it is one thing, others another. Often one and the same person responds
differently, for when he is sick, it is health; when poor, wealth. And when
they are aware of their own ignorance, they wonder at[19] those who say   25
something that is great and beyond them. Certain others, in addition,
used to suppose that the good is something else, by itself, apart from these
many good things, which is also the cause of their all being good.

Now, to examine thoroughly all these opinions is perhaps rather pointless; those opinions that are especially prevalent or are held to have a cer-   30
tain reason to them will suffice. But let it not escape our notice that there
is a difference between the arguments that proceed *from* the principles[20]
and those that proceed *to* the principles. For Plato too used to raise this
perplexity well and investigate it, whether the path is going from the principles or to the principles, just as on a racecourse one can proceed from   1095b
the judges to the finish line or back again. One must begin from what is
known, but this has a twofold meaning: there are things known to us, on
the one hand, and things known simply, on the other. Perhaps it is necessary for us, at least, to begin from the things known to us. Hence he who
will listen adequately to the noble things and the just things, and to the   5
political things generally, must be brought up nobly by means of habituation.[21] For the "that" is a principle, and if this should be sufficiently ap-

---

16 · *Hoi polloi*: literally, "the many" or "the majority," but in Greek as in English, the
expression often carries a decidedly negative connotation.

17 · *Eudaimonia*, the first appearance of this central term; see the glossary and introduction.

18 · The expression Aristotle here uses (*eu prattein*) means in the first place "to act
well," but carries the extended meaning "to fare well," with the implication that those
who act well will indeed fare well: Aristotle's investigation of happiness emphasizes the
centrality of good action to happiness.

19 · Or, "admire" (*thaumazein*).

20 · Or, more simply, "beginning points," "origins" (*archai*, the plural of *archē*).

21 · Some MSS, and the ancient commentator Aspasius, read here "by means of customs (usages, [moral] characters)" (*ēthesin*) rather than the "habituation" (in the plural: *ethesin*) of one MS; Burnet accepts the former on the grounds that "[w]e have not
settled yet that *ēthos* comes from *ethos*" (alluding to the beginning of book 2); Stewart
and Bywater accept the latter reading.

parent, there will be no need of the "why" in addition, and a person of the sort indicated has or would easily get hold of principles. As for him to whom neither of these is available, let him listen to the words of Hesiod:

10   This one is altogether best who himself understands all things

. . . .

But good in his turn too is he who obeys one who speaks well.
But he who neither himself understands nor, in listening to another,
Takes this to heart, he is a useless man.[22]

CHAPTER FIVE

Let us speak from the point where we digressed. For on the basis of the
15 lives they lead, the many and crudest seem to suppose, not unreasonably, that the good and happiness are pleasure. And thus they cherish the life of enjoyment. For the especially prominent ways of life are three: the one just mentioned, the political, and, third, the contemplative.

20   Now, in choosing a life of fatted cattle, the many appear altogether slavish; but they attain a hearing, because many people in positions of authority experience passions like those of Sardanapallus.[23] The refined and active, on the other hand, choose honor, for this is pretty much the end of the political life. But it appears to be more superficial than what is be-
25 ing sought, for honor seems to reside more with those who bestow it than with him who receives it; and we divine that the good is something of one's own and a thing not easily taken away. Further, people seem to pursue honor so that they may be convinced that they themselves are good; at any rate, they seek to be honored by the prudent,[24] among those to whom they are known, and for their virtue.[25] It is clear, then, that in the case of
30 these people at least, virtue is superior.

22 · Hesiod, *Works and Days* 293, 295–97. The line Aristotle omits is: "Reflecting on what is better subsequently and in the end." The term translated as "good" is not *agathos* but the more poetic *esthlos* (see also book 2, n. 18); "heart" is *thumos*, elsewhere rendered as "spiritedness" or "spirit."

23 · An Assyrian king (ruled ca. 669–627) renowned for, and apparently boastful of, his extravagant way of life and sensual indulgences. Aristotle mentions him also in the *Eudemian Ethics* (1216a16).

24 · The first appearance of this adjective, related to the intellectual virtue of prudence (*phronēsis*).

25 · This is the first appearance of the term *aretē*, which refers to the excellence specific to a given thing or being. It will be translated throughout as "virtue," but one should

And perhaps someone might in fact suppose that virtue is to a greater degree the end of the political life. Yet it too appears to be rather incomplete. For it seems to be possible for someone to possess virtue even while asleep or while being inactive throughout life and, in addition to these, while suffering badly and undergoing the greatest misfortunes. But no one would deem happy somebody living in this way, unless he were defending a thesis. But enough about these things: they have been spoken about adequately also in the circulated writings.[26]

1096a

Third is the contemplative life, about which we will make an investigation in what will follow.[27]

5

The moneymaking life is characterized by a certain constraint, and it is clear that wealth is not the good being sought, for it is a useful thing and for the sake of something else. Thus someone might suppose that the previously mentioned things are ends to a greater degree than is money, for at least they are cherished for their own sakes. But they do not appear to be ends either, and many arguments have been widely distributed in opposition to them.[28] So let these things be dismissed.

10

CHAPTER SIX

As for the universal [good],[29] perhaps it is better to examine it and to go through the perplexities involved in the ways it is spoken of, although undertaking such an inquiry is arduous, because the men who introduced

---

keep in mind that it is possible to refer in Greek to the "virtue" not only of human beings but also of other animals and even of inanimate objects.

26 · It is unknown precisely what Aristotle here refers to; the extended meaning of the term may be "routine" or "everyday," and the general sense is that these writings are not the most exacting.

27 · For Aristotle's explicit discussion, see 10.6–8.

28 · Reading, with Gauthier and Jolif, the *kai* (and) of some MSS, rather than the *kaitoi* (although) of others, and taking *pros* in its not uncommon sense of "against" or "in opposition to." The other reading could be rendered: "although many arguments have been widely distributed relating to them."

29 · Or, "general" (*kathalou*), here referring to the Platonic *idea* of the good as a self-subsisting whole separate from any particular good thing. The word order in Greek suggests at first blush that the subject of the chapter will be "the universal better" (*to de kathalou beltion*), and indeed Aristotle will argue that our experience of better and worse does not permit us access to a universal "good."

the forms[30] are dear.[31] But perhaps it might be held to be better, and in fact to be obligatory, at least for the sake of preserving the truth, to do away
15 with even one's own things, especially for those who are philosophers. For although both are dear, it is a pious thing to honor the truth first.

Now, those who conveyed this opinion did not make *ideas*[32] pertain to those cases in which they spoke of the prior and posterior; hence they did not set up an *idea* of numbers either. But the good is spoken of in relation
20 to *what* something is, and in relation to what *sort* of thing it is, and as regards its *relation* to something; but that which is the thing in itself—that is, the being—is prior by nature to any relation it has (for this is like an offshoot and accident of the being). As a result, there would not be any common *idea* pertaining to these things.

And further, the good is spoken of in as many ways as is the term *is*—for the good is spoken of in relation to *what* something is (for example,
25 the god and intellect[33]); as for what *sort* of thing something is, the good is spoken of as the virtues; as for *how much* something is, it is spoken of as the measured amount; in its *relation* to something, as what is useful; as regards *time*, as the opportune moment; as regards *place*, as the [right] location; and other things of this sort. [Since all this is so,] it is clear that the good would not be something common, universal, and one. For if that were the case, it would not be spoken of in all the categories but in one alone.

30 And further, since there is a single science of things that pertain to a single *idea*, there would also be some single science of *all* the good things. But as things stand, there are many sciences even of things that fall under a single category—for example, the opportune moment: in war, it is gen-

---

30 · *Eidē* (singular, *eidos*): a term closely associated with Plato or the Platonists. Like *idea*, the term that will shortly follow, the primary sense of *eidos* is "that which is seen," in particular, the "form" or "shape" of a thing. In the Platonic doctrine of the forms, to which Aristotle refers here, the *eidē* are the self-subsisting forms that give each particular thing its class character and hence are in some sense responsible for the existence of a thing as what it is.

31 · Or, "friends" (*philoi*).

32 · A transliteration of the term made famous by Plato and closely associated with *eidos*, or "form." It is related to the verb *to see* and means most simply the outward look or appearance of a thing and, by extension, the class to which a group of things with similar looks belong; see also n. 58.

33 · The first appearance of the term *theos*, "god," and of the term *nous*, translated throughout as "intellect," with the exception of 1110a11, 1112a21, and 1115b9, where it is translated as "sense."

eralship, in illness, medicine; and in the case of the measured amount of
nourishment, on the one hand, it is medicine, but in that of physical exertions, on the other, it is gymnastic training.

But someone might be perplexed as to whatever they mean by "thing-   35
as-such," if in fact the very same account of human being pertains both to   1096b
"human being-as-such" and to a given human being. For in the respect in
which each is a human being, they will not differ at all. And if this is so,
[then neither the good-as-such nor a good thing will differ] in the respect
in which each is good. Moreover, the good will not be good to a greater
degree by being eternal either, if in fact whiteness that lasts a long time
will not be whiter than that which lasts only a day.

The Pythagoreans[34] seem to speak more persuasively about it by pos-   5
iting the One in the column of the goods, and it is indeed they whom
Speusippus[35] seems to follow. But about these things let there be another
argument.

A certain dispute over the points stated begins to appear, because the
arguments made [by the proponents of the forms] do not concern every
good: things pursued and cherished by themselves are spoken of in refer-   10
ence to a single form, but what produces these (or in some way preserves
them or prevents their contraries) is spoken of as being good on account
of the former sorts of goods and in a different manner. It is clear, then,
that the good things would be spoken of in two senses: those that are
good in themselves, others that are good on account of these.

Separating the things good in themselves from those that are advanta-   15
geous, then, let us examine whether the former are spoken of in reference
to a single *idea*. What sorts of things might someone posit as being good
in themselves? Is it so many things as are in fact pursued for themselves
alone — for example, exercising prudence and seeing, as well as certain
pleasures and honors? For even if we pursue these on account of something else as well, nonetheless one might posit them as being among the
things that are good in themselves. Or is nothing good in itself except   20
the *idea*? The result will be that the form [abstracted from all individual
good things] is pointless. But if in fact these things [that is, exercising prudence, seeing, and the like] are among the things good in themselves, the

34 · Little is known about Pythagoras, a famous thinker of the sixth century hailing
from Samos; but he, or his followers, became particularly well known for their mathematical investigations.

35 · An Athenian philosopher (ca. 407–339) who succeeded Plato as head of the Academy in Athens. Though he was a prolific writer, only fragments of his work remain.

definition of the good will need to manifest itself as the same in *all* cases, just as the definition of whiteness is the same in the case of snow and in that of white lead. But the definitions of honor, prudence, and pleasure are dis-
25   tinct and differ in the very respect in which they are goods. It is not the case, therefore, that the good is something common in reference to a single *idea*.

But how indeed are they spoken of [as good]? For they are not like things that share the same name by chance. Is it by dint of their stemming from one thing or because they *all* contribute to one thing? Or is it more that they are such by analogy? For as there is sight in the body, so there is intellect in the soul, and indeed one thing in one thing, another in an-
30   other. But perhaps we ought to leave these considerations be for now: to be very precise about them would be more appropriate to another phi-losophy. The case is similar with the *idea* as well: even if there is some one good thing that is predicated [of things] in common, or there is some sep-arate thing, itself by itself, it is clear that it would not be subject to action or capable of being possessed by a human being. But it is just some such thing that is now being sought.

35   Perhaps someone might be of the opinion that it is better to be familiar
1097a   with it, with a view to those goods that *can* be possessed and *are* subject to action. By having this [universal good] as a sort of model, we will to a greater degree know also the things that are good for us; and if we know them, we will hit on them. Now, the argument has a certain persuasive-ness, but it seems to be inconsistent with the sciences. For although all
5   sciences aim at some good and seek out what is lacking, they pass over knowledge of the good itself. And yet it is not reasonable for *all* craftsmen to be ignorant of so great an aid and not even to seek it out.

A further perplexity too is what benefit the weaver or carpenter might gain, in relation to his own art, by knowing this same good, or how he
10   who has contemplated the *idea* itself will be a more skilled physician or general. For it appears that the physician does not examine even health this way, but inquires rather into the health of a human being and even more, perhaps, into that of this particular human being. For he treats pa-tients individually.

And let what pertains to these things be stated up to this point.

CHAPTER SEVEN

15   Let us go back again to the good being sought, whatever it might be. For it appears to be one thing in one action or art, another in another: it is a

different thing in medicine and in generalship, and so on with the rest. What, then, is the good in each of these? Or is it that for the sake of which everything else is done? In medicine, this is health; in generalship, victory; in house building, a house; and in another, it would be something   20 else. But in *every* action and choice, it is the end involved, since it is for the sake of this that all people do everything else. As a result, if there is some end of *all* actions, this would be the good related to action; and if there are several, then it would be these. So as the argument proceeds, it arrives at the same point. But one ought to try to make this clearer still.   25

Since the ends appear to be several, and some of these we choose on account of something else—for example, wealth, an aulos,[36] and the instrumental things generally—it is clear that not all ends are complete,[37] but what is the best appears to be something complete. As a result, if there is some one thing that is complete in itself, this would be what is being sought, and if there are several, then the most complete of these. We say   30 that what is sought out for itself is more complete than what is sought out on account of something else, and that what is never chosen on account of something else is more complete than those things chosen both for themselves and on account of this [further end]. The simply complete thing, then, is that which is always chosen for itself and never on account of something else.

Happiness above all seems to be of this character, for we always choose   1097b it on account of itself and never on account of something else. Yet honor, pleasure, intellect, and every virtue we choose on their own account—for even if nothing resulted from them, we would choose each of them—but we choose them also for the sake of happiness, because we suppose that,   5 through them, we will be happy. But nobody chooses happiness for the sake of these things, or, more generally, on account of anything else.

The same thing appears to result also on the basis of self-sufficiency, for the complete good is held to be self-sufficient. We do not mean by *self-sufficient* what suffices for someone by himself, living a solitary life, but what is sufficient also with respect to parents, offspring, a wife, and, in   10 general, one's friends and fellow citizens, since by nature a human being is political. But it is necessary to grasp a certain limit to these; for if one

36 · A double-reed instrument not unlike the modern oboe; the noun here is plural in the Greek.

37 · Or, "perfect" (*teleios*); the adjective is related to the noun *telos* and suggests that which reached or fulfilled the end or goal appropriate to a given thing (see also n. 3 above).

extends these to include the parents [of parents],[38] and descendants, and the friends of friends, it will go on infinitely. But this must be examined
15   further later on. As for the self-sufficient, we posit it as that which by itself makes life choiceworthy[39] and in need of nothing, and such is what we suppose happiness to be.

Further, happiness is the most choiceworthy of all things because it is not just one among them—and it is clear that, were it included as one among many things, it would be more choiceworthy with the least addition of the good things; for the good that is added to it results in a superabundance of goods, and the greater number of goods is always
20   more choiceworthy. So happiness appears to be something complete and self-sufficient, it being an end of our actions.

But perhaps saying that "happiness is best" is something manifestly agreed on, whereas what it is still needs to be said more distinctly. Now,
25   perhaps this would come to pass if the work[40] of the human being should be grasped. For just as in the case of an aulos player, sculptor, and every expert, and in general with those who have a certain work and action, the relevant good and the doing of something well seem to reside in the work, so too the same might be held to be the case with a human being, if in fact there is a certain work that is a human being's. Are there, then, certain works and actions of a carpenter and shoemaker, but none of a human
30   being: would he, by contrast, be naturally "without a work"[41]? Or just as there appears to be a certain work of the eye, hand, and foot, and in fact of each of the parts in general, so also might one posit a certain work of a human being apart from all these?

So whatever, then, would this work be? For living appears to be something common even to plants, but what is peculiar [to human beings] is
1098a   being sought. One must set aside, then, the life characterized by nutrition as well as growth. A certain life characterized by sense perception would be next, but it too appears to be common to a horse and cow and in fact to every animal. So there remains a certain active life of that which possesses

---

38 · This additional phrase, not present in the MSS, seems necessary in order to make the text consistent with 1097b9–10; it is suggested by Rassow and accepted by both Burnet and Gauthier and Jolif.

39 · Some MSS add at this point the words "and sufficient" (*arkion*) (or, "sufficient and choiceworthy").

40 · *To ergon*: see n. 3 as well as the glossary.

41 · *Argon*: literally, without an *ergon*, a work, task, or function, and so by extension idle.

reason; and what possesses reason includes what is obedient to reason, on the one hand, and what possesses it and thinks, on the other. But since   5 this [life of reason in the second sense] also is spoken of in a twofold way, one must posit the life [of that which possesses reason] in accord with an activity, for this seems to be its more authoritative meaning.[42] And if the work of a human being is an activity of soul in accord with reason, or not without reason, and we assert that the work of a given person is the same in kind as that of a serious[43] person, just as it would be in the case of a cithara[44] player and a serious cithara player, and this would be so in   10 all cases simply when the superiority in accord with the virtue is added to the work; for it belongs to a cithara player to play the cithara, but to a serious one to do so well. But if this is so[45]—and we posit the work of a human being as a certain life, and this is an activity of soul and actions accompanied by reason, the work of a serious man being to do these things well and nobly, and each thing is brought to completion well in accord   15 with the virtue proper to it—if this is so, then the human good becomes an activity of soul in accord with virtue, and if there are several virtues, then in accord with the best and most complete one.

But, in addition, in a complete life. For one swallow does not make a spring, nor does one day. And in this way, one day or a short time does not make someone blessed and happy either.

Let the good have been sketched in this way, then, for perhaps one   20

---

42 · The subject of the sentence is unclear, and we supply the immediately preceding referent, the life in accord with the part of the soul that possesses reason and thinks; of this part, there is both an activity and a characteristic (*hexis*); and, as Aristotle will argue in 1.8, happiness consists in the activity or use rather than the mere possession of a characteristic. Burnet recommends dropping the immediately preceding phrase, which distinguishes the two parts of the soul; he argues that the phrase "interrupts the argument and destroys the grammar." On his reading, the referent would be simply the active life of that which possesses reason.

43 · The first appearance of the term *spoudaios*. The "serious" (*spoudaios*) human being is characterized by the correct devotion to and exercise of moral virtue, although Aristotle extends the term to anything that does its own "work" well, including horses and eyes: see 2.6.

44 · A plucked instrument with a tortoiseshell soundboard.

45 · Bywater brackets everything within the dashes on the grounds that it is both awkward and a repetition of points already raised. The grammar here is difficult; Burnet, who accepts the text, confesses that he "hardly [likes] to put a limit to the capacity of Aristotle for long and complicated protases even when they involve repetitions and grammatical awkwardnesses."

ought to outline it first and then fill it in later. It might seem to belong to everyone to advance and fully articulate things whose sketch is in a noble condition, and time is a good discoverer of or contributor to such things:
25 from this have arisen the advances in the arts too, for it belongs to everyone to add what is lacking.

But one must remember the points mentioned previously as well, to the effect that one must not seek out precision in all matters alike but rather in each thing in turn as accords with the subject matter in question and insofar as is appropriate to the inquiry. For both carpenter and geom-
30 eter seek out the right angle but in different ways: the former seeks it insofar as it is useful to his work; the latter seeks out what it is or what sort of a thing it is, for he is one who contemplates[46] the truth. One ought to act in the same manner also in other cases, so that things extraneous to the
1098b works involved not multiply. And one should not demand the cause in all things alike either; rather, it is enough in some cases to have nobly pointed out the "that"—such is the case in what concerns the principles—and the "that" is the first thing and a principle. Some principles are observed[47] by means of induction,[48] some by perception, some by a certain habituation,
5 and others in other ways. One ought to try to go in search of each in turn in the manner natural to them and to be serious about their being nobly defined. For they are of great weight in what follows from them: the beginning[49] seems to be more than half of the whole, and many of the points being sought seem to become manifest on account of it.

CHAPTER EIGHT

One must examine what concerns it,[50] not only on the basis of the conclu-
10 sion and the premises on which the argument rests, but also on the basis of things said about it. For with the truth, all the given facts harmonize; but with what is false, the truth soon hits a wrong note.

46 · Or, is an "observer," "spectator" (theatēs); the term is related to the words translated as "contemplation" and "contemplative" (theōretikē, theōretikos).
47 · Again, "contemplated," "beheld," or "seen" (theōrein).
48 · A technical term of Aristotelian logic (epagōgē); see also 6.3.
49 · Archē: "principle" or "beginning point" (see n. 20).
50 · The nearest grammatical subject is "beginning" or "principle" (archē). Gauthier and Jolif (following Susemihl) object to this and suggest making a relatively small change in the reading of the MSS (from autēs to autou) such that the referent would be "the good" rather than "principle."

Now, although the good things have been distributed in a threefold manner—both those goods said to be external, on the one hand, and those pertaining to soul and to body, on the other—we say that those pertaining to soul are the most authoritative and especially good. And we posit as those "goods pertaining to soul," the soul's actions and activities. As a result, the argument[51] would be stated nobly, at least according to this opinion, which is ancient and agreed to by those who philosophize. It would be correct too to say that certain actions and activities are the end, for in this way the end belongs among the goods related to soul, not among the external ones.

And that the happy person both lives well and acts well harmonizes with the argument, for [happiness] was pretty much said to be a certain kind of living well and good action.[52] It also appears that *all* the things being sought pertaining to happiness are included in what was said: in the opinion of some, happiness is virtue; of others, prudence; of others, a certain wisdom; in the opinion of still others, it is these or some of these things, together with pleasure or not without pleasure. And others include alongside these the prosperity related to external goods as well. Many of the ancients say some of these things, a few men of high repute say others of them; and it is reasonable that neither of these two groups be wholly in error, but rather that they be correct in some one respect, at least, or even in most respects.

The argument, then, is in harmony with those who say that [happiness] is virtue or a certain virtue, for the activity in accord with virtue belongs to virtue. But perhaps it makes no small difference whether one supposes the best thing to reside in possession or use, that is, in a characteristic[53] or an activity. For it is possible that, although the characteristic is present, it accomplishes nothing good—for example, in the case of some-

---

51 · The main verb is without an expressed subject; we follow the suggestion of Burnet and assume *logos*, here rendered as "argument," although "definition" (of happiness) is another possibility.

52 · "Good action" or "faring well" (*eupraxia*): the abstract noun here used is related to the word translated as "action" throughout (*praxis*); and the previous terms in the sentence, "acts well" (*euprattein*), can also be translated as "fares well"; see n. 18.

53 · This is the first appearance of the important term *hexis*, which is related to a verb (*echein*) that means to have, hold, or possess, and in conjunction with an adverb, to be in a given state. A *hexis* in the context of the *Ethics* is an ordered disposition or state of soul, produced by habituation, and active especially in the face of pleasures and pains; as Aristotle notes at the end of book 1, the praiseworthy characteristics are the (moral) virtues.

one who is asleep or has been otherwise hindered. But this is not possible when it comes to the activity: of necessity, a person will act, and he will act well. For just as it is not the noblest and strongest who are crowned with the victory wreath in the Olympic Games but rather the competi-
5   tors (for it is certain of these who win), so also it is those who act correctly who attain the noble and good things in life.

But their life is also pleasant in itself; for feeling pleasure is among the things related to the soul, and there is pleasure for each person in connection with whatever he is said to be a lover[54] of—for example, a horse
10   is pleasant to the horse lover, a play to the theater lover. In the same manner too, the just things are pleasant to the lover of justice, and in general, things in accord with virtue are pleasant to the lover of virtue. Now, things pleasant to the many do battle with one another, because such things are not pleasant by nature; but to the lovers of what is noble, the things pleasant by nature are pleasant. Such too are the actions in accord with virtue, with the result that they are pleasant both to such people and in them
15   selves. Indeed, the life [of those who love what is noble] has no need of additional pleasure, like a sort of added charm, but possesses pleasure in itself. For, in addition to the points mentioned, he who takes no delight in noble actions is not good either; for no one would say that somebody
20   who does not delight in acting justly is just or who does not delight in liberal actions is liberal, and similarly in the other cases as well. And if this is so, then the actions in accord with virtue would, in themselves, be pleasant. But certainly these actions *are* good as well as noble;[55] and they will be each of these especially, if in fact the serious person judges nobly about them—and he judges as we said.
25   Happiness, therefore, is the best, noblest, and most pleasant thing; and these are not separated, as the inscription at Delos has it:

Noblest is what is most just, but best is to be healthy;
And most pleasant by nature is for someone to attain what he passionately desires.

For *all* these are present in the best activities, and we assert that happiness
30   is these activities—or the best one among them.
Nonetheless, it[56] manifestly requires external goods in addition, just

54 · The love here indicated is *philia*, friendship or friendly love, not *erōs* or erotic desire.
55 · One MS reads "noble, as well as good."
56 · Either "happiness" or "the best activity" is a grammatically possible subject.

as we said. For it is impossible or not easy for someone without equipment to do what is noble: many things are done through instruments,   1099b
as it were—through friends, wealth, and political power. Those who
are bereft of some of these (for example, good birth, good children, or
beauty) disfigure their blessedness,[57] for a person who is altogether ugly
in appearance,[58] or of poor birth, or solitary and childless cannot really
be characterized as happy; and he is perhaps still less happy, if he should   5
have altogether bad children or friends or, though he did have good ones,
they are dead. Just as we said, then, [happiness] seems to require some
such external prosperity[59] in addition. This is why some make good fortune equivalent to happiness, and others, virtue.

CHAPTER NINE

This is also why the perplexity arises as to whether happiness is something that can be gained through learning or habituation or through   10
some other practice, or whether it comes to be present in accord with a
sort of divine allotment or even through chance.

   Now, if there is in fact anything that is a gift of the gods to human beings, it is reasonable that happiness is god given, and it especially among
the human concerns insofar as it is the best of them. But perhaps this
would be more appropriate to another examination—yet it appears that
even if happiness is not god sent but comes to be present through virtue   15
and a certain learning or practice, it is among the most divine things. For
the prize of virtue or its end appears to be best and to be something divine
and blessed. It would also be something common to many people, for it
is possible for it to be available, through a certain learning and care, to all
who have not been rendered defective in point of virtue. And if it is better   20
to be happy in this way rather than through chance, it is reasonable that
this is how [happiness is acquired]—if in fact what accords with nature
is naturally in the noblest possible state, and similar too is what accords

57 · The terms translated as "bereft" and "disfigure" in this clause are poetic or tragic
and hence rare in Aristotle.
58 · Aristotle here uses the term *idea*, characteristic of the Platonic "doctrine of ideas,"
in its primary sense of outward appearance or look (see n. 32 above).
59 · This phrase attempts to capture a word (*euēmeria*) whose components suggest
"having a good day" or spending one's days cheerfully; the word then came to mean
being successful or enjoying good luck. The same word appears also at 1178b33.

with art and with cause as a whole, and especially the best [art or cause]. To entrust the greatest and noblest thing to chance would be excessively discordant.

25   What is being sought is manifest also on the basis of the argument [or definition], for happiness was said to be a certain sort of activity of soul in accord with virtue. Now, of the remaining goods, some must necessarily be present, others are coworkers and by nature useful in an instrumental way. And these points would be in agreement also with those made at the

30   beginning: we posited the end of the political art as best, and it exercises a very great care to make the citizens of a specific sort—namely, good and apt to do the noble things. It is to be expected, then, that we do not say that either a cow or a horse or any other animal is at all happy, for none

1100a   of them are able to share in such an activity. It is because of this too that a child is not happy either: he is not yet apt to do such things, on account of his age, though some children are spoken of as blessed on account of the expectation[60] involved in their case. For, as we said, both complete virtue

5   and a complete life are required: many reversals and all manner of fortune arise in the course of life, and it is possible for someone who is particularly thriving to encounter great disasters in old age, just as the myth is told about Priam in the Trojan tales.[61] Nobody deems happy someone who deals with fortunes of that sort and comes to a wretched end.

CHAPTER TEN

10   Should one, then, not deem happy any human being for so long as he is alive; but must one look instead, as Solon[62] has it, to his end? But if indeed it is necessary to posit such a thesis, then is in fact a person happy when he is dead? Or is this, at least, altogether strange, especially for us who say that happiness is a certain activity? But if we do not say that the

15   dead person is happy—and this is not what Solon means either—but say rather that someone might safely deem a human being blessed only once he is already at a remove from bad things and misfortunes, this too admits

60 · Or, "hope" (elpis).

61 · Priam, the highly respected king of Troy in Homer's Iliad, witnesses the destruction of his city in the course of the Trojan War and so loses all that his great virtue and fortune had bestowed on him, not least his fifty sons (see Homer, Iliad 24.493–94; compare 24.248–52, 686–88, 751–53).

62 · An Athenian statesman, legislator, and poet (ca. 638–558); for his conversation with King Croesus of Lydia, here alluded to, see Herodotus 1.32.

of some dispute. For it is held that both something bad and something good can befall the dead person, if in fact they can befall the living person who does not perceive it—for example, honors and dishonors, and the faring well or the misfortunes of his offspring and descendants generally.

But these things too are perplexing: for someone who has lived bless-edly until old age and come to his end accordingly,[63] it is possible that many reversals may occur involving his descendants, just as some of these descendants may be good and attain the life that accords with their merit, but others the contrary. Yet it is clear that it is possible for these descen-dants to be of varying degrees of remove from their ancestors. Indeed, it would be strange if even the dead person should share in reversals and become now happy, now wretched again. But it would be strange too if nothing of the affairs of the descendants should reach the ancestors, not even for a certain time.

But one must return to the perplexity previously mentioned, for per-haps what is now being sought might also be contemplated on the basis of it. If indeed one does have to see a person's end and at that time deem each person blessed, not as being blessed [now] but as having been such previ-ously—how is this not strange if, when he is happy, what belongs to him will not be truly attributed to him? [This strange consequence arises] on account of our wish not to call the living happy, given the reversals that may happen, and of our supposition that happiness is something lasting and by no means easily subject to reversals, while fortunes often revolve for the same people. For it is clear that if we should follow someone's fortunes, we will often say that the same person is happy and then again wretched, declaring that the happy person is a sort of chameleon and on unsound footing.

Or is it not at all correct to follow someone's fortunes? For it is not in these that doing well or badly consists. Rather, human life requires these fortunes in addition, just as we said; yet it is the activities in accord with virtue that have authoritative control over happiness, and the contrary ac-tivities over the contrary.

The perplexity just now raised also bears witness to the argument, since in none of the human works is anything so secure as what pertains to the activities that accord with virtue. For such activities seem to be more lasting than even the sciences; and the most honored of them seem to be more lasting, because those who are blessed live out their lives en-

63 · Literally, "in accord with reason [*logos*]."

gaged, to the greatest degree and most continuously, in these activities. This seems to be the cause of our not forgetting such activities. Indeed, what is being sought will be available to the happy person, and he will be such throughout life. For he will always or most of all act on and contem-
20   plate what accords with virtue, and he—at least he who is truly good and "four-square, without blame"[64]—he will bear fortunes altogether nobly and suitably in every way.

Now, many things occur by chance, and they differ in how great or small they are. The small instances of good fortune, and similarly of its
25   opposite, clearly do not tip the balance of one's life, whereas the great and numerous ones that occur will make life more blessed (since these naturally help adorn life, and dealing with them is noble and serious). But those fortunes that turn out in the contrary way restrict and even ruin one's blessedness, for they both inflict pains and impede many activities.
30   Nevertheless, even in the midst of these, nobility shines through, whenever someone bears up calmly under many great misfortunes, not because of any insensitivity to pain but because he is wellborn and great souled.[65]

And if the activities have authoritative control over life, just as we said,
35   then no one who is blessed would become wretched, since he will never do things that are hateful and base. For we suppose that someone who
1101a is truly good and sensible bears up under all fortunes in a becoming way and always does what is noblest given the circumstances, just as a good general makes use, with the greatest military skill, of the army he has and
5   a shoemaker makes the most beautiful shoe out of the leather given him. It holds in the same manner with all the other experts as well. And if this is so, the happy person would never become wretched—nor indeed would he be blessed, it is true, if he encounters the fortunes of Priam. He would not be unstable and subject to reversals either, for he will not be
10   easily moved from happiness, and then not by any random misfortunes but only by great and numerous ones. And as a result of such things he would not become happy again in a short time; but, if in fact he does, he will do so in the completion of some lengthy time during which he comes to attain great and noble things.

15   What, then, prevents one from calling happy someone who is active in accord with complete virtue and who is adequately equipped with exter-

64 · From Simonides, a lyric and elegiac poet (ca. 556–468); see also Plato *Protagoras* 339b, where parts of the poem from which this line is taken are quoted and discussed.
65 · Or, "magnanimous." This is the first appearance of this important virtue (*megalopsychia*), which Aristotle will analyze at 4.3.

nal goods, not for any chance time but in a complete life? Or must one posit in addition that he will both live in this way and meet his end accordingly[66]—since the future is immanifest to us, and we posit happiness, wholly and in every way, as an end and as complete? And if this is so, we will say that those among the living who have and will have available to   20
them the things stated are blessed—but blessed human beings.

Let what pertains to these things too be defined up to this point.

CHAPTER ELEVEN

But that the fortunes of a person's descendants and all his friends contribute nothing whatsoever [to his happiness] appears to be excessively opposed to what is dear[67] and contrary to the opinions held. And because the things that may befall us are many and differ in various respects—   25
some hitting closer to home, other less so—thoroughly distinguishing each appears to be a long and even endless task. But perhaps for the matter to be stated generally and in outline would be adequate.

Just as some of the misfortunes that concern a person himself have a certain gravity and weight as regards his life but others seem lighter, so   30
also the misfortunes that concern all his friends are similar; and if, concerning each thing suffered, it makes a difference whether the friends are alive or have met their end, far more than if the unlawful and terrible things in tragic plays occur before the action of the play or during it, then one must indeed take this difference into account—and even more, perhaps, when it comes to the perplexity raised concerning those who have   35
passed away,[68] that is, whether they share in something good or in the opposite. For it seems, on the basis of these points, that even if anything   1101b
at all does get through to them, whether good or its contrary, it is something faint and small, either simply so or to them. And if this is not so, then what gets through to them is, at any rate, of such a degree and kind that it does not make happy those who are not such or deprive those who   5
are happy of their blessedness. The friends' faring well, then, appears to make some contribution to the condition of those who have passed away, as does, similarly, their faring ill—but a contribution of such a kind and degree as not to make the happy unhappy or anything else of that sort.

66 · Or, "according to reason" (see n. 63).
67 · Or, perhaps, "excessively unfriendly" or even "hateful" (*aphilon*).
68 · Literally, "those who have grown weary," a euphemistic term, characteristic of tragedy, that can be applied either to the sick or to the dead.

CHAPTER TWELVE

10   With these things defined, let us examine closely whether happiness is something praised or rather honored, for it is clear that it does not belong among the capacities, at any rate.[69] Now, everything praised appears to be praised for its being of a certain sort and for its condition relative to something: we praise the just person, the courageous person, and, in gen-

15   eral, the good person as well as virtue itself, on account of the actions and works involved; and we praise the strong man and the swift runner and each of the rest for their being, by nature, of a certain sort and for their condition in relation to something good and serious. This is clear also on the basis of the praises offered to the gods, since it is manifestly laughable

20   for them to be compared to us; but this happens because praise arises through comparison, as we said. And if praise is of things of that sort, it is clear that not praise but something greater and better than praise applies to the best things, as in fact appears to be the case: the gods we deem blessed and happy, and the most divine of men we deem blessed.[70]

25   The case is similar with the good things too: none praise happiness the way they praise justice; rather, people deem happiness a blessed thing, on the grounds that it is something more divine and better. And Eudoxus too seems to have nobly pleaded his case that the first prize belongs to pleasure. For the fact that it is not praised as being among the good things re-

30   veals, he supposed, that it is superior to the things praised; and such, he supposed, is the god and the good. For it is to these that all else is compared. Indeed, praise belongs to virtue: people are apt to do noble things as a result of virtue, whereas encomiums belong to the works of both body and soul alike. But perhaps being very precise about these things is more

35   appropriate to those who have labored over encomiums; to us it is clear,
1102a   on the basis of what has been said, that happiness belongs among the things that are honored and complete. This seems to be the case also on account of its being a principle: it is for the sake of this that we all do everything else, and we posit the principle and the cause of the good things as being something honorable and divine.

---

69 · For a possible interpretation of this line, see Aristotle's treatment of capacities in 2.1 and 2.5.

70 · The reading of the MSS. Burnet, following the text of Bywater and the suggestion of Susemihl, deletes the final verb such that the emended text would read in translation, "we deem blessed and happy the gods as well as the most divine of men."

CHAPTER THIRTEEN

Now, since happiness is a certain activity of soul in accord with complete   5
virtue, what concerns virtue would have to be examined. For perhaps in
this way we might better contemplate happiness as well. And the politician in the true sense seems to have labored over this especially, for he
wishes to make the citizens good and obedient to the laws. We have as
models of these the lawgivers of the Cretans and Lacedaimonians, and   10
any others of that sort there might have been. And if this examination is
a part of the political art, it is clear that the investigation would be in accord with the choice made at the beginning.

But that we must examine the virtue distinctive of a human being is
clear, for we were seeking both the human good and human happiness.   15
We mean by "virtue distinctive of a human being" not that of the body
but that of the soul, and by "happiness" we mean an activity of soul. But
if these things are so, then it is clear that the politician ought to know
in some way about the soul, just as also someone who is going to treat
the eye must know the whole body as well—and even more so inasmuch   20
as the political art is more honorable and better than medicine. Those
physicians who are refined take very seriously what pertains to knowledge of the body, and the politician too ought to contemplate the soul;
but he ought to contemplate it for the sake of these things and up to the
point that is adequate for what is being sought: to be more precise is per-   25
haps too difficult given the tasks set forth. But some points concerning
the soul are stated sufficiently even in the exoteric[71] arguments, and one
ought to make use of them—for example, that one part of it is nonrational, another possesses reason. Yet whether these things are divided,
like the parts of the body and every divisible thing, or whether they are
two in speech but naturally inseparable, like the convex and the concave   30
in the circumference of a circle, makes no difference with a view to the
present task.

Of the nonrational, one part seems to be that which is held in common and vegetative—I mean that which causes nutrition and growth.
For someone could posit that such a capacity of the soul is in all things   1102b
that are nourished and in embryos, and that this same capacity is present
in the completed things as well, for this is more rational than positing

---

71 · Evidently a reference to writings intended for a wider or more popular audience;
see also n. 26.

some other capacity. A certain virtue belonging to this capacity, then, appears to be common and not distinctive of a human being. For this part
5   and its capacity seem particularly active in sleep, but the good person and the bad would be least distinct in sleep. (So it is that people assert that for half of life, the happy do not differ at all from the wretched, and this is to be expected: sleep is an idleness of that in reference to which the soul is said to be serious or base.) Unless, that is, certain motions do reach them
10   to a small degree, and in this way the dreams of the decent[72] are better than those of people at random. But enough about these things: let the nutritive part be, since it does not naturally share in human virtue.

Yet there seems to be also a certain other nature of the soul that is nonrational, although it does share in reason in a way. For in the case of the self-restrained person and of the one lacking self-restraint, we praise their
15   reason and that part of their soul possessing reason, since it correctly exhorts them toward the best things. But there appears to be something else in them that is by nature contrary to reason, which does battle with and strains against reason. For just as when we choose to move paralyzed parts
20   of the body to the right and they are, to the contrary, borne off to the left, so also with the soul: the impulses of those lacking self-restraint are toward things contrary [to their reason]. Yet whereas in the case of bodies, we see the thing being borne off, in the case of the soul we do not see it. But perhaps one must hold there to be, no less in the case of the soul too,
25   something contrary to reason that opposes and blocks it. How it is different does not matter at all; it too appears to share in reason, as we said. In the case of the self-restrained person, at any rate, it is obedient to the commands of reason—and perhaps it heeds those commands still more readily in the case of the moderate or courageous person, since then it is in all respects in harmony with reason.

It appears, therefore, that the nonrational part is twofold, for the veg-
30   etative part has nothing in common with reason; but that part characterized by desire, and by longing in general, shares somehow in reason inasmuch as it heeds it and is apt to be obedient to its commands. Thus we assert that [he who is in this way obedient to the commands] of his father and friends in some manner possesses reason—and not that he does so in the manner of [someone knowledgeable in] mathematics. That the nonrational part is somehow persuaded by reason is indicated both by

72 · *Epieikēs*, here in its general sense of "decent," is also rendered as "equitable" in the discussion of justice and equity in 5.10.

admonition and by all criticism as well as exhortation. But if we must as-   1103a
sert that this part too possesses reason, then that which possesses reason
will be twofold as well: what possesses it in the authoritative sense and in
itself, on the one hand, and, on the other, what has it in the sense of being
apt to listen as one does to one's father.

Virtue too is defined in accord with this distinction, for we say that
some of the virtues are intellectual, others moral:[73] wisdom, comprehen-   5
sion, and prudence being intellectual, liberality and moderation being
moral. For in speaking about someone's character, we do not say that he
is wise or comprehending but that he is gentle or moderate. Yet we praise
the wise person too with respect to the characteristic that is his, and we
say that of the characteristics, the praiseworthy ones are virtues.   10

---

73 · *Ēthikos*, here in the plural, from *ēthos*, the same word appearing in 1.3 (see n. 14
above) and, as a plural adjective, in the title of the work. When it is used in relation to
virtue or the virtues, we will always translate it as "moral," in deference to the traditional translation, "moral virtue."

Book 2

CHAPTER ONE

Virtue, then, is twofold, intellectual and moral. Both the coming-into-being and increase of intellectual virtue result mostly from teaching—hence it requires experience and time—whereas moral virtue is the result of habit, and so it is that moral virtue got its name [*ēthikē*] by a slight alteration of the term *habit* [*ethos*]. It is also clear, as a result, that none of the moral virtues are present in us by nature, since nothing that exists by nature is habituated to be other than it is. For example, a stone, because it is borne downward by nature, could not be habituated to be borne upward, not even if someone habituates it by throwing it upward ten thousand times. Fire too could not be borne downward, nor could anything else that is naturally one way be habituated to be another. Neither by nature, therefore, nor contrary to nature are the virtues present; they are instead present in us who are of such a nature as to receive them, and who are completed[1] through habit.

Further, in the case of those things present in us by nature, we are first provided with the capacities associated with them, then later on display the activities, something that is in fact clear in the case of sense perceptions. For it is not as a result of seeing many times or hearing many times that we came to have those sense perceptions; rather, it is, conversely, because we have them that we use them, and not because we use them that we have them. But the virtues we come to have by engaging in the activities first, as is the case with the arts as well. For as regards those things we must learn how to do, we learn by doing them—for example, by building houses, people become house builders, and by

[handwritten marginalia: never clear on how to get either virtue]

---

1 · Or, "who are perfected." The same participle (*teleioumenois*) may be taken to be in the middle rather than the passive voice: "and who complete or perfect themselves through habit."

playing the cithara, they become cithara players. So too, then, by doing $\quad$ 1103b
just things we become just; moderate things, moderate; and courageous
things, courageous. What happens in the cities too bears witness to this,
for by habituating citizens, lawgivers make them good, and this is the
wish of every lawgiver; all who do not do this well are in error, and it is in $\quad$ 5
this respect that a good regime[2] differs from a base regime.

Further, as a result of and on account of the same things, every virtue both comes into being and is destroyed,[3] as is similarly the case also
with an art. For it is as a result of playing the cithara that both good and
bad cithara players arise, and analogously with house builders and all the $\quad$ 10
rest: as a result of building houses well, people will be good house builders; but as a result of doing so badly, they will be bad ones. If this were
not the case, there would be no need of a teacher, but everyone would
come into being already good or bad. So too in the case of the virtues: by
doing things in our interactions with human beings, some of us become $\quad$ 15
just, others unjust; and by doing things in terrifying circumstances and
by being habituated to feel fear or confidence, some of us become courageous, others cowards. The case is similar as regards desires and bouts of
anger. For some people become moderate and gentle, others licentious
and irascible, the former as a result of conducting themselves in the one $\quad$ 20
way, the latter as a result of doing so in the other. And so, in a word, the
characteristics come into being as a result of the activities akin to them.
Hence we must make our activities be of a certain quality, for the characteristics correspond to the differences among the activities. It makes
no small difference, then, whether one is habituated in this or that way
straight from childhood but a very great difference—or rather the whole $\quad$ 25
difference.

CHAPTER TWO

Now, since the present subject is taken up, not for the sake of contemplation, as are others—for we are conducting an examination, not so that we
may know what virtue is, but so that we may become good, since otherwise there would be no benefit from it—it is necessary to examine matters pertaining to actions, that is, how one ought to perform them. For $\quad$ 30

2 · The first appearance of this important political term (*politeia*), which refers to the
authoritative ruling element in a political community. Aristotle's sixfold classification
of regimes is found in 8.10.
3 · Or, perhaps, "ruined," "corrupted" (*phtheirein*).

these actions have authoritative control over what sorts of characteristics come into being, just as we have said. Now, "acting in accord with correct reason"[4] is commonly granted, and let it be posited for now—what pertains to it will be spoken of later, both what "correct reason" is and how it relates to the virtues.[5]

1104a   But let it be agreed to in advance that every argument concerned with what ought to be done[6] is bound to be stated in outline only and not precisely—just as we said at the beginning as well, that the demands made of given arguments should accord with the subject matter in question. Matters of action and those pertaining to what is advantageous have nothing
5   stationary about them, just as matters of health do not either. And since such is the character of the general argument, still less precise is the argument concerned with particulars, for it does not fall under an art or any set of precepts. Instead, those who act ought themselves always to examine what pertains to the opportune moment [when it presents itself], as is the
10   case with both medicine and piloting. Although such is the character of the present argument, one must nonetheless attempt to be of assistance.

This, then, is the first thing that must be contemplated. Such things [as the virtues] are naturally destroyed through deficiency and excess, just as we see in the case of strength and health (for one ought to make use
15   of manifest things as witnesses on behalf of what is immanifest): excessive as well as deficient gymnastic exercises destroy strength, and, similarly, both drink and food destroy health as they increase or decrease in quantity, whereas the proportionate amounts create, increase, and preserve health. So it is too with moderation, courage, and the other virtues:
20   he who avoids and fears all things and endures nothing becomes a coward, and he who generally fears nothing but advances toward all things becomes reckless. Similarly, he who enjoys every pleasure and abstains from none becomes licentious; but he who avoids every pleasure, as the boorish do, is a sort of "insensible" person.[7] Moderation and courage are

---

4 · This famous phrase (*orthos logos*), which translators have often rendered as "right reason," is as ambiguous as its components: what is "correct" (*orthos*) may or may not be true, and a *logos* may be a rational argument or merely a "speech," rational or not.
5 · Literally, "to the other virtues."
6 · The reading of the principal MSS accepted by Burnet, but Bywater, following Bekker and Susemihl, emends the text to read in translation: "concerned with actions."
7 · That is, someone lacking in sense perception (*anaisthētos*); Aristotle will note later (1107b8) that there really is no name for such persons, since they "do not come into being very much" (see also 1108b21, 1109a4, 1114a10, and 1119a7).

indeed destroyed by excess and deficiency, but they are preserved by the   25
mean.[8] —→ *middle*

But not only do the coming-into-being and increase [of the virtues], as
well as their destruction, occur as a result of the same things and through
the same things, but the activities [associated with the virtues] too will be
found in the same things [as are responsible for their coming-into-being
and increase]. For this is the case also with other, more manifest things—   30
for example, in the case of strength: it comes into being as a result of
taking much nourishment and enduring many exertions, and he who is
strong would especially be able to do just these things. So too in the case
of the virtues, for as a result of abstaining from pleasures, we become
moderate; and by so becoming, we are especially able to abstain from   35
them. Similar is the case of courage as well: by being habituated to dis-   1104b
dain frightening things and to endure them, we become courageous, and
by so becoming, we will be especially able to endure frightening things.

CHAPTER THREE

The pleasure or pain that accompanies someone's deeds ought to be taken   5
as a sign of his characteristics: he who abstains from bodily pleasures and
enjoys this very abstention is moderate, but he who is vexed in doing so is
licentious; he who endures terrifying things and enjoys doing so, or at any
rate is not pained by it, is courageous, but he who is pained thereby is a
coward. For moral virtue is concerned with pleasures and pains: it is on account of the pleasure involved that we do base things, and it is on account   10
of the pain that we abstain from noble ones. Thus one must be brought
up in a certain way straight from childhood, as Plato asserts, so as to enjoy as well as to be pained by what one ought, for this is correct education.

Further, if the virtues are concerned with actions and passions, and
pleasure and pain accompany every passion and every action, then on this   15
account too virtue would be concerned with pleasures and pains. Punishments are indicative of this as well, since they arise through these [pains]:
they are a sort of curative treatment, and curative treatments naturally
take place through contraries.

Further, as we said just recently too, every characteristic of soul shows
its nature in relation to and in its concern for the sorts of things by which   20

8 · The first appearance of this famous term (*hē mesotēs*) in Aristotle's account of the
moral phenomena.

it naturally becomes worse or better: it is through pleasures and pains that people become base, by pursuing and avoiding these, either the pleasures and pains that one ought not to pursue or avoid, or when one ought not, or as one ought not, or in as many other such conditions as are defined by reason.[9] Thus people even define the virtues as certain dispassionate and calm states, though such a definition is not good; for they say simply this much but not "as one ought," "as one ought not," "when," and any other things posited in addition. Virtue, therefore, has been posited as being such as to produce the best [actions] in relation to pleasures and pains, and vice as being the contrary.

But that [virtue and vice] are concerned with the same things might become manifest to us also from these considerations: there being three objects of choice and three of avoidance—the noble, the advantageous, and the pleasant together with their three contraries, the shameful, the harmful, and the painful—in all these the good person is apt to be correct, the bad person to err, but especially as regards pleasure. For pleasure is common to the animals and attendant upon all things done through choice, since both what is noble and what is advantageous appear pleasant.

Further, pleasure has been a part of the upbringing of us all from infancy; it is difficult to remove this experience, since our life has been so ingrained with it. We also take pleasure and pain as the rule of our actions, some of us to a greater degree, some to a lesser. It is on account of this, then, that one's entire concern necessarily pertains to pleasure and pain, for taking delight and feeling pain make no small contribution to our actions' being well or badly done.

Further, it is more difficult to battle against pleasure than against spiritedness, as Heraclitus[10] asserts, and art and virtue always arise in connection with that which is more difficult: the doing of something well is better when it is more difficult. As a result, and on account of this, the whole

---

9 · Or, "the argument" (*ho logos*). The phrase may well refer to "[correct] reason"; see also n. 4 above.

10 · Heraclitus of Ephesus lived in the late sixth century and is numbered among the most famous of the pre-Socratic philosophers. It is uncertain what remark Aristotle here refers to, and the fragment most frequently cited by commentators ("with *thumos* it is difficult to do battle / for whatever it craves is purchased at the price of soul") appears to use *thumos* (translated in the text above by "spiritedness," its usual meaning in later Attic Greek) as an equivalent of, rather than in contrast to, craving or desire (see Gauthier and Jolif). Aristotle cites this line also in the *Politics* (1315a30–31) and *Eudemian Ethics* (1223b23).

matter of concern in both virtue and the political art is bound up with pleasures and pains. For he who deals with these well will be good, but he who does so badly will be bad.

Let it be said, then, that virtue concerns pleasures and pains; that it both increases as a result of those actions from which it comes into be-   15
ing and is destroyed when these are performed in a different manner; and that it becomes active in just those activities as a result of which it also came into being.

CHAPTER FOUR

But someone might be perplexed as to what we mean when we say that to become just, people must do just things or, to become moderate, do moderate things. For if they do just and moderate things, they already *are*   20
just and moderate, just as if they do what concerns letters and music, they are by that fact skilled [or artful] in letters and in music. Or is this not so even in the case of the arts? For it is possible to do something skillful in letters by chance or on the instructions of another. A person will actually be skilled in letters, then, when he both does something skillful and does it in a skillful way, and this is what accords with the art of letters that re-   25
sides within the person himself.

Further, what pertains in the arts is not at all similar to what pertains in the virtues. For the excellence in whatever comes into being through the arts resides in the artifacts themselves. It is enough, then, for these artifacts to be in a certain state. But whatever deeds arise in accord with the virtues are not done justly or moderately if they are merely in a cer-   30
tain state, but only if he who does those deeds is in a certain state as well: first, if he acts knowingly; second, if he acts by choosing and by choos-
ing the actions in question for their own sake; and, third, if he acts while being in a steady and unwavering state. But these criteria are irrelevant when it comes to possessing the arts—except for the knowledge itself   1105b
involved. But when it comes to the virtues, knowledge has no, or little, force, whereas the other two criteria amount to not a small part of but rather the whole affair—criteria[11] that are in fact met as a result of our doing just and moderate things many times. Matters of action are said to   5

11 · The reading of the MSS (*haper*). Perhaps better is Bywater's slight emendation of the text (*eiper*), adopted also by Burnet and Gauthier and Jolif, which might be ren-dered as follows: "the whole affair, if in fact [the virtues] are gained as a result of doing just and moderate things many times."

be just and moderate, then, when they are comparable in kind to what the just or moderate person would do. And yet he who performs these actions is not by that fact alone just and moderate, but only if he also acts as those who are just and moderate act.

It is well said, then, that as a result of doing just things, the just person comes into being and as a result of doing moderate things, the moderate person; without performing these actions, nobody would become good. Yet most people [or the many] do not do them; and, seeking refuge in argument, they suppose that they are philosophizing and that they will in this way be serious, thereby doing something similar to the sick who listen attentively to their physicians but do nothing prescribed. Just as these latter, then, will not have a body in good condition by caring for it in this way, so too the former will not have a soul in good condition by philosophizing in this way.

CHAPTER FIVE

After this, what virtue is must be examined. Now, since there are three things that are present in the soul—passions, capacities, and characteristics—virtue would be one of these. I mean by *passions* the following: desire, anger, fear, confidence, envy, joy, friendly affection,[12] hatred, yearning, emulation, pity—in general, those things that pleasure or pain accompany. And *capacities* are those things in reference to which we are said to be able to undergo these passions—for example, those in reference to which we are able to feel anger, pain, or pity. But *characteristics* are those things in reference to which we are in a good or bad state in relation to the passions; for example, if we feel anger intensely or weakly, we are in a bad condition, but if in a measured[13] way, we are in a good condition, and similarly with the other passions as well. Neither the virtues nor the vices, then, are passions, because we are not said to be serious or base in reference to the passions but in reference to the virtues and vices, and because we are neither praised nor blamed in reference to the passions simply (for neither he who is afraid nor he who is angry is praised,

12 · Or, "friendship." Although Aristotle uses exactly the same word (*philia*) for both the moral virtue taken up in 4.6 and the association of two friends discussed in books 8–9, he argues that the former does not really have a name, "though it seems most like friendship," and that the latter is finally something other than moral virtue.

13 · Or, in a manner characteristic of the middle (*mesōs*), a term related to Aristotle's doctrine of moral virtue as a "mean" (*mesotēs*) or "middle" (*to meson*). See also n. 15 below.

nor is he who is simply angry blamed, but only he who is such in a certain   1106a
way). Rather, it is in reference to the virtues and vices that we are praised
or blamed. Further, we are angry and afraid in the absence of choice, but
the virtues are certain choices or not without choice. In addition to these
considerations, in the case of the passions we are said to be moved; but   5
in that of the virtues and vices, we are not said to be moved but rather to
have a certain disposition.

On account of these considerations as well, the virtues and vices are
not capacities either. For we are not said to be either good or bad by dint
of possessing the capacity simply to undergo the passions, nor are we
praised or blamed. Further, we are possessed of capacities by nature, but
we do not by nature become good or bad. But we spoke about this before.   10

If, then, the virtues are neither passions nor capacities, it remains that
they are characteristics. What virtue is with respect to its genus, then, has
been said.

CHAPTER SIX

Yet one ought to say not only this—that virtue is a characteristic—but
also what sort of characteristic it is. So it must be stated that every virtue   15
both brings that of which it is the virtue into a good condition and causes
the work belonging to that thing to be done well. For example, the virtue of the eye makes both the eye and its work excellent,[14] for by means
of the virtue of the eye, we see well. Similarly, the virtue of a horse makes   20
the horse both excellent and good when it comes to running, and carrying its rider, and standing its ground before enemies. If indeed this is so
in all cases, then the virtue of a human being too would be that characteristic as a result of which a human being becomes good and as a result of
which he causes his own work to be done well. And how this will be, we
have already stated.

But virtue will be further manifest also as follows—if we contemplate   25
what sort of thing its nature is. In everything continuous and divisible, it
is possible to grasp the more, the less, and the equal, and these either in
reference to the thing itself or in relation to us. The equal is also a certain
middle term[15] between excess and deficiency. I mean by "a middle term   30

14 · Or, "serious" (*spoudaios*), here and in the next sentence.

15 · *To meson* (the middle term, the middle—though not necessarily the literal center
of something) as distinguished from *hē mesotēs*, which will always be rendered as "the
mean." The two are etymologically close.

of the thing" that which stands at an equal remove from each of the extremes, which is in fact one and the same thing for all; though in relation to us, it is that which neither takes too much nor is deficient. But this is not one thing, nor is it the same for all. For example, if ten is much but two is few, six is a middle term for those who take it in reference to the thing itself. For it both exceeds and is exceeded by an equal amount, and

35   this is the middle term according to the arithmetic proportion. But one
1106b ought not to grasp in this way the middle term relative to us, for if eating ten pounds is a lot but two pounds too little, the trainer will not prescribe six pounds, since perhaps even this is a lot or a little for him who will take it: for Milo,[16] it would be too little; for someone just starting gymnastic training, it would be too much. It is similar in the case of running and in that of wrestling.

5   Thus every knower of the excess and the deficiency avoids them, but seeks out the middle term and chooses this—yet not a middle belonging to the thing in question but rather the one relative to us. Indeed, every science in this way brings its work to a good conclusion, by looking to the

10   middle term and guiding the works toward this. Hence people are accustomed to saying that there is nothing to take away from or add to works that are in a good state, on the grounds that the good state is destroyed by excess and deficiency but the mean preserves it; and the good craftsmen, as we say, perform their work by looking to this. Virtue is more precise

15   and better than every art, as is nature as well. If all this is so, then virtue would be skillful in aiming at the middle term.

But I mean moral virtue, for it is concerned with passions and actions, and it is in these that excess, deficiency, and the middle term reside. For example, it is possible to be afraid, to be confident, to desire, to be angry,

20   to feel pity, and, in general, to feel pleasure and pain to a greater or lesser degree than one ought, and in both cases this is not good. But to feel them when one ought and at the things one ought, in relation to those people whom one ought, for the sake of what and as one ought—all these constitute the middle as well as what is best, which is in fact what belongs to virtue. Similarly, in the case of actions too, there is an excess, a deficiency,

25   and the middle term. Virtue is concerned with passions and actions, in which the excess is in error and the deficiency is blamed;[17] but the middle

16 · A famous wrestler of the late sixth century, hailing from Croton. He is said to have won six victories in the Olympic Games and six in the Pythian.

17 · The reading of the MSS defended by Gauthier and Jolif. Bywater, followed by Burnet and others, deletes the verb translated as "is blamed."

term is praised and guides one correctly, and both [praise and correct guidance] belong to virtue. Virtue, therefore, is a certain mean, since it, at any rate, is skillful in aiming at the middle term.

Further, while it is possible to be in error in many ways (for what is bad is unlimited [or indeterminate], as the Pythagoreans used to conjecture, what is good, limited [or determinate]), there is only one way to guide someone correctly. And thus the former is easy, the latter hard: it is easy to miss the target, hard to hit it. On account of these considerations, then, to vice belongs the excess and the deficiency, to virtue the mean.

For [people] are good[18] in one way, but in all kinds of ways bad

Virtue, therefore, is a characteristic marked by choice, residing in the mean relative to us, a characteristic defined by reason and as the prudent person would define it.[19] Virtue is also a mean with respect to two vices, the one vice related to excess, the other to deficiency; and further, it is a mean because some vices fall short of and others exceed what should be the case in both passions and actions, whereas virtue discovers and chooses the middle term. Thus, with respect to its being and the definition that states what it is, virtue is a mean; but with respect to what is best and the doing of something well, it is an extreme.

But not every action or every passion admits of the mean, for some have names that are immediately associated with baseness—for example, spitefulness, shamelessness, envy, and, when it comes to actions, adultery, theft, and murder. For all these things, and those like them, are spoken of as being themselves base, rather than just their excesses or deficiencies. It is never possible, then, to be correct as regards them, but one is always in error; and it is not possible to do what concerns such things well or not well—by committing adultery with the woman one ought and when and as one ought. Rather, doing any of these things whatever is simply in error. Similar to this, then, is thinking it right that, as regards committing injustice, being a coward, and acting licentiously, there is a mean, an excess, and a deficiency: in this way there will be a mean of an excess and of a deficiency, an excess of an excess, and a deficiency of a deficiency! And just as there is no excess and deficiency of moderation and courage, on ac-

18 · Not the usual word translated as "good" (*agathos*) but the more poetic *esthlos*. The author of the verse is unknown.

19 · An alternative reading suggested by Alexander of Aphrodisias, among others, and adopted by Bywater, would give the following translation: "residing in the mean relative to us, a mean defined by that argument by which the prudent person would define it."

count of the middle term's being somehow an extreme, so too there would
not be a mean or an excess and a deficiency of those [base acts mentioned
25   above]; rather, however they are done, they are in error. For in general
there is neither a mean of an excess and of deficiency nor an excess and
deficiency of a mean.

CHAPTER SEVEN

One must not only state this [definition] in general terms but also make
30   it harmonize with the particulars involved. For in the case of arguments
concerning actions, the general arguments are of wider application,[20]
whereas those pertaining to a part are truer: actions concern particulars,
and it is with these that the arguments ought to accord. One must grasp
these particulars from the [following] outline.

Concerning fear and confidence, then, courage is a mean. Among
1107b   those characterized by an excess, he who is excessive in fearlessness is
nameless (in fact, many of these characteristics are nameless), and he who
is excessive in feeling confident is reckless; he who is excessive in being
afraid and deficient in feeling confident is a coward. Concerning plea-
5   sures and pains—not all of them, and to a lesser degree as regards pains—
the mean is moderation, the excess, licentiousness. But those who are deficient when it comes to pleasures do not arise very much, and thus people
of this sort too have not attained a name; let them be "the insensible."

Concerning the giving and taking of money, the mean is liberality, the
10   excess and deficiency, prodigality and stinginess[21] respectively. But they
are excessive and deficient in contrary respects: the prodigal person is excessive in spending but deficient in taking, whereas the stingy is excessive
in taking but deficient in spending. Now, at present we are speaking in
15   outline and summarily, being satisfied with just that, but later what pertains to them will be defined more precisely. Concerning money, there
are also other dispositions: the mean is magnificence (for the magnificent
person differs from the liberal, the former being concerned with great
things, the latter with small); the excess is vulgarity and crassness; the de-
20   ficiency, parsimony. These differ from matters related to liberality, but
how they differ will be stated later.

20 · Or, "are common to more things" (*koinoteroi*). Some translators and commentators follow an alternative reading (*kenōteroi*) that might be rendered as follows: "the
general arguments are emptier."
21 · Literally, "illiberality" (*aneleutheria*).

Concerning honor and dishonor, the mean is greatness of soul; the excess, what is said to be a certain vanity; the deficiency, smallness of soul. And just as we were saying that liberality bears a relation to magnificence, though it differs by being concerned with small things, so also there is a   25
certain [other] virtue that bears a relation to greatness of soul, the latter being concerned with great honor, the former with small. For it is possible to long for honor as one ought and more or less than one ought; the person who is excessive in his longings in this regard is said to be ambitious,[22] the deficient unambitious, while the one in the middle is nameless. And the dispositions are in fact nameless, except the ambition   30
of the ambitious person. This is why people at the extremes lay claim to the middle ground, and we sometimes call the person in the middle "ambitious," sometimes "unambitious"; and sometimes we praise the ambi-   1108a
tious person, sometimes the unambitious one. What the cause is, on account of which we do this, will be stated subsequently. For now, let us speak about what remains in the manner that has guided us thus far.

In what concerns anger too there is an excess, a deficiency, and a mean; and although these are pretty much nameless, let us call the mean gentle-   5
ness, since we speak of the person in the middle as gentle. Of those at the extremes, let he who is excessive be irascible, the vice irascibility, and let he who is deficient be a sort of "unirascible" person, the deficiency "unirascibility."

There are also three other means, and though they bear a certain simi-   10
larity to one another, they also differ from one another. For all are concerned with our sharing in speeches and actions, but they differ because one of them is concerned with the truth in such speeches and actions, the others with what is pleasant in them. Of these latter, one is found in times of play, the other in all that relates to life [as a whole]. One must speak about these too, then, so that we may see better that in all things, the   15
mean is praiseworthy and the extremes are neither praiseworthy nor correct but instead blameworthy. Now, the majority of these are nameless, and yet one must try, as in the case of the others as well, to fashion a name for them for the sake of clarity and ease of following along.

Concerning the truth, then, let the person in the middle be said to be somebody truthful and the mean, truthfulness; the pretense that exag-   20
gerates is boastfulness, and he who possesses it, a boaster, whereas that which understates is irony and he who possesses it, an ironist. As for what

22 · Literally, "a lover of honor" (*philotimos*).

is pleasant in times of play, he who is in the middle is witty and the disposition, wittiness; the excess is buffoonery and he who possesses it, a
buffoon, while he who is deficient is a sort of boor, and the characteristic, boorishness. As for the remaining part of what is pleasant, which is
found in life [as a whole], he who is pleasant as he ought to be is friendly
and the relevant mean, friendliness.[23] But he who is friendly in excess is
obsequious, if he is such for no reason, but if he is excessively friendly for
his own advantage, he is a flatterer; he who is deficient and is in all things
unpleasant is a sort of quarrelsome and surly person.

   There are also means in the passions and concerning the passions. For
a sense of shame is not a virtue, but he who is bashful[24] is praised: in these
things too there is one person said to be in the middle, another who is in
excess, like the shy person who feels shame in everything. He who is deficient in this or is generally ashamed of nothing is shameless, whereas
he who is in the middle is bashful. Indignation[25] is a mean between envy
and spitefulness, and these concern pleasure and pain at the fortunes that
befall one's neighbors: the indignant person is pained at those who fare
well undeservedly; the envious person exceeds him because he is pained
at anyone's faring well; the spiteful is so deficient in feeling pain [at the
misfortune of others] that he even delights in it. But about these types,
there will be an opportunity to speak elsewhere.

   As for justice, since it is not spoken of in a simple way, after we have
gone through each [of the meanings of *justice*], we will say how they are
means, and similarly also with the rational virtues.[26]

CHAPTER EIGHT

There are, then, three dispositions, two of them vices—one relating to
an excess, the other to a deficiency—and one of them a virtue, namely,

23 · Or simply, "friendship" (*philia*). Books 8 and 9 examine *philia*, understood there
not as a moral virtue but as a kind of community or association that the virtues help
make possible.

24 · The word translated as "bashful" (*aidēmōn*) shares the same root as the word translated as "a sense of shame" (*aidōs*), which can also refer to the "awe" or "reverence" due
to the gods and the divine things, for example.

25 · Literally, "nemesis," also the name of a Greek goddess, the divine personification
of righteous indignation or revenge (see Hesiod, *Works and Days* 200, *Theogony* 223
and contexts).

26 · The phrase "rational virtues" (*logikai aretai*) appears nowhere else in the *Nicomachean Ethics*.

the mean. All are in some way opposed to all: the extremes are contrary both to the middle disposition and to each other, while the middle disposition is contrary to the extremes. For just as the equal is greater when compared to what is lesser and lesser when compared to what is greater, so the middle characteristics are excessive when compared to the deficient characteristics but deficient when compared to the excessive, in both passions and actions. For the courageous person appears reckless when compared to the coward, but when compared to the reckless, a coward. And similarly, the moderate person appears licentious when compared to the "insensible" one, but when compared to the licentious, "insensible"; the liberal person, when compared to the stingy, appears prodigal, but when compared to the prodigal, stingy. Hence each of those at the extremes pushes the person in the middle over to the other extreme: the coward calls the courageous man reckless, the reckless calls him a coward, and analogously in the case of the others. And although these are opposed to one another in this way, the greatest contrariety lies with the extremes in relation to each other rather than in relation to the middle term; for these extremes stand at a greater remove from each other than they do from the middle term, just as the great stands at a greater remove from the small and the small from the great than either stands from the equal.

Further, there appears to be a certain similarity of some extremes to the middle term, as recklessness has some similarity to courage and prodigality to liberality, but the extremes have the greatest dissimilarity to one another. (Things at the greatest remove from one another are defined as contraries, with the result that the more they are removed from one another, the more they are contraries of one another.)

In some cases, it is the deficiency that is more opposed to a given middle term, in some cases it is the excess. For example, it is not recklessness, which is an excess, but rather cowardice, which is a deficiency, that is more opposed to courage. Then again, it is not "insensibility," which is a deficiency, but rather licentiousness, an excess, that is more opposed to moderation. This occurs through two causes, one being the result of the thing itself: by dint of the one extreme's being closer and more similar to the middle, we set not this extreme but rather its contrary in greater opposition [to the middle term]. For example, since recklessness seems more similar and closer to courage, but cowardice less similar, we posit cowardice as being in greater opposition [to the middle term than is recklessness]: things at a greater remove from the middle term seem to be more contrary to it. This, then, is one cause, which results from the thing itself.

The other cause results from us ourselves. For those things to which
15 we somehow more naturally incline appear to a greater degree contrary
to the middle term. For example, we ourselves are naturally more inclined
toward pleasures; hence we have a greater propensity toward licentiousness than orderliness. We say, then, that those things toward which our
tendency is greater are to a greater degree contraries [of the mean]; and
on this account licentiousness, which is an excess, is more contrary to
moderation [than is "insensibility"].

CHAPTER NINE

20 That moral virtue is a mean, then, and how it is such; that it is a mean between two vices, the one relating to excess, the other to deficiency; and
that it is such on account of its being skilled in aiming at the middle term
in matters of passion and action, have been stated adequately. Hence it
25 is in fact a task to be serious, for in each case it is a task to grasp what resides in the middle. For example, to grasp the middle of a circle belongs
not to everyone but to a knower. And so too, to become angry belongs to
everyone and is an easy thing, as is also giving and spending money; but
to whom [one ought to do so], how much, when, for the sake of what,
and how—these no longer belong to everyone nor are easy. Thus in fact
30 acting well is rare, praiseworthy, and noble. Hence he who aims at the
middle term must first depart from what is more contrary to it, just as
Calypso too advises:

From this smoke and swell, keep the ship²⁷

For of the extremes, the one is more in error, the other less. Now, since it
is difficult to hit on the middle with extreme precision, we must, in accord
35 with "the second sailing,"²⁸ as they say, grasp the least of the bad things,
1109b and this will occur most of all in the way we are speaking of.
But one must examine what we ourselves readily incline toward, for

27 · In the text of Homer's *Odyssey* as it has come down to us, these words are spoken
by Odysseus to his men, as the result of Circe's advice (*Odyssey* 12.219). According to
Burnet, "[s]ome inferior MSS. have *Kirkē* [Circe, rather than Calypso] which is more
nearly right."
28 · A proverbial expression roughly equivalent to "the next best thing." Socrates, for
example, uses the expression of his turn away from the natural philosophy of his predecessors and to his characteristic examination of "the speeches": see Plato, *Phaedo* 99c9–
d1 and context. See also *Philebus* 19c2–3; *Statesman* 300c2.

some of us naturally incline to some things, others to other things. This [object of our inclination] will be recognizable from the pleasure and the pain that occur in our case. And we must drag ourselves away from it toward its contrary; for by leading ourselves far from error, we will arrive at the middle term, which is in fact what those who straighten warped lumber do. But in everything one must be especially on guard against the pleasant and pleasure, for we do not judge it impartially. What the town elders felt toward Helen, then, is what we too ought to feel toward pleasure; and in all cases we ought to utter their remark, for by thus dismissing pleasure, we will err less.[29] By doing these things, then—to speak in summary fashion—we will be most able to hit on the middle term.

But perhaps this is hard, and especially so in particular cases; for it is not easy to define how, with whom, at what sorts of things, and for how long a time one ought to be angry: sometimes we praise those who are deficient and assert that they are gentle, sometimes those who are harsh, calling them manly. But he who deviates a little from what is well done is not blamed, whether he does so in the direction of what is more [than the mean] or in that of what is less than it. But he who deviates more than that *is* blamed, for he does not go unnoticed. Yet at what point and to what extent he is blameworthy is not easy to define by means of argument, for neither is anything else that is subject to perception; such things reside in the particulars involved, the relevant decision too residing in the perception [of the particulars].

This much, then, is clear: the middle characteristic in all cases is praiseworthy, but one ought to incline sometimes toward the excess, sometimes toward the deficiency, for in this way we will most easily hit on the middle term and what is well done.

29 · See *Iliad* 3.154–160:

And when they saw Helen moving along the city walls
Softly they uttered winged words to one another:
"No indignation [*nemesis*: see n. 25] at the Trojans and well-greaved Achaeans,
Who for the sake of this woman have long suffered pains.
Terribly does she resemble, in our eyes, immortal goddesses.
But, even such as she is, let her go home in the ships
And not remain, for us and our children, a calamity hereafter."

Book 3

1109b30 Since virtue concerns passions as well as actions, and voluntary [actions] elicit praise and blame, whereas involuntary ones elicit forgiveness[1] and sometimes even pity, it is perhaps necessary for those who are examining virtue to define the voluntary and the involuntary. Doing so is useful also

35 for lawgivers with a view to both honors and punishments.

1110a Now, things that come about as a result of force or on account of ignorance seem to be involuntary. That which is forced[2] is something whose origin is external, since it is the sort of thing to which the person who is acting or undergoing something contributes nothing—for example, if a wind, or people who have control over someone, should carry him off somewhere.

But as for all that is done on account of fear of greater harm or on ac-

5 count of something noble—for example, if a tyrant should order someone to do something shameful while the tyrant has control over his parents and offspring, and if he should do it, they would be saved, but if not, they would be killed—whether this kind of thing is involuntary or voluntary admits of dispute. Something comparable occurs also when it comes

10 to casting off cargo in storms; for, in an unqualified sense, no one voluntarily jettisons cargo, but when one's own preservation and that of the rest are at issue, everyone who has sense[3] would do it. These sorts of actions, then, are mixed, though they are more voluntary [than involuntary], for

---

1 · We translate the term *sungnōmē* in book 3 as "forgiveness," but as "sympathy" in 6.11 and 7.2, 6, and 7.

2 · The term that Aristotle uses here (*biaios*) has both an active sense—that which is doing the forcing—and, more frequently in the *Ethics*, a passive one—that which is being forced.

3 · Here "sense" translates *nous*, which is elsewhere "intellect."

they are choiceworthy at the time they are done and the
accords with what is opportune at the moment.

Both what is voluntary and involuntary, then, must l
reference to when someone acts. And [in the case at h
acts voluntarily, for in fact the origin of the movement o
body] that serve as instruments in such actions is in th
And in those cases in which the origin is in the person himself, it is also up
to him to act or not to act. Such cases, therefore, are voluntary—though
in an unqualified sense, they are perhaps involuntary. For no one would
choose anything of this sort in itself. In such actions, people are some-   20
times even praised, whenever they endure something shameful or painful
in return for great and noble things. But should the contrary occur, they
are blamed, for it belongs to a base person to endure shameful things in
the service of nothing noble or measured.

In some actions, not praise but forgiveness arises, whenever someone
does what he ought not to do because the matters involved surpass hu-   25
man nature and could be endured by no one. Some things, perhaps, it is
not possible to be compelled to do; one ought instead to die while suffering the most terrible things. Indeed, the considerations that compelled
Euripides's Alcmaeon to commit matricide appear laughable.[4] But it is
difficult sometimes to decide what sort of thing one ought to choose in   30
return for what, and what ought to be endured in return for what. It is still
more difficult to abide by the judgments one makes in each case, since,
for the most part, the things people anticipate in such circumstances are
painful and those they are compelled to do are shameful, which is why
praise and blame are dependent on whether the people in question are
compelled or not to act as they do.

What sorts of actions, then, must be declared to be "forced"? Or in an   1110b
unqualified sense do forced actions occur whenever their cause is found
in external things and the person who acts contributes nothing to them?
But as for the actions that are in themselves involuntary and yet choiceworthy at the present moment in return for specific things and whose origin is in the person who acts—these actions in themselves are involun-   5

---

4 · We have only fragments of Euripides's play to which Aristotle refers here; see also
1136a13, where Aristotle quotes from the play. According to the scholiast, Alcmaeon's
father was persuaded to fight at Thebes by his wife Eriphyle, who had been bribed by
the promise of a necklace. He was killed at the battle but had learned of her treachery,
and while he was dying, he commanded his son to kill his mother, placing a curse on
him should he not comply.

y, but, at the present moment and in return for these specific things, they are voluntary. Yet they are more like voluntary actions, for actions reside in particulars, and these are voluntary. What sort of thing ought to be chosen in return for what is not easy to explain, for there are many distinctions involved in the relevant particulars.

If someone should declare that pleasant things and noble things are characterized by force (for they exercise compulsion, while being external), then in this way everything would be forced: it is for the sake of these things that everyone does everything. And people who act as a result of force and involuntarily, do so painfully, while those who act on account of what is pleasant and noble do so with pleasure. But it is laughable to attribute to external things the cause[5] of one's being easily snared by such things, rather than to attribute the cause to oneself, as is attributing the cause of noble things to oneself but that of shameful ones to pleasures. That which is forced, then, appears to be something whose origin is external, while he who is forced contributes nothing thereto.

What is done on account of ignorance is in every case not voluntary, but it is involuntary [only] when it causes the person who acts to feel pain and regret. For the person who does anything whatever on account of ignorance, while feeling no degree of disgust at the action, has not acted voluntarily, since he, at least, did not know what he was doing; and yet he has not in turn acted involuntarily either, since he is not pained by so acting. In the case of what is done on account of ignorance, then, he who feels regret seems to act involuntarily; but as for the person who is without regret, since he is different, let his action be "nonvoluntary." For since they differ, it is better that each have his own name.

Acting on account of ignorance seems different also from acting in ignorance, for he who is drunk or angry is not held to act on account of ignorance but rather on account of one of the things stated, [drunkenness or anger,] and not with knowledge but in ignorance. Everyone who is corrupt, then, is ignorant of what he ought to do and to abstain from; and through this sort of error, people become unjust and bad in general. But one does not wish to use the term *involuntary* when somebody is ignorant of what is advantageous; for the ignorance involved in one's choice is the cause, not of what is involuntary, but of one's corruption. Nor is the ignorance of the relevant general [principle] the cause of an act's being in-

5 · The verb here translated as "to attribute the cause to" (*aitiasthai*) can also carry the sense of moral condemnation, "to blame."

voluntary (for people are indeed blamed on account of this sort of general ignorance); the cause, rather, is the ignorance pertaining to the various particulars, both the circumstances of the action and what it concerns. In these latter cases, there is both pity and forgiveness, since he who is ignorant of any of these particulars acts involuntarily.

1111a

Perhaps, then, it is not the worst thing to distinguish what and how many these particulars are—that is, who acts, what he does, and with respect to what or in what circumstances, and sometimes also with what (for example, with an instrument), for the sake of what (for example, preservation), and how (for example, gently or violently). Now, no one could be ignorant of *all* these things, unless he were mad; and it is clear that he would not be ignorant of the person who is acting either, for how could he be ignorant of himself? But someone could be ignorant of what he is doing—for example, people declare that they had a slip of the tongue while speaking; or that they did not know that what they said was forbidden, as Aeschylus said about the Mysteries;[6] or that, as the fellow said about the catapult, he set it off while wishing simply to exhibit it. Someone might also suppose that his own son is an enemy, just as Merope did,[7] that the pointed spear has been blunted, or that the stone is pumice. Or, by giving someone a drink to save him, one might kill him. Or wishing only to touch, as sparring partners do, someone might land a blow. So, since there may be ignorance about all these things that constitute an action, he who is ignorant of any them is held to have acted involuntarily, and especially so in the case of the most authoritative of them—the most authoritative seeming to be those particular circumstances that constitute the action and the end for the sake of which it is done. Although an action is said to be involuntary in reference to this sort of ignorance, it must still be painful to the person in question and done with regret.

5

10

15

20

Since what is involuntary is that which is the result of force and done on account of ignorance, what is voluntary would seem to be something whose origin is in the person himself, who knows the particulars that constitute the action. For perhaps it is not nobly said that involuntary actions are those done on account of spiritedness or desire: in that case, in

25

6 · According to this famous story, the great tragic poet Aeschylus (ca. 525–456) was brought before the Areopagus and charged with divulging secrets of the Eleusinian Mysteries. He defended himself by arguing that he had never been initiated into the Mysteries and said only what came to his lips. He was acquitted of the charges.

7 · A story from another lost play of Euripides. Merope recognizes her son just in time to avoid killing him. See also Aristotle, *Poetics* 1153b3–54a10.

the first place, none of the other animals will ever act voluntarily, nor will children. Second, do we do nothing stemming from desire and spiritedness voluntarily, or do we do noble things voluntarily and only the shameful ones involuntarily? Or is this laughable, since they both arise from one cause? It is perhaps strange to declare to be involuntary those things for which one ought to long; and one ought both to be angry at certain things and to desire certain things—for example, health and learning. It seems too that involuntary things are painful, but that what accords with our desire is pleasant. Further, what difference does it make, with respect to their being involuntary, whether errors are made by way of calculation or spiritedness? For both kinds of error are to be avoided. And the non-rational passions[8] seem to be no less characteristically human [than calculation or reason], such that the actions resulting from spiritedness and desire too belong to a human being. It is strange, then, to set these down as involuntary.

CHAPTER TWO

Since both the voluntary and the involuntary have been defined, going through what pertains to choice comes next. For choice seems to belong very much to virtue and to distinguish people's characters more than actions do. Now, choice appears to be something voluntary, but not the same thing as the voluntary; rather, what is voluntary is wider in scope. For both children and animals share in what is voluntary but not in choice, and we say that sudden actions are voluntary but do not stem from choice.

Those who say that choice is desire, spiritedness, wish, or some specific opinion do not seem to speak correctly. For choice is not something shared by nonrational animals, but desire and spiritedness are. And the person lacking self-restraint acts out of desire, but he does not do so from choice; the self-restrained person, conversely, acts from choice but not out of desire. And whereas desire opposes choice, desire does not oppose desire. Desire has to do with what is pleasant and painful, whereas choice has to do with neither the painful nor the pleasant. Still less is choice spiritedness. For what arises through spiritedness seems least of all to stem from choice.

8 · Burnet argues that the word for "passions" (*pathē*) is rightly omitted from the best MSS. If so, the line would read: "And what is nonrational is held to be no less characteristically human."

Yet choice is not wish either, although it appears to be closely related   20
to it. For choice does not have impossibilities [as its object], and if someone should claim to choose something impossible, he would be held to
be foolish. But wish may be for things that are impossible—for example,
immortality. And wish is also concerned with things that could not come
about through one's own doing, such as wishing that a certain actor or
athlete win a victory. No one chooses these sorts of things, but only those   25
that a person supposes may come about through his own doing. Further, wish has more to do with the end, whereas choice has to do with
things conducive to that end—for example, we wish to be healthy,
whereas we choose those things by which we will become healthy; and
we wish to be happy and we declare this, whereas to say that we choose to
be happy is not appropriate. For, on the whole, choice appears to be con-   30
cerned with things that are up to us.

Choice would also not be opinion, then, since opinion seems to be
concerned with all matters and to be no less concerned with things eternal or impossible than with those that are up to us. And opinion is divided
into false and true, not into bad and good, whereas choice is divided more
into these latter two. Perhaps, then, no one even says that choice is the   1112a
same as opinion generally. But it is not the same as some specific opinion
either. For it is by choosing the good or bad things that we are of a certain
sort, not by opining about them. And we choose to take or to avoid one   5
of these sorts of [good or bad] things, but we opine about what it is, or to
whom or in what manner it is advantageous, and we really do not opine
about taking or avoiding them. Choice is also praised more for being directed at what it ought to be or for being correctly made,[9] whereas opinion is praised for how true it is. And we choose what we know most of all
to be good, whereas we opine about what we do not know at all well. The
same people do not seem both to choose and to opine what is best; rather,
some opine what is better, yet, on account of their vice, they choose what   10
they ought not. But whether opinion precedes choice or accompanies it
makes no difference, for we are not examining this but whether it is the
same thing as some specific opinion.

What or what sort of thing is choice, then, since it is none of the things
mentioned? It indeed appears to be something voluntary, but not everything voluntary is an object of choice. But is it, therefore, at least an object   15

9 · This first clause could also be translated: "And choice is praised more for being directed at what it ought to be *than* for being correctly made."

of prior deliberation? For choice is accompanied by reason and thought. Even the name appears to signify this, as though it refers to something "taken before other things."[10]

CHAPTER THREE

Do people deliberate about all things and is everything an object of deliberation, or about some things is there no deliberation? Perhaps it must be said that an object of deliberation is not something that a foolish or mad person would deliberate about, but rather something a person with sense[11] would deliberate about. And about eternal things no one deliberates—for example, about the cosmos or about the fact that the diagonal and the side of a square are incommensurable. But neither does anyone deliberate about things that are in motion but that always come into being in the same ways, whether from necessity or also by nature (or on account of some other cause)—for example, about solstices and sunrises. Nor does anyone deliberate about things that are different at different times—for example, droughts and rains—or about what arises from chance—for example, the discovery of treasure. But neither is there deliberation about *every* human concern: for example, no Lacedaimonian deliberates about how the Scythians might best govern themselves. For none of these things could come into being through us.

But we do deliberate about things that are up to us and subject to action, and these are in fact what remain. For nature, necessity, and chance seem to be causes, but so too are intellect and all that comes about through a human being. When it comes to human beings, each deliberates about actions that come about through his own doing. And as for those sciences marked by precision and self-sufficiency, there is no deliberation involved—for example, concerning letters (for we do not doubt how one must write). Rather, we deliberate about all those things that come about through us but that do not always do so in the same way—for example, what pertains to the arts of medicine and moneymaking—and we deliberate more about the art of piloting than about gymnastic training, insofar as the former has attained less precision. And further, the case is similar with the remaining arts or sciences, but more so with the arts than the sciences, for we have more doubt in the case of the arts. But deliberat-

10 · The Greek is *proairesis*, which means literally "taking [*-airesis*] before [*pro-*]" other things and so choosing or preferring some things over others.
11 · Literally, with "intellect" or "mind" (*nous*).

ing occurs in matters that are for the most part so, where it is unclear how they will turn out and in which something is undetermined. We also take counselors when it comes to great matters, distrusting ourselves on the grounds that we are not adequate to determine them.

We deliberate not about the ends but about things conducive to the ends. For a doctor does not deliberate about whether he is to make some-one healthy, an orator whether he is to persuade, or a politician whether he is to produce good order—in fact, nobody else deliberates about the end either. Rather, having set down the end, they examine how and through what things it will exist. And if the end in question appears to come about in several ways, they examine the easiest and noblest way it will do so. But if it will come to completion through only one means, they examine how it will come about through this means and how this one, in turn, will arise through some other means, until they arrive at the first cause, which is the last in the process of discovery. For he who deliber-ates seems to investigate and to analyze in the manner just spoken of, as he would in the case of a geometrical figure (and it appears that not ev-ery investigation is a deliberation—for example, mathematical investiga-tions—but every deliberation is an investigation); and what is last in the analysis is first in the process of coming into being. If people happen on something impossible, they leave it be—for example, they need money,[12] but it is impossible for this to be furnished—but if it appears possible, they undertake to do it. Possible things are those that could come to be through us; for what comes to be by way of our friends is in a way through us, since the origin is in us. Sometimes what is sought out are the instru-ments needed, sometimes the use of them; and similarly too in the case of all else, sometimes what is sought out is that through which the end will come about, sometimes in what way or through whom it will come about.[13]

It seems, then, as has been said, that a human being is an origin of his actions. Deliberation is concerned with actions that happen through one's own doing, and the actions are for the sake of something else. For not the end, but rather the things conducive to the end, would be the ob-ject of deliberation. So deliberation is not about particular facts either— for example, whether this is a loaf of bread or whether it has been baked

12 · Or, "goods," "property" (*chrēmata*).
13 · As Stewart points out, this clause is awkward. It is not clear, for example, what the phrase "all else" refers to, or whether "through whom" should be translated as "through what" and thus as explanatory of "in what way."

as it ought to have been—for these belong to sense perception. And if a person will always be deliberating about them, the process will go on infinitely. The object of deliberation and the object of choice are the same thing, except that the object of choice has already been determined, for that which has been decided by deliberation is what is chosen: each person ceases investigating how he will act when he traces the origin [of the action] back to himself and to what it is in himself that leads the way, since this is what chooses. This is clear also from the ancient regimes, which Homer portrayed: the kings used to announce to the people what they had chosen. Since what is chosen is a certain longing, marked by deliberation, for something that is up to us, choice would in fact be a deliberative longing for things that are up to us. For in deciding something on the basis of having deliberated about it, we long for it in accord with our deliberation.

Let choice, then, be thus spoken of in outline—both the sorts of things it is concerned with and that it has to do with things conducive to ends.

CHAPTER FOUR

That wish is concerned with the end has been said. But in the opinion of some people, wish is for the good; in the opinion of others, it is for what appears good. Yet for those who say that the object of wish is the good, it turns out that if someone chooses incorrectly, then what he wishes for is not actually an object of wish (for if it will be an object of wish, it will also be good, whereas if someone were to choose incorrectly, it would in fact be bad). But for those, in turn, who say that the apparent good is the object of wish, it turns out that there is no object of wish by nature but only what seems to be good to each. But different things appear good to different people, and, should it so happen, even contrary things.

But if, then, these [consequences] are not satisfactory, must it be declared that the object of wish in the unqualified and true sense is the good, but that for each person it is what appears to him to be good? To the serious person, then, the object of wish is to be in a true sense [or, is what exists in a true sense], whereas to the base person, it is whatever chances to appear good, just as is the case also with bodies: to those who are in good condition, things that are truly healthful appear to be such, whereas to those who are sick, the healthful things appear to be different from these, as is similarly the case with what is bitter, sweet, hot, cold, and each of the rest. For

the serious person judges each case correctly, and in each case what is true   30
appears to him. For with respect to each characteristic, there are noble and
pleasant things peculiar to it; and the serious person is distinguished perhaps most of all by his seeing what is true in each case, just as if he were a
rule and measure of them. But in the case of most people [or the many], a
deception appears to occur on account of the pleasure involved, for what is
not good appears to them as good. They choose the pleasant, then, on the   1113b
grounds that it is good, and they avoid pain on the grounds that it is bad.

CHAPTER FIVE

Since the object of wish is the end, whereas the objects of deliberation
and choice are the means conducive to the end, actions pertaining to
these latter would accord with choice and be voluntary. And the activi-   5
ties of the virtues pertain to these means. Virtue too, then, is up to us, and
similarly vice is as well. For in the cases in which it is up to us to act, so too
is not acting; and where there may be a "no," there may also be a "yes." As a
result, if acting, when it is noble to do so, is up to us, then also not acting,
when it is shameful not to do so, will be up to us; and if not acting, when   10
it is noble not to, is up to us, then also acting, when it is shameful to do
so, is up to us. If doing the noble and the shameful things is up to us, and
similarly also not doing them—and this, as we saw, amounts to our being
good or bad—it is, therefore, up to us to be decent or base.

But the saying that "no one is voluntarily wicked or involuntarily   15
blessed"[14] appears to be in one respect false and in another respect true.
For no one is involuntarily blessed, but corruption is voluntary. Otherwise, one would have to dispute the points now being made, at least, and
deny that a human being is the origin and begetter of his actions, as he is
also of his offspring. But if these points appear to be the case, and we are
not able to trace the origins [of our actions] to any other origins apart from   20
those within us, then these very actions are up to us and voluntary. And
these considerations appear to be born witness to both in the case of each
person individually and in that of lawgivers themselves. For they punish
and seek revenge on those who do corrupt things (insofar as the latter do

14 · The source of this saying is uncertain, though the scholiast suggests that it is a fragment or adaptation of a line from the poet Epicharmus. The idea that no one is voluntarily bad recurs in Plato's dialogues; see, e.g., *Laws* 731c, 734b, 863b, 868c; *Protagoras*
345d; *Timaeus* 86d.

not act as a result of force or on account of an ignorance of which they are
25   not themselves the cause[15]), and they honor those who do noble things,
on the grounds that they will thereby exhort the latter and punish the former. And yet nobody exhorts us to do those things that are neither up to
us nor voluntary, on the grounds that it is pointless to persuade someone
not to feel heat or suffer pain or be hungry or any other such thing, since
we will suffer them nonetheless.

30   For in fact [lawgivers] do punish the ignorance that depends on oneself, if someone is held to be a cause of his own ignorance—for example,
in the case of those who are drunk, the penalties are doubled.[16] For the origin [of the ignorance] is in oneself, since one is in control of not getting
drunk, and it is drunkenness that is the cause of the ignorance in question. Also, they punish those who are ignorant of anything in the laws,
which people ought to know and which it is not difficult to know. The
1114a   case is similar in other matters as well, whenever people seem to be ignorant through carelessness, on the grounds that it was up to them not to be
ignorant, since they are in control of taking the appropriate care.

But perhaps someone is the sort of person who does not take that ap-
5   propriate care. Yet by living loosely, people are themselves the causes of
their becoming such a sort and of their being unjust and licentious—the
former, by doing vicious things; the latter, by passing the time in drinking bouts and the like. For the activities that pertain in each case produce
people of a corresponding sort. This is clear from those who take the appropriate care with a view to any contest or action whatever, for they are
continually engaged in the relevant activity. To be ignorant, then, that the
10   corresponding characteristics come from engaging in a given activity is
exactly the mark of someone who is insensible.

Further, it is unreasonable [to say] that he who commits injustice does
not wish to be unjust or that he who is licentious does not wish to be licentious. If someone who is not acting in ignorance does those things as a
result of which he will be unjust, then he would be voluntarily unjust—it
is surely not the case that if somebody who is unjust merely wishes to cease
to be unjust, he will cease being it in fact and thus be just: neither will the
15   sick person in this way become healthy. And if it did happen in this way,

15 · Or, "are not themselves to blame."
16 · At *Politics* 1274b19, Aristotle notes that this was a law peculiar to Pittacus (ca. 650–
570), one of the Seven Sages, who was for ten years a dictator of his city, Mytilene. See
also *Rhetoric* 1402b10.

then the person in question is sick voluntarily, as a result of living his life without self-restraint and in disobedience to his doctors. At one time, then, it was possible for him not to be sick; but in letting himself go, it is no longer possible, just as it is not possible for someone to toss away a stone and then retrieve it. Nonetheless, the throwing was up to him, because the origin [of the throwing] is in him. In this way too, it was possible at the beginning for both the unjust person and the licentious one   20
not to become such as they are, and hence they are what they are voluntarily; but once they become such, it is no longer possible for them to be otherwise.

Not only are the vices of the soul voluntary, but, for some people, so too are the vices of the body, namely, for those people whom we in fact censure. For nobody censures those who are ugly on account of nature, whereas people do censure those who are ugly through want of exercise and failing to take the appropriate care. Similar too is the case of feeble-   25
ness or defects, for no one would reproach somebody who is blind by nature or from sickness or suffering a blow; rather, one would pity such a person. But he who is blind from drunkenness or other licentiousness, everyone would censure. Hence, with respect to the vices of the body, those that are up to us are censured, those not up to us are not censured. If this is so, then in the case of the other vices too, those that are censured would   30
be up to us.

But someone might say that while all people aim at what appears good to them, they do not have control over that very appearance;[17] rather, the end appears to each according to whatever sort of person he is. If, then,   1114b
each person is somehow a cause of his own characteristic, he himself will somehow be a cause also of the appearance [of the good]. Otherwise — if he is not such a cause — then no one is a cause of his own bad actions. Rather, it is on account of a person's ignorance of the end that he performs these bad actions, because he supposes that, through them, what is   5
best will be his; and in this case, his aiming at the end is not self-chosen. Instead, one must simply be born as someone who has, as it were, the vision by which he will judge nobly and take hold of the true good, and he is of a good nature to whom this noble [capacity] belongs by nature. For when it comes to the greatest and noblest thing — which it is not possible

---

17 · Here the term is *phantasia*, which can also mean "imagination," the soul's ability to present or represent appearances or images.

10   either to get or to learn from another, but rather one is simply such by
      birth as to have this—to have been born so well and nobly in this respect
      would constitute natural goodness in the complete and true sense.

          If these things are true, how, then, will virtue be any more voluntary
      than vice? For to both alike, to both the good person and the bad, the end
      appears and is set down by nature (or in whatever way); and by referring
15   to this, they do all else in whatever way they do it. Whether, then, the end
      (of whatever sort it may be) does not appear to each person by nature but
      is in some respect dependent on the person himself, or whether, granting
      that the end is indeed natural, yet because the serious person does all else
      voluntarily, his virtue too is a voluntary thing—[in either case,] vice too
20   would be no less voluntary [than virtue]. For [just as in the case of the ac-
      tions taken by the good person,] so the actions taken by the bad person
      are similarly traceable to him himself, even if that is not so when it comes
      to the end [that guides him]. If, then, just as is said, the virtues are volun-
      tary (and indeed we ourselves are somehow joint causes of our character-
      istics, and by being of a certain sort, we set down this or that sort of end),
25   the vices too would be voluntary, for their case is similar [to that of the
      virtues].

          As for what concerns the virtues taken together, then, their genus was
      stated by us in outline: that they are means and that they are character-
      istics; that they are in themselves productive of the actions out of which
      they come to be; that they are up to us and voluntary; and that [they
30   prompt us to act] in the way correct reason commands. But actions and
      characteristics are not voluntary in a similar way. For in the case of ac-
      tions, from the beginning up to the end we exercise authoritative control
      over them, knowing the particulars involved; whereas in the case of the
      characteristics, we are in control of the beginning of them, but at each
1115a moment, the growth [that results from the relevant activity] is not no-
      ticed, just as in the case of illnesses. But because it was once in our power
      to make use of [the characteristics] in this or that way, they are voluntary.

          But taking up each virtue again, let us say what they are, what sorts of
5   things they are concerned with, and in what way. At the same time, how
      many there are will be clear as well.

CHAPTER SIX

And first let us speak about courage. Now, that it is a mean with respect
to fear and confidence has already become apparent. It is clear that we

fear frightening things, and these are, to speak unqualifiedly, bad things. Hence people also define fear as the anticipation of a bad thing.[18] We fear, then, all the bad things—for example, disrepute, poverty, sickness, friendlessness, and death—but the courageous person is not held to be concerned with all of these. For some things one even ought to fear, and it is noble to do so and shameful not to—for example, disrepute, since he who fears this is decent and bashful, whereas he who does not is shameless, though he is said by some to be courageous in a metaphorical sense: he bears a certain likeness to the courageous man because the courageous man is in fact a sort of fearless person. One ought not to fear poverty, perhaps, or sickness, or, in general, anything that is not the result of vice or one's own doing. But he who is fearless concerning these things is not courageous either, though we do say that he too is fearless by dint of a certain similarity [to the truly courageous]. For though some may be cowards in the dangers of war, they are nonetheless liberal and cheerfully confident in the face of a loss of money. And someone who is afraid of wanton violence against his children and wife, or of malicious envy or something of this sort, is not a coward. Nor if a person is confident when he is about to be flogged is he courageous.

With what sort of frightening things, then, is the courageous man concerned? Or is he concerned with those that are such to the greatest degree? For no one more steadfastly endures terrible things. And the most frightening thing is death, for it is a limit [or end], and there seems to be nothing else for the dead, nothing either good or bad. But the courageous man would seem not to be concerned with death in any or every circumstance—for example, death at sea or by way of illnesses. In what circumstances, then? Or is it in the noblest? Such deaths are those that occur in war, for they happen amid the greatest and noblest danger. In agreement with these considerations are also the honors given in cities and by monarchs.

In the authoritative sense, then, a courageous man could be said to be someone who is fearless when it comes to a noble death and to any situation that brings death suddenly to hand. What pertains to war is above all of this character. Yet surely the courageous man is fearless also at sea and in sicknesses, though not in the way that sailors are. For the courageous man despairs of his preservation and is disgusted with this sort of death, whereas the sailors are of good hope, given their experience. But at

18 · See, e.g., Plato, *Protagoras* 358d6–7 and *Laches* 198b8.

the same time too, the courageous act like men[19] in circumstances where
5　prowess in battle is possible or dying is noble; but in the sorts of destruction mentioned, by contrast, neither such prowess nor nobility is possible.

CHAPTER SEVEN

What is frightening is not the same for all, and we say that there is a certain frightening thing that is too much for a human being to bear. This is
frightening to everyone, then, at least to everyone who has sense; whereas
the frightening things that are within the scope of what is humanly bear-
10　able differ in magnitude, that is, in being greater or lesser, and similarly
too do the things that inspire confidence differ.

　　But the courageous man is as undaunted as a human being can be. He
will fear things of this sort, then, but he will endure them in the way that
he ought and as reason commands, for the sake of the noble, for this is
the end of virtue. It is possible to fear these things more and less [than
15　one ought] and, further, to fear things that are not frightening as if they
were. One of the errors that arise is to fear what one ought not, another is
to fear in a way one ought not, and yet another is to fear when one ought
not or something of this sort. The case is similar also with things that inspire confidence. He, then, who endures and fears what he ought and for
the sake of what he ought, and in the way he ought and when, and who is
20　similarly confident as well, is courageous. For the courageous man suffers
and acts in accord with what is worthy and as reason would command.
Moreover, the end of every activity is that which accords with the characteristic, and to the courageous man, courage is noble.[20] Such too, therefore, is the end, for each thing is defined by its end. For the sake of the
noble, therefore, the courageous man endures and does what accords
with courage.

　　As for those who are marked by excess, he who exceeds in fearlessness
25　is nameless (it was previously said by us that many [characteristics] are
nameless), but someone would be mad or insensitive to pain if he should
fear nothing, neither earthquake nor floods, as people claim about the

19 · The root of the verb here (*andrizein*) is *anēr*, a male in an emphatic sense, a "real
man"; it is related also to the moral virtue *andreia*, which we translate as "courage" but
which means literally "manliness."

20 · Rassow suggests an alternative reading: "This is also the case for the courageous
man, and courage is noble."

Celts. He who exceeds in confidence when it comes to frightening things is reckless, and the reckless person is held to be both a boaster and a pretender to courage; at any rate, as the courageous man actually is with respect to frightening things, so the reckless wishes to appear to be. In the circumstances in which he is able to do so, then, he imitates the courageous man. Hence the majority of them are in fact "reckless cowards," for although they are reckless where circumstances permit it, they do not endure frightening things.

He who exceeds in being fearful is a coward, for he fears what one ought not and in the way one ought not, and all the things of that sort that follow. He is also deficient in feeling confidence, but it is in his exceeding in feeling pain that he is more conspicuous. The coward, therefore, is someone of faint hope, for he fears everything. The courageous man is the opposite, since to feel confident is to be of good hope.

The coward, the reckless, and the courageous are concerned with the same things, then, but they differ in relation to them. For the former two exceed and are deficient respectively, whereas the latter holds to the middle and in the way he ought. The reckless are also impetuous, and though prior to the dangers they are willing, in the midst of them they withdraw, whereas courageous men are keen in the deeds but quiet beforehand.

In accord with what has been said, then, courage is a mean with respect to what inspires confidence and fear in the situations spoken of, and it chooses and endures what it does because it is noble to do so, or because it is shameful not to. But dying in order to flee poverty, erotic love, or something painful is not the mark of a courageous man but rather of a coward. For it is softness to flee suffering, and such a person endures death not because it is noble to do so but in order to avoid a bad thing.

CHAPTER EIGHT

Courage is something of this sort, then, but there are also other kinds of courage spoken of, in five ways. First is the courage found in the citizen,[21] since it seems most like courage properly speaking. For citizens seem to endure dangers on account of the legal penalties and reproaches involved, as well as on account of the honors at stake. For this reason too people seem to be most courageous wherever cowards are dishonored and the

21 · More literally, "political courage," the *andreia* that is *politikē*.

courageous honored. And such are those whom Homer depicts—for example, Diomedes and Hector:

Polydamas will be the first to lay a reproach upon me.[22]

And:

25   For Hector will one day declare among the Trojans, speaking in the assembly,
"The son of Tydeus, by me...."[23]

This most closely resembles the courage spoken of before, because it arises through virtue, that is, through a sense of shame and longing for what is noble (since it is for honor) and through avoiding reproach, since it is shameful.

30   Someone might put in the same category also those who are compelled by their rulers [to fight], but they are inferior insofar as they do what they do not through a sense of shame but on account of fear, and because they are fleeing not what is shameful but what is painful to them. For those in authority compel them, just as does Hector:

Him whom I might spy far off from the battle, crouching in fear,
35   It is certain that he will not be able to flee the dogs.[24]

And if those who assign military posts drive their men back into their
1116b   ranks by beating them,[25] they do the same thing, as do those who station their men in front of trenches and such things. For all are using compulsion, and one ought not to be courageous on account of compulsion but because it is noble to be such.

But experience of particular things seems to be courage as well. So it
5   is that Socrates too supposed courage to be knowledge.[26] Yet different people are experienced in different things, and in matters of war, it is the

---

22 · Homer, *Iliad* 22.100.

23 · Ibid., 8.148. The full line is, "The son of Tydeus, by me being put to flight, ran for the ships."

24 · Ibid., 2.391. It is Agammenon, not Hector, who speaks. See *Politics* 1285a, where Aristotle correctly attributes the speech to Agammenon.

25 · According to some commentators who take Herodotus 7.223 as their source, this was a practice of the Persians, who used whips to force their troops forward at Thermopylae.

26 · Or, "science" (*epistēmē*). See the definition of courage at *Laches* 199a10–b1 and *Protagoras* 360d4–5.

professional soldiers who are such. For there seem to be many false alarms in war, which professional soldiers especially see through. Hence they appear courageous, because the others do not know what these false alarms are. Then too, professional soldiers are especially able to make an attack and not to suffer one, as a result of their experience, since they are able to use their weapons and possess the sorts of things that are most excellent for both making an attack and not suffering one oneself. They, then, are like armed men fighting unarmed ones or trained athletes contesting with private amateurs. And indeed, in these sorts of contests, it is not the most courageous who are fittest for battle but those who are especially strong and have the best bodies. But professional soldiers become cowards when the danger outstrips them and they are lacking in numbers and preparations. For they are the first to flee, whereas the citizen soldiers, who remain in place, die, just as happened at the temple of Hermes.²⁷ For to citizen soldiers, it is shameful to flee and death is more choiceworthy than preservation of the kind indicated; whereas those who from the very beginning were taking risks on the supposition that they were the stronger ones, once they realize they are not, they flee, because they fear death more than shame. But a courageous man is not of this sort.

People refer to spiritedness as courage because those who act on account of spiritedness do in fact seem to be courageous (like brute animals who turn on those who have wounded them) and because the courageous are spirited. For spiritedness renders a person most ready to face dangers, and so it is that Homer said, "he infused strength into his spirit," and "he roused up his might and his spirit," and "strength piercing his nostrils," and "his blood boiled."²⁸ For everything of this sort seems to signal the awakening and impulse of spiritedness. Courageous men, then, act on account of the noble, though their spiritedness does work together with them, whereas brute animals act on account of pain, as a result of being struck or afraid: if they are in the forest or the marshland, they do not approach. Hence it is not courage to rush impulsively into danger, being driven by pain and spiritedness, without seeing in advance any of the terrible things

27 · According to the scholiast, this refers to a battle during which the Coroneans, having been betrayed to the Phocian commander Onomachus, nonetheless stood their ground and were slaughtered while their Boeotian auxiliaries fled.
28 · The first phrase refers to *Iliad* 14.151 and 16.529, the second to *Iliad* 5.470. The third phrase refers to the *Odyssey* 24.318, but the fourth does not come from the texts of Homer as we have them. The scholiast indicates that it comes from Theocritus; see also *De Anima* 403a31.

involved. In this way, at any rate, even asses would be courageous when they are hungry; for although they are being beaten, they nonetheless do not move off from their grazing. And adulterers too, on account of their desire, do many daring things.[29]

Yet the courage that arises through spiritedness appears to be the most natural kind; and if it includes choice and that end for the sake of which [the act ought to be done], it is courage. And certainly when human beings are angry, they feel pain; but when they exact revenge, they feel pleasure. Those who fight on account of anger or revenge are fit for battle, but they are not courageous, since they fight not on account of the noble or as reason commands but on account of their passion. Yet they are in possession of something closely resembling courage.

Nor indeed are those of good hope courageous. Because they have won many victories on many occasions, they are confident in the midst of dangers, and they do resemble the courageous, since both are confident. But courageous men are confident on account of the points stated previously, whereas the hopeful are confident because they suppose they are strongest and would suffer nothing in the event. Those who are drunk also do this sort of thing, for they come to be of good hope. But when such things as they hope for do not turn out for them, they flee. Yet, as we noted, it belongs to the courageous man to endure what is and appears to be frightening to a human being because it is noble to do so and shameful not to. Hence it also seems that it is more courageous to be fearless and calm amid unforeseen dangers than amid those that are clear beforehand: the former reaction would depend more on one's characteristic, since fearlessness in the face of such unforeseen dangers would stem less from preparation. In the case of foreseen dangers, a person would make his choice on the basis of calculation and reason, whereas in the case of sudden dangers, he would choose in accord with his characteristic.

But the ignorant too appear courageous, and they are not far from those who are of good hope. Yet they are inferior insofar as they have no claim to merit, whereas those of good hope do. Hence the latter in fact remain in their station for a certain time. But if those who have been deceived discern that things are different from what they surmise, they flee,

---

29 · A line that follows—"It is not courage, therefore, to rush impulsively into danger on account of pain or spiritedness"—largely repeats a previous line and is omitted in the best MS.

just as happened to the Argives when they encountered the Laconians, supposing them to be Sicyonians.[30]

Of what sort the courageous are, as well as those who merely seem courageous, has been stated.

CHAPTER NINE

Now although courage is concerned with confidence and fear, it is not similarly concerned with both but is instead more concerned with frightening things. For he who is calm in frightening situations and is as he ought to be in the face of them is courageous, more so than he who is as he ought to be when it comes to what inspires confidence. It is because they endure painful things, as was said,[31] that people are spoken of as courageous. Hence courage is in fact a painful thing and is justly praised, since it is more difficult to endure painful things than to abstain from pleasures. Nevertheless, the end that pertains to courage would seem to be pleasant but to be obscured by the circumstances that surround it, as occurs, for example, in gymnastic contests. For to boxers, the end—the crown and the honors—for the sake of which they fight is pleasant, but being struck is grievous and, given that they are made of flesh and blood, painful, as is all the exertion involved. And because there are many such painful things involved, the end for the sake of which boxers fight, being a small thing, appears not to be pleasant at all.

If, therefore, what concerns courage is this sort of thing, then death and wounds will be painful to the courageous man and he will endure them involuntarily, but he will endure them because it is noble to do so or because it is shameful not to. And the more he possesses complete virtue and the happier he is, the more he will be pained at the prospect of death. For to this sort of person, living is especially worthwhile, and he is deprived of the greatest goods knowingly—and this is a painful thing. Yet he is not less courageous for that, but perhaps even more so, because he chooses what is noble in war instead of these [greatest goods]. Hence the activity is not pleasant in the case of *all* the virtues, except insofar as the virtue attains its end. But perhaps nothing prevents those who are not of this sort from nonetheless being the most excellent

30
35
1117b
5
10
15

30 · See Xenophon, *Hellenica* 4.4.10.
31 · See 1115b7–13.

soldiers—those who are less courageous, yet possess nothing else good.
20   For such men are ready to face dangers, and they exchange their lives for small gain.

Let what concerns courage, then, be stated up to this point. But it is not difficult to grasp what it is, in outline at least, from what has been said.

CHAPTER TEN

After this virtue, let us speak about moderation, for these seem to be the virtues of the nonrational parts [of the soul]. Now, that moderation is
25   a mean with respect to pleasures has been stated by us, for it is less concerned with pains than with pleasures, and it is concerned with each in dissimilar ways; licentiousness too is manifest in the same things. Let us now define the sorts of pleasures with which they are concerned.

Let the bodily pleasures, then, be distinguished from those that belong to the soul—for example, love of honor [or ambition], love of learning—
30   for, of these latter pleasures, each person enjoys the one he is disposed to love, his body not being at all affected by them but rather his thought. People who are concerned with such pleasures are not spoken of as either moderate or licentious, nor, similarly, are those concerned with any of the other nonbodily pleasures. As for people who are lovers of myth and
35   disposed to storytelling and who while away the days on whatever chance matters they may happen on—we say that they are idle chatterers but not
1118a   licentious. Nor do we say that those who are pained over money or friends are licentious.

Moderation would be concerned with the bodily pleasures, and not even with all of them. For people who enjoy the pleasures stemming from sight—for example, colors, shapes, and drawings—are not spoken of as
5   either moderate or licentious, and yet it would seem possible to enjoy these things too in the way one ought as well as in an excessive or deficient way. This is similarly the case also with hearing, for no one calls licentious those who take excessive enjoyment in melodies or dramatic oratory, nor does anyone call moderate those who enjoy them in the way they ought. Nor does anyone speak this way about people taken up with smells, ex-
10   cept incidentally, for we do not say that people who enjoy the smell of apples, roses, or incense are licentious, but rather those who enjoy the smell of fancy perfume or gourmet foods. For the licentious enjoy these because, through such smells, they come to have a memory of things they

desire. One could see others too enjoying the smell of foods when they are hungry, but enjoying such things belongs to a licentious person, since for him they are objects of desire. In the case of the other animals, there is no pleasure associated with these perceptions, except incidentally, for it is not the smell of hares that the hounds enjoy but their meat, and the smell produces the perception [of the meat to be enjoyed]. The lion too enjoys not the sound of the cow's voice but the eating of the cow, though the fact that the cow was nearby he perceived through the sound of its voice, and so he appears to enjoy this. And, similarly, the lion does not take enjoyment because he sees "a deer or a goat in the fields,"[32] but because he will have its meat.

Moderation and licentiousness are concerned with the sorts of pleasures that the rest of the animals also share in—which is why these pleasures appear slavish and brutish—namely, the pleasures of touch and taste. But in fact moderation and licentiousness appear to deal with taste only to a small extent or not at all. For it belongs to the sense of taste to discriminate among flavors, which is just what people who test wines and season meats do. But they do not even enjoy these things very much, or at least not if they are licentious; instead, the licentious enjoy the delight that comes about entirely through touch, in food, drink, and the matters said to belong to Aphrodite. Hence a certain gourmand[33] prayed for his throat to become longer than a crane's, on the grounds that he takes his pleasure through touch. So licentiousness pertains to the most common[34] of the senses; and it might be held to be justly subject to the greatest reproach, because it belongs to us not inasmuch as we are human but inasmuch as we are animals. To enjoy these sorts of things, then, and to be fond of them most of all, is brutish. The most liberal[35] of the pleasures that arise through touch are excepted—for example, those in the gymnasia connected with massage and heat—since the touch that is of interest to the licentious person does not concern the whole body but only certain parts.

15

20

25

30

1118b

5

---

32 · The phrase alludes to *Iliad* 3.24.

33 · This gourmand is identified in the *Eudemian Ethics* (1231a17) as Philoxenos, son of Eryxis.

34 · The term (*koinos*) suggests in the first place "widely shared" but also, by extension, "ordinary" or "vulgar."

35 · The substantive use of the adjective *eleutherios*, which refers most generally to the quality or qualities that distinguish a free man—above all, in the *Ethics*, the freedom from any slavish attachment to money.

CHAPTER ELEVEN

Of the desires, some seem to be common, others idiosyncratic and ac-
10   quired. For example, the desire for food is natural, for everyone who lacks
it desires dry or wet food, and sometimes both; and as Homer asserts, one
who is young and in the bloom of youth desires a "marriage-bed."[36] But
beyond this, not everyone desires this or that sort of thing, or the same
things; hence [the object of desire] appears to be peculiarly our own.
Nevertheless, it has at least something natural about it too, for different
things are pleasant to different people, and some things are more pleasant
15   to all than are just any chance ones.

In the natural desires, then, few people err and in only one direction,
namely, toward what is too much. For to eat random things or to drink
until one is overfull is to exceed the quantity that accords with nature,
since the natural desire is for the satisfaction of need. Hence these people
20   are said to be gluttons on the grounds that they gorge themselves beyond
what is needful, and those who are extremely slavish become people of
this sort.

With respect to the idiosyncratic pleasures, many people err and in
many different ways. For although the lovers of this or that sort of thing
are said to enjoy what they ought not, or to enjoy something more than
25   most people do, or in a way they ought not, the licentious exceed in all
these ways. For they both enjoy some things they ought not (these are
hateful things); and if they enjoy some of the sorts of things one ought
to enjoy, they do so more than they ought or more than most people
do. That the excess with respect to the pleasures is licentiousness and is
blameworthy, then, is clear.

Concerning pains, it is not for enduring them (as in the case of cour-
30   age) that a person is spoken of as moderate, nor is he spoken of as licentious for not doing so. Rather, he is spoken of as licentious for being
pained more than he ought to be because he does not attain his pleasures
(and, for him, pleasure produces pain as well), whereas a person is spoken of as moderate for not being pained by the absence of pleasure and
1119a   for abstaining from pleasure. The licentious person, then, desires all the
pleasures or the especially pleasant ones, and he is led by his desire so that
he chooses these instead of other things. Hence he is pained both by fail-

36 · *Iliad* 24.129.

ing to obtain his desire and by desiring itself. For desire is accompanied
by pain, though it seems strange to be pained on account of pleasure.   5

Those who are deficient when it comes to pleasures and enjoy them
less than they ought do not arise very often, because this sort of "insensibility" is not characteristically human; even the rest of the animals distinguish among their foods and enjoy some but not others. And if there is
someone for whom nothing is pleasant or who does not distinguish one
thing from another, he would be far from human. And this sort of person   10
has not obtained a name because he does not arise very often.

The moderate person takes the middle path with respect to these
things. He does not take pleasure in those things that are particularly
pleasant to a licentious person—rather, he is disgusted by them—and
in general the moderate person does not take pleasure in things he ought
not or in any such thing to an excessive degree; and when pleasures are
absent, he neither feels pain as a result nor desires them, or does so only
in a measured way and not more than he ought, or when he ought not, or   15
anything of this sort in general. But as for all the pleasures that are conducive to health or good conditioning, these the moderate person will long
for in a measured way and as he ought; he will long also for such other
pleasures as do not impede the healthy pleasures, or are not opposed to
what is noble, or do not outstrip his resources. For he who *is* disposed to
the contrary is fond of such pleasures more than they are worth, whereas
the moderate person is not of this sort but is as correct reason commands.   20

CHAPTER TWELVE

Licentiousness seems more voluntary than cowardice, for the former
arises on account of pleasure, the latter on account of pain; and of these
two, pleasure is something we choose, pain something we avoid. And
pain unhinges a person and destroys the nature of him who undergoes it,
whereas pleasure does no such thing. So it is more voluntary and hence   25
more subject to reproach. Indeed, it is easier to be habituated in relation
to pleasures, for there are many such things in life; and the processes of
habituation in the case of pleasures are free from danger, but it is the reverse in the case of frightening things. And it might seem that cowardice is not voluntary in the same way as the particular instances of it are.
For cowardice itself is without pain, whereas in the particular instances
of cowardice, people are unhinged on account of the pain they undergo,

30   such that they both throw down their weapons and do other unseemly
things. Hence these things seem to be forced as well. In the case of the
licentious person, to the contrary, the particular instances are voluntary
(since he desires and longs for something), whereas the whole [character-
istic] is less so, for no one desires to be licentious.

We apply the name "licentiousness" also to the errors of children, for
1119b   there is a certain resemblance.[37] Which is named for which makes no difference to the present considerations, yet it is clear that what comes later
is named for what comes earlier. And the transferring of this meaning
seems not to have been badly done, since whatever longs for shameful
5   things and can undergo much growth ought to be chastised, and desire
and a child are especially of this description: children too live according
to desire, and the longing for pleasure is present in them especially. If,
then, this longing will not be obedient and placed under that which rules,
it will grow too great, for the longing for pleasure is insatiable and bom-
bards from all sides someone who lacks sense; the activity of the desire
10   increases the innate desire, and if the desires are great and intense, they
drive out calculation. Hence they ought to be measured, and few, and in
no way opposed to reason—we say that a thing of that sort is "obedient"
and "chastised"—and just as a child ought to live in accord with the command of his tutor, so too the desiring part ought to live in accord with
15   reason. Hence the desiring part of the moderate person ought thus to be
in harmony with reason: the target for both is the noble, and the moderate person desires what he ought and in the way that he ought and when.
It is also in this way that reason commands.

Let these things, then, be stated by us concerning moderation.

---

37 · The term used here (*akolastos*) can be used of children who are "spoiled." It literally means "unchecked" or "unpunished" and so is related to the term translated as
"chastise" (*kolazein*).

Book 4

Let us speak next in order about liberality. It seems, then, to be a mean with respect to money.[1] For the liberal person is praised not in situations of war or in those in which the moderate person is praised, or, again, in those that involve legal adjudications. Rather, he is praised when it comes to the giving and taking of money, and more with regard to the giving of it. (We mean by *money* all those things whose worth is measured in legal currency.) Prodigality and stinginess are excesses and deficiencies pertaining to money; and while we always ascribe stinginess to those who are more serious about money than they ought to be, we sometimes assign the term *prodigality* to a combination of things, for we call prodigal those who lack self-restraint and who, in their licentiousness, spend lavishly. Hence the prodigal are held to be very base people, since they have many vices simultaneously. But in fact they are not appropriately called by this name, because a "prodigal person" means someone who has one vice, namely, ruining his own resources.[2] For a prodigal person is destroyed by his own doing, since the destruction of one's own resources seems to be a kind of self-destruction, on the grounds that it is through these resources that one is able to live. We take prodigality, then, in this sense.

Regarding things that have a use, it is possible to use them either well or badly, and wealth belongs among things useful to us. In each case, the person who has the virtue pertaining to a given thing uses it best. Hence he who has the virtue pertaining to money uses wealth best, and this is the

1119b25

30

1120a

5

1 · Or, "goods," "property" (*chrēmata*), as distinguished from "legal currency" (*nomisma*).

2 · "Resources" here translates *ousia*, a noun derived from the verb *to be* that can in philosophical contexts be translated as "being." Hence to destroy one's "resources" is in a sense to destroy one's being.

liberal person. The use of money seems to consist in spending and giving
it, whereas taking and safeguarding money seem to constitute more its
acquisition. Thus it belongs to the liberal person more to give to whom
he ought than to take from whom he ought or to refrain from taking from
whom he ought not, since it belongs to virtue more to act well than to
fare well and to do what is noble than not to do what is shameful. It is also
not unclear that acting well and doing what is noble correspond with giving, while faring well and not acting shamefully correspond with taking.
Moreover, gratitude flows to one who gives and not to one who refrains
from taking, and praise even more so. It is also easier to refrain from taking than it is to give, for people are less inclined to give away their own
property than they are to refrain from taking that of another. And those
who give are spoken of as liberal, whereas those who refrain from taking
are praised, not with a view to liberality, but more with a view to justice;
those who take are not praised at all. Of all those who act on the basis of
virtue, liberal human beings are perhaps loved most, for they are advantageous to others, and this consists in giving.

Actions that accord with virtue are noble and for the sake of the noble.
The liberal person too, then, will give for the sake of the noble and correctly: he will give to whom he ought and as much as and when he ought,
and anything else that accompanies correct giving. Moreover, he will do
these things with pleasure or without pain, since what accords with virtue
is pleasant or not painful—in fact, least of all is it painful. But the person
who gives to whom he ought not, or who gives not for the sake of what
is noble but for some other cause, will not be spoken of as liberal but as
something else, which is the case also with the person who is pained by
giving. For he would choose money rather than noble action, and this is
not the mark of a liberal human being. The liberal person will also refrain from taking from where he ought not, since someone who does not
honor money will not engage in this sort of taking; he would not even be
apt to ask [for money], since someone who is a benefactor is not readily
the recipient of a benefit. And the liberal person will take from where he
ought—for example, from his own possessions—not on the grounds that
it is noble to do so but on the grounds that it is necessary, so that he may be
able to give to others. But he is not careless with his own possessions, since
he wishes, at least, to aid some people through these very possessions. And
he will not give to just anyone, so that he may be able to give to whom he
ought and when and where it is noble to do so. Yet it very much belongs

to the liberal person also to exceed in giving, such that there is little left   5
for himself, for it is typical of a liberal person not to look out for himself.

Liberality is spoken of in reference to a person's resources, since what is
liberal consists not in the specific amount given but in the characteristic
of the giver, and the characteristic relates to his resources.[3] In fact, noth-   10
ing prevents the person who gives a lesser amount from being the more
liberal one, if he gives from a lesser total amount. And those who did not
acquire what they themselves own but inherited it seem more liberal, for
they are without the experience of need; and all people are fonder of the
works [or products] that are their own, just as parents and poets are.[4] It is
also not easy for a liberal person to be wealthy, since he is inclined neither   15
to accept nor to safeguard money; rather, he is inclined even to throw it
away, since he does not honor money on its own account but rather for
the sake of giving it. Hence the accusation is leveled against chance that
those who most deserve wealth are the least wealthy in fact. Yet this happens not without reason, for it is not possible to possess money without taking the requisite care so as to have it, just as is the case with other   20
things. The liberal person surely will not give to whom he ought not and
when he ought not or any other such thing, since he would then no longer
be acting in accord with liberality; and by spending on these things, he
would not be able to spend on the things he ought. For, just as was said,
he who spends in accord with his resources and on what he ought is liberal, whereas he who exceeds these is prodigal. Hence we do not speak   25
of tyrants as prodigal, because for them to exceed their great wealth,
through gifts and expenditures, seems no easy thing.

Since, then, liberality is a mean with respect to the giving and taking
of money, the liberal person will both give and spend on what he ought
and as much as he ought, in things small and great alike, and he will do so   30
with pleasure. Moreover, he will take from where he ought and as much
as he ought: since the virtue is a mean with respect to both giving and
taking, he will do both as he ought, for this sort of taking corresponds
with equitable giving, whereas what is not of this character is contrary.
The giving and taking that correspond with each other, then, arise simultaneously in the same person, but the contrary kinds clearly do not. If he   1121a

3 · The translation of the final phrase follows Bywater and Burnet; another reading is
suggested by Stewart: "this person gives in accord with his resources."
4 · Aristotle's remark here recalls a similar one of Socrates in Plato's *Republic* (330c3–6);
consider also below, 1167b28–1168a2.

happens to spend contrary to what he ought and to what is noble, he will be pained, though in a measured way and as he ought, since it belongs to virtue to feel both pleasure and pain at the things one ought and as one ought. The liberal person, moreover, is easy to deal with in money mat-
5　ters, for he can be done injustice, since he does not honor money, at any rate; and he is more vexed if he fails to spend what he ought than pained if he does spend what he ought not, and he is not content with the view of Simonides.[5] The prodigal person thoroughly errs in these matters too, for he neither takes pleasure in the things he ought or as he ought, nor is he pained. This will be more manifest as we proceed.
10　　　It was stated by us, then, that prodigality and stinginess are excesses and deficiencies, and in two ways—in giving and in taking—for we put spending in the category of giving. Now, prodigality exceeds in giving and not taking, and is deficient in taking, whereas stinginess is deficient
15　in giving but exceeds in taking, though only in small things. The different parts of prodigality, then, do not all fit together, since it is not easy to give to all while taking from none: resources quickly run out for those who give their own possessions to others, and these are the very people who are held to be prodigal. Yet this sort of person, at least, would seem to be bet-
20　ter, and in not a small way, than the stingy person, because he is easily cur-able, by the effects of both age and want, and he can arrive at the middle term because he possesses the traits of the liberal person: he both gives and does not take, but in neither case does he do so as he ought or well. If, then, he should be habituated in the manner indicated, or changed in some other way, he would be liberal, for he will give to whom he ought
25　and not take from where he ought not.[6] Hence too his character does not seem to be base, since to exceed in giving and in not taking is the mark of neither a corrupt nor a lowborn person, but of a foolish one. He who is prodigal in this manner is held to be much better than the stingy per-son, both on account of the points stated and because the prodigal person benefits many and the stingy no one, not even himself.
30　　　But the majority of those who are prodigal, as has been said, also take from where they ought not and are in this respect stingy [or illiberal].

---

5 · Simonides of Ceos (ca. 506–468) was a fifth-century poet, known for his greed. According to a story Aristotle tells in his *Rhetoric* (1391a8), when Simonides was asked by the wife of the tyrant Hiero whether it was better to be wealthy or wise, he replied, "Wealthy, for I see that the wise hang about the doors of the rich."

6 · Or, according to some MSS, "he will give to whom he ought and take from where he ought."

They become disposed to taking because they wish to spend but are not able to do so readily, since their own possessions are quickly depleted. They are compelled, therefore, to supply resources from some other quarter; at the same time too, on account of having no thought for what is noble, they care little about taking from any and all quarters. For they desire to give, and how [they supply the necessary resources] or from where they do so makes no difference to them. Because of this very thing, their acts of giving are not liberal, since they are not noble or for the sake of what is noble, nor are they done as they ought to be. Rather, sometimes they make wealthy those who ought to labor, and they might give nothing to those whose characters are measured, whereas they would give much to those who flatter them or furnish some other pleasure. Hence many of the prodigal are also licentious, for they spend readily and are lavish in their licentious pursuits; and because they do not live with a view to what is noble, they incline in the direction of pleasures. The prodigal person who is without guidance, then, changes in these directions, yet one who obtains the requisite care could arrive at the middle term and at what is proper.

But stinginess is both incurable (for it seems that age and every infirmity make people stingy) and inborn in human beings to a greater degree than is prodigality. For most people [or the many] are lovers of money more than they are inclined to giving it, and this disposition extends widely and is of multiple kinds, since there seem to be many ways to be stingy. Because stinginess is divided into two categories—deficiency in giving and excess in taking—it is not present as a complete whole in everyone but is sometimes divided: some people exceed in taking, while others are deficient in giving. For all those who have such names as "thrifty," "penny-pincher," and "miser" are deficient in giving, but they do not aim at the property of others or wish to take from others. Some people are like this on account of a certain decency and their avoidance of shameful things. For some seem to guard their money, or so at least they assert, precisely so that they will not be compelled at some point to do something shameful—among these fall also the skinflint and everyone of that sort, who are so named because they exceed in giving nothing. Some, in turn, abstain from the property of others out of fear, on the grounds that it is not easy for somebody to take the property of others and not have those others take his in return. They are satisfied, then, neither to take from nor to give to another. But still other people exceed when it comes to taking, in the sense that they take from anywhere and anything—for example, those who perform illiberal tasks, such as brothel keepers and all of their

1121b

5

10

15

20

25

30

1122a ilk, and usurers who lend small amounts at high interest.⁷ For all these
people take from where they ought not and in quantities they ought not.
Shameful greediness for gain appears to be what they have in common,
since they all endure reproach for the sake of gain, and small gain at that.
For we do not call stingy those who take great amounts from where they
5 ought not or of what they ought not—for example, tyrants who plunder
cities and pillage temples—but we speak of them more as wicked, impi-
ous, and unjust. Yet a gambler and a thief⁸ do belong among the stingy,
since they are greedy for gain in a shameful way: both engage in their
10 business and endure reproach for the sake of gain, thieves running the
greatest risks for the sake of loot, while gamblers gain from their friends
to whom they ought rather to give. Since both types, then, wish to gain
from where they ought not, their greediness for gain is shameful, and so
all such kinds of taking are marked by stinginess.

Stinginess is appropriately said to be the contrary of liberality, both be-
15 cause it is the greater vice than prodigality and because people err more in
the direction of this [extreme] than in the direction of prodigality.

As for what concerns liberality, then, and the vices opposed to it, let
this much have been said.

CHAPTER TWO

Going through what concerns magnificence as well would seem to follow next. For this too seems to be a certain virtue pertaining to money,
20 although, unlike liberality, it does not extend to all actions involving
money but concerns only expenditures; and in these expenditures, it surpasses liberality in greatness. For just as the name itself signifies, magnificence is a fitting expenditure on a great thing.⁹ But greatness is relative,
since the expenditure is not the same for someone who outfits a trireme
25 as for the sponsor of a sacred embassy.¹⁰ What is fitting, then, is relative to
the person involved and to the thing on which as well as that for which he

---

7 · The MSS vary. Another possible reading for the final phrase is "who perform small
tasks for much money."

8 · Following Aspasius, we delete a third term, *pirate*, particularly in light of the next
two references to "both."

9 · *Megaloprepeia*: the prefix, *mega*, signifies the connection of the virtue to "greatness,"
prepeia to what is fitting or appropriate thereto.

10 · These are examples of both ordinary and extraordinary public offices or services
that would have been expected of wealthy citizens. See also 1122b19–23.

makes the expenditure. But he who spends on small or measured things in accord with their worth is not said to be magnificent—as, for example, in the line, "I often used to give to a wanderer"[11]—but only he who does so on great things. For the magnificent person is liberal, but the liberal person is not thereby magnificent. The deficiency of this sort of characteristic is called parsimony, whereas the excess is called crassness and vulgarity and all such things. The excess here resides, not in the magnitude of the expenditure for the things one ought to spend on, but in making an ostentatious display in the circumstances one ought not and in a way one ought not. We will speak about these [the deficiency and the excess] later.

But the magnificent person resembles a knower, since he is able to contemplate what is fitting and to spend great amounts in a suitable way. For just as we said in the beginning, the characteristic is defined by the corresponding activities and their objects. The expenditures of the magnificent person, then, are great and fitting; such too, therefore, are the works involved, since in this way the expenditure will be great and fitting to the work. As a result, the work ought to be worthy of the expenditure, the expenditure worthy of the work, or even to exceed it. The magnificent person will make these sorts of expenditures for the sake of what is noble, for this is common to the virtues. Further, he will do so both with pleasure and unstintingly. For strict accounting is a mark of parsimony. He would examine how to spend most nobly and fittingly rather than how much the work will cost or how to produce it most cheaply. It is necessary, then, that the magnificent person also be liberal, since the liberal person too will spend what he ought and as he ought. But in these considerations resides precisely what is great in the magnificent person, that is, his "greatness"; for although liberality is concerned with these matters, even from an equal expenditure the magnificent person will produce the more magnificent work.[12] For the virtue of a possession and that of a work are not the same. The possession whose price is greatest (such as gold) is the most valued, but the most valued work is the great and noble one (for the contemplation[13]

30

35

1122b

5

10

15

---

11 · Homer, *Odyssey* 17.420.

12 · The translation of this line is much disputed among modern commentators, since it is unclear whether Aristotle intends to draw a contrast between liberality and magnificence, as our translation suggests, or to continue to show their likeness in contrast to the vices associated with magnificence.

13 · Or, "beholding" (*theōria*). Here we see the connection suggested by *kalos* between "noble" and "beautiful," the nobility of the work being related to its beauty.

of such a work is wondrous, and what is magnificent is wondrous); and the virtue of a work, its magnificence, resides in its greatness.

Of expenditures, we say that some kinds are honorable, such as those
20   that concern the gods—votive offerings, [sacred] buildings, and sacrifices—and similarly too those that concern the entire divine realm and are proper objects of ambition in common affairs: for example, if people should suppose that they ought to endow a chorus splendidly or outfit a trireme or even provide a feast for the city. But in *all* cases, as was said, the
25   expenditure is referred to the person who is acting—who he is and what resources are available to him—for the expenditure must be worthy of these and be fitting not only to the work but also to the person producing it. Hence a poor man could not be magnificent, since he does not have the resources from which he might fittingly spend large amounts, and the person who tries to do this is foolish. Doing so would be contrary to what is worthy and proper, whereas spending correctly accords with virtue. But magnifi-
30   cence is fitting to those who possess these sorts of resources to begin with— whether on their own account or through their ancestors or relations—and to those who are wellborn, of good repute, and all such things, for all these things possess greatness and worthiness. The magnificent person, then, is this kind of person especially, and magnificence consists in these sorts of
35   expenditures, as was said, since they are greatest and most honored.
1123a   As for private expenditures, there are all those that occur just once (such as a wedding or anything of this sort) and anything the whole city or people of worth take seriously, as well as anything connected with the receiving and sending off of foreign guests or the giving and reciprocat-
5   ing of gifts. For the magnificent person is lavish not on himself but on the common affairs, and his gifts have a certain resemblance to votive offerings. Yet it also belongs to the magnificent person to furnish his home in a way fitting to his wealth (since this, too, is a certain ornament); and with respect to these furnishings, he will spend more on those works that endure over time (since these are noblest) and spend what is fitting in
10   each case. For the same thing is not suitable for gods and human beings, or in the case of a temple and that of a burial tomb. Now, each expenditure is great within its class (great expenditure on a great thing is most magnificent simply, whereas what is most magnificent in this or that circumstance is what is great in it); and what is great in the case of a given work differs from what is great in the case of the expenditure, for the most
15   beautiful ball or oil flask is magnificent as a gift for a child, though its cost is small and cheap. Since these things are so, it belongs to the magnificent

person to produce things in a magnificent way in whatever category he should produce something (for such production is not easily surpassed) and in a way worthy of the expenditure. The magnificent person, then, is of this sort.

But he who is excessive and vulgar exceeds in spending beyond what is 20 needful, as has been said. For on small things, he lavishes much expense and makes an ostentatious display of himself contrary to what is proper— for example, in giving a club dinner in the manner of a wedding feast or leading a comic chorus clothed in purple in its entrance on stage, just as they might do in Megara. And he will do all such things not for the sake 25 of the noble but to display his wealth; and for these reasons he supposes that he makes himself an object of wonder. He will spend little on what he ought to spend much, and he will spend much on what he ought to spend little. But the parsimonious person will be deficient in all respects, and after spending great amounts, he will destroy the noble for some trifle; he continually examines how to spend the least amount on whatever he may 30 produce, lamenting even this expenditure, and, in every case, supposing that he spends more than he ought.

These characteristics, then, are vices. Nevertheless, they do not bring reproach, because they are neither harmful to a neighbor nor extremely unseemly.

CHAPTER THREE

Greatness of soul[14] seems, even from its name, to be concerned with great 35 things, and let us first grasp what sort of great things it concerns. It makes no difference whether we examine the characteristic or the person who 1123b accords with the characteristic.

He, then, who deems himself worthy of great things and *is* worthy of them is held to be great souled.[15] For he who does this in a manner con-

14 · *Megalopsychia* is often translated "magnanimity," from the Latin, but this term in English has come to mean generosity or liberality rather than the sense intended by Aristotle. The more literal translation, "greatness of soul," captures better the full meaning of the virtue, both the greatness of its possessor in terms of his virtue and his awareness of this greatness.

15 · "To deem oneself worthy" (*axioun*), in accord with one's worth (*axia*), is a central idea in Aristotle's treatment of greatness of soul, and the verb and its cognates occur more than thirty times in this chapter alone. Here, *axia* is always translated as "worth"; it can also mean "merit," as we translate it in the discussion of justice in particular.

trary to his real worth is foolish, and no one who acts virtuously is foolish or mindless. The person spoken of, then, is great souled. For he who
is worthy of small things and deems himself worthy of them is moderate[16] but not great souled, since greatness of soul resides in greatness, just
as beauty involves a body of great stature: those who are small may be el-
egant and well proportioned but not beautiful. He who deems himself
worthy of great things while *not* being worthy of them is vain, though not
everyone who deems himself worthy of things greater than he is worth
is vain. He who deems himself worthy of less than he is worth is small
souled—whether he is worthy of great things or of measured things or
even if, being worthy of small things, he deems himself worthy of still less.
And most small-souled of all would seem to be the person who is in fact
worthy of great things [but does not deem himself so], for what would he
do if he were not worthy of so much?

The great-souled man, then, is an extreme in terms of greatness, but he
is in the middle in terms of his acting as one ought, since he deems himself
worthy of what accords with his worth, whereas the others exceed or are
deficient [in judging their own worth]. If, then, he deems himself worthy
of great things, while being worthy of them, and especially of the greatest things, he would be concerned with one matter most of all. Worth is
spoken of in relation to external goods, and we would posit as the greatest
of these that which we assign to the gods, that at which people of worth
aim, and that which is the prize conferred on the noblest people. Honor
is such a thing, since it is indeed the greatest of the external goods. The
great-souled man, then, is concerned with honor and dishonor in the way
that he ought to be. Even in the absence of argument, the great-souled appear to be concerned with honor, for they[17] deem themselves worthy of
honor most of all, in accord with their worth. But the small-souled person is deficient in relation to his estimation of himself and the worthiness of the great-souled man; the vain person is excessive when it comes
to himself, though not, of course, in relation to the great-souled man.

The great-souled man, if indeed he is worthy of the greatest things,
would be the best, for he who is better is always worthy of what is greater,
and he who is best is worthy of the greatest things. He who is truly great
souled, therefore, must be good, and what is great in each virtue would

16 · The term is *sōphron*. In his discussion of the virtue of moderation (*sophrōsunē*),
Aristotle confines its sphere to the bodily appetites or desires, whereas here it has a
general meaning of "sensible."

17 · Bywater brackets as an interpolation the terms *the great* that appear here in the MSS.

seem to belong to the great-souled man. It would in no way be suitable   30
for a great-souled man to flee with arms swinging or to commit injustice:
for the sake of what will he do shameful things, he to whom nothing is
great?[18] And to anyone who thoroughly examines each characteristic, it
would appear entirely laughable if the great-souled man were not good.
He would not be worthy of honor, either, if he were base, for honor is the   35
prize of virtue and is assigned to those who are good. Greatness of soul,
then, seems to be like a kind of ornament[19] of the virtues, for it makes   1124a
them greater and does not arise without them. For this reason, it is difficult, in truth, to be great souled, for it is not possible without gentlemanliness.[20]

It is especially with matters of honor and dishonor, then, that a great-   5
souled man is concerned. And he will take pleasure in a measured way
in great honors and those that come from serious human beings, on the
grounds that he obtains what is proper to him or even less—for there
could be no honor worthy of complete virtue, but he will nevertheless accept it inasmuch as they have nothing greater to assign to him. As for honor
that comes from people at random, or small honors, he will have complete   10
contempt for them, since it is not of these that he is worthy. The case of dishonor is similar, for it will not justly pertain to him. The great-souled man,
then, is, as was said, especially concerned with honors, but he will surely
also be disposed in a measured way toward wealth and political power as   15
well as all good and bad fortune, however it may occur: he will be neither
overjoyed by good fortune nor deeply grieved by bad fortune. For he is not
disposed even toward honor as though it were a very great thing, and political power and wealth are choiceworthy on account of the honor they
bring; at any rate, those who possess them wish to be honored on account
of them. But to him for whom honor is a small thing, so also are these other
concerns. Hence the great-souled are held to be haughty.   20

But instances of good fortune too seem to contribute to greatness of
soul, since the wellborn deem themselves worthy of honor, as do those who
possess political power or wealth. For they are in a position of superiority,
and everything superior in point of goodness is more honorable. Hence

18 · Aristotle repeats this phrase at 1125a3 and 15. Compare Plato, *Republic* 486a8–10,
for a similar remark in reference to the philosopher.
19 · Or, "adornment," "crown" (*kosmos*). It is used also at 1123a6–7 to refer to the way
that someone who possesses magnificence furnishes his home.
20 · *Kalokagathia*, literally "nobility and goodness," is the term typically applied in
Greek to the "gentleman," *the* exemplar of the moral virtues.

these sorts of things render people more great souled, since they are honored by some as a result. Yet in truth, only the good human being is honorable, though he who has both goodness and good fortune is deemed even
worthier of honor. But those who possess such goods in the absence of virtue do not justly deem themselves worthy of great things, nor are they correctly spoken of as great souled: in the absence of complete virtue, neither
of these is possible. And people who possess such goods become haughty
and hubristic because, in the absence of virtue, it is not easy to deal with
the goods of fortune in a suitable manner. Although not in fact being able
to deal with these goods and supposing themselves to be superior to others, they look down on them, while they themselves act in whatever random way. For they imitate the great-souled man without being like him,
and they do this wherever circumstances permit. They do not perform the
deeds that accord with virtue, then, but they look down on others nonetheless. For the great-souled man justly looks down on others (since he holds a
true opinion of himself), whereas the many do so in a random fashion.

The great-souled man is not one to hazard trifling dangers and he is
not a lover of danger either, since he honors few things. But he will hazard
great dangers, and when he does so, he throws away his life, on the grounds
that living is not at all worthwhile.[21] He is also the sort to benefit others
but is ashamed to receive a benefaction; for the former is a mark of one
who is superior, the latter of one who is inferior. He is disposed to return
a benefaction with a greater one, since in this way the person who took
the initiative [with the original benefaction] will owe him in addition and
will have also fared well thereby. But those who are great souled seem in
fact to remember whatever benefaction they may have done, yet not those
that they have been done (for he who receives the benefit is inferior to him
who performed it, whereas the great-souled man wishes to be superior);
and they seem to hear about the former with pleasure, but about the latter
with displeasure. Hence Thetis too did not speak of the benefactions she
had done for Zeus, nor did the Laconians speak of those they had done
for the Athenians but only those they had been done.[22] It belongs to the

21 · Translators often render this ambiguous phrase as "living at any cost is not worthwhile," perhaps rightly. The alternative we offer, while arresting in its import, makes
sense of the suggestion that the great-souled man will "throw away" his life and of Aristotle's repeated statement that "nothing is great" to such a man.

22 · For the reference to Thetis, see *Iliad* 1.503–4. In fact, she does refer to the good
she has done Zeus, though only in general terms: "Father Zeus, if ever I benefited you
among the immortals, either by word or by deed ..." It is not certain what the claim

great-souled also to need nothing, or scarcely anything, but to be eager to be of service, and to be great in the presence of people of worth and good fortune, but measured toward those of a middling rank. For it is a difficult   20 and august thing to be superior among the fortunate, but easy to be that way among the middling sorts; and to exalt oneself among the former is not a lowborn thing, but to do so among the latter is crude, just as is using one's strength against the weak. It belongs to the great-souled man also not to go in for the things that are generally honored or in which others hold first place, and he is idle and a procrastinator, except wherever either a great honor or a great deed is at stake; he is disposed to act in few affairs,   25 namely, in great and notable ones. He is necessarily open in both hate and love, for concealing these things is the mark of a fearful person, as is caring less for the truth than for people's opinion. He necessarily speaks and acts in an open manner: he speaks freely because he is disposed to feeling contempt for others, and he is given to truthfulness, except inasmuch as   30 he is ironic toward the many. And he is necessarily incapable of living with a view to another—except a friend—since doing so is slavish. Hence too   1125a all flatterers are servile, and all lowly types are flatterers.

The great-souled man is also not given to admiration,[23] since nothing is great to him. But neither is he one to remember evils done him; for it does not belong to a great-souled man to recall things with a grudge, in particular evils done him, but rather to overlook them. He is also not one   5 for personal conversation: he will speak neither about himself nor about another, since he does not care either to be praised himself or for others to be blamed. Nor, in turn, is he given to praising others. Hence he is not one to speak ill, not even of his enemies, except where insolence is involved.[24] When it comes to necessities or small concerns, he is least of all given to lamentation and requests for help, since it is the mark of a serious person   10 to be thus disposed toward these. He is such as to possess beautiful and useless things more than useful and beneficial ones, for this is more the mark of a self-sufficient person. Also, slowness of movement seems to be the mark of a great-souled man, as well as a deep voice and steady speech;

about the Laconians refers to. According to a scholiast, who quotes the historian Callisthenes, it refers to an event in 369 when the Spartans sought Athenian aid against the Thebans. But if so, Xenophon's account of the relevant Spartan speeches does not bear out Aristotle's claim; see Xenophon, *Hellenica* 6.5.33–34.

23 · Or, "wonder" (*thaumastikos*).

24 · Commentators disagree about the meaning of this final phrase: is the insolence (*hubris*) that of the great-souled man or of his enemy?

15   for he who is serious about few things is not given to hastiness, nor is anyone ever vehement who supposes that nothing is great, whereas a shrill
voice and quickness result from these things.

Such, then, is the great-souled man, whereas he who is deficient is
small souled, and he who exceeds is vain. Now, these people too do not
seem to be bad (since they are not malefactors), though they do err. For
20   the small-souled person, even though he is worthy of good things, deprives
himself of those he is indeed worthy of, and he seems to be in some way bad,
as a result of not deeming himself worthy of good things, and to be ignorant
of himself; he otherwise would long for the things he is worthy of, since they
are good. Nonetheless, such people are held not to be foolish but, rather,
25   timid. Yet such an opinion seems to make them even worse; for everyone
aims at those things that accord with his worth, whereas the small-souled
refrain even from noble actions and pursuits, on the grounds that they are
unworthy of them, as is similarly the case also with external goods.

But vain people are foolish and ignorant of themselves, and manifestly
so; for although they are not worthy,[25] they try their hand at the things
30   people honor, and then they are found out. They deck themselves out
when it comes to their dress and appearance and things of that sort; they
wish for the things of good fortune and for these to be manifestly theirs;
and they speak about these things,[26] on the grounds that they will be honored as a result.

But smallness of soul is more opposed to greatness of soul than vanity
is, for it both occurs more often and is worse.

35   Greatness of soul, then, is concerned with great honor, just as has been
said.

CHAPTER FOUR

1125b   But there seems to be a certain virtue also concerned with honor, just as
was said in the first discussions,[27] which would seem to stand in a similar
way to greatness of soul as liberality stands to magnificence: both are at
a remove from what is great but dispose us to be such as we ought to be
5   when it comes to measured and small things. Just as there is a mean, an
excess, and a deficiency in the taking and giving of money, so also in the
longing for honor one can have more or less of such a longing than one

25 · Or, according to some MSS, "as if they are worthy."
26 · Or, according to some MSS, "they speak about themselves."
27 · In the enumeration of the virtues in 2.7 (1107b24–31); consider also 1.5 (1095b22–30).

ought, and one can seek honor from where and in the way one ought. For
we blame the ambitious person,[28] on the grounds that he aims at getting
honor more than he ought and from where he ought not; and we blame   10
the unambitious person, on the grounds that he chooses not to be honored even in the case of what is noble. But sometimes we praise the ambitious person as manly and a lover of what is noble, and praise the unambitious person as measured and moderate, just as we said in the first
discussions as well. Yet it is clear that since we speak of the "lover of such
and such" in various ways, we do not always apply the phrase "lover of   15
honor" [or ambitious person] to the same thing; when we are offering
praise, we apply the term to those who love honor more than the many
do, but when we are speaking in terms of blame, to those who love honor
more than they ought. Since the mean is nameless, the extremes seem to
dispute over it as if it were unclaimed. But where there is excess and deficiency, there exists also a middle term, and people long for honor both
more than they ought and less; and, therefore, it is possible to do so as   20
one ought. It is this characteristic that is praised, then, although the mean
with respect to honor is nameless. In relation to ambition, it appears as
lack of ambition; in relation to lack of ambition, it appears as ambition;
and in relation to both, it somehow appears as both. This seems to be the
case also with the other virtues, but here it is the extremes that appear to   25
be opposites of each other, because the middle term has not been named.

CHAPTER FIVE

Gentleness is a mean with respect to anger. Since the middle term is
nameless, as the extremes also pretty much are, we confer the name "gentleness" on the middle term, since it inclines in the direction of the deficiency, which is nameless. The excess might be said to be a certain irascibility, for the passion involved is anger, though what produces anger is   30
manifold and varied.

The person who gets angry at the things and with whom he ought,
then, and, further, in the way, when, and for as much time as he ought, is
praised. Hence this person would be gentle, if indeed gentleness is praised.
The gentle person wishes to be calm and not led by his passion, but rather   35
as reason may command, and so to be harsh regarding the things he ought

28 · The ambitious person (*philotimos*) is literally a "lover of honor," while the one who
lacks ambition is *aphilotimos*, "without the love of honor."

1126a   and for the requisite time. But he seems to err more in the direction of
the deficiency, since the gentle person is given not to revenge but rather to
forgiveness. The deficiency, whether it is a certain lack of anger or something else, is blamed. For those who do not get angry at the things they
5   ought are held to be foolish, as are those who do not get angry in the way
they ought or when or with whom they ought. For such a person seems
to lack perception and even not to feel pain; since he does not get angry,
he seems not apt to defend himself against an attack. Yet to hold back in
this way after having been treated insolently, and to overlook such treatment of one's kin, is held to be slavish.

The excess arises in all these respects (that is, getting angry at whom
10   one ought not and at the things one ought not, more than one ought, and
more quickly and for too much time), though surely not *all* these happen
to one and the same person: this would not be possible, since what is bad
destroys even itself, and if it is complete in all its parts, it becomes intoler-
able. Irascible people, then, get angry rapidly, with whom they ought not,
15   at things they ought not, and more than they ought; but they rapidly cease
being angry, which is in fact their best trait. This happens to them because
they do not hold on to their anger but retaliate in a manifest way on account of the quickness of their temper, and then they leave off. The choleric are exceedingly quick tempered and irascible toward everyone and at
everything; hence too the name.[29] But bitter people are resistant to recon-
20   ciliation and are angry for a long time, because they constrain their spirit.
Yet it does come to a halt when they retaliate, since revenge makes anger
cease, thus producing pleasure instead of pain. Whenever this does not occur, bitter human beings carry a heavy weight: because their anger is not
25   manifest, no one persuades them out of it, and time is needed to digest it in
oneself. Such people are most troublesome to themselves and their closest
friends. We speak of harsh people as those who are harsh regarding matters
not requiring it, who are harsher than they ought to be and for too long
a time, and who cannot be reconciled unless they inflict their revenge or
punishment. We set the excess in question as more opposed to gentleness
30   [than the deficiency], for it also occurs more often, since to seek revenge is
more characteristically human, and harsh people are worse to live with.

What was said earlier is clear also from the points being discussed: it
is not easy to determine how, with whom, at what sort of things, and for

---

29 · The Greek term *akrocholos* has the sense similar to that of the English *choleric* or
bilious, meaning "an excess of *cholē*," choler or bile, the humor thought to cause anger.

how much time one ought to be angry, as well as up to what point this is correctly or erroneously done. For he who deviates a little is not blamed, 35 whether in the direction of more [than the mean] or in that of less than it, since sometimes we praise those who are deficient and assert that they 1126b are gentle, and sometimes we praise those who are harsh as manly, on the grounds that they are capable of ruling. How much and in what way he who deviates is blameworthy, then, is not easy to render by means of argument. For in each circumstance, the relevant decision resides in the perception in question. But this much at least is clear: the middle char- 5 acteristic is praiseworthy, in accord with which we are angry with whom we ought to be, at the things we ought, in the way we ought, and everything of this sort; whereas the excesses and deficiencies are blameworthy—slightly so if they are small in degree, more so if in greater degree, and extremely so if in great degree. It is clear, therefore, that one must cleave to the middle characteristic.

Let the characteristics that pertain to anger, then, be stated in this way. 10

CHAPTER SIX

In our associations with one another, both in living together and in sharing in speeches and actions, some people are held to be obsequious: those who praise everyone with a view to pleasing them and oppose nothing, but rather suppose they ought not to cause pain to anyone they may meet. At the opposite extreme to them are those people who oppose everything 15 and give no thought whatever to causing others pain, people who are called surly and quarrelsome. It is not unclear, then, that the characteristics spoken of are blameworthy and that the middle term with respect to these— in accord with which a person will approve of what he ought and in the way he ought, and similarly also disapprove—is praiseworthy. But a specific name has not been given to this characteristic, though it seems most 20 like friendship [or friendliness]. For someone who accords with the middle characteristic here is the sort of person we mean by an equitable friend, if his disposition also goes together with feeling affection for the other. This characteristic differs from friendship, however, because it is without the relevant passion, that is, the feeling of affection for those with whom one associates: it is not as a result of friendly affection[30] or hatred that the

30 · For "the feeling of affection" and "friendly affection," Aristotle uses forms of two different verbs, *stergein* and *philein*, respectively; the first usually connotes familial affection, and the second the affection connected with friendship proper (*philia*).

person in question approves of each matter as he ought, but as a result of
25   being the sort of person he is. For he will act similarly in the case of both
those he does not know and those he does know, of both those who are intimates and those who are not—except that he will also do what is suitable in
each case. For it is not proper to give similar thought to one's intimates as to
strangers, nor, in turn, to be similarly concerned about causing each pain.

It has been stated in general, then, that this person will associate with
others in the way he ought; and by referring to what is noble and advanta-
30   geous, he will aim either at not causing others pain[31] or at contributing to
their pleasure. For he seems to be concerned with the pleasures and pains
that arise in the course of our associations; and in all cases in which it is
not noble, or is harmful, for him to contribute to their pleasure, he will
disapprove of doing so, and he will choose to cause them pain. If something would bring no little disgrace or harm to the person doing it, while
35   opposing it would cause little pain, he will not approve but rather disapprove of it. He will also associate differently among people of worth
than among people at random, just as he will associate differently also
1127a   with those who are more or less known to him, and similarly in the case
of other relevant differences, assigning to each what is fitting. And while
he chooses to contribute to the pleasure of others for its own sake and is
cautious about causing others pain, he is guided by the consequences at
5   stake—I mean if what is noble and advantageous may be greater [than
the pleasure or pain involved]. And for the sake of a great pleasure in the
future, he will cause a little pain now. Such, then, is the person marked by
the middle characteristic, but he does not have a name.

As for contributing to pleasure, he who aims at being pleasant for no
ulterior motive is obsequious, whereas he who does so in order to gain
some benefit for himself, in money and all that comes from money, is
10   a flatterer. But he who disapproves of everyone was said to be surly and
quarrelsome. And the extremes appear to be opposed to each other because the middle term is nameless.

CHAPTER SEVEN

Concerning pretty much the same things, there is also the mean related to
15   boasting, but it too is nameless. Yet it is not the worst thing to go through

31 · Or, according to a suggestion of Susemihl and Gauthier and Jolif, "he will aim at
causing them pain."

considerations of this kind as well, since we would know better what pertains to character by going through each of them, and we would trust that
the virtues are means by seeing plainly that this is so in each case.

When it comes to living together, then, those who associate with a view
to pleasure and pain have been spoken of. Let us speak similarly also about   20
those who tell the truth as well as those who state falsehoods[32] related to
speeches and actions, that is, in relation to what it is they pretend to. The
boaster, then, seems apt to pretend to qualities held in high repute,
both qualities he does not actually possess and those that are greater than
the ones he does possess, whereas the ironist, conversely, seems to deny the
qualities he actually possesses or to make them less; and the person in the
middle between them is a kind of "plain dealer,"[33] since he is given to truthfulness, both in his life and his speech, acknowledging that the qualities he   25
possesses are his own and neither exaggerating nor diminishing them.

It is possible to act in each of these ways either for the sake of some goal
or for none. The sorts of things each person says and does, and thus how he
lives, are determined by the sort of person he is—if he is not acting for the
sake of some goal. In itself, what is false is base and blameworthy, whereas
what is true is noble and praiseworthy. In this way too, he who is given to   30
truthfulness, being characterized by the middle term, is praiseworthy; but
both of those given to falsehoods are blameworthy, though more so the
boaster. Yet let us speak about each, and first about the truthful person.

Now, we are speaking not about truthfulness in the case of agreements
or anything that extends into the realm of injustice or justice (for this
would belong to another virtue). Rather, in the situations in which noth-   1127b
ing of that sort is involved, the person we are speaking of is truthful both
in speech and in life because such is his characteristic. A person of this
sort would seem to be decent because he is a lover of truth; and if he is
truthful in the situations in which being such makes no difference, still   5
more so will he be truthful in the situations in which it does. For he will
guard against what is false on the grounds that it is shameful, especially
when he is also used to guarding against it in itself. And such a person is
praiseworthy. He will incline more in the direction of [saying] less than
what is true, for this appears more refined, given the irksomeness of the
excesses in this regard.

He who pretends to qualities greater than he possesses for no partic-

32 · Or, "who tell lies," here and throughout.

33 · The term used here (*authekastos*) refers to someone who "calls things by their right
names"—who "calls a spade a spade."

10   ular purpose resembles a base person (for otherwise he would not enjoy
     lying), and yet he appears more silly than bad. But when some goal is at
     issue, he who pretends to more than he is for the sake of reputation or
     honor is not overly blameworthy as a boaster, whereas he who does this
     for money (or anything that would lead to money) is more unseemly. (It is
     not in having the capacity to boast but in making the choice to do so that
15   someone is a boaster, for choice accords with one's characteristic, and he
     is a boaster because he is that sort of person.) In this same way too, some-
     one given to falsehood either enjoys falsehood in itself or longs for repu-
     tation or gain. Some who boast for the sake of reputation, then, pretend
     to the sorts of qualities that are praised or are thought to bring happiness;
     others, who boast for the sake of gain, pretend to qualities that please
20   their neighbors, the false pretense to which can go unnoticed—for ex-
     ample, when they pretend to be a prophet, a wise man, or a doctor.[34] On
     this account, most people pretend to and boast of such things, since the
     criteria just mentioned are present in [those areas of expertise].
        Ironists, who tend to say less than they are, appear more refined in their
     characters. For they seem not to speak for the sake of gain but as people
25   who avoid bombast. And they especially deny having qualities held in high
     repute—as, for instance, Socrates used to do. Those who deny small and
     manifest things are said to be humbugs and are rather contemptible, and
     sometimes such denial appears as boasting—as in the dress of the Spar-
     tans, for example.[35] For both excess and extreme deficiency are boastful,
30   but those who use irony in a measured way and concerning things that are
     not extremely obvious come to sight as refined in their irony. The boaster
     appears to lie opposite the truth teller, since he is worse than the ironist.

CHAPTER EIGHT

But since rest [or relaxation] too is a part of life, and a part of rest involves
passing the time[36] with playful amusement, it seems that here too there is

---

34 · As an alternative reading, Gauthier and Jolif, following Rackham, suggest "in pretending to be a doctor or wise prophet." This reading is supported by some MSS, and the figures of the doctor and prophet or soothsayer were often comically presented as charlatans.
35 · The Spartans adopted an ostentatiously simple mode of dress that masked differences of wealth: consider, e.g., Thucydides 1.6.4.
36 · This is the first appearance of diagōgē, the meaning of which can range from "passing the time" in the simple sense to "the conduct of one's life." It appears again at
1171b13, 1176b12 and 14, and 1177a9 and 27.

a certain suitable manner of association, that is, both certain things one   1128a
ought to say to others and a certain manner of doing so, and similarly also
with listening to others. It will also make a difference what sorts of people
one speaks among and to what sorts one listens. It is clear that, regarding
these matters as well, there is an excess and a deficiency with respect to a
middle term.

Those who are excessive in provoking laughter, then, are held to be buf-
foonish and crude, intent on doing anything for a laugh and aiming more   5
at producing laughter than at saying something seemly or at not causing
pain to the person who is the butt of the joke. On the other hand, those
who would say nothing funny themselves and who are disgusted with
those who do are held to be boorish and dour. But those who are playful
in a suitable manner are called witty, as in those who are "versatile,"[37] since   10
such witticisms seem to be movements of their character; and characters,
like bodies, are judged by their movements. Since something laughable
is always near to hand, and since most people enjoy playfulness and joking more than they ought, even buffoons are addressed as witty as if they   15
were refined. But that the two differ, and not a little, is clear from what
has been said.

Tact too is proper to the middle characteristic, and it belongs to the
tactful person to say and listen to the sorts of things suited to a decent and
liberal person. For certain things are fitting for such a person to say in his   20
turn at play, and to listen to, and the playfulness of a liberal person differs from that of a slavish one as the play of an educated person does from
that of an uneducated one. Someone could see this also from the ancient
and new comedies,[38] for in the former, foul language used to be laughable,
whereas in the latter, innuendo is more so, and these differ in no small way
in point of decorum. Must one, then, define the person who jokes well as   25
he who says what is not inappropriate for a liberal human being,[39] or as
he who does not cause pain to the listener (or even causes him delight)?
Or is this sort of thing indefinable too? For different things are hateful as
well as pleasant to different people. Such also are the things someone will

37 · Aristotle playfully traces the etymological origin of *eutrapelos* ("easily turning" and
so "witty") and of *eutropos* (versatile) to the verb *trepein*, "to turn."
38 · As commentators note, the distinction Aristotle makes here is not the official one
of the later grammarians between the "old" comedy of Aristophanes and the "new"
comedy of Menander and his successors, but a distinction between the comedies of the
fifth century, including of course those of Aristophanes, and those of Aristotle's day.
39 · Or, as some MSS read, "as he who says what is fitting for a liberal human being."

listen to, since what he endures listening to, he is held also to do. [The tactful or witty person] will not do just anything or everything, of course, since a joke is a kind of slander and legislators prohibit the slandering of some things, but they perhaps ought also to prohibit joking about some things. The refined and liberal person, then, is disposed in this way, he being like a law unto himself. The person characterized by the middle term, then, is of this sort, whether he is said to be tactful or witty.

But the buffoon cannot resist a laugh, sparing neither himself nor others if he will produce laughter, and saying the sorts of things that a refined person would never say—and some that he would not even listen to. The boor is useless in these sorts of associations because, contributing nothing to them, he is disgusted with everything.

Rest and play seem to be necessary in life. The three means that are found in life, then, have been spoken of, and all are concerned with certain speeches and actions related to community. They differ in that one is concerned with truth, whereas the others are concerned with what is pleasant. Of those concerned with the pleasant, one has to do with what is pleasant in matters of play, the other with what is pleasant in the associations connected with the rest of life.

CHAPTER NINE

It is not fitting to speak about a sense of shame as a particular virtue, for it seems more like a passion than a characteristic. It is defined, at any rate, as a certain fear of disrepute, and it turns out to resemble the fear of terrible things, for those who feel shame blush and those who fear death turn pale. Both, then, appear in some way to be bodily, which seems to be more a mark of a passion than of a characteristic. But this passion is appropriate, not to every age but to the young; for we suppose that the young ought to be bashful because the many errors they make, in living by passion, are checked by a sense of shame. And we praise those of the young who are bashful, but no one would praise an older man because he is given to shame: we suppose that he ought not to do anything that incurs shame. Shame does not belong to a decent person either, since it occurs in connection with base things (for one must not do such things). And whether these are shameful truly or shameful according to opinion makes no difference, for neither is to be done; as a result, one should not feel shame. And to be the sort of person to do anything shameful is the mark of someone base. But to be disposed to feel shame at doing any such thing, and on *this* account to suppose that one is decent, is strange. For shame attaches to voluntary acts, but the decent person will never voluntarily do base things. Yet a sense of shame might be a decent thing on the   30 basis of a given hypothesis: if a person were to do something base, he would feel shame. But this does not pertain to the virtues: if shamelessness (or not being ashamed to do shameful things) is base, it is still no more the case that he who is ashamed to do these sorts of things is decent.

Self-restraint is not a virtue either, but something mixed. Yet what concerns it will be pointed out in what comes later.[40]

But now let us speak about justice.   35

40 · See 7.1–10.

Book 5

1129a5 Concerning justice and injustice, we must examine what sort of actions they happen to be concerned with, as well as what sort of mean justice is and of what things the just is a middle term.[1] Let our examination be in accord with the same method of inquiry employed in the matters discussed earlier.

Now, we see that everyone wishes to say that justice is the sort of characteristic on the basis of which people are disposed to do just things and on the basis of which they act justly and wish for just things. It is the same

10 way also concerning injustice—that it is that on the basis of which people are unjust and wish for unjust things. Hence for us too, let these things first be set down as an outline.

What holds in the case of the sciences and capacities does not hold in that of the characteristics: the same capacity or science seems to pertain to opposites,[2] but a characteristic does not seem to pertain to opposites.

15 For example, as a result of health, one does not do things opposed to one another [—things characteristic of health and those of sickness, for example—], but only what is healthy: we say that it is a healthy walk when one walks as a healthy person would. Many times, then, the one characteristic is known from its opposite; but many times too, the characteristics are known from the things in which they are found. For if the good con-

20 dition is manifest, then the bad condition too becomes manifest; from what is conducive to it, the good condition becomes manifest, and from this good condition, what is conducive to it also becomes manifest: if the

1 · Aristotle uses two terms here to refer to justice: *dikaiosunē*, which we always translate as "justice," and *to dikaion*, the noun derived from the adjective *dikaios*, which we variously translate as "the just," "the just thing," or "what is just."

2 · Or, "contraries" (*ta enantia*), here and throughout.

good condition is firm flesh, then the bad condition is necessarily flabby flesh, and what is conducive to the good condition necessarily produces firmness in the flesh.

It follows for the most part that if one of two terms is spoken of in various ways, then the other is spoken of in various ways as well—for example, if the just is spoken of in various ways, then so too is the unjust.[3] Now, it seems that justice and injustice are spoken of in various ways, but because their meanings are close, their sharing of the same name is not noticed and is not as clear as it is in cases in which the meanings are far apart (for then the difference in their outward appearance[4] is great)—as in the case, for example, of what is called by the same name "*kleis*," either the collarbone of animals or that with which people lock doors.

So let us grasp in how many ways the unjust person is spoken of. The lawbreaker, then, is held to be unjust, as is he who grasps for more[5] and is unequal.[6] It is clear as a result that the just person will be both lawful and equal. The just, therefore, is what is lawful and what is equal; the unjust is what is unlawful and what is unequal.

Since the unjust person grasps for more, he will be concerned with the good things—not all goods but so many as good fortune and misfortune concern, which are those that are always good unqualifiedly but not always good for a particular person. Yet human beings pray for and pursue these things, though they ought not; rather, they ought to pray that the things that are good unqualifiedly be good also for them, and they ought to choose the things that are good for them in fact.

The unjust person does not always choose the greater share but chooses also the lesser share of things unqualifiedly bad. Yet because the lesser of what is bad also seems to be in some way good, and since to be grasping is to be after what is good, it is on this account that the unjust person is held to be grasping for more. He is unequal as well, for this [inequality] com-

25

30

1129b

5

10

3 · This is the reading adopted by Bekker and Bywater. Other MSS suggest the following: "for example, if the just and justice are spoken of in various ways, so too are the unjust and injustice."

4 · Aristotle uses the term *idea* here in its literal sense of outward appearance. See book 1, nn. 32 and 58.

5 · The term is *pleonektēs*, meaning literally "the having of more" and by extension the desiring of more than one is due; hence being greedy or grasping.

6 · The term is *anisos*, meaning literally "unequal," though many translate it also as "unfair." We retain the literal term, given that the notion of equality is central to the two forms of particular justice, distributive and corrective, and to law.

prehends and is common [to taking both the greater share of the good and the lesser of the bad].

Since, as noted before, he who is a lawbreaker is unjust and he who is lawful just, it is clear that all lawful things are somehow just. For matters defined by the legislative art are lawful, and each of these we declare to be just. The laws pronounce on *all* things, in their aiming at the common advantage, either for all persons or for the best or for those who have authority, either in accord with virtue[7] or in some other such way. As a result, we say that those things apt to produce and preserve happiness and its parts for the political community are in a manner just. The law orders us to do the deeds of the courageous person (for example, not to leave the order of battle or to flee or to throw down our weapons), and those of the moderate person (for example, not to commit adultery or outrage), and those of the gentle person (for example, not to strike or to slander someone), and similarly also in the case of the other virtues and corruptions; the law commands the ones and forbids the others—correctly, in the case of the law laid down correctly, and in a worse way, in the case of the law laid down haphazardly.

This justice, then, is complete[8] virtue, though not unqualifiedly but in relation to another person. And on account of this, justice is often held to be the greatest of the virtues, neither the evening star nor the morning dawn being so wondrous. And, speaking in proverbs, we assert that "in justice, every virtue is summed up."[9] Further, it is the most complete virtue because it is the use of complete virtue; it is complete because he who possesses it is able to use virtue also in relation to another, and not only as regards himself. For many people are able to use virtue in dealing with the members of their household, but in their affairs regarding another, they are unable to do so. And on this account, the saying of Bias seems good, that "office will show the man."[10] For he who rules is already in relation to another and within the community. And on account of this same thing too, justice alone of the virtues is held to be another's good, because it relates to another. For it does what is advantageous to another, either to a ruler or to someone who shares in the community.

Worst, then, is he who treats both himself and his friends in a corrupt

7 · The phrase "in accord with virtue" is omitted in one MS.

8 · Or, "perfect" (*teleios*).

9 · According to the scholiast, this is a saying of Theognis (ll.145–46), an elegiac poet from Megara (fl. 544–541).

10 · Bias is one of the traditional Seven Sages or wise men of Greece.

way, but best is he who makes use of virtue not in relation to himself but in relation to another. For this is a difficult task. This justice, then, is not a part of virtue but the whole of virtue, and the injustice opposed to it is not 10 a part of vice but the whole of vice. In what respect virtue and this justice differ is clear from what has been said. For they are the same, though in their being, they are not the same; rather, in the respect in which it bears a relation to another, it is justice; in the respect in which it is simply a characteristic of this sort, it is virtue.

CHAPTER TWO

But we, at any rate, are investigating the justice that is a part of virtue— for there is some such one, as we assert—and similarly also the injustice 15 that is a part [of vice]. And there is a sign that it exists. For he who acts in accord with the other kinds of corruption commits injustice but is not at all grasping for more—for example, someone who throws down his shield through cowardice, who speaks viciously on account of his harshness, or who does not donate money for another's aid on account of his stinginess. Yet when a person grasps for more, he often does so, not in 20 connection with any one of these sorts of things, and even less in connection with them all, but rather in relation to a certain wickedness (for we blame it), namely, injustice. There is, therefore, some other injustice as a part of the whole, and something unjust that is a part of injustice as a whole, this latter being what is contrary to the law.

Further, if someone commits adultery for the sake of gain and profits in addition thereby, whereas another spends money and suffers a loss on 25 account of his desire, the latter would be held to be licentious rather than grasping for more, the former to be unjust but not licentious. It is clear, therefore, that he is such on account of the gain he receives.

Further, concerning all other acts of injustice, reference is always made to a specific corruption—for example, if a person commits adultery, one refers to his licentiousness; if he deserts his comrade in arms, to his cow- 30 ardice; if he strikes someone, to his anger—but if he makes a gain, we refer to no corruption other than injustice. It is manifest, as a result, that there is a certain other, partial injustice, apart from the whole [of injustice understood as vice], which has the same name because its definition falls in the same genus. For both exercise their capacity in what concerns 1130b another person; but the one injustice pertains to honor, money, or preservation—or to some one thing if we were able to encompass all these by a

single name—and arises on account of the pleasure associated with gain.
5   The other injustice pertains to *all* the things with which a serious person is concerned.

That the justices are multiple, then, and that there is also a certain other justice besides the whole of virtue, is clear. But one must grasp what and what sort of thing it is. Now, the unjust has been defined as both the unlawful and the unequal, the just as both the lawful and the equal. It
10 is then to the unlawful that the injustice previously mentioned [that is, complete injustice] pertains. Since the unequal and the unlawful are not the same thing but different, as part in relation to whole—for everything unequal is unlawful, but not everything unlawful is unequal—so also the unjust and injustice [in the partial sense] are not the same but different from [the unjust and injustice in the complete sense], the former as parts
15 and the latter as wholes. For this injustice is a part of injustice as a whole, and similarly also this justice is a part of justice as a whole. As a result, one must speak also about both partial justice and partial injustice, and in like manner about the just and unjust that correspond to them.

Let us put aside, then, the justice and injustice ordered in accord with
20 the whole of virtue, the former being the use of the whole of virtue in relation to another, the latter being the use of the whole of vice. But it is manifest how one must define both the just and the unjust that accord with these. For roughly speaking the majority of the lawful things are those commanded[11] on the basis of the whole of virtue: the law commands us to live in accord with each virtue and forbids us to live in accord with each
25 corruption. Things productive of the whole of virtue are all those legislative acts pertaining to the education to the common [good].[12] But as for the education pertaining to the individual, in reference to which he is a good man simply—whether this education belongs to the political art or to another one, must be determined later. For perhaps it is not the same thing in every case to be a good man and to be a good citizen.

30 One form of partial justice, and of the just thing that accords with it, is found in the distributions of honor or money or any of the other things divisible among those who share in the regime (for in these things it is possible for one person to have a share that is either unequal or equal to

11 · Most MSS read here "the things that are done [*prattomena*] on the basis of the whole of virtue"; we follow the reading of one MS, adopted by Bywater.
12 · The Greek is *to koinon*, "the common," but having the meaning of the common affairs and well-being of the political community.

another's). The other form of such justice is the corrective one involved   1131a
in transactions, and of this latter there are in turn two parts; for some
transactions are voluntary, others involuntary. The voluntary ones are of
the following kinds: selling, buying, money lending, pledging security,
investing, making deposits, and letting for hire (they are said to be voluntary because the beginning point of these transactions is voluntary). Of   5
the involuntary transactions, some are covert, such as theft, adultery, poi-
soning, procuring, slave stealing, slaying by treachery, and bearing false
witness; others are violent, such as assault, imprisonment, death, rape,
maiming, slander, and outrage.

CHAPTER THREE

Since the unjust person is unequal and what is unjust is unequal, it is clear   10
that there is also a certain middle term associated with what is unequal.
And this is the equal, for in whatever sort of action in which there are degrees, the more and the less, there is also the equal. If, then, the unjust is
unequal, the just is equal, which is in fact what is held to be the case by
everyone, even without argument.

Since the equal is a middle term, the just would be a certain middle
term. The equal involves at least two things. It is necessary, accordingly,   15
for the just to be a middle term as well as equal, both in relation to something and for certain persons. In the respect in which it is a middle term,
it is between certain things (these are the more and the less); in the respect in which it is equal, it involves two things; and in the respect in
which it is just, it is for certain persons. It is necessary, therefore, for the
just to involve at least four terms: the persons for whom it happens to
be just are two, and the things involved—the matters of concern—are   20
two. And there will be the same equality for the persons and the things
involved: as the latter (the things in the given circumstances) are related,
so also are the former. For if the people are not equal, they will not have
equal things. Rather, from this arise fights and accusations, either when
people who are equal have or are distributed unequal things, or when
people who are unequal have or are distributed equal things.

Further, this is clear from what accords with merit, for all agree that   25
what is just in distributions ought to accord with a certain merit. Nevertheless, all do not mean the same thing by *merit*; rather, democrats say it
is freedom; oligarchs, wealth; others, good birth; aristocrats, virtue. The

30   just, therefore, is a certain proportion. Proportion is not peculiar to abstract number alone, but belongs to number generally. For proportion is
an equality of ratios,[13] and it involves at least four terms.

That the discrete proportion involves four terms, then, is clear. But so
too does the continuous proportion, for it employs the one term as two
1131b and names it twice—for example, as line α is to line β, so line β is to line γ.
Thus line β is named twice, so that if line β is set down twice, there will
be four proportional terms. The just too is divided into at least four terms
5   and the ratio is the same, for it is divided similarly between the persons
and the things involved. Therefore, as the term α is to β [the persons], so
also γ is to δ [the things]; and so too alternately, as α is to γ, so β is to δ.
So too, as a result, is the whole to the whole $[(α + γ) : (β + δ) :: α : β]$—
which is what the distribution links; and if they are put together in this
way, it links them justly. Therefore, the combination of term α with γ and
10   of term β with δ is what is just in the distribution; and the just here is a
middle term, whereas the unjust is what is contrary to the proportion, for
the proportion is a middle term and the just is a proportion. The math-
ematicians call this sort of proportion "geometric," for in the geometric
proportion, it follows also that whole is to whole as each part is to each
15   part. But this proportion is not continuous, for there is not a single numerical term for person and thing.

The just in this case, then, is the proportional; the unjust is what is contrary to the proportion. The unjust, therefore, is both what is more [than
the proportion], on the one hand, and what is less than it, on the other,
which is in fact what happens when it comes to our deeds: he who acts
20   unjustly has more of the good, and he who suffers injustice, less, and the
reverse in the case of what is bad. For the lesser share of what is bad, compared with the greater share of it, falls into the definition of what is good:
the lesser bad is more choiceworthy than the greater; what is choiceworthy is good; and the more choiceworthy it is, the greater a good it is.

This, then, is one form of the just.

CHAPTER FOUR

25   The remaining form of the just is the corrective, which occurs in transactions, both voluntary and involuntary. The just in this sense has a differ-

---

13 · The term translated as "ratios" is the plural of *logos*; it appears below also in the
singular.

ent form from the previous one, for the just in the distribution of things held in common always accords with the proportion spoken of. And in fact if the distribution comes out of common resources, it will accord   30 with the same ratio that the contributions have toward each other. The unjust that is opposite to the just in this sense is contrary to the proportion.

The just in transactions is a certain equality, and the unjust, a certain inequality, yet not in accord with the proportion just indicated but in ac-   1132a cord with an arithmetic one. For it makes no difference at all whether a decent person robs a base one, or a base person a decent one, or if a decent or a base person commits adultery. Rather, the law looks only at the dif-   5 ference that stems from the harm done, and it treats persons as equals: if the one person acts unjustly, the other suffers injustice; and if the one did harm, the other was harmed. As a result, since the unjust in this sense is an inequality, the judge tries to restore equality. For indeed, if one person is struck and the other strikes, or if he also kills him and the other dies, the suffering and the doing involved are divided into unequal segments. But the judge tries to restore equality by inflicting a loss,[14] thereby tak-   10 ing away the gain. For the term *gain* is used as a way of speaking simply in such circumstances (even if in certain cases it would not be the proper name—for example, for the person who struck another), and the term *loss* is used for him who suffered. But, at any rate, whenever the suffering is measured, the one is called a loss, the other a gain. As a result, the equal is a middle term with respect to what is more and less, while the gain and   15 the loss are more and less in opposite ways: more of the good and less of the bad is gain, the reverse is loss. The middle term with respect to these is, as we noted, the equal, which we say is just; as a result, the just that is corrective[15] would be the middle term when it comes to loss and gain.

Hence when people dispute with one another, they find refuge before   20 a judge. To go to a judge is to go to the just, for a judge wishes to be, as it were, the just ensouled. And people seek a judge as a middle way,[16] and some call them mediators, on the grounds that, if they hit on the middle term, they will have hit on the just. The just, therefore, is a certain middle way, if in fact the judge is as well. The judge also restores equality, just as,   25

14 · The word (*zēmia*) also means "penalty."

15 · Here Aristotle uses a slightly different term for "corrective" (*epanorthōtikos* instead of *diorthōtikos*).

16 · *Meson*, translated here and in the next sentence as "middle way," is the same term that we usually translate as "middle term."

in the case of a line cut into unequal parts, one subtracts that by which the larger part exceeds the half and adds it to the smaller part. When the whole is divided in two, then people assert that they have what is theirs whenever they receive what is equal. The equal is the middle term of the larger and the smaller in accord with the arithmetic proportion. On this account as well, it has its name "just" [*dikaion*], because it is divided in two [*dicha*], just as if one were to say "divided" [*dichaion*], and of the judge [*dikastēs*] that he is a "divider" [*dichastēs*].[17] For when, of two equal things, a part is subtracted from one and added to the other, then the latter exceeds by twice the part subtracted from; for if the one is subtracted from, but the other not added to, then the latter exceeds only by one. Therefore, the latter exceeds the middle term by one, and the middle term exceeds the one subtracted from by one. By this, then, we will know both what we ought to subtract from the person who has the greater share and what we ought to add to him who has the lesser: we ought to add that which exceeds the middle term to the person with the lesser, and to subtract from the one who has the greatest that by which the middle term is exceeded. The lines αα', ββ', γγ' being equal to one another, subtract from αα' the part αε and add it to γγ' as part, so that the whole, δγγ', exceeds εα' by δγ and γζ, and hence ββ' by δγ.[18]

These names, both "loss" and "gain," have come from voluntary transactions; for to have more than what is one's own is spoken of as "gaining," and to have less than what one had at the beginning, as "suffering a loss"—in buying and selling, for example, and in as many other transactions as the law has permitted. When people have neither more nor less but the very things they have contributed, they declare that they have what is their own and that they have neither suffered a loss nor gained. As

17 · Aristotle's etymology is suspect: he obviously plays on the terms *dicha*, *dikastēs*, and *dichastēs*, as if the judge were a "divider"; but the root of *dikastēs*, as of *dikaion*, is *dik-* and not *dicha*, as he suggests here. According to pseudo-Alexander of Aphrodisias, Aristotle's etymology here has Pythagorean roots.

18 · The lines would be as follows:

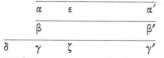

With Bywater, we omit what appears to be an interpolation from 1133a14–16: "This is the case also in the other arts, for they would perish if the maker did not make both so much and such a kind of a given product, and the recipient did not receive both the same amount and same kind of product."

a result, in transactions that are contrary to what is voluntary, the just is a middle term between a certain gain and loss—it is to have what is equal both before and after the transaction.   20

CHAPTER FIVE

Reciprocity[19] is also held by some to be the just unqualifiedly, as the Pythagoreans asserted, for they used to define the just unqualifiedly as reciprocity toward another. But reciprocity fits neither with the just in the distributive sense nor with the just in the corrective sense—although   25 people want this reciprocity to mean also what is just according to Rhadamanthus:[20]

If he should suffer the things he did, then justice[21] would be straight.

For in many cases, there is a discrepancy [between reciprocity and what is just]: for example, if a ruler strikes another, he ought not to be struck in return; but if someone strikes a ruler, he ought to be not only struck   30 but also punished. Further, there is a great difference between what is voluntary and what is involuntary. But in communities concerned with exchange, the just in this sense—reciprocity in accord with proportion and not in accord with equality—holds them together, for the city stays together by means of proportional reciprocity. For either people seek to reciprocate harm for harm—if they do not, that is held to be slavish—or   1133a they seek to reciprocate good for good. And if they do not do this, there is no mutual exchange, and people stay together through mutual exchange. Hence too people place a shrine to the Graces[22] along the roadway, to foster reciprocal giving, for this belongs to gratitude: one ought to serve in return someone who has been gracious, and ought oneself, the next time,   5 to take the lead in being gracious.[23]

19 · The word (*antipeponthos*) stems from the verb meaning "to suffer in turn" and can have the sense of "eye for an eye."

20 · In Greek mythology, Rhadamanthus was the son of Zeus and Europa who served as a ruler and judge of the dead. See, e.g., Plato, *Apology of Socrates* 41a–c as well as *Laws* 624b5 and *Gorgias* 523e8.

21 · Here the term is *dikē* rather than *dikaiosunē*. It can refer more precisely to the process of arbitration and a specific judgment regarding justice.

22 · The Graces (*charites*) were goddesses, fathered by Zeus, embodying *charis*—grace, gratitude, and charm. See, e.g., Hesiod, *Theogony* 64, 907.

23 · The translation of the last verb (*charizesthai*) secures the connection to grace but obscures its relation to benefaction.

The combination that aligns with the diagonal produces proportional reciprocal giving. For example, let α be a house builder, β a shoemaker, γ a house, and δ a sandal.[24] The house builder, then, ought to take from the shoemaker the work he produces and give in exchange a share of his own
10   work. If, then, there is first proportional equality and then reciprocal exchange occurs, the proportional reciprocity spoken of will take place. If not, the exchange is not equal and does not endure. For nothing prevents the work of the one person from being superior to that of the other. These things ought, therefore, to be equalized. This is the case also in the other
15   arts, for they would perish if the maker did not make both so much and such a kind of a given product, and the recipient did not receive both the same amount and same kind of product. For no community comes into existence out of two doctors but rather out of a doctor and a farmer and, in general, out of those who are different and not equal. But these [differing types] must be equalized.

Hence all that is exchanged must somehow be capable of being com-
20   pared. For this purpose, money[25] has arisen and become in a way a middle term. For it measures everything—both excess and deficiency—so that it measures however many sandals are equal to a house or to food. Accordingly, as a house builder stands in relation to a shoemaker, so a given number of sandals must stand in relation to a house or food. For if this is not the case, then there will be no exchange or community, and this will not
25   be the case if the terms should not be somehow equal.

All things, therefore, must be measured by some one thing, as was said earlier. This thing is, in truth, need, which holds all things together. For if people should not need anything, or not in the same way, then

---

24 · To achieve proportional reciprocal giving, α must conjoin with δ and β with γ, and so, in the simplest sense, the equation must work out along the diagonal as $α + δ = β + γ$.

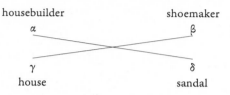

But for the mathematical proof of reciprocity in this sense, see Euclid, *Elements* 6.15.
25 · Or, "legal currency." The term Aristotle here uses (*nomisma*) means "anything sanctioned by current or established usage" (*nomos*) and so "current coin" or "money" (LSJ). In 6.1 we translate *chrēmata* as "money" and *nomisma* as "legal currency," but here in book 5 we follow English idiom and for the most part translate the term as "money."

there will either not be exchange or not the same sort of exchange. But money has become, by agreement, a kind of exchangeable representative of need; and on account of this it has its name [*nomisma*, literally "legal currency"], because it exists not by nature but by law [*nomos*], and it is up to us to change it or render it useless.

Therefore, there will be reciprocity when terms are made equal, and the result will be that, as a farmer stands in relation to a shoemaker, so the work of the shoemaker stands in relation to that of the farmer. But one must not bring the works into the figure of the proportion after they have been exchanged (if they are, one of the extremes will have both excesses), but one must do so instead when people still have their own things. In this way, they will be equals and partners in a community, since it is possible for this equality to arise in their cases. Let the farmer be α, his food γ, the shoemaker β, the work of his that is being equalized [to γ], δ; if it were not possible to have reciprocity in this way, then there would be no community.

That need holds people together as if they were some single entity is clear. For when either both parties or one of them is not in need of the other, they do not undertake exchange, as does happen when someone needs what another has—for example, because they are in need of wine, people give their license to export corn.[26] Therefore, this [exchange] must be made equal. As for the exchange that will occur in the future, if there is no such need of it now, money is like a guarantee for us that it will occur when there is need of it, since someone who brings money ought to attain what he needs. Now, money undergoes this same thing as well, for it is not always possible for it to be equal. Nevertheless, it tends to stay more constant [than does the value of particular commodities]. Hence all things ought to have a value assigned to them; for in this way there will always be exchange, and if there is exchange, then there will be community. Hence by making things commensurate, money, just like a measure, equalizes them. For there is no community if there is no exchange, or exchange if there is no equality, or equality if there is no commensurability.

Now, in truth, it is impossible for things that differ greatly from one another to become commensurable, but it is possible, to a sufficient de-

26 · This last phrase, which is ungrammatical, is suspected by Bywater, who suggests that the text may have a lacuna. One might insert a negative: "as is the case whenever one does not possess what someone needs—for example, he needs wine, while people are giving their license to export corn." But doing so raises other difficulties, so there is no obvious solution in translating this phrase.

gree, in relation to need. So there must be some one thing [that serves as a measure], and this is based on a presupposition; hence it is called "legal currency" [*nomisma*].[27] For it makes all things commensurable, since all things are measured by currency. Take a house as α, ten minae as β, a couch as γ. α is half of β if the house is worth or equal to five minae, and the couch, γ, is one-tenth a part of β.[28] Accordingly, it is clear how many couches are equal to a house, namely, five. That there used to be exchange in this way before the advent of money is clear, for it makes no difference at all whether five couches are exchanged for a house, or for however much money five couches are worth.

What the unjust and the just are, then, has been stated. And with these things defined, it is clear that just action is a middle term with respect to doing injustice and suffering injustice, for the former is to have more and the latter is to have less [than one ought]. Justice is also a certain mean, not in the same way as in the other virtues, but because it is bound up with a middle term, whereas injustice belongs to the extremes. And justice refers to that by which the just person is said to be disposed to act according to his choice of what is just, and to distribute things to himself in relation to another (and to another person in relation to a third), not in such a way as to distribute more of what is choiceworthy to himself and less to his neighbor, and of harm the reverse, but rather to distribute what is equal in accord with the proportion (and similarly also in the case of another person in relation to a third).

But injustice involves the opposite [distribution] with regard to what is unjust, and this is excess or deficiency of the beneficial or harmful respectively, contrary to what is proportional. Hence injustice is excess and deficiency, since it is bound up with an excess and a deficiency—an excess in one's own case of what is unqualifiedly beneficial and a deficiency of what is harmful. And, in the case of the others involved, injustice is as a whole similar. But it is contrary to what is proportional in one way or another [whether by assigning too little benefit or too great a harm to others], as the case may be. With respect to the wrong done, the lesser wrong is to suffer injustice, the greater is to commit injustice.

27 · See n. 25 above.

28 · A mina was the equivalent of one hundred drachmae, and in the course of the Peloponnesian War, a drachma a day was a good wage for a soldier. A house worth five minae, then, or five hundred drachmae, would take such a soldier approximately sixteen months to pay for (assuming, of course, no other expenses).

As for what concerns justice and injustice, then—that is, what the na-   15
ture of each is—let it have been stated in this way, and similarly also what
concerns the just and unjust in the general sense.

CHAPTER SIX

Since it is possible that he who does injustice is not yet an unjust person,
what sort of wrongs does someone who is in fact unjust commit, in the
case of each sort of injustice—for example, a thief, an adulterer, or a pirate? Or, in this respect, will it not make any difference? For someone
could have intercourse with a woman, knowing who she is, but this has   20
its origin not in one's choice but in one's passion. He who does injustice,
then, is not unjust—for example, he is not a thief, though he stole, and
he is not an adulterer, though he did commit adultery, and similarly also
in the other cases.[29]

Now, how reciprocity stands in relation to the just has been stated earlier. But it must not escape our notice that what is being sought is also   25
the just unqualifiedly, that is, the just in the political sense.[30] And this
exists among those who share a life in common with a view to being self-
sufficient, who are free and equal, either in accord with a proportion or
arithmetically. As a result, for all those for whom this does not exist, there
is nothing politically just in relation to one another, but only something
just in a certain sense and by way of a similarity. The just exists for those   30
for whom there is also law pertaining to them, and law exists among those
for whom there is injustice. For justice is a judgment[31] about the just and
the unjust. Among those for whom there is injustice, there is also the doing of injustice among them (though among those for whom there is the

29 · Some commentators believe that this opening passage is imported from another
section of the text, since it would indeed seem to belong to the subject matter of 5.8
and following. But there is no evidence based on the MSS that the passage does not
belong here.

30 · Another translation is possible: "But it must not escape our notice that what is being sought is both the just unqualifiedly and the just in the political sense." It is unclear,
that is, whether "what is being sought" is one or two things; the singular "this" (*touto*)
at the beginning of the next sentence suggests (although it does not require) that the
singular is intended.

31 · The term here for "justice" is *dikē* (see n. 21 above), and for "judgment," *krisis*,
which we have translated elsewhere as "decision" and, at the beginning of 4.1, as "legal adjudication."

doing of injustice, not all are marked by injustice), and this is to distribute more of the unqualifiedly good things to oneself and less of the un-
35   qualifiedly bad than one ought. Hence we do not permit a human being
to rule, but rather law,[32] because a human being makes this distribution
1134b   [of things good and bad] for himself and so becomes a tyrant. But a ruler
is a guardian of the just, and if of the just, then also of the equal. For it
seems that he gains nothing for himself, if he is indeed just: he does not
distribute more of what is unqualifiedly good to himself, unless it is pro-
5   portional in relation to himself. Hence he labors for another, and on account of this, people declare that justice is the good of another, as was
said also before. Some wage, therefore, must be given to him, and this is
honor and privilege. But those for whom these sorts of things are not sufficient become tyrants.

   The just peculiar to a slave master and to a father are not the same as
these [political senses of justice], though they are similar. For there is no
10   injustice in an unqualified sense toward one's own things, but one's property or offspring (until the latter is of a certain age and independent) is
like a part of oneself, and nobody chooses to harm himself. Hence there
is no injustice in relation to oneself, nor, therefore, is there what is unjust
and just in the political sense. For, as we saw, these accord with law and ex-
15   ist among those for whom law is natural, namely, those for whom there is
equality in ruling and being ruled. Hence the just exists more in relation
to a wife than in relation to one's offspring and possessions, for this is the
just pertaining to household management. But this too is different from
the just in the political sense.

CHAPTER SEVEN

Of the just in the political sense, one part is natural, the other, conventional.[33] The natural [part of political justice] is that which has the same
20   capacity everywhere and is not dependent on being held to exist or not,
whereas the conventional part is that which at the beginning makes no
difference whether it is thus or otherwise, but once people have set it
down, it does make a difference: for example, the sum of money to offer for ransom, or to sacrifice a goat rather than two sheep, or, further, all

32 · Given the context, we accept here the reading of one MS, *nomos*; other MSS have
instead *logos* (reason).
33 · That is, it is legal or accords with law (*nomikos*).

that people legislate in each particular case—for example, to sacrifice to Brasidas,[34] and specific decrees.

In the opinion of some people, all [just things] are of this character, be-   25
cause what is by nature is unchangeable and has the same capacity everywhere, just as fire burns both here and in Persia, whereas they see the just
things being changed. But this is not the way it is—or rather, it is this way
in a sense: while among the gods, at any rate, it is perhaps not at all this
way, among us there is in fact something that is [just] by nature, though
it is altogether changeable. Nevertheless, in one respect it is by nature, in   30
another it is not by nature.

It is clear what sort of thing is by nature, among the things that admit
of being otherwise, and what sort is not by nature but is conventional and
by agreement, if indeed both are similarly changeable. The same distinction will apply also in other cases: by nature, the right hand is stronger,   35
although it is possible for all to become ambidextrous. As for things that
are just by agreement and in reference to advantage, they are like mea-   1135a
sures: the measures for wine and corn are not everywhere equal; rather,
where wine and corn are bought, the measures are greater, and where they
are sold, smaller. And similarly, the just things that are not natural but human are not everywhere the same, since the regimes are not either; but
everywhere there is only one regime that is in accord with nature, the best   5
regime.

Each of the just and lawful things is related [to the various acts that accord with them] as universals are to the several particulars. For whereas
there are many particular acts, each of the just and lawful things is one,
since it is universal. An act of injustice[35] differs from the unjust, and an
act of justice differs from the just. For what is unjust is by nature or by en-   10
actment, but this very thing becomes an act of injustice once it is done;
yet until what is unjust is done, it is not yet an act of injustice, though it
is unjust. The case is similar also for an act of justice (though this is more
commonly called a "just action" [*dikaiopragēma*], whereas an "act of justice" [*dikaiōma*] is a correction of an act of injustice).

In reference to each of these, we must examine later what forms it   15

34 · Brasidas was an extraordinary Spartan general in the Peloponnesian War who lib-
erated several Greek cities, most notably Amphipolis, from Athenian control. After his
death, he was worshiped as a "hero" by the Amphipolitans: see Thucydides 4.102–8
and 5.6–11.

35 · Elsewhere translated as "a wrong" (*adikēma*).

takes, how many forms there are, and with what sorts of things each happens to be concerned.[36]

CHAPTER EIGHT

Since the just and the unjust things are as stated, someone acts unjustly or performs a just act when he does these things voluntarily; when he does them involuntarily, he neither acts unjustly nor performs a just act, except incidentally. For people do just and unjust things incidentally, but an un-
20 just and a just act are defined in terms of the voluntary and involuntary: when the act is voluntary, it is blamed, and at the same time it is then also an unjust act, so that there will be something unjust but not yet an unjust act if voluntariness is not present in addition. I mean by *voluntary*, as has been stated earlier as well,[37] whatever act is up to a person and he
25 performs knowingly, not in ignorance of either the person acted on, the means used, or that for the sake of which he acts. For example, he strikes someone with something and for the sake of something, and he does each of these not incidentally or under compulsion (as if someone, taking another's hand, were to strike yet another with it; this would not be voluntary since it is not up to the person in question). It is possible that the person being struck is his father, and for someone to know that he who is
30 struck is a human being or among those present, but to be ignorant that he is his father. And let this sort of distinction be similarly made concerning both that for the sake of which he acts and the action as a whole.

Hence that which a person is ignorant of, or which he is not ignorant
1135b of but is not up to him, or that which is forced, is involuntary. For we do and suffer knowingly many things that happen by nature, but they are neither voluntary nor involuntary—for example, to age or to die. Similarly, in the case of unjust and just things, there is also that which is done incidentally. In fact, someone could give back something deposited in trust
5 involuntarily and through fear; one must deny that such a person either does what is just or acts justly, except incidentally. Similarly too one must assert that he who, under necessity and involuntarily, does not give back something deposited with him in trust acts unjustly or does unjust things only incidentally. Some voluntary things we do because we have chosen them, others we do though we have not chosen them: we choose all those
10

36 · Aristotle does not take up again the distinctions he makes here.
37 · Consider 3.1–5.

we deliberated about beforehand, and those not chosen are those not deliberated about beforehand.

Now, since there are three types of harm that arise in communities, those that are done in ignorance are errors whenever the person acted on, the act, the means, or that for the sake of which the act is done is not as the person acting assumed. For he supposed that he was either not throwing or not with this thing or not at this person or not for the sake of this end; but the result is not the one he supposed would occur — for example, he supposed that he acted not in order to wound but only to prick, or not to wound this person, or not with this thing.

Whenever, then, contrary to reasonable expectation, harm occurs, it is an unfortunate thing. Whenever harm occurs not contrary to reasonable expectation but without vice, it is an error (for one errs when the origin of the cause is in oneself, whereas one is unfortunate when it is external). But whenever harm is done knowingly yet without prior deliberation, it is an unjust act — for example, whatever is done through spiritedness and all other passions that necessarily or naturally befall human beings. For in inflicting these harms and making these errors, people do injustice, and these are acts of injustice. Still, these people are not yet unjust or wicked for these reasons, for the harm done does not arise through any corruption. But whenever the harm arises from choice, the person involved is unjust and corrupt.

Hence it is noble to judge acts that arise from spiritedness as not stemming from forethought, since he who acts from spiritedness is not the origin of the act; rather, the person who made him angry is. Further, what did or did not happen is not the subject of dispute but rather what is just in the given circumstance, since anger depends on an apparent injustice. For it is not the case, as it is in contracts, that people dispute about what happened, in which case it is necessary for one of the two parties to be corrupt (unless they dispute out of forgetfulness). Rather, they agree about the matter at hand, but they dispute about which side justice lies on (whereas someone who plotted against another is not ignorant [that what he has done is unjust]), with the result that the one party supposes that he is suffering an injustice, the other that the former is not.

But if a person harms someone from choice, he acts unjustly; and it is in reference to *these* acts of injustice that he who does them is himself unjust, whenever the act is contrary to what is proportional or equal. Similarly too a person is himself just whenever he performs a just act, having chosen to do so; but he performs a just act if he simply acts voluntarily.

15

20

25

30

1136a

5   Of involuntary acts, some are forgivable,[38] others are not forgivable.
For all the errors that people commit, not only in ignorance but also on
account of ignorance, are subject to forgiveness, whereas all errors not
committed on account of ignorance but while people are in a state of ignorance as a result of a passion that is neither natural nor human are not
subject to forgiveness.

CHAPTER NINE

10   But if what concerns the suffering and the doing of injustice has been adequately defined, someone might be perplexed, first, as to whether it is as
Euripides said, putting it oddly:

> "I killed my mother, brief is my speech."

> "You voluntarily and she voluntarily,
> Or she [not] voluntarily and you not voluntarily?"[39]

15   For is it truly possible to suffer injustice voluntarily, or is it not, rather,
entirely involuntary, just as also the doing of injustice is entirely voluntary? [But then again,] is in fact suffering injustice either one way or the
other—entirely voluntary or entirely involuntary[40]—or is it sometimes
voluntary and sometimes involuntary? Similar too is the case of being
treated justly, for performing a just act is entirely voluntary [just as performing an unjust act is entirely voluntary]. As a result, it is reasonable
20   for there to be a similar opposition in each case, and so for suffering injustice and being treated justly to be either [entirely] voluntary or [entirely]
involuntary. Yet it would seem to be strange in the case of being treated
justly, if, that is, being treated justly were entirely voluntary: some who are
treated justly do not submit to it voluntarily.
       Next, someone might be perplexed also about this: whether everyone
who has suffered something unjust always thereby suffers injustice, or
whether what pertains in the case of the doing pertains also in the case of

38 · Or, "subject to sympathy, sympathetic understanding." The root of this word
(*sungnōmika*) is the same one translated as "sympathetic judgment" in 6.11.
39 · The passage is from Euripides's lost *Alcmaeon*. See also 1110a28, where Aristotle alludes to the same play. Bywater emends the text by adding the negative in the last line;
as Burnet notes, "the sense seems to require an antithesis to *hekousan* [voluntarily]" in
the previous phrase.
40 · Bywater brackets here a phrase, "just as also the doing of injustice is entirely voluntary," that appears to be repeated from the previous line.

the suffering. For it is possible, in the case of both doing and suffering, to   25
share incidentally in just things. Similarly, it is clear that this is also possible in the case of unjust things; for to do unjust things is not the same as
to be unjust, to suffer unjust things is not the same as to suffer injustice,
and similarly also in the case of performing a just act and being treated
justly. For it is impossible to suffer injustice if another does not do an in-   30
justice, or to be treated justly if another person does not do something
just. If to do injustice is simply to harm someone voluntarily, and the person who acts voluntarily knows whom he is harming, with what, and in
what manner, and the person who lacks self-restraint harms himself voluntarily, then in that case he would do injustice voluntarily and it would
be possible for him to do injustice to himself.

And this too is one of the perplexing questions: whether it is possible   1136b
for someone to do injustice to himself. Further, [there is perplexity as
to whether] someone, on account of his lack of self-restraint, could be
harmed voluntarily by another who acts voluntarily, such that it could
be possible for him to suffer injustice voluntarily. Or is the definition not
correct, and must one rather add to "doing harm knowing to whom, with
what, and in what manner" the phrase "against the other's wish"? Some-   5
one is harmed voluntarily and suffers unjust things, then, but no one voluntarily suffers injustice, for no one wishes for this, not even the person
lacking self-restraint. Rather, he acts against his own wish. For no one
wishes for what he supposes not to be of serious worth, and the person
lacking self-restraint supposes that he ought not to do what he proceeds
to do. The person who gives away his own things—just as Homer asserts
that Glaucus gave to Diomedes "gold for bronze, the worth of a hundred   10
cattle for nine"[41]—does not suffer injustice. For the giving is up to him,
but suffering injustice is not up to him. Rather, there must be someone
who commits injustice. As for suffering injustice, then, it is clear that it is
not voluntary.

Of the things we chose to speak of, two remain: whether he who dis-   15
tributes more than is merited is ever unjust, or whether the unjust person
is the one who receives that greater share; and whether it is possible for
someone to do injustice to himself. For if the first statement is possible,
and he who distributes what is more than is merited does injustice, but
not he who receives it, then if someone knowingly and voluntarily distributes more of his own things to another, this person does injustice to

41 · Homer, *Iliad* 6.236.

20 himself, which is the very thing that those of a measured disposition are held to do, since the decent person is disposed to taking less for himself. Or is not even this a simple thing? For, as may happen, [the decent person] is grasping for more than his share of another good—for example, of reputation or of what is unqualifiedly noble.

Further, this perplexity is resolved by referring to what distinguished the doing of injustice, for whoever gives more of his own goods than is merited suffers nothing contrary to his own wish. The result is that he does not suffer injustice on this account, at least, but if he suffers anything at all, it is harm only. But it is manifest too that he who distributes more than is merited does injustice, though not always he who receives more. For what is unjust belongs not to the person who simply does injustice but to the one who does it voluntarily. This rests in him who is the origin of the action, which is in the person who distributes but not in the one who receives.

30 Further, since "to do" [poiein] is spoken of in many ways, and it is possible for inanimate things to kill—also for a hand and a house slave who is so commanded—the person who receives a greater share is not acting unjustly, though he does "do" [poiein] unjust things. Further, if the distributor judged in ignorance, he does not do injustice according to what is legally just, and neither is his judgment unjust, though it is in a sense unjust: what is legally just is different from what is just in the primary sense. But if he judged unjustly, while recognizing this fact, then he himself too is grasping for more, either of gratitude or of vengeance. Just as if, then, someone should receive a share of an unjust distribution, so too he who judges unjustly because of these things [gratitude or vengeance] receives more than his share. For if he were to make a judgment about land on this basis, then he would take not land but money.

5 Human beings suppose that doing injustice is up to them and hence also that what is just is easy. But it is not. For to have intercourse with the neighbor's wife, to strike someone nearby, and to put money into someone's hand is, they suppose, easy and up to them, but to do these things while being in a certain state is neither easy nor up to them. Similarly

10 too, people suppose that to know the just and unjust things is in no way to be wise, because it is not difficult to comprehend what the laws say (but these are not the just things, except incidentally). But how the just things are done and how they are distributed—this is indeed a greater task than to know what is conducive to health, since even here to know

15 about honey, wine, hellebore, cauterizing, and cutting is easy, but to know

1137a

how one must administer them with a view to health, and to whom and when, is as great a task as to be a physician.

On account of this very thing too, people suppose that doing injustice belongs no less to the just person [than to the unjust], because the just person would be no less able but even more able to act both justly and unjustly. For he could, they suppose, have intercourse with another's wife and   20
strike another, and the courageous man could throw down his shield and, turning every which way, run in whatever direction. But being a coward or doing injustice is not doing these things, except incidentally, but rather doing them when one is in a certain state, just as being a doctor or healing someone does not consist in cutting or not cutting someone, or prescribing   25
drugs or not prescribing them, but in doing these things in a certain way.

The just things exist among those who share in the unqualifiedly good things and who have an excess or a deficiency of them. For some, there is no excess of these goods, for example, the gods, perhaps; for others—for the incurably bad—there is no beneficial portion of them but all of them do harm; and for still others, there is a beneficial portion up to a certain   30
amount. On account of this, [justice] is something human.[42]

CHAPTER TEN

What concerns equity[43] and the equitable—how equity stands in relation to justice and the equitable in relation to the just—is the next thing to speak of. For they appear, to those who examine them, to be neither simply the same thing nor each in a different genus. And sometimes we   35
praise what is equitable and this sort of man, such that when we bestow praise also on other things, we use the term *equitable* in place of *good*, thus   1137b
making it clear that what is more equitable is better. But sometimes it appears strange, to those who follow up the argument, if the equitable is something praiseworthy, despite its being other than the just. For, if they are different, either the just is not a serious thing or the equitable is itself not just;[44] or, if both are serious, they are the same thing.   5

42 · The reading of the MSS. An ancient translation, however, suggests an original text that would read, "Hence this [i.e., the good] is something human." Burnet, among others, prefers this emended version, since the text as it stands has no expressed, or even clearly implied, subject.

43 · *Epieikeia*, which we elsewhere translate as "decency."

44 · The reading of one MS: "either the equitable is not a serious thing or it is not just, if they are different."

The perplexity concerning what is equitable, then, arises for pretty much these reasons. But all such considerations are in a certain way correct and do not stand in any opposition to one another. For the equitable, though it is better than the just in a certain sense, is just, and it is not because it belongs to a different class of thing that it is better than
10   the just. Therefore, the just and the equitable are the same thing, and although both are serious, the equitable is superior. This is what produces the perplexity, because although the equitable is just, it is not what is just according to law. The equitable is instead a correction of the legally just. The cause of this is that all law is general, but concerning some matters it is not possible to speak correctly in a general way. In those cases, then, in
15   which it is necessary to speak generally, but it is not possible to do so correctly, the law takes what is for the most part the case, but without being ignorant of the error involved in so doing. And the law is no less correct for all that: the error resides not in the law or in the lawgiver but in the nature of the matter at hand. For such is simply the stuff of which actions
20   are made. Whenever the law speaks generally, then, but what happens in a given case constitutes an exception to the general rule, then it is correct, where the lawgiver omits something and erred by speaking unqualifiedly, to rectify that omission with what the lawgiver himself would have said if he had been present and, if he had known of this case, what he would have legislated.

Hence equity is just and better than what is just in a certain sense—
25   not what is just unqualifiedly but the error that arises through its being stated unqualifiedly. This is in fact the nature of the equitable: a correction of law in the respect in which it is deficient because of its being general. For this is the cause also of the fact that all things are not in accord with law: it is impossible to set down a law in some matters, so that one must have recourse to a specific decree instead. For the rule [or measure]
30   of something indeterminate is indeterminate too, just as is the case with the lead rule used in house building in Lesbos:[45] the lead rule changes in relation to the shape of the stone and does not stay the same; and so too the specific decree changes in relation to the matters at hand.

45 · Some scholars have suggested that Aristotle here refers to a flexible piece of lead that was used in fitting polygonal stones together in "Cyclopean building," such as at Tiryns (see Burnet). But Stewart suggests, and Burnet concurs, that Aristotle has in mind a certain molding, typical of Lesbos, which was "undulating, not a simple hollow like the Dorian" (Burnet), and was shaped to the surface of one rock and then used to determine stones that would best match it.

What the equitable is, then—that it is both just and better than the just in a certain sense—is clear. It is manifest from this also who the equitable person is: he who is disposed to choose and to do these sorts of things and is not exacting to a fault about justice, but is instead disposed to take less for himself even though he has the law on his side, is equitable. And this characteristic is equity, it being a certain sort of justice and not some other characteristic.

CHAPTER ELEVEN

Whether it is possible to do injustice to oneself or not is manifest from what has been said. For some just things have been arranged by the law in reference to the whole of virtue—for example, the law does not command one to kill oneself, and what the law does not command, it forbids. Further, when, contrary to law, a person harms another voluntarily, and not because he is retaliating, he thereby does injustice; and he does so voluntarily when he knows both whom he harms and with what. A person who, on account of his anger, kills himself voluntarily does this contrary to correct reason,[46] which the law does not permit. Therefore, he does injustice. But to whom? Is it to the city but not to himself? For he suffers voluntarily, and no one suffers injustice voluntarily. Hence the city imposes a penalty, and a certain dishonor attaches to him who destroys himself, on the grounds that he does the city an injustice.

Further, in the case where someone who does injustice is only unjust but not wholly base, it is not possible to do injustice to oneself. (This latter case is different from the former one: there is a sense in which the unjust person, like the coward, is wicked in such a way that he is not wholly wicked. So he too is not unjust in the sense of being wholly wicked.) For [if it were possible to be unjust to oneself,] the same thing would have been simultaneously taken away from and added to the same person. But this is impossible. Rather, it is always necessary for the just and the unjust to involve more than one person. Further, the unjust is voluntary, stems from choice, and is prior in time [to the harm one undergoes]. For the person who, because he suffered some harm, also reciprocates the same thing is not held to do injustice; but if the same person does these things to himself, he simultaneously both suffers and does them. Further, [if someone could do himself an injustice,] it would be possible for him to

---

46 · Some MSS have *nomos* (law) rather than *logos* (reason).

have suffered injustice voluntarily. And, in addition to these consider-
25   ations, no one does injustice without committing particular acts of injustice—no one commits adultery with his own wife, breaks into his own
house, or steals his own things. On the whole, the perplexing question of
one's being able to do injustice to oneself is resolved also by the distinction made concerning whether a person suffers injustice voluntarily.

It is manifest too that both—both suffering injustice and doing injustice—are base [or bad]. For suffering injustice is to have less and doing
30   injustice to have more than the middle term, just as is also the case with
health in medicine and good condition in gymnastic training. But, nevertheless, doing injustice is worse. For doing injustice is accompanied by
vice and is blameworthy, and this vice is either complete and unqualified
or nearly so (for not *every* unjust act done voluntarily is accompanied by
35   injustice). Yet suffering injustice is without vice and injustice. In itself,
then, suffering injustice is less base [or bad], though nothing prevents it
1138b from producing incidentally the greater harm. But this is of no concern
to the art involved; rather, medicine calls pleurisy a greater malady than
stumbling, although sometimes the latter might be worse incidentally if
5   it should turn out that he who stumbles is seized by enemies or killed because he fell.

Metaphorically and in reference to a certain similarity, there is something just that pertains, not to a person in relation to himself, but to certain parts of himself; this is not the just in every sense of the term but
rather that peculiar to the slave master or household manager. In these
sorts of arguments,[47] the part of the soul possessing reason is set apart
10   from the nonrational; hence to those who look to these considerations,
there does in fact seem to be injustice in relation to oneself, because in
these parts of the soul, it is possible to suffer something contrary to their
respective longings. Just as for ruler and ruled, then, there seems to be
something just in relation to each other, so also in the case of these parts
of the soul.

Concerning justice and the other moral virtues, then, let the distinctions be made in this manner.

47 · See, e.g., Plato's *Republic* 435a and following.

Book 6

CHAPTER ONE

Now, since we happen to have said previously that one ought to choose the middle term—not the excess and not the deficiency—and that the middle term is what correct reason states it to be, let us define this. For 1138b20 in all the characteristics mentioned (just as in the others as well), there is a certain target that he who possesses reason[1] looks to and so tightens or loosens;[2] and there is a certain defining boundary[3] of the middle,[4] which middle, we assert, is between the excess and the deficiency, since it is in accord with correct reason.

But speaking in this way is, though truthful, not at all clear. For in all 25 the other concerns too about which a science exists, it is true to say that one ought not to strain or slacken either too much or too little, but as accords with the mean and as correct reason states. Yet if somebody should possess this alone, he would be no further ahead in his knowledge—for 30 example, he would not know what sorts of things ought to be applied to the body if somebody should say, "so many things as the art of medicine commands and as he who possesses that art commands." Hence in the case of the characteristics of the soul too, not only ought this to be stated truly, but what correct reason is must also be defined, that is, what its defining boundary is.

1 · Literally "the reason," which may refer to "correct reason."
2 · As Burnet notes, "Here the metaphor changes from 'hitting the mark' to 'tuning a lyre.'"
3 · This phrase translates a single word, *horos*, whose first meaning is simply a stone or other marker indicating a boundary line.
4 · Plural in the Greek.

1139a   When defining the virtues of the soul, we asserted that some are virtues of character,[5] others of thinking. Now, as for the moral virtues, we have gone through them; but as for those that remain, let us speak first about soul, and do so as follows.

It was stated previously, then, that there are two parts of the soul, the one possessing reason as well as the nonrational part. But now we must divide the part possessing reason in the same manner. Let it be posited that the parts possessing reason are two: one part is that by which we contemplate all those sorts of beings whose principles do not admit of being otherwise, one part that by which we contemplate all those things that do admit of being otherwise. For when it comes to beings that differ in kind from one another, the part of the soul that naturally relates to each is also different in kind, if in fact it is by dint of a certain similarity and kinship that knowledge is available [to the rational parts of the soul]. And let it be said that one of these is "the scientific," the other "the calculative."[6] For deliberating and calculating are the same thing, and nobody deliberates about things that do not admit of being otherwise. The calculative, as a result, is one part of that which possesses reason. So it is necessary to grasp what the best characteristic of each of these two parts is, for this is the virtue of each, and virtue is relative to the work belonging to each thing.

CHAPTER TWO

There are three things in the soul that are authoritative over action and truth: sense perception, intellect, and longing. But of these, sense perception is not the origin[7] of any action, and this is clear from the fact that beasts have sense perception but do not share in action.[8]

What affirmation and denial are in the case of thinking, pursuit and avoidance are in the case of longing for something. As a result, since moral virtue is a characteristic marked by choice, and choice is longing marked by deliberation, then on account of these considerations, the reasoning involved must be true and the longing correct, if in fact the choice is a serious one, and what the reasoning asserts must be the same as what the longing pursues. This, then, is the thinking and the truth concerned with

5 · That is, moral virtue, as the next sentence makes clear. See also 2.1, beginning.

6 · "The scientific" here is *to epistēmonikon*, "the calculative" *to logistikon*.

7 · Or, "beginning," "originating source," "principle" (*archē*).

8 · In *praxis*, i.e., in morally relevant action that is the basis of justified praise or blame.

action.[9] But in contemplative thinking, on the other hand, and not that characterized by action or making, thinking well or badly consists in the true and the false respectively (for this is the work of the thinking part as a whole), whereas practical thinking is well done when truth is in agreement with the correct longing.

Of action, then, choice is the origin—that from which the motion arises but not that for the sake of which one moves; and of choice, the origin is one's longing and the reasoning that indicates what it is for the sake of which one acts. Hence there cannot be choice either in the absence of intellect and thinking or in the absence of a moral characteristic, for there cannot be acting well or its contrary in action in the absence of thinking and character. Now, thinking itself moves nothing, but thinking that is for the sake of something and concerned with action does, for it serves as the starting point[10] also of an art concerned with making something: it is for the sake of something that every maker makes what he does, and the thing made is not an end simply (rather, it is an end only relative to something and of a given person), but the action performed is an end simply. For acting well[11] is an end, and one's longing is for this end. Hence choice is either intellect marked by a certain longing or longing marked by thinking [*dianoētikē*], and a starting point of this sort *is* a human being.

But nothing that has already come into being is an object of choice. For example, nobody now chooses to have sacked Troy in the past, and nobody deliberates, either, about what has already come into being but rather about what will be and admits of happening; what has already come into being does not admit of not having come into being. Hence Agathon[12] has it correctly:

For of this alone even a god is deprived:
To make undone[13] whatever things have been done.

9 · Or, "practical thinking and the practical truth."

10 · Or, "origin," or even, perhaps, "rules over": the verb here (*archein*) is related to the noun *archē* and shares in its ambiguity.

11 · Or, "faring well": the abstract noun here used (*eupraxia*) is related to the word translated as "action" throughout (*praxis*), but the phrase "to act well" can also mean in idiomatic Greek to "fare well"; consider, e.g., the last line of Plato's *Republic*. It is of course a great question in the *Ethics* whether or in what sense acting well *is* to fare well.

12 · A celebrated tragic poet (died ca. 401) who appears as a character in Plato's *Symposium*. Only fragments of his work survive.

13 · Literally, to make "ungenerated" (*agenēta*), the same word Aristotle uses just below at 1139b24.

So of both of the intellectual parts [of the soul], the work [or task] is truth. The characteristics, then, by which each part will to the greatest degree attain the truth are the virtues of the two parts respectively.

CHAPTER THREE

15   Beginning, then, from a point further back,[14] let us speak about them again. So let those things by which the soul attains the truth, by way of affirmation and denial, be five in number. These are art, science, prudence, wisdom, and intellect (for through conviction[15] and opinion, one can be mistaken[16]).

20   Now, what science is—if one ought to speak precisely and not attend to things merely resembling it—is manifest from this: we all suppose that what we know scientifically[17] does not admit of being otherwise. As for the things that do admit of being otherwise, whenever they come into being without being observed,[18] it escapes one's notice whether they exist or do not exist. Therefore, what is knowable scientifically exists of necessity. Therefore it is eternal, for the things that exist of necessity in an unqualified sense are all eternal, and eternal things are not subject to generation and do not perish.

25   Further, every science seems to be teachable, and what is knowable scientifically can be learned; and all teaching proceeds from things previously recognized—just as we say in the *Analytics* as well[19]—some teaching occurring through induction,[20] some by means of syllogism. Induction is in fact the starting point [or principle] of the universal, whereas syllogism

30   proceeds *from* the universals. There are, therefore, principles from which

14 · Literally, "higher up" (*anōthen*); see also n. 56 below.

15 · Or, "supposition" (*hypolēpsis*); the related verb (*hypolambanomai*) is translated as "suppose," as in the next sentence.

16 · Or, perhaps, "deceived" (*diapseudesthai*).

17 · *Epistasthai*, related to *epistēmē*, "science." In book 6, the term signifies the possession of "scientific" knowledge, as opposed to knowledge acquired in some other way. To indicate the instances it appears, we use the expression "to know scientifically" or "to have scientific knowledge."

18 · Or, "contemplated" (*theōrein*).

19 · Consider the beginning of the *Posterior Analytics*.

20 · The word (*epagōgē*) means literally a bringing or leading of someone to something, or introducing him to it: "induction" occurs when one is brought to see a given universal from prior familiarity with the relevant particulars (consider, e.g., *Posterior Analytics* 71a7–9; *Topics* 103b3 and context, 105a10–19).

a syllogism proceeds, but of which there is no syllogism; these are due instead, therefore, to induction. Science, therefore, is a characteristic bound
up with demonstration, and so many other things as we add to its definition in the *Analytics*.[21] For whenever someone trusts in[22] something in a
certain way, and the principles are known to him, he has scientific knowledge; for if [he does not know those principles] to a greater degree than
the conclusion, he will be in possession of the science [only] accidentally.   35
   As for what concerns science, then, let it be defined in this manner.

CHAPTER FOUR

Both a thing made and an action performed belong to what admits of   1140a
being otherwise, but making[23] and action are different (and concerning
them, we trust in even the exoteric arguments). As a result, the characteristic bound up with action that is accompanied by reason is different from
the characteristic bound up with making that is accompanied by reason.
Hence the one is not contained in the other, for action is not making and   5
making is not action. Since house building is a certain art and is in that respect a certain characteristic bound up with making that is accompanied
by reason, and since there is no art whatever that is not a characteristic
bound up with making and accompanied by reason (nor is there any such
thing that is not an art), an art and a characteristic bound up with making   10
that is accompanied by true reason would be the same thing. And every
art is concerned with the process of coming-into-being, that is, with artfully contriving and contemplating[24] how something that admits of either
existing or not existing may come into being, the origin of which lies in
the person making but not in the thing made. For of the things that exist
or come into being of necessity, there is no art, nor is there of those that   15
do so according to nature, for these have their origin within themselves.

21 · Consider *Posterior Analytics* 71b9–72b4, 73a21–74a3.
22 · The verb (*pisteuein*) means in the first place simply to trust or have faith in something and then, following from this, the sense of confidence or certainty one may feel as
a result of such trust or faith. Aristotle himself uses the verb in the first sentence of 6.4.
23 · Or, "production" (*poiēsis*), as many translators render it; it is also the term for "poetry" and "poem." Here, as in 6.2, *poiēsis*, the making or production that is art, is distinguished from *praxis*, "action."
24 · Some editors alter the text in such a way as to make of "artfully contriving" (*to tech-
nadzein*) a new subject: "and artful contrivance is contemplating how ..." But Bywater,
followed by Burnet, defends the reading of the MSS.

Now, since making and action are different, an art is necessarily concerned with making but not with action. And in a certain manner, chance
and art are concerned with the same things, just as Agathon too asserts:
"art is fond of chance and chance of art."[25] An art, then, as was stated, is a
certain characteristic bound up with making that is accompanied by true
reason; and artlessness [or lack of skill], to the contrary, is a characteristic bound up with making, accompanied by false reason, and concerned
with what admits of being otherwise.

CHAPTER FIVE

As for what concerns prudence, we might grasp it by contemplating
whom we say to be prudent. It seems to belong to a prudent person to be
able to deliberate nobly about things good and advantageous for himself,
not in a partial way—for example, the sorts of things conducive to health
or to strength—but about the sorts of things conducive to living well in
general. A sign of this is that we say that people are in fact prudent about
something whenever they calculate well with a view to some serious end
in matters of which there is no art. As a result, the person skilled in deliberating would in general also be prudent.

But nobody deliberates about things that cannot be otherwise, or
about things that he himself cannot act on. As a result, if in fact science is
accompanied by demonstration, but no demonstration is possible when
it comes to things whose origins [or principles] admit of being otherwise (for all such things admit of being otherwise as well), and if it is
not possible to deliberate about the things that exist of necessity, then
prudence would not be a science or an art: not a science, because the
thing bound up with the relevant action admits of being otherwise; not
an art, because the genus of action is different from that of making. It remains, therefore, that prudence is a true characteristic that is bound up
with action, accompanied by reason, and concerned with things good
and bad for a human being. For of making, the end is something other
than the making itself, whereas of action, there would not be any other
end: acting well itself is an end. On account of this, we suppose Pericles[26] and those of that sort to be prudent—because they are able to ob-

25 · The line contains an alliterative jingle: *"technē tuchēn ... tuchē technēn."*
26 · Pericles (ca. 495–429) was Athens's leading democratic statesman at the peak of
his city's powers. He is perhaps best remembered today for his powerful praise of democratic Athens in the funeral speech reported by Thucydides (2.34–46).

serve²⁷ the good things for themselves and those for human beings. We
hold that skilled household managers and politicians are of this sort too.   10
This is why in fact we call "moderation" by its name, on the grounds
that it "preserves prudence,"²⁸ and it does preserve the sort of conviction
indicated.

For it is not *every* conviction that the pleasant and painful ruin²⁹
and distort—for example, that the triangle has or does not have [angles   15
whose sum is equal to] two right angles—but rather those convictions
concerning action. For the principles of actions are that [end] for the sake
of which the actions are undertaken, but to someone who has been ruined on account of pleasure or pain, the principle immediately fails to appear—it is not manifest to him that he ought to choose all things and to
act for the sake of this and on account of it. For vice is ruinous of the principle. As a result, prudence is necessarily a characteristic accompanied by   20
reason, in possession of the truth, and bound up with action pertaining
to the human goods.³⁰

And although there is a virtue of an art, there is not of prudence; in
the case of an art, it is more choiceworthy for one to err voluntarily, less
choiceworthy in the case of prudence (as also in the virtues). It is clear,
then, that prudence is a certain virtue and not an art. And since there are   25
two parts of the soul having reason, prudence would be the virtue of one
of them, namely, the part involved in the formation of opinions. For both
opinion and prudence are concerned with what admits of being otherwise. Yet prudence is also not solely a characteristic accompanied by reason, a sign of which is that it is possible to forget such a characteristic, but
not to forget prudence.³¹   30

27 · Or, "contemplate" (*theōrein*).

28 · Aristotle's etymology is untranslatable: he indicates that "moderation" (*sōphrosunē*)
contains within it the suggestion that it "preserves" (*sōdzousan*) "prudence" (*phronēsin*).
Consider also Plato, *Cratylus* 411e.

29 · Or, "corrupt," "destroy" (*diaphtheirein*).

30 · The MSS differ here, and another translation is possible: "prudence is necessarily a characteristic accompanied by true reason and bound up with action pertaining
to the human goods."

31 · Consider here St. Thomas Aquinas: prudence "is not connected with reason alone,
as art or science, but it requires rectitude of the appetitive faculty. A sign of this is that
a habit in the reason alone can be forgotten (for example, art and science), unless the
habit is a natural one like understanding. Prudence, however, is not forgotten by dis-
use, but it is destroyed by the cessation of right desire which, while remaining, is continually engaged with the things belonging to prudence, so that oblivion cannot come

CHAPTER SIX

Now, since science is a conviction concerning universals and the things that exist of necessity, and since there are principles of demonstrable things and of every science (for science is accompanied by reason), then regarding the principle of what is known scientifically, there would be

35   neither a science nor an art nor prudence. For what is known scientifically is demonstrable, and art and prudence happen to be concerned with

1141a   things that admit of being otherwise. Nor, indeed, is there wisdom with regard to these principles, for it belongs to the wise person to have a demonstration about some things.

So if the ways by which we attain the truth and are never mistaken

5   about things that do not (or even do) admit of being otherwise are science, prudence, wisdom, and intellect, and it cannot be any one of these three—I mean by "three" prudence, science, and wisdom—it remains that it is intellect that pertains to the principles.

CHAPTER SEVEN

Wisdom in the arts too we ascribe to those who are most precise in the

10   arts—for example, Pheidias was a wise sculptor in marble and Polycleitus a wise sculptor in bronze[32]—signifying by "wisdom" here nothing other than a virtue belonging to an art. But we suppose that there are some wise people who are wise generally and not partially, or in some other respect, just as Homer asserts in the *Margites*:

15   But him gods made neither digger nor ploughman,
     Nor wise in some other respect.[33]

It is clear, as a result, that the most precise of the sciences would be wisdom. The wise person, therefore, ought not only to know what proceeds

---

along unawares" (*Commentary on Aristotle's "Nicomachean Ethics,"* lec. 1174 = Aquinas 1964, p. 372).

32 · Pheidias of Athens (born ca. 490) is best known for the statue of Athena made for the Parthenon, and for the depiction of a seated Zeus fabricated for the temple of Zeus at Olympia. Polycleitus of Argos was a leading sculptor of the second half of the fifth century. His most famous work was the chryselephantine statue of Hera made for the Heraeum at Argos.

33 · The *Margites*, a comic poem no longer extant, is mentioned also in the *Poetics*, 1448b28 and following.

from the principles but also to attain the truth *about* the principles. Wisdom, as a result, would be intellect and science, a science of the most honorable matters that has, as it were, its capstone.[34]   20

For it is strange if someone supposes the political art or prudence to be most serious, if a human being is not the best of things in the cosmos. If indeed what is healthful and good is different for human beings and for fish, but what is white or straight is always the same, all would say that what is wise is the same thing but that what is prudent differs: they would   25 assert that that which observes[35] the good condition for each sort of thing is prudent, and they would entrust such concerns to this.[36] Hence they assert that certain beasts too are prudent, namely, all those that manifestly have the capacity for forethought concerning their own life. It is manifest too that wisdom and the political art would not be the same: if people say that the art concerned with things advantageous to themselves is wis-   30 dom, there will be many wisdoms; for there is not one wisdom concerned with the good of all the animals but a different one for each, unless there is in fact a single medical art concerned with all the beings. And whether a human being is the best in comparison with the other animals makes no difference, for there are other things whose nature is much more divine   1141b than that of a human being—to take only the most manifest example, the things of which the cosmos is composed.

So on the basis of what has been said, it is clear that wisdom is a science and intellectual grasp [*nous*] of the things most honorable by nature. Hence people deny that Anaxagoras, Thales, and the wise of that   5 sort are prudent when they see them being ignorant of the things advantageous to themselves, and they assert that such men know things that are extraordinary,[37] wondrous, difficult, and daimonic[38]—yet useless too,

34 · Literally, its "head." The meaning is that the science is complete.

35 · Or, "contemplates."

36 · There is some disagreement here in the reading of the MSS. We follow in the main Burnet's suggestions, which are generally supported by Gauthier and Jolif. Another possible translation is "they would assert that that which observes well the various particulars concerning itself is prudent, and they would entrust such things to this."

37 · The word (*peritta*) can also mean "superfluous," "excessive," "extravagant." See n. 40 below and the last of the lines of Euripides there quoted.

38 · That is, characteristic of a daimon, a divine power or agency that, in Plato's presentation, occupies the realm between human beings and gods; the term can also be used colloquially to mean "most surprising" or "wondrous": "you daimonic fellow!" (see, e.g., Plato, *Symposium* 223a1).

because they do not investigate[39] the human goods. But prudence is concerned with the human things and with those about which it is possible
10   to deliberate. For we assert this to be the work of the prudent person especially—deliberating well—and nobody deliberates about things that
cannot be otherwise, or about so many things as are without some end,
an end, moreover, that is a good attainable through action. He who is a
good deliberator simply is skilled in aiming, in accord with calculation,
at what is best for a human being in things attainable through action.
15   And prudence is not concerned with the universals alone but must also
be acquainted with the particulars: it is bound up with action, and action concerns the particulars. Hence even some who are without knowledge—those who have experience, among others—are more skilled in
acting than are others who do have knowledge. For if someone should
know that light meats are easily digestible and healthful, but is ignorant of
20   what sorts are light, he will not produce health; rather, he who does know
that poultry is light and healthful will to a greater degree produce health.
      Prudence is bound up with action. As a result, one ought to have
[knowledge of] both [universals and particulars], but more so of the latter. But here too there would be a certain architectonic [art or knowledge].

CHAPTER EIGHT

And in fact the political art [or expertise] and prudence are the same
25   characteristic [or state], though their being is not the same. Of the prudence that is concerned with a city, one part is an architectonic prudence,
namely, the legislative art; the other, concerned with particulars, bears
the name that is common to them, "the political art," and is bound up
with action and deliberation. For a specific decree is a matter of action,
as it is the last [or ultimate] thing [in the process of deliberation]. Thus
people say that only those [who issue decrees] are engaged in political life,
for they alone act, just as craftsmen do.
      In addition, the prudence that pertains to oneself—that is, the in-
30   dividual—is held to be prudence especially, and it is this that bears the
common name "prudence." Of the other kinds of prudence, one part is
household management, another legislation, another the political art;
and of this last, one part is deliberative, the other judicial. Now, one form
of knowledge would be knowing about what concerns oneself, but this

39 · Or, "seek out."

differs very much [from political prudence]. In fact, he who knows about　1142a
and spends his time on things that concern himself is held to be prudent,
whereas the politicians are held to be busybodies. Thus Euripides:

> And how could I be prudent, who might have been free of busyness,
> Numbered among the many of the army,
> Enjoying an equal share ... ?　　　　　　　　　　　　　　　　　5
>
> . . . .
> For those who are extraordinary and a little too active.... [40]

For people seek out their own good, and they suppose that this is what
they ought to do. From this opinion, then, has arisen the view that these
people are prudent. Yet perhaps one cannot do well for oneself in the absence of household management or a regime. Further, how one ought to　10
manage one's own affairs is unclear and must be examined.

One sign of what has been said is the fact that the young become skilled
in geometry and mathematics, and are wise in such things, but a young
person does not seem to be prudent. The cause is that prudence is also of
particulars, which come to be known as a result of experience, but a young　15
person is inexperienced: a long period of time creates experience. And then
someone might examine this as well: on account of what indeed might a
boy become skilled in mathematics, but not wise or well versed in nature?
Or is it because the former subjects exist through abstraction, whereas the
principles of the latter come from experience? And do the young not have　20
any settled convictions[41] about these latter but [merely] speak of them,
whereas, with mathematics and geometry, what they are is not unclear?

Further, error in deliberation concerns either the universal or the particular, for one can err in deliberating either about the fact that all heavy
water is bad, or about the fact that this water here is heavy.[42]

40 · The lines quoted are taken from the prologue to Euripides's lost *Philoctetes* and
are said to have been uttered by Odysseus. The complete third line quoted in the text
is "Enjoying an equal share with the wisest?" The context of the last line is as follows:

> For nothing is by nature so haughty as a man,
> For we honor those who are extraordinary and a little too active,
> And hold them to be men in the city.

41 · Not the usual word translated here as "conviction" (*hypolēpsis*) but the verb that
can mean "trust" or "have faith in" (*pisteuein*); see also n. 22 above.

42 · Burnet here cites Athenaeus's quotation of Theophrastus: "And the heavier [wa-
ters] are worse ... for they are harder to digest ... because they contain much soil" (Athenaeus 42c).

And that prudence is not science is manifest: prudence concerns the
25   ultimate particular thing, as was said, for the action performed is of this
kind. Indeed, prudence corresponds to intellect, for intellect is concerned
with the defining boundaries,[43] of which there is no rational account; and
prudence is concerned with the ultimate particular thing, of which there
is not a science but rather a perception, and a perception not of things peculiar to one of the senses, but a perception of the sort by which we perceive that the ultimate particular thing, in mathematics, is a triangle.[44]
30   For here too there will be a stop. But this is perception rather more than
prudence, though perception of a form different from that [of one of the
senses].

CHAPTER NINE

Investigating and deliberating differ, for deliberating is a sort of investigating. But one ought to grasp what good deliberation is as well, whether it is
some science, opinion, good guesswork, or is some other kind[45] of thing.

Now, it is certainly not science, for people do not investigate the things

43 · That is, of the *horoi*, an ambiguous term meaning most simply a defining marker
or definition of a thing, but also by extension a term of a logical proposition; consider
n. 3 above and nn. 48 and 53 below.

44 · As Gauthier and Jolif note, this sentence has occasioned two principal interpretations. According to the first, put forth by St. Albertus Magnus and followed in the main
by Burnet among others, the triangle is an ultimate (*to eschaton*) in the sense that it is
the last thing in one's analysis (consider here 1112b20–24). So Burnet: "The case supposed is that of the geometer who breaks up his figure till he comes to something—say
a triangle—which enables him to start the construction or proof at which he aims. It
is in this way, for example, that the properties of parallelograms are discovered." The
second interpretation, stated by St. Thomas Aquinas and adopted by Gauthier and Jolif among others, is to the effect that Aristotle is here illustrating the thought that we
simply perceive a given particular thing (*to eschaton*) as what it is and must rely on that
perception in whatever we may go on to say about it, be it a triangle or any other geometric figure. Thus St. Thomas Aquinas: "prudence is concerned with an ultimate, i.e.,
a singular practicable that must be taken as a principle in things to be done. Yet there is
no scientific knowledge of the singular ultimate, for it is not proved by reason; there is,
though, sensitive knowledge [i.e., perception] of it because this ultimate is perceived by
one of the senses. However, it is ... apprehended ... by the inner sense which perceives
things sensibly conceivable. Similarly, in mathematics we know the exterior triangle, or
the triangle conceived as singular, because there we also conform to a sensibly conceivable singular" (*Commentary*, lec. 1214 = Aquinas 1964, pp. 384–85).

45 · Literally, "genus."

they know, but good deliberation is a kind of deliberation, and he who   1142b
deliberates, investigates and calculates. But neither is it good guesswork.
For good guesswork is both unaccompanied by reasoned argument and
something swift, whereas people deliberate for a long time and assert
that while they ought to do swiftly what has been deliberated about, they
ought to deliberate slowly.   5

Further, shrewdness is something other than good deliberation,
though shrewdness is a sort of good guessing. And neither is good deliberation any opinion. But since someone who deliberates badly errs and
he who deliberates well does so correctly, it is clear that good deliberation
is a sort of correctness — but not correctness of either science or opinion.
For of science, there is no correctness (nor is there error), and correctness   10
of opinion is truth; at the same time too, everything of which there is an
opinion is already determined. Yet surely good deliberation is accompanied by reasoned argument, and so it remains that good deliberation is
correctness of thinking, for thinking is not yet an assertion: opinion is
not an investigation into something but is already a specific assertion,
whereas he who deliberates — whether he deliberates well or even delib-   15
erates badly — is investigating something and calculating.

Good deliberation is, rather, a certain correctness of deliberation.
Hence one must investigate first what deliberation is and what it is concerned with. Now, since *correctness* has various senses, it is clear that correctness of deliberation is not every kind of correctness; for the person
lacking self-restraint or the base person will hit on,[46] as a result of calculation, whatever he sets before himself as obligatory,[47] with the result that
he will have deliberated correctly but nonetheless have gotten hold of   20
something very bad. But to have deliberated well seems to be something
good, for such correctness of deliberation is good deliberation, which is
apt to hit on what is good. But it is possible to hit on this also as the result
of a false syllogism and to hit on what one ought to do but through the
means one ought not to use, the middle term[48] being false. As a result, not

46 · Or, "attain" (*tuchein*), here and throughout.

47 · The word translated as "obligatory" (*dein*), derived from the medieval translation
of Robert Grosseteste, and with apparently some manuscript authority, is a slight departure from the difficult (Burnet: "meaningless") reading of the majority of the MSS
(*idein*); the reading adopted in the text is defended by Burnet as well as by Gauthier
and Jolif.

48 · Not the term elsewhere translated as "middle term" or "middle" (*to meson*) but
rather *ho mesos horos*, here used in its technical (logical) sense; consider *Prior Analyt-*

25   even that deliberation, through which one hits on what one ought but
not by the proper means, would yet be good deliberation.

Further, it is possible for someone to hit on what he ought by deliberating for a long time, while another does so quickly. Lengthy deliberation,
then, is not yet good deliberation either; rather, it is the correctness that
accords with what is beneficial and aims at what one ought, in the right
manner, and at the right time.

Further, it is possible to have deliberated well both simply and with a
30   view to a certain end: good deliberation simply is that which guides us
correctly toward the end simply, but a specific sort of deliberation is what
guides us correctly toward some particular end. So if having deliberated
well belongs to those who are prudent, good deliberation would be a correctness that accords with what is advantageous in relation to the end,
about which end prudence is a true conviction.

CHAPTER TEN

There is also comprehension and good comprehension, in reference to
1143a   which we speak of those who comprehend or comprehend well. Comprehension is in general neither the same thing as science, nor the same thing
as opinion (in which case everyone would have comprehension); nor is it
any one of the particular sciences—for example, medicine, which is con-
5   cerned with matters of health, and geometry, with magnitudes. Comprehension is concerned neither with beings that are eternal and unmoved
nor with just any or every one of the things that come into being, but
rather with the things about which someone might be perplexed and deliberate. Hence it is concerned with the same things as prudence. Comprehension and prudence are not the same thing, however, for prudence
is characterized by the giving of commands: its end is what one ought or
10   ought not to do. But comprehension is characterized by decision[49] alone.
For comprehension and good comprehension, as well as those who comprehend and those who do so well, are the same thing. And comprehen-

---

ics 24b16 and context (on this meaning of *horos*) as well as 25b33 and following (on the
"middle term" of a syllogism).

49 · Or, "judgment." The phrase "characterized by decision" attempts to render a single
Greek word (*kritikē*), whose root is the verb meaning to distinguish, judge, decide, or
determine (*krinein*); related to both is the English *crisis*, i.e., the moment when the crucial decision or determination will be made.

sion is neither the possession of prudence nor the gaining of it. Rather, just as "learning" is said to be comprehending, whenever it makes use of science,[50] so comprehension is said to consist in making use of opinion to render a decision about what someone else says, regarding the matters   15
that prudence is concerned with—and rendering such a decision nobly. For doing something well is the same as doing it nobly. And from this, the name "comprehension"—in reference to which we speak of those who are of good comprehension—has arisen, namely, from the comprehension involved in learning.[51] For we often say "learning" when we mean "comprehending."

CHAPTER ELEVEN

And what is called "judgment," in reference to which we assert that people are sympathetic judges and have judgment,[52] is the correct decision as to   20
what is equitable. There is a sign of this: we assert that the equitable person is especially characterized by sympathetic judgment and that having sympathy in some matters is an equitable thing. Sympathetic judgment is a judgment characterized by a correct decision as to what is equitable, it being correct because it grasps what is truly equitable.

It is only reasonable that all the characteristics tend toward the same   25
thing, for in attributing judgment, comprehension, prudence, and intellect to the same people, we mean that they have judgment and intellect already and are prudent and comprehending. For all these capacities are concerned with things ultimate and particular—and someone's being comprehending and of good or sympathetic judgment consists in his being skilled in deciding the matters with which the prudent person is   30
concerned. For the equitable things are common to *all* good human beings in their being directed toward another, and *all* matters of action fall

---

50 · Here Aristotle makes use of an ambiguity in the verb *manthanein*, which, as he himself notes in the *Topics* (165b32), can mean both to learn, i.e., to get hold of science or knowledge, or to have learned and so now to understand, i.e., to have "the comprehension that makes use of science [*epistēmē*]."

51 · Or, "in having learned something" and so understanding it. Again, Aristotle makes use of the ambiguity of the verb *to learn* (*manthanein*): see the preceding note.

52 · The phrase "sympathetic judges" translates a single word (*sungnōmonas*) whose root is the word translated as "judgment" (*gnōmē*); "sympathetic judgment" (*sungnōmē*) may be translated also as "forgiveness," as we translate it in 3.1.

among things particular and ultimate: the prudent person must recognize them, and both comprehension and judgment concern actions performed, which are ultimate things.

Moreover, intellect is concerned with the ultimate things in both directions, for [what grasps] both the first defining boundaries[53] and the ultimate particulars is intellect and not reason. That is, on the one hand, intellect pertaining to demonstrations grasps the unchanging first defining boundaries; on the other hand, intellect in matters of action grasps also the ultimate particular thing that admits of being otherwise, that is, the minor premise. For these ultimate particulars are the principles [or starting points] of that for the sake of which one acts: the universals arise from the particulars. Of these, then, one must have a perception, and this perception is intellect. Hence these things are also held to be natural, and though nobody is held to be wise by nature, a person is held to have judgment, comprehension, and intellect by nature. A sign of this is that we suppose these accompany the various times of life, and that a given time of life is possessed of intellect and judgment, on the grounds that nature is the cause of them. Hence intellect is both a beginning and an end, for the demonstrations arise from these and concern them.[54] As a result, one ought to pay attention to the undemonstrated assertions and opinions of experienced and older people, or of the prudent, no less than to demonstrations, for because they have an experienced eye, they see correctly.

What prudence and wisdom are, then, with what each of them happens to be concerned, and that each is the virtue of a different part of the soul has been said.

CHAPTER TWELVE

But about these matters, someone might be perplexed as to why wisdom and prudence are useful. For wisdom, on the one hand, will not contemplate anything as a result of which a human being will be happy (since wisdom is not concerned with anything that is coming-into-being), while prudence, on the other hand, does pertain to this. But for the sake of what does one need prudence? If in fact it is concerned with the things just, noble, and good for a human being, and these are the things it belongs to

53 · *Horoi*, the plural of *horos*.
54 · As Burnet notes, "These words break the argument here," and Bywater, together with several modern editors (though not Burnet), suggests placing this sentence immediately after the sentence above that ends, "and this perception is intellect."

a good man to do, we are no more skilled in the relevant action by dint of knowing them, if in fact the virtues are characteristics, just as in the case of things healthful or distinctive of good conditioning—all such things as are said to exist, not simply as a result of one's doing something, but as a result of one's possessing the relevant characteristic. For we are not more skilled in the actions that correspond to health by possessing the arts of medicine and gymnastic training.

But if it must be said that one is prudent not for the sake of these things, [that is, knowing what is just, noble, and good,] but rather for the sake of becoming such, prudence would be of no use to those who already are serious, or, for that matter, to those who do not have [such seriousness].[55] For it will make no difference whether they themselves have prudence or obey others who have it, and that would be enough for us, just as it is also in what concerns health: although we wish to be healthy, nonetheless we do not learn the art of medicine.

And, in addition to these considerations, it would seem strange if prudence, though inferior to wisdom, will exercise greater authority than it, for what makes or produces each thing rules over and arranges that thing.

It is about these matters, then, that it is necessary to speak; for, as things stand, only the perplexities about them have been raised.

First, then, let us say that wisdom and prudence are necessarily choice-worthy in themselves, since each of them is a virtue of each part [of the soul], even if neither one of them makes or produces anything. Second, they do in fact make or produce something, not as the art of medicine produces health, but, rather, just as health produces health, so wisdom produces happiness. For wisdom, being a part of the whole of virtue, makes one happy by being possessed and by being active. Further, the relevant work is completed in accord with prudence and moral virtue. For virtue makes the target correct, prudence the things conducive to that target. (But of the fourth part of the soul, the nutritive, there is no such virtue, since acting or not acting does not at all apply in its case.)

As for our being, on account of prudence, no more skilled in action when it comes to things noble and just, it is necessary to begin from a point a little further back,[56] taking this as our starting point. For just as we say that some people who do just things are not yet just—for example,

---

55 · The fifteenth-century scholar John Argyropoulos adopted a reading that would translate as "or, further, to those who are not [serious]," which, according to Burnet, "gives a clearer sense."

56 · Literally, "higher up" (*anōthen*): see also n. 14 above.

15   those who do what has been ordered by the laws but do so either involuntarily, through ignorance, or on account of something else and not on
account of the orders themselves (though they *do* do what they should,
namely, all the things that the serious human being ought to do)—so
also, as it seems, it is possible for someone to perform each thing in turn
while being in a certain state, with the result that he is good—I mean,
20   that is, through choice and for the sake of the actions themselves. As for
the choice involved, then, virtue makes it correct; but as for doing all that
is naturally done for the sake of that choice, this belongs not to virtue but
to another capacity.

But we must stop here and speak more clearly about these things. There
is indeed a capacity that people call "cleverness,"[57] and this is of such a
25   character as to be capable of doing what is conducive to the target posited and so of hitting it. If, then, the target is a noble one, the cleverness
is praiseworthy; but if base, it is mere cunning. Hence we assert that even
the prudent are terribly clever and cunning. Prudence is not the capacity
30   in question, though it does not exist without this capacity, and this "eye of
the soul" does not acquire the characteristic [of prudence] in the absence
of virtue, as was said and is clear. For the syllogisms dealing with matters
of action have a principle [or starting point], "since the end, that is, what
is best, is of such-and-such a character," whatever it may be (let it be, for
the sake of argument, any chance thing), but this end does not appear to
35   someone if he is not good. For corruption distorts and causes one to be
mistaken[58] about the principles bound up with action. As a result, it is
manifest that it is impossible for someone who is not good to be prudent.

CHAPTER THIRTEEN

1144b   So it is necessary to examine virtue once again. For in fact the case of virtue resembles that of prudence in its relation to cleverness—it is not the
same thing as cleverness but is similar to it—and so also does natural virtue stand in relation to virtue in the authoritative sense. For all people
5   are of the opinion that each of the several characters [or traits] is in some
way present by nature: we are just, inclined to be moderate, and are cou-

---

57 · This noun (*deinotēta*) and the adjective associated with it (*deinos*) are ambiguous—as Aristotle's use of the noun here suggests—and can connote that which is terrible, frightening, and awful, or what is clever or shrewd, including what is a little too
clever; "terribly clever" will often be used to convey the sense of *deinos*.
58 · Or, "to be deceived about."

rageous and the rest, immediately from birth. But nevertheless we are seeking something else, namely, the good in the authoritative sense and such things as are present in us in another manner. For in both children and beasts, the natural characteristics are present, but they are manifestly harmful in the absence of intellect. Yet this much does seem to be seen — that just as a strong body moving without eyesight will end up stumbling with considerable force because it is without sight, so it is also in this case [of having the natural virtues in the absence of intellect]. But if someone gains intellect, his actions will alter accordingly; and the characteristic he possesses, though similar to what it was, will then be virtue in the authoritative sense. As a result, just as there are two forms of that which is concerned with the formation of opinion, namely cleverness and prudence, so also there are two of that which is concerned with moral character, namely natural virtue and virtue in the authoritative sense; and of these, virtue in the authoritative sense does not arise in the absence of prudence.

So it is that some people assert that all the virtues are kinds of prudence, and Socrates used to investigate it correctly in one respect, but in another respect he erred. For he erred when he supposed that all the virtues are kinds of prudence, but he spoke nobly when he said that they do not exist in the absence of prudence. And there is a sign of this. For even now when all define virtue, after speaking of the given characteristic and the things to which it is related, they set down in addition, "the characteristic in accord with correct reason," and the reason that accords with prudence is correct. Indeed, all seem somehow to divine that such a characteristic is virtue, namely, the one that accords with prudence.

But one ought to make a small change. For virtue is not only the characteristic that accords with correct reason, but also the one that is *accompanied* by correct reason. And prudence is correct reason concerning such sorts of things. Socrates, then, used to suppose that the virtues are reasoned accounts [*logoi*] (for, he supposed, all are kinds of scientific knowledge), but we hold that they are accompanied by reason. It is clear, then, on the basis of what has been said, that it is not possible to be good in the authoritative sense in the absence of prudence, nor is it possible to be prudent in the absence of moral virtue.

But in this way the argument that someone might make in a dialectical manner[59] would also be resolved, to the effect that the virtues are sepa-

59 · Or, more simply, "in conversation" (*dialegesthai*). Socrates, for one, takes up just this argument made by Protagoras in Plato's *Protagoras*.

rate from one another. For the same person will not have a most excellent
nature with a view to *all* the virtues, so that he will have one virtue while
not yet having another. This can happen in the case of the natural virtues,
but as for those virtues in reference to which someone is said to be good
unqualifiedly, it cannot happen. For all the virtues will be present when
the one virtue, prudence, is present. And it is clear that, even if prudence
were not bound up with action, it would be needed on account of its being the virtue of a part [of the soul]. It is clear too there will be no correct
choice in the absence of prudence, nor in the absence of virtue; for the
latter makes one carry out[60] the end, the former the things conducive to
the end. And yet prudence does not exercise authoritative control over
wisdom or the better part [of the soul], just as the art of medicine does
not do so over health either, for it does not make use of health but rather
sees how it comes into being; it is for the sake of health, then, that medicine issues commands, but it does not issue them to health. Furthermore,
it would be just as if someone should assert that the political art rules over
the gods because it issues commands about all things in the city.

---

60 · Or, "do," perhaps "fashion" (*prattein*). This striking line, which has occasioned
some commentary, suggests that virtue prompts us to carry out or "do" the end of virtue, while prudence is responsible for making clear to us the means appropriate to the
end of moral virtue, which is not chosen but given.

Book 7

After these matters, we must make another beginning and say that there   1145a15
are three forms of things pertaining to character that must be avoided:
vice, lack of self-restraint, and brutishness.[1] The contraries of two of these
are clear: the one contrary we call virtue, the other self-restraint. But as
for the contrary of brutishness, it would be especially fitting to speak of
the virtue that is beyond us, a certain heroic and divine virtue—just as   20
Homer has written, when Priam says about Hector that he was exceedingly good, "and he did not seem to be a child of any mortal man, but
of a god."[2] As a result, if (as people assert) human beings become gods
through an excess of virtue, it is clear that something of this sort would
be the characteristic opposite to brutishness. For just as a brute animal   25
has neither vice nor virtue, so also a god does not either; rather, the characteristic belonging to a god is more honorable than virtue and that belonging to a brute animal is of some genus other than vice. And since it
is rare for a man to be divine—just as the Laconians[3] are accustomed
to addressing someone, when they greatly admire him, as "a divine man,"[4]
they assert—so also the brutish person is rare among human beings, he   30
being present among barbarians especially, though some cases also arise
through both diseases and defects. And such is the bad name, "brutish,"
we give to those human beings who exceed the rest in vice. But some men-

1 · Or, "savagery." The term (*thēriotēs*) is related to the word elsewhere translated as
"beast" or "brute animal" (*thērion*).
2 · Homer, *Iliad* 24.258.
3 · That is, the Spartans.
4 · Aristotle's quotation contains the Laconian variant of the word for "divine" (*seios*
instead of *theios*). Consider also Plato, *Meno* 99d7–9 and *Laws* 626c4–5.

tion of this sort of disposition must be made later; what concerns vice was
35   spoken of before.

But as for what concerns lack of self-restraint, softness, and delicacy,
this must be spoken about, as well as what concerns self-restraint and
steadfastness. For it must not be assumed either that each of the two
[—that is, self-restraint or lack of self-restraint, steadfastness or softness—]
1145b   concerns the same characteristics as virtue and corruption respectively
or that each is of a different genus. But, just as in other cases as well, after
positing the phenomena[5] and first raising perplexities about them, one
5   ought in this way to bring to light especially all the received opinions
about these experiences[6] or, failing that, the greatest number and most authoritative of those opinions. For if the vexing questions[7] are solved and
the received opinions remain standing as well, then the matter would be
adequately explained.

Now, self-restraint and steadfastness seem to fall among things serious and praiseworthy, lack of self-restraint as well as softness among
10   things base and blameworthy; the self-restrained person seems to be the
same as someone who abides by his calculation, the person lacking
self-restraint to be one who departs from his calculation. Moreover,
the person lacking self-restraint, knowing that what he does is base, acts
on account of his passion, while the self-restrained person, knowing
that his desires are base, does not follow them, on account of his reason. And [though it is said that] the moderate person is self-restrained
15   and steadfast, some assert that a person of this latter sort is moderate
in all respects, while others deny it. And some assert that the licentious
person lacks self-restraint and the person lacking self-restraint is licentious, without discriminating between them, but others assert that they
are different. And sometimes people deny that the prudent person can
be without self-restraint, whereas sometimes they assert that some who
are prudent and terrifically clever do lack self-restraint. Further, people
20   are said to lack self-restraint also in point of spiritedness, honor, and
gain.

These, then, are the statements made on the subject.

5 · Literally, "the things that appear" or "come to sight" (*ta phainomena*).
6 · Or, "the passions" (*ta pathē*). "The word *pathos* is loosely used here of all states of
soul.... Really they are *hexeis* [characteristics]" (Burnet).
7 · The word (*dyscherē*) can also mean disagreeable or offensive things.

CHAPTER TWO

But someone might be perplexed as to how a person, though he forms a correct conviction,[8] lacks self-restraint. Some, then, deny that a person who has scientific knowledge can lack self-restraint; for it would be a terrible thing, when science is present (as Socrates used to suppose), for something else to overpower it and drag it around as if it were a slave.[9] For Socrates used to battle against this argument in its entirety, on the grounds that no such thing as lack of self-restraint exists: nobody acts contrary to what is best while supposing that he is so acting; he acts instead through ignorance.

This argument, then, is in contention with the phenomena that come plainly to sight, and one must investigate, if in fact this experience occurs through ignorance, what the character of the ignorance is. For it is manifest that before he is in the grip of passion, a person who lacks self-restraint does not think, at least, [that he ought to act as he then proceeds to act]. And there are some people who concede this in certain respects but not in others: they agree, on the one hand, that there is nothing superior to science, but they disagree, on the other, that nobody acts contrary to the opinion held of what is better; and it is for this reason they assert that the person lacking self-restraint is overpowered by pleasures because he possesses not science but opinion. But if in fact it is opinion and not science at issue, and a person's conviction that resists is not a strong but a mild one, as in the case of people given to hesitation, there is sympathy for someone who does not stick by those convictions in the face of strong pleasures. Yet for corruption there is no sympathy, nor is there for anything else blameworthy.

Is it, therefore, prudence that resists [pleasures]? For prudence is a very strong thing. This contention, however, is strange. For the same person will be simultaneously prudent and lacking self-restraint, and not one person would assert that it belongs to a prudent human being to do voluntarily the basest things. In addition to these points, it has been shown before that the prudent person is skilled in action, at least—for he is someone concerned with ultimate particular things—and possesses the other virtues.

Further, if a person is self-restrained in having strong and base desires,

---

8 · Or, "supposition" (*hypolambanōn*).
9 · Consider Plato, *Protagoras* 352a8–c7.

the moderate person will not be self-restrained or the self-restrained moderate. For it does not belong to a moderate person to have either excessive or base desires. And yet the self-restrained person *must* have such desires, for if his desires are worthy,[10] the characteristic that prevents him from following them will be base, with the result that not all self-restraint

15 will be of serious worth. But if his desires are weak and not base, it is nothing august to resist them, and if they are base and weak, it is nothing great to do so.

Further, if self-restraint renders a person apt to abide by every opinion, it is base—for example, if it prompts someone to abide by even a false opinion. And if lack of self-restraint renders a person apt to depart from every opinion, some lack of self-restraint will be of serious worth, as in the

20 example of Neoptolemus in Sophocles's *Philoctetes*. For he is praiseworthy because he does not abide by what he was persuaded of by Odysseus, on account of his being pained at telling a lie.[11]

Further, Sophistic argument prompts perplexity. For on account of the Sophists' wish to refute their opponents by way of paradox, so that they may be terrifically clever when they succeed, the very syllogism that

25 results becomes a perplexity. For one's thinking is tied up in knots whenever, on account of its being dissatisfied with the conclusion reached, it does not wish to stay put but at the same time is unable to proceed because it is unable to refute the argument. So it results from a certain argument that foolishness, when accompanied by lack of self-restraint, is a virtue. For in that case a person, on account of his lack of self-restraint, does things contrary to what he supposes; and he supposes that things

30 actually good are bad and that he therefore ought not to do them—with the result that he will do what is actually good and not bad.

Further, he who, because he has been so persuaded, does and pursues pleasant things, and chooses accordingly, might be held to be better than someone who acts, not from calculation, but through lack of self-restraint. For the former person is easier to cure, because he might be persuaded otherwise; while the person lacking self-restraint is subject to

35 the proverb in which we assert, "when the water chokes, what should you

1146b drink?"[12] For if he had been persuaded to act as he does, then upon being subsequently persuaded to stop, he would have done so. But as it is,

10 · Or, perhaps, "good" (*chrēstai*).

11 · See Sophocles, *Philoctetes*, especially 54–122 and 895–916.

12 · The proverb is otherwise unknown.

though he has been persuaded of one thing, he does other things none-theless.

Further, if self-restraint and its lack pertain to all things, who is the person lacking self-restraint in an unqualified sense? For nobody has *all* forms of the lack of self-restraint, but we do assert that some people are lacking self-restraint in an unqualified sense.

Such, then, are some of the perplexities that result; and of these, one ought to do away with some but leave others remaining. For the resolu-tion of a perplexity is a discovery.

CHAPTER THREE

First, then, is to examine whether those who act without self-restraint do so knowingly or not, and how they might do so knowingly. Next one must set down the sorts of things that the persons lacking self-restraint and the self-restrained are concerned with—I mean whether they are concerned with every pleasure and pain or with certain particular ones, and, as regards the self-restrained and the steadfast, whether they are the same person or different, and similarly for all other points belonging to this study.[13]

A starting point of the examination is whether the self-restrained per-son and the person lacking self-restraint are distinguishable by *what* they are concerned with or by *the way* in which they are so concerned. I mean this: whether it is solely by being concerned with these or those things that the person is lacking in self-restraint; or, if that is not the case, then instead because of the way in which he is so concerned; or, if not that, then instead as a result of both considerations. Second, one must exam-ine whether lack of self-restraint and self-restraint pertain to all things or not. For the person lacking self-restraint in an unqualified sense is not concerned with *all* things but rather with those with which the licen-tious person is concerned. Nor is he lacking self-restraint simply by be-ing concerned with these—in that case, lack of self-restraint would be the same thing as licentiousness—but by being concerned with them in a certain way. For the licentious person is led on by what he chooses, hold-ing that he ought always to pursue the present pleasure, whereas the per-son lacking self-restraint does not think that, but pursues the pleasure anyway.

13 · Or, "contemplation" (*theōria*).

As for its being true opinion but not science [or knowledge] against
25   which those who lack self-restraint act, it makes no difference to the argument. For some people, when they opine about something, are without
hesitation but think they know things precisely. If, then, those who opine
will act contrary to their conviction more than do those who possess science, solely on account of their having a weak conviction,[14] then [as a
matter of fact] science will not differ from[15] opinion; for some are no less
30   convinced of what they opine about than are other people of what they
know[16]—and Heraclitus makes this clear.[17] But since we say "to know" in
two senses—both the person who has the science but is not using it and
he who uses it are said to know—it will make a difference whether someone who does what he ought not to do has the relevant knowledge but is
not actively contemplating it, or whether he is actively contemplating it.
35   For this latter does seem to be a terrible thing, but not so if he is not actively contemplating [the science he nonetheless has].

Further, since there are two kinds of premises, [namely, the univer-
1147a   sal and the particular,] nothing prevents someone who holds both from
acting contrary to the science he possesses because he makes use of the
universal premise but not the particular one, matters of action being of
course particulars. There is also a relevant difference pertaining to the
universal premise, for there is the universal relating to the person himself
5   and the one relating to the matter of concern at hand: for example, that
dry foods are advantageous for every human being and that he himself is
a human being, or that this sort of thing here is dry. As to whether this
particular food here is of a particular character, however, the person lacking self-restraint either does not have that knowledge or is not exercising
it. And so, given these different ways of knowing, a massive difference will
arise, such that for the person lacking self-restraint to know in the one
way, [that is, to know in principle the relevant universal but not to know
or to be activating his knowledge of a given particular,] seems to be noth-

---

14 · Not the word usually translated as "conviction" (*hypolambanein* and related terms),
but *pisteuein*, as also in the next clause of this sentence ("convinced of"), which can also
mean simply "trust" or "have faith in."
15 · Or, "will not be superior to."
16 · *Epistasthai*, "to know scientifically," here and in the next two instances of "to know."
17 · The famous pre-Socratic philosopher of Ephesus. The precise reference is uncertain; some commentators suggest that Aristotle may here allude to Heraclitus's oracular style of arguing, itself a response to the impossibility of certain knowledge of the
world, which is fundamentally in "flux."

ing strange, but in the other way, [that is, knowing and having active in him both kinds of premises,] it would indeed be a cause for wonder.[18]

Further, another way of having science, different from those just now mentioned, is available to human beings. For in the case of having but not using science, we see that the "having"[19] is different, such that a person both has it in a way and does not have it—for example, someone who is asleep, mad, or drunk. But surely those in the grip of the passions are disposed in this way; for outbursts of spiritedness, the sexual desires, and certain other such things clearly bring about a change in the body too, and in some people they even cause madness. It is clear, then, that those lacking self-restraint must be said to be in a state similar to such people. But stating the arguments that proceed from science is not a sign of anything, for even people in the grip of these passions state demonstrations and verses of Empedocles,[20] and those who are first learning will put together arguments but not yet understand them. For one must grow naturally into the knowledge, and that requires time. As a result, it must be supposed that those who lack self-restraint speak just as actors do.

Further, someone might also look at the cause of the lack of self-restraint in terms of nature, as follows. For the universal premise is an opinion; the other premise concerns particulars, over which perception is authoritative from the start. And whenever one conclusion arises from the universal and particular premises, the soul must necessarily assert it, but in the case of a conclusion bound up with making [or doing] things, the soul must immediately act. For example, if one ought to taste everything sweet, and this thing here is sweet (it being some one particular thing), someone who is so capable and not prevented from doing so must

18 · As Aquinas here says: "it is possible that a man knows, both habitually and actively, the universal considered in itself but either he does not grasp the universal considered in this particular object, i.e., the universal is not known in an habitual way, or he does not bestir himself, i.e., the universal is not actually known. Therefore ... it does not seem unreasonable for a man, who acts incontinently [i.e., without self-restraint], to have one kind of knowledge, viz., universal alone or even particular—if it is habitual and not actual. But it would seem unreasonable for the man who acts continently [i.e., with self-restraint] to have another kind of knowledge, i.e., actual, concerned with this particular."

19 · The term translated as "the having" (*hexis*) is elsewhere translated as "characteristic." Aristotle here makes use of the fact that the noun is derived from the verb meaning (among other things) "to have" (*echein*): see also the glossary.

20 · Empedocles of Sicily (ca. 493–433) was a famous pre-Socratic philosopher, two of whose poems, *On Nature* and *Purifications*, survive in fragmentary form.

at the same time necessarily also carry out this action. Whenever, then, the universal premise is present that forbids us from tasting sweet things, and another universal is also present, to the effect that every sweet thing is pleasant, and this thing here is sweet (and this premise is active), and by chance the relevant desire is present in us, the one premise says to avoid this; but the desire for it leads the way, for it is able to set in motion each of the parts [of the body]. It turns out, as a result, that someone can come to be without self-restraint by a reasoned account [*logos*], in a way, and by opinion, an opinion that is not in itself but incidentally contrary to correct reason—for the desire involved, not the opinion, is contrary to correct reason. As a result, on this account as well, brute animals do not lack self-restraint, because they do not possess a universal conviction but rather an image and memory of particular things.

But as to how the ignorance involved is undone, and the person lacking self-restraint becomes again a knower, the same argument pertains also to the case of someone drunk or asleep and is not peculiar to this experience—an argument one must hear from those who study nature. Now, since the final premise is both an opinion pertaining to an object of perception and authoritative over our actions, someone in the grip of the relevant passion either does not have this final premise or has it in such a way that his having it does not amount to his knowing it;[21] instead he merely speaks, as a drunk man states the sayings of Empedocles. And because the ultimate term[22] is not universal and seems not to be knowable as the universal is knowable, it seems also that what Socrates was seeking turns out to be the case. For it is not when science in the authoritative sense seems to be present that the experience of the lack of self-restraint occurs, nor is it this science that is dragged around on account of passion, but rather that [knowledge] which is bound up with perception.

So about the knower and non-knower, and how a knower can lack self-restraint, let this much be said.

CHAPTER FOUR

But it must be stated next in order whether anyone lacks self-restraint in an unqualified sense, or whether all who lack self-restraint do so in some

21 · Here again and in the next line, to know "scientifically," or in the strict sense.
22 · The *eschatos horos*: see *defining boundary* in the glossary.

partial respect, and, if this latter is the case, with what sorts of things the person lacking self-restraint is concerned.

Now, it is manifest that self-restrained and steadfast people, as well as those who lack self-restraint or are soft, are concerned with pleasures and pains. Some things productive of pleasure are necessary, and others are choiceworthy in themselves but susceptible to excess. The bodily ones are   25
necessary (I mean such sorts of pleasures as those bound up with nourishment and the sexual need, and the sort of bodily pleasures that we posited as being the concern of licentiousness and moderation), whereas the other pleasures are not necessary but choiceworthy in themselves (I mean, for   30
example, victory, honor, wealth, and the good and pleasant things of that sort). Given this, when it comes to the people who are excessively concerned with these sorts of pleasures, contrary to the correct reason that is within them, we do not say that they lack self-restraint in an unqualified sense, but instead we set down in addition "lacking self-restraint in regard to money" (or gain, honor, or spiritedness). We do not say that they lack self-restraint without qualification, on the grounds that they are different and are spoken of as such only in reference to a certain similarity they   35
share, just as with Anthropos ["Human Being"], the Olympic victor: in his case, the common definition [*logos*] differed little from the definition   1148a
[*logos*] peculiar to him, but nonetheless it was different.[23] And there is a sign of this. For lack of self-restraint is blamed not only on the grounds that it is an error, but also on the grounds that it is a certain vice, either without qualification or in some partial way, but none of those who lack self-restraint in some specific respect are blamed in this way.

Among those who are concerned with such bodily enjoyments as we   5
say are the concern of the moderate person and the licentious one, there is the person who pursues the excesses of the pleasures (and avoids the pains) bound up with hunger, thirst, heat, cold, and all those pleasures and pains associated with taste and touch; but he acts in this way not from choice but contrary to his choice and thinking. This person is said to lack self-restraint not with reference to some additional qualification,   10
to the effect that he is concerned with this or that, as in the case of someone lacking self-restraint when it comes to anger; rather, he is only said to be lacking self-restraint unqualifiedly. And there is a sign of this: people

23 · According to several sources, recorded in Burnet's commentary, there was an Olympic boxing champion by the name of Anthropos—"Human Being"—in 456.

are said to be soft when it comes to these pleasures, but not when it comes
to any of the other ones. On this account too we set down the person lacking self-restraint and the licentious person in the same category, as well
as the self-restrained and moderate—but not so in the case of any of the
15   other [vicious or virtuous types]—and we do so because they are somehow concerned with the same pleasures and pains: they are concerned
with the same things but not in the same way, for the licentious choose
the pleasures in question, those lacking self-restraint do not choose them.
Hence we would call anyone who pursues excessive pleasures, while not
desiring them or desiring them only mildly, and who avoids measured
20   pains, more licentious than someone who acts in these ways on account
of strong desires. For what would the former person do if youthful desire should arise in him and the strong pain associated with the necessary
needs?

Some desires and pleasures fall in the class of noble and serious things
(for some pleasures are by nature choiceworthy), some are the contrary
25   of these, and still others are in the middle between them, just as we defined them earlier—for example, money, gain, victory, and honor. And it
is in regard to *all* these, both the pleasures of this sort and those of the in-
between kind, that people are blamed, not for undergoing them, desiring
them, and loving them, but rather for doing so in a certain way, namely,
in excess. Hence all those who, contrary to reason, are either overpowered
30   by or pursue something by nature noble and good [are not corrupt]²⁴—
for example, those who are more serious than they ought to be about
honor, or about their offspring and parents, for these concerns are in fact
good and those who are serious about them are praised. But nevertheless there is a certain excess in these things too, if someone, like Niobe,
should fight against even the gods, or as Satyrus, nicknamed "Philopator,"
1148b was disposed toward his father.²⁵ For he was held to be exceedingly silly.
There is, then, no corruption concerning these things on account of the
point mentioned—that by nature each of them is choiceworthy in itself,

24 · This complex sentence does not have a main verb; we supply what we take to be
missing, following Burnet.
25 · Accounts of Niobe differ, but she seems to have represented (excessive) mourning:
after Niobe boasted of her worth as compared to Leto, Leto's two children, Artemis
and Apollo, are said to have killed all of Niobe's many children. Burnet suggests that
Satyrus may have been a fourth-century king of the Bosporos who deified his father,
although commentators differ; "Philopater" means literally "father-lover" or "friend
to one's father."

but their excesses are base and to be avoided. Similarly, there is no lack   5
of self-restraint pertaining to them either. For lack of self-restraint is not
only something to be avoided but also blameworthy. But on account of
a similarity to the relevant experience, people say "lack of self-restraint"
while specifying something additional about each case, as people say, for
example, "bad doctor" or "bad actor" about someone they would not say
is bad simply. Just as, then, one would not in these cases speak of their
being bad simply, because each of these conditions is not vice but only   10
similar to it by way of analogy, so it is clear, in this case too, that only that
which is concerned with the same things as are moderation and licentiousness should be supposed to be lack of self-restraint and self-restraint,
whereas we speak about lack of self-restraint in point of spiritedness by
way of a certain similarity only. Hence we assert that someone is lacking
self-restraint, adding also "when it comes to spiritedness," just as in the
cases of honor and gain as well.

CHAPTER FIVE

Now, some things are pleasant by nature—and of these, some are pleasant   15
without qualification, others are such according to the various kinds of
animals and human beings involved. Certain things, by contrast, are not
pleasant by nature but do become pleasant, some on account of people's
defects, others through habits, and still others on account of people's corrupt natures. Since this is so, it is possible to see, in each of these cases,
characteristics closely resembling them. I mean the brutish characteristics—for example, the human female who, they say, rips open pregnant   20
women and devours the infants; or the sorts of things that, people assert,
certain of the savages living around the Black Sea[26] enjoy, some of whom
enjoy raw meat, others human flesh, and still others trade their children
with one another to feast on them; or what is said about Phalaris.[27] These
are brutish characteristics, and other such characteristics arise through ill-   25
ness as well as through madness in some cases, like the man who made a
sacrifice of his mother and ate her, and the person who ate the liver of his
fellow slave; and still others are marked by disease or arise from habit—

---

26 · More literally, "around Pontus," a region of northern Asia Minor on the south
shore of the Black Sea, famous for the brutality or barbarism of some of its tribes; see
also *Politics* 1338b19–24.

27 · Phalaris was tyrant of Acragas (ca. 570–549) and notorious for his inventive cruel-
ties: he was known to have roasted his victims alive in a hollow brazen bull, for example.

for example, plucking out one's hair and gnawing on one's fingernails, or even on coal and dirt, and, in addition to these, the pleasure of sex with males. For some of these arise by nature, others from habit—for example, in those who are wantonly abused[28] from childhood.

As for those people, then, whose condition is caused by nature, no one would say that they lack self-restraint, just as one would not say it of women because they are passive rather than active in marital relations; nor, similarly, would one say it of all those who are in a diseased condition through a given habit. Each of these conditions falls outside the defining boundaries of vice, as does brutishness as well. And for someone who has such a condition, overpowering it or being overpowered[29] by it is not a matter of a simple lack of self-restraint, but this only by way of a certain similarity to it. For just as someone who, when it comes to spiritedness, undergoes this passion may be said to lack self-restraint by way of a certain similarity, yet he ought not to be said to lack self-restraint simply. In every instance of excessive foolishness, cowardice, licentiousness, and harshness, some people are marked by brutishness, others by disease. For someone who is by nature such as to be afraid of everything, even if a mouse makes a noise, is a coward whose cowardice is brutish, whereas that fellow who was afraid of the weasel was a coward through disease. And of the foolish, some who are irrational as a result of nature and live by sense perception alone, like certain tribes of distant barbarians, are brutish; others who are such through disease, for example, epileptics, or through madness are diseased.

Now, it is sometimes possible for someone just to have one of these characteristics but not to be overpowered by it—I mean, for example, if Phalaris had kept in check his desire to eat a child or to enjoy a strange sexual pleasure. But it is also possible to be overpowered by it, not merely to have it. Just as in the case of corruption too, then, there is the corruption spoken of in its unqualified sense, in reference to a human being, and there is the corruption spoken of in reference to some additional qualification—that it is corruption stemming from brutishness or disease, but not corruption without qualification—so in the same manner there is clearly also the lack of self-restraint that is brutish and the lack of it that stems from disease. But only that which relates to human licentiousness is lack of self-restraint in the unqualified sense.

28 · Literally "treated with hubris."
29 · Aristotle uses here the active and passive forms of *kratein*, the verb related to the terms for "self-restraint" (*enkrateia*) and "lack of self-restraint" (*akrasia*).

It is clear, then, that lack of self-restraint and self-restraint are concerned only with the matters to which licentiousness and moderation
pertain; and that the lack of self-restraint pertaining to other things is
another form of it, which is spoken of as lack of self-restraint only metaphorically and not unqualifiedly.

CHAPTER SIX

But let us observe[30] also that the lack of self-restraint related to spirit-   25
edness is less shameful than that pertaining to desires. For spiritedness
seems to hear reason in some way, but to mishear it, like swift servants
who run off before they hear what is said in its entirety and then err in
carrying out the command, or as dogs bark if there is merely a knock
at the door, before examining whether it is a friend. So spiritedness, be-   30
cause of its heated and swift nature, hears something, and though it does
not hear an order, it sets off after revenge. For speech or imagination has
made clear that there is a hubristic insult or slight; and spiritedness, as if it
inferred from a syllogism that one ought to wage war against such a thing,
immediately becomes harsh. But as for desire, if reason or sense percep-   35
tion merely says that something is pleasant, it sets off after enjoyment.
As a result, spiritedness follows reason in a way, but desire does not. De-   1149b
sire, then, is more shameful. For someone who lacks self-restraint when it
comes to spiritedness is in a way conquered by reason, whereas the other
person is conquered by desire and not by reason.

Further, there is greater sympathy [or forgiveness] for someone who
follows the natural longings, since there is more sympathy also for those   5
who follow such desires as are common to all and insofar as they are common. Spiritedness and harshness are more natural than are the desires for
what is excessive, that is, the unnecessary desires—just like the person
who defended himself for striking his father by saying, "And he struck his
father, and his father struck his," and, pointing to his own son, said, "and   10
he will strike me, when he becomes a man: it runs in our family!" And the
man who was being dragged by his son bade him stop by the doors, for he
himself dragged his own father only that far.

Further, those who hatch plots are more unjust [than are those who
act from spiritedness]. The man characterized by spiritedness, then, is
not a plotter, nor is spiritedness itself; rather, it is open, whereas desire is   15

30 · Or, "contemplate."

just as they assert of Aphrodite: "a weaver of wiles, Cyprus-born,"[31] and as Homer says of her embroidered girdle, "its alluring words, which stole the mind even of one who is most sensible."[32] As a result, if in fact this lack of self-restraint is more unjust and more shameful than that bound up with spiritedness, it is also lack of self-restraint unqualifiedly and, in a way, vice as well.

20   Further, no one acts hubristically while feeling pain, but everyone who does something in anger, does so while feeling pain, whereas the hubristic person acts with pleasure. If, then, those things are more unjust, at which it is especially just to be angry, so also is the lack of self-restraint connected with desire, for in spiritedness there is no hubris. It is clear, then, that the lack of self-restraint pertaining to desire is more shame-
25   ful than that pertaining to spiritedness, and that there is in fact a self-restraint and lack of self-restraint pertaining to bodily desires and pleasures.

But one must grasp the distinctions among these very desires and pleasures. For, just as was said at the beginning, some are human and natural in both kind and magnitude, but others are brutish, and some arise
30   through defects and diseases. Of these, it is only with the first ones that moderation and licentiousness are concerned. Hence too we do not say of brute animals that they are either moderate or licentious, except metaphorically, and only if some one kind of animal differs as a whole from another in hubris, destructiveness, and voraciousness. For they do not pos-
35   sess choice or calculation but do depart from the natural, just as madmen
1150a   do among human beings. But brutishness is a lesser thing than vice, even though it is more frightening, for the better part [of the soul] has not been ruined in the case of a brute animal, as it has been in a human being who is vicious; rather, the brute animal does not have that better part. It is similar, then, to comparing an inanimate thing to an animate one, as to which is worse: baseness that does not possess its own starting point [or
5   principle] is always less harmful than that which does possess it, and intellect is such a starting point. It is akin, then, to comparing injustice itself to an unjust human being, for there is a way in which each is worse than the other: a bad human being could produce ten thousand times more bad things than could a brute animal.

31 · The author of this line is unknown.
32 · Homer, *Iliad* 14.214, 217.

CHAPTER SEVEN

But as for the pleasures, pains, desires, and aversions that arise through   10
touch and taste—which both licentiousness and moderation were earlier
defined as being concerned with—it is possible for someone to be such
as to be defeated by those that the majority of people[33] are stronger than;
and it is possible to be such as to overpower those by which the majority are defeated. In these cases, one person lacks self-restraint concerning
pleasures, another is self-restrained, one person is soft when it comes to
pains, another steadfast. But the characteristic belonging to most people
is in between these, even if people incline more toward the worse char-   15
acteristics.

Now, some pleasures are necessary, others not, and the former are necessary only up to a certain point (those that are excessive are not necessary, and neither are the deficient ones); and what concerns desires and
pains is similar. Given all this, the person who pursues the excessive pleasures, in an excessive way or through choice, doing so for the sake of the   20
pleasures themselves and for nothing else that results from them, is licentious. For this person necessarily feels no regret and so is incurable, since
the person without regret is incurable. But he who falls short is the opposite, he who is in the middle, moderate. And similar is the case of someone who avoids the bodily pains not because he is defeated by them but
through choice.

Now, among those who do not choose, one type is led by pleasure, an-   25
other by avoiding the pain arising from desire, and so they differ from
each other. It would seem to everyone to be worse if someone should do
something shameful, though he felt no desire for it or only a mild one,
than if he should so act because of a strong desire, just as it would seem
to be worse if someone should strike another without being angry at him
than if he did so in anger. For what would such a person do, were he in the   30
grip of a passion? Hence the licentious person is worse than the one lacking self-restraint. So, of the characteristics mentioned, the one is rather a
form of softness, whereas the other person is licentious.

He who lacks self-restraint lies opposite the self-restrained person, the
steadfast opposite the soft. For being steadfast consists in holding out
against something, whereas self-restraint consists in overpowering it; and   35

---

33 · Or, "the many" (*hoi polloi*), here and in the next clause.

holding out is different from overpowering, just as not being defeated is different from winning. Hence self-restraint is also more choiceworthy than steadfastness. But the person who falls short in relation to what the majority[34] strain against and are capable of—he is soft and delicate. For such delicacy is in fact a sort of softness: for example, he who lets his cloak drag, so that he not suffer the pain of lifting it up, and who, though he imitates someone sickly, does not suppose that he himself is wretched, similar though he is to the wretched.

The case is similar also as regards self-restraint and lack of self-restraint. For if someone is defeated by strong and excessive pleasures or pains, that is not to be wondered at. Rather, he is apt to receive sympathy if he at least strains against them, just as Theodectes's Philoctetes did when struck by the viper, or Cercyon in the *Alope* of Carcinus, and just like those who, though they attempt to restrain their laughter, burst out laughing all at once, such as happened to Xenophantes.[35] But it *is* to be wondered at if somebody is defeated by and unable to strain against those pleasures and pains that the majority are able to hold out against, when this is not due to the nature of one's stock[36] or to illness—like the softness of the Scythian kings due to their stock, and as the female is distinguished from the male. And someone fond of amusement is held to be licentious but is actually soft; for play is relaxation, if in fact it is recreation [or rest], and the person fond of amusement is among those who are excessive when it comes to this.

One part of the lack of self-restraint is impetuosity, another weakness; some people deliberate but then do not abide by their deliberations on account of the relevant passion, while others, because they do not deliberate, are led by the passion. For just as those who anticipate being tickled are unaffected by being tickled, so too some who perceive and see in advance what is coming, and so rouse themselves and their calculation in

34 · Or, "the many," as in the preceding note.

35 · Theodectes (ca. 375–334), author and orator, was born in Lycia but probably lived mostly at Athens, where he is said to have studied with Plato and Aristotle, among others. His *Philoctetes* does not survive. Carcinus, son of the tragedian Carcinus, is said to have authored 160 plays; Aristotle mentions him also in the *Poetics* (1454b23) and *Rhetoric* (1400b10, 1417b10). According to the scholiast, quoted by Burnet, when Cercyon learned of his daughter's marriage, he asked her whom she had married, saying that "if you should tell me this, I would not be altogether pained"—yet he found the pain of living too great once he heard her answer and so chose to die. The Xenophantes here mentioned may have been a musician in the court of Alexander (see Seneca, *de Ira* 2.2).

36 · *Genos*: class, kind, race.

advance, are not defeated by the relevant passion, whether it is pleasant or   25
painful. And it is especially the keen and the melancholic[37] whose lack of
self-restraint is of the impetuous sort; for neither the former, on account
of their swiftness, nor the latter, on account of the intensity of their passion, stick with reason, they being apt to follow imagination instead.

CHAPTER EIGHT

The licentious person, as was said, is not characterized by regret, for he   30
abides by his choice. But every person lacking self-restraint is apt to feel
regret. Hence the perplexity at issue is not in fact as we encountered it;[38]
rather, the licentious person is incurable, the person lacking self-restraint
curable. For corruption seems to be like such diseases as dropsy and con-
sumption; whereas lack of self-restraint is like epileptic seizures, the former defective[39] condition being continuous, the latter not continuous.
And in general, the genus to which lack of self-restraint belongs is dif-   35
ferent from that to which vice belongs; for vice escapes the notice of one
who has it, whereas lack of self-restraint does not escape the notice of
those lacking self-restraint. Among people lacking self-restraint, those apt   1151a
to be impulsive[40] are better than those who are in possession of an argument [*logos*] but do not abide by it. For these latter are defeated by a lesser
passion than that which overwhelms the impulsive and are not without a
prior deliberation, as are the impulsive. The person lacking self-restraint
in this latter sense is similar to those who get drunk quickly and on little
wine, that is, on less wine than do most people.   5
    It is manifest, then, that lack of self-restraint is not vice (but perhaps it
is in a certain way): lack of self-restraint is contrary to one's choice, vice
in accord with one's choice. Nevertheless, they are similar, at least when
it comes to actions, just as in Demodocus's saying about the Milesians—
"Milesians are not stupid, but they do the things stupid people do"[41]—and

---

37 · Or, "excitable"; those with an excess of black bile and so given to agitation or un-
ease.
38 · Consider 1146a31–b2.
39 · The word (*ponēria*) is elsewhere translated as "wickedness."
40 · *Ekstatikoi*: the same word was translated as "one who departs" (from one's calculation) at 1145b11–12; here the word seems roughly equivalent to the "keen and the melancholic."
41 · Originally from the small island of Leros, lying just opposite Miletus, Demodocus
is today best known for the comic lines here quoted.

10 those lacking self-restraint are not unjust, though they will commit injustices. The person lacking self-restraint is such as to pursue the bodily pleasures that are excessive and contrary to correct reason, without his having been persuaded to do so, whereas the licentious person has been so persuaded, on account of his being the sort of person to pursue them. Given this, it is the person lacking self-restraint who can easily be per-

15 suaded otherwise, the licentious not. For virtue preserves and corruption destroys the principle; and in actions, that for the sake of which one acts is the principle, just as the given hypotheses are in mathematics. So in neither case is reason [or argument] such as to teach the principles, but virtue—either natural or habitual—is apt to teach one to hold the correct

20 opinion[42] about the principle in question. Such a person, then, is moderate; his contrary, licentious.

There is also a sort of person who is apt, on account of his passion, to depart[43] from correct reason, a person whom passion overpowers, such that he does not act in accord with correct reason. Yet the passion in question does not overpower him so that he becomes the sort of person to be persuaded that he ought to pursue pleasures of this kind without restraint. This is the person lacking self-restraint, who is better than the li-

25 centious and is not unqualifiedly base: what is best in him, the principle, is preserved. Another sort is his contrary, [that is, the self-restrained person,] who is apt to abide by and not depart from correct reason, at least not on account of passion. So it is manifest from these considerations that the one characteristic is serious, the other base.

CHAPTER NINE

30 Is, then, a self-restrained person someone who abides by any argument whatever and any choice whatever, or does he abide by only the correct choice? And is a person lacking self-restraint someone who fails to abide by any choice whatever and any argument whatever, or does he fail to abide by the argument that is not false and by the choice that is correct, as in the perplexing question encountered before?[44] Or is it only incidentally that the argument and choice involved are of this or that sort, but it is the true argument and the correct choice in themselves that

42 · The verb translated as "to hold the correct opinion" (*orthodoxein*) contains the elements of the English word *orthodoxy*.

43 · *Ekstatikos*: see n. 40 above.

44 · Consider 1146a16–21.

the self-restrained abides by and the other does not abide by? For if some-   35
one chooses or pursues this given thing on account of that given thing, he   1151b
pursues and chooses this latter in itself, the former only incidentally. And
by "in itself" we mean "unqualifiedly." As a result, in one sense the self-
restrained person abides by any opinion whatever, while the person lacking self-restraint departs from it; but in an unqualified sense, it is the true
opinion that the one abides by and the other departs from.

There are also some who are inclined to abide by their opinion, whom   5
people call obstinate; such people are hard to persuade and, once persuaded, not easily changed. They have a certain similarity to the self-
restrained person, just as the prodigal has to the liberal and the reckless
to the confident, but they are different in many respects. For the one, the
self-restrained person, does not change on account of passion and desire,
but it may sometimes happen that he will be readily persuadable [by rea-   10
son]; whereas the obstinate are not persuadable, when they take hold of
given desires, and in fact many of them are led by pleasures. Obstinate
types are the opinionated, the ignorant, and the boorish, the opinionated
being such on account of the pleasure and pain at stake: they delight in
the victory they gain, if their persuasion undergoes no change, and they   15
are pained if their own opinions become null and void, like decrees. As a
result, they resemble more the person lacking self-restraint than they do
the self-restrained.

There are also some who do not abide by their opinions, but not on
account of a lack of self-restraint—for example, Neoptolemus in Sophocles's *Philoctetes*. It was, however, on account of pleasure that he did not
abide by his opinion—albeit a noble pleasure: telling the truth was noble   20
in his eyes, but he was persuaded by Odysseus to lie. For not everyone
who does something on account of pleasure is licentious or base or lacking self-restraint; rather, he who does something on account of a shameful pleasure is such.

But since there is also a sort of person who enjoys the bodily pleasures
less than one ought and who does not abide by reason, the self-restrained
person is in the middle between this person and the one lacking self-   25
restraint: the person lacking self-restraint does not abide by reason because he enjoys something more than he ought, this person because he enjoys something less than he ought, while the self-restrained person abides
by reason and does not change on either account. If in fact self-restraint
is something serious, both of these contrary characteristics ought to be
base, just as they in fact appear to be. But because the characteristic that   30

leads one to enjoy pleasure less than one ought appears in few people and on few occasions, then just as moderation is held to be the sole contrary of licentiousness, so too self-restraint is held to be the sole contrary of the lack of self-restraint.

Since many things are spoken of by way of a certain similarity they may share, it has followed that we speak of the self-restraint of the moderate person by way of a certain similarity they share: the self-restrained person is such as to do nothing, on account of the bodily pleasures, that is contrary to reason, and so too is the moderate person. But the one person has, and the other does not have, base desires; and the one is such as not to feel pleasure contrary to reason, the other such as to feel the pleasure but not to be led by it. Those lacking self-restraint and the licentious are similar as well, though they are in fact different: both pursue the bodily pleasures, but the one does so while supposing he ought to, the other while supposing he ought not to.

CHAPTER TEN

The same person does not admit of being at the same time both prudent and lacking self-restraint; for it was shown that, as regards his character, a prudent person is at the same time serious as well.[45] Further, a person is prudent not only by dint of what he knows, but also because he is skilled in action. But the person lacking self-restraint is not skilled in action. (Yet nothing prevents the clever person from lacking self-restraint. Hence there are times when some people are even held to be prudent and lacking self-restraint, because cleverness differs from prudence in the manner stated in the first arguments; and although they are close to each other, in reference to their respective definitions, they do differ when it comes to the choice each makes.) And so the person lacking self-restraint does not resemble someone who knows and contemplates something, but resembles rather someone who is asleep or drunk. Although he acts voluntarily—for in a certain manner he knows both what he is doing and for the sake of what he does it—he is not wicked: his choice is decent, such that he is only half-wicked. He is also not unjust, for he is not a plotter: one sort of person lacking self-restraint is not apt to abide by the results of his deliberation, whereas another, melancholic sort is not even apt

45 · Consider 1144a36–b1, b30–32.

to deliberate at all. So the person lacking self-restraint is like a city that votes for all that it ought to vote for and has serious laws, yet it makes use   20 of none of them, just as Anaxandrides joked:

> The city wished to, the one that cares for none of its laws.[46]

But the wicked person [is like a city that] makes use of the laws, though the laws it uses are wicked.

Lack of self-restraint and self-restraint are concerned with what goes   25 beyond[47] the characteristic typical of the many; for the self-restrained person abides by his deliberations more, the person lacking self-restraint less, than is within the capacity of most people. And among those who lack self-restraint, that of the melancholic type is more readily curable than is the lack of self-restraint of those who deliberate but do not abide by their deliberations; and those lacking self-restraint as a result of habit- uation are more curable than those who are such by nature. For a habit is   30 easier to change than nature: it is for this reason that habit too is difficult [to change]—because it seems like nature—just as Evenus[48] says as well:

> I assert that it is a practice of long duration, friend, and so
> In the end this is nature for human beings.

What is self-restraint, then, and what lack of self-restraint, what stead- fastness and what softness, and how these characteristics relate to one an-   35 other has been stated.

CHAPTER ELEVEN

Contemplating what concerns pleasure and pain belongs to him who phi-   1152b losophizes about the political art. For he is the architect of the end with a view to which we speak of each thing as being bad or good in an unquali- fied sense. Further, it is also necessary to examine what concerns them, for we posited[49] both moral virtue and vice as being concerned with pains   5

---

46 · Anaxandrides, originally from Rhodes but a resident of Athens, was a fourth-century comic poet, of whose works only forty-one titles and some eighty citations survive.
47 · Elsewhere translated as "in excess" (*to hyperballon*).
48 · Evenus hailed from Paros and was active as a Sophist and poet in the fifth century. Plato mentions him in the *Apology of Socrates* (20a–c), *Phaedrus* (267a), and *Phaedo* (60d–61a).
49 · Consider 1104b8–13.

and pleasures, and most people assert that happiness is accompanied by pleasure. Hence they have even derived the name of the "blessed" person from the feeling of "enjoyment."[50]

By some people, then, no pleasure is held to be good, either in itself or incidentally, for the good and pleasure are held not to be the same thing. But by certain others, some pleasures are held to be good, though they hold the majority of them to be base. And further, the third view: even if all pleasures are good, nonetheless pleasure does not admit of being the best thing.

In general, then, pleasure is not good, because every pleasure is a perceptible process of coming into its nature; but no coming-into-being belongs to the same class as the ends we pursue—for example, no house building belongs to the same class as a house. And further, the moderate person avoids pleasures. Further, the prudent person pursues what is painless, not the pleasant. Further, pleasures are an impediment to prudent thinking, and the more delight they supply, the more an impediment they are—for example, sexual pleasure: nobody would be able to think about anything while in its grip. Further, there is no art of pleasure, though everything good is the work of an art. Further, children and brute animals pursue pleasures.

As for pleasures not all being of serious worth, that is because there are pleasures that are both shameful and subject to reproach, and because there are harmful ones, some pleasures having the character of diseases. As for pleasure's not being the best thing, that is because it is not an end but a process of coming-into-being.

These, then, are pretty much the things said.

CHAPTER TWELVE

But that it does *not* turn out that, on account of these things, pleasure is not good, or even not the best thing, is clear from the following points. First, since the good is twofold—there is the good unqualifiedly and the good for some particular person—it will follow that both natures and characteristics are good in a twofold sense. The result of this is that motions [or changes] and processes of coming-into-being will be good in a twofold sense as well. Some of the base motions and processes seem to be

50 · The rather fanciful etymology Aristotle here reports is untranslatable: the term *blessed* (*makarios*) supposedly derives from the verb meaning "to feel enjoyment" or "to delight in something" (*apo tou chairein*).

base unqualifiedly, whereas for a particular person, they are not such but   30
are even choiceworthy for him, while some are not choiceworthy for him
but are such only on a given occasion and for a short time, though not
unqualifiedly. Some of these are not even pleasures, but merely appear
to be—all those that are accompanied by pain and for the sake of medical
treatment, like those the sickly undergo, for example.

Further, since one part of the good is an activity, another a characteristic, whatever restores us to our natural characteristic is pleasant only
incidentally. But there is an activity, involving the desires, of our char-   35
acteristic and our nature when these remain unimpaired, since there
are also pleasures unaccompanied by pain and desire—for example, the
activity[51] bound up with contemplation when one's nature is not defi-   1153a
cient. A sign of this is that people do not enjoy the same pleasure when
their nature is undergoing restoration [or replenishment] and when it
is has been restored; rather, the restored nature enjoys the unqualified
pleasures, but the nature that is undergoing restoration enjoys even the
contrary pleasures, for people then enjoy both sharp and bitter things,   5
none of which are pleasant by nature or pleasant unqualifiedly. Neither, as a result, are the pleasures involved, for as the various pleasant
things stand in relation to one another, so do the pleasures arising from
them.

Further, it is not necessary for there to be something else that is
better than pleasure, in the way that some assert that the end is better than the process of coming-into-being. For pleasures are not processes of coming-into-being, nor are all pleasures even accompanied by
a coming-into-being; rather, they are activities and an end, and they do   10
not occur when there is a coming-into-being but when [our capacities]
are put to use. And not all pleasures have something else as an end, but
only the pleasures belonging to those who are being led toward the completion of their nature. Hence also it is not a noble thing to assert that
pleasure is a perceptible process of coming-into-being; one ought rather
to say that it is an activity of the characteristic that accords with nature,
and instead of "perceptible," one ought to say "unimpeded." But pleasure   15
is held by some to be a process of coming-into-being, because it is good
in an authoritative sense. For they suppose that activity is a process of
coming-into-being, but in fact it is something else.

51 · The MSS differ here somewhat, and other readings are possible: "for example, the
pleasures of contemplation" or "for example, the activities bound up with contemplation."

But saying that pleasures are bad[52] because some pleasant things cause diseases is the same thing as saying that some healthful things are bad because they are bad when it comes to moneymaking. In this respect, then, both pleasant and healthful things are bad; but that, at least, does
20   not make them bad in themselves, since even contemplating may at some point harm one's health.

And neither prudence nor any characteristic is impeded by the pleasure arising from either. Rather, the pleasures foreign to them are impediments, since those pleasures arising from contemplating and learning will only make us contemplate and learn more.

But that no pleasure is the work of an art happens reasonably, for there
25   is no art of any other activity either, only of a capacity, although both the art of perfume making and the art of fine cookery are held to be arts of pleasure.

But that the moderate person avoids pleasure, that the prudent person pursues a life without pain, and that children and brute animals pursue pleasure—all these perplexities are resolved by the same consideration. For since it was said in what sense pleasures are good unqualifiedly, and
30   in what sense not all are good, both brute animals and children pursue the sorts of pleasures that are accompanied by desire and pain, that is, the bodily pleasures (for these pleasures are such) and the excesses of these pleasures; the prudent person seeks out freedom from the pain associated with these same pleasures—pleasures in reference to which the licentious person is licentious. Hence the moderate person avoids these pleasures,
35   since there are pleasures belonging to a moderate person as well.

CHAPTER THIRTEEN

1153b   Now, that pain is indeed bad is agreed to,[53] so too that it is something to be avoided: one kind of pain is bad unqualifiedly, another is bad by dint of its being in some way an impediment. And the contrary of something to be avoided, insofar as it is to be avoided and bad, is good. It is necessary,
5   then, that pleasure be something good. For as Speusippus[54] attempted to resolve the perplexity—that pleasure is just like the greater in its opposi-

52 · Or, "base" (*phaulos*), rather than *kakos*, here and in what follows.
53 · Consider 1148a22 and following.
54 · Speusippus (ca. 407–339) was an Athenian philosopher, related to Plato, who took over leadership of the Academy from 347 to 339. Only fragments of his many writings remain. See also 1096b7.

tion to both the lesser and the equal—no resolution actually follows, for he would not assert that pleasure is in itself something bad.

And nothing prevents a certain pleasure from being the best thing, even if some pleasures are bad,[55] just as there is nothing to prevent a certain science from being the best thing, though some sciences may be bad.

If in fact there are unimpeded activities of each characteristic—whether happiness is constituted by the activity (provided it is unimpeded) of all these characteristics or by the unimpeded activity of a certain one of them—perhaps it is even necessary that this activity be most choiceworthy. But this is pleasure. As a result, a certain pleasure would be the best thing, even though many pleasures may be, as it happens, unqualifiedly base.

For this reason, all people suppose the happy life to be pleasant, and they weave pleasure into happiness—reasonably so. For no activity is complete when it is impeded, but happiness is among the things that are complete. Hence the happy person needs in addition the goods residing in the body as well as external goods and chance, so that he not be impeded in these respects. And those people who claim that somebody being tortured on the wheel or meeting with great misfortune is happy—if he is good—make no sense, either voluntarily or involuntarily. It is because one needs chance in addition that good fortune is held by some to be the same thing as happiness, though it is not; since even good fortune, when in excess, acts as an impediment—and perhaps it is not just to call this "good fortune" any longer, for its definition[56] is relative to happiness.

And that *all* things—both brute animals and human beings—pursue pleasure is a sort of sign that it is somehow the best thing:

There is no talk that dies down entirely, which many peoples ...[57]

But since neither the same nature nor the same characteristic is or is held to be the best [for all], all do not pursue the same pleasure, though all do pursue pleasure. Yet perhaps they pursue not the pleasure they suppose or would assert they pursue, but in fact the same pleasure, for all things by nature possess something divine. But the bodily pleasures have appropriated as theirs alone the name "pleasure," because, most often, people

55 · Here again and in the next line, the term is *phaulos*, which can also mean "base."
56 · *Horos*: see *defining boundary* in the glossary.
57 · Hesiod, *Works and Days* 763. The poem continues: "spread about. She [i.e., "talk" or "rumor"] too is a certain goddess." As the context makes clear, Hesiod is warning against acting in such a way as to permit "talk" to spread about and so to exact its penalties.

35   steer toward them and all share in them. Because these pleasures alone
      are known to them, then, people suppose that only these pleasures exist.
1154a   But it is manifest also that if pleasure and activity are not good, the
      happy person will not live pleasantly: for the sake of what would he need
      pleasure, if in fact it is not good? Rather, it is possible for him even to live
5   his life in pain; for pain would be neither bad nor good, if in fact pleasure
      were not either. As a result, on what account would he avoid pain? And
      so the life of the serious person would be no more pleasant [than anyone
      else's] either, if his activities were not more pleasant as well.

CHAPTER FOURTEEN

      But what concerns the bodily pleasures must be examined by those who
      say that some pleasures, at least, are highly choiceworthy—for example,
      the noble ones—but that the bodily pleasures are not, that is, those plea-
      sures with which the licentious person is concerned. But why is it, then,
10   that the pains contrary to the bodily pleasures are bad [or corruptions]?
      For good is contrary to bad. Or are the necessary pleasures good only in
      the way that what is not bad is good? Or are they good only up to a certain
      point? For in the case of all those characteristics and motions that do not
      admit of an excess of what is good, there would not be an excess of plea-
      sure either; but for all those characteristics and motions that *do* admit of
15   such an excess, there would be an excess also of pleasure. Now, there is an
      excess of bodily goods; and a person is base because he pursues that excess,
      but not because he pursues the necessary pleasures—for all in some way
      enjoy refined foods, wines, and sex, but not all do so as they ought. But
      the contrary holds in the case of pain: one does not avoid just excessive
20   pain, but rather pain in general; for pain is not the contrary of excessive
      pleasure, except for someone who pursues that excess.
          Now, one ought to state not only the truth but also the cause of the
      falsehood, for this contributes to the trust[58] one has. For whenever a rea-
      sonable explanation comes to sight as to why a thing appears to be but is
25   not true, this makes for greater trust in the truth. One must, as a result, say
      why it is that the bodily pleasures appear more choiceworthy than other
      pleasures. First, then, they expel pain. Because of excessive pain, people
      seek out excessive pleasure, and bodily pleasure in general, as though it
30   were a cure. And such cures become intense—the reason people do in

58 · Or, "conviction" (*pistis*): see n. 14.

fact pursue them—because they come to sight in contrast with their opposite. Pleasure is also held not to be of serious worth for these two reasons, as has been said: some pleasures are actions belonging to a base nature—either base from birth, as in the case of a brute animal, or through habit, as in the example of the pleasures of base human beings; and some pleasures act as cures for a deficient nature, and it is better to be complete, rather than to be in the process of becoming so. These pleasures, because they arise only for those still in the process of becoming complete, are of serious worth only incidentally.   1154b

Further, bodily pleasures are pursued on account of their intensity by those who are incapable of enjoying other pleasures. At any rate, people foster in themselves certain thirsts; and when these are harmless, this is not reproachable, but when they are harmful, it is base. For such people   5
do not have other things from which they derive enjoyment, and that which is neither painful nor pleasant is painful to many, given their nature. For a living animal is always toiling—just as those who study nature also bear witness: as they assert, seeing and hearing are painful, though by now we are accustomed to them. And similarly, during youth, because   10
of the process of growth that then occurs, people are in a condition like that of those who are drunk, and youth is as a result pleasant. But those who are melancholy[59] in nature, on the other hand, are always in need of a cure; for their body is continually being stung because of the blending [of the humors within it], and they are always in the grip of an intense longing. And pleasure drives out pain, both the pleasure contrary to the relevant pain and any chance pleasure, provided it is intense. It is for these   15
reasons too that people become licentious and base.

But the pleasures unaccompanied by pains do not have an excess, and these fall among the things pleasant by nature and not incidentally. I mean by "things pleasant incidentally," those that serve as cures: because it happens that people are cured when that which remains healthy in them acts, these cures seem to be pleasant. But things pleasant by nature are those that prompt an action belonging to a healthy nature.   20

Yet the same thing is not always pleasant on account of our nature's not being simple. Rather, something else is present in us as well (hence we are subject to destruction)[60] such that when the one part acts, this is contrary

59 · See n. 37 above.

60 · Following the reading of Bywater (*phthartoi*), itself based on the commentary of Aspasius. The reading of the MSS (*phtharta*) would give: "But something else is present in us as well (hence [or: insofar as] these things are subject to destruction)."

to nature with respect to the other nature; and when both are equally balanced, the action performed seems to be neither painful nor pleasant. For if someone's nature were simple, the same actions would always be most pleasant. Hence the god always enjoys a pleasure that is one and simple, for there is an activity not only of motion but also of motionlessness, and pleasure resides more in rest than in motion. But "change in all things is sweet," as the poet has it,[61] on account of a certain defective condition.[62] For just as the defective person is a human being who readily undergoes change, so also the nature in need of change is defective, for it is neither simple nor decent.

What concerns self-restraint and lack of self-restraint, then, and what concerns pleasure and pain, has been stated—both what each is and how it is that some of them are good, others bad. But in what remains, we will speak also about friendship.

61 · Euripides, *Orestes* 234.
62 · The term Aristotle here uses (*ponēria*) is usually translated as "wickedness"; he may here be playing on the fact that the term has both a moral and a nonmoral use.

Book 8

It would follow, after these matters, to go through what concerns friendship. For friendship is a certain virtue or is accompanied by virtue; and, further, it is most necessary with a view to life: without friends, no one   1155a5
would choose to live, even if he possessed all other goods; and indeed those who are wealthy or have acquired political offices and power[1] seem to be in need of friends most of all. What benefit would there be in such prosperity if one were deprived of [the opportunity to perform] a good deed, which arises and is most praiseworthy in relation to friends especially? Or how could one's prosperity be guarded and preserved without   10
friends? For the more prosperity one has, the more precarious it is. In poverty as well as in other misfortunes, people suppose that friends are their only refuge. And friendship is a help to the young, in saving them from error, just as it is also to the old, with a view to the care they require and their diminished capacity for action stemming from their weakness; it is a help also to those in their prime in performing noble actions, for   15
"two going together"[2] are better able both to think[3] and to act.

By nature, friendship seems to be inherent in a parent for offspring and in offspring for a parent,[4] not only in human beings but also in birds and most animals; it is inherent too in those that are alike in kind to one another, and especially in human beings, which is why we praise people who   20

---

1 · The term here translated as "power," *dunasteiai* (dynasties), is omitted in the best MS.

2 · Homer, *Iliad* 10.224.

3 · Or, "to perceive by the mind," "to apprehend" (*noēsai*).

4 · The first phrase "in a parent for offspring" is omitted in some of the MSS; the second, "in offspring for a parent," is omitted in others.

are "lovers of humankind."[5] One might see in one's travels too that every human being is kindred to every other human being and a friend[6] to him.

It seems too that friendship holds cities together and that lawgivers are more serious about it than about justice. For like-mindedness[7] seems to resemble friendship, and lawgivers aim at this especially and drive out discord because it especially produces hatred. When people are friends, they have no need of justice, but when they are just, they do need friendship in addition; and in the realm of the just things, the most just seems to be what involves friendship. Yet friendship is not only necessary but also noble, for we praise those who love their friends,[8] and an abundance of friends is held to be a noble thing. Further, people suppose good men and their friends to be one and the same.

But not a few things about friendship are in dispute. For some set it down as a certain likeness and friends as those who are alike, which is why they assert that "like is to like," "jackdaw to jackdaw,"[9] and such things. Others, to the contrary, assert that all such persons are "potters" to one another.[10] And concerning these very points, people seek out something higher and pertaining more to nature, Euripides claiming that "the parched earth loves the rain" and that "the august heaven, when full of rain, loves to fall to earth,"[11] Heraclitus that "opposition is advantageous,"[12] that "the noblest harmony comes from things that differ," and "all things come into being in accord with strife." Contrary to

5 · *Philanthropoi*, from which is derived our *philanthropic*.

6 · Or, "dear" (*philos*), a term that can be translated either by an adjective, "loved," "beloved," "dear," or by a noun, "a friend."

7 · *Homonoia*, "oneness of mind."

8 · *Philophiloi*, "those who love their friends," though some MSS read simply *philoi*, "friends."

9 · This phrase has the same meaning as our proverbial saying "birds of a feather flock together." For the phrase "like to like," see in particular Plato, *Lysis* 214a3–b4.

10 · That is, each vies with each, just as potter does with potter. Aristotle here alludes to Hesiod, *Works and Days* 25–26; this particular strife, according to Hesiod, is good for mortals. The line is also quoted in Plato's *Lysis* 215c8, but the context in that case is the question of whether the good are most hostile to the good.

11 · These verses of Euripides come from a play no longer extant, fragments of which are preserved by Athenaeus. The verb for "love" in these passages is not *philein* (see n. 15 below), the root of "friendship" (*philia*), but *eran*, generally signifying passionate or erotic love.

12 · Or, perhaps, "what is in opposition holds together"; according to Grant, this saying reflects the "oracular style" of the famous Heraclitus of Ephesus (ca. 540–475). Only the last fragment is preserved by another source (Origen) apart from Aristotle.

these are still others, including Empedocles, who claim that like aims at like.[13]

Now, let us leave aside those perplexing questions bound up with matters of nature (for they are not proper to the present examination), and let us examine instead those that are bound up with what is distinctively human and that involve characters and passions: for example, whether friendship arises in all people or whether it is impossible for the wicked to be friends; and whether there is one form of friendship or more. Those who suppose that there is only one form, because it admits of degrees, the more and the less, have trusted in an insufficient indication, for things different in form also admit of more and less. But what pertains to them was spoken of before.[14]

CHAPTER TWO

Perhaps what concerns these matters would become apparent if what is lovable[15] should become known. For not everything seems to be loved but only what is lovable, and this seems to be what is good, pleasant, or useful. But what is useful would seem to be that through which something good or pleasant arises, with the result that what is good as well as what is pleasant would be lovable as ends. Is it the good, then, that people love or is it the good for themselves? For sometimes these conflict, as is the case also with the pleasant. For it seems that each person loves what is good for himself and that, while in an unqualified sense the good is what is lovable, what is lovable to each is what is good for each. Yet each in fact loves not what *is* good for him but what *appears* so. Yet this will make no difference at all, since it will be what *appears* lovable [that each will in fact regard as good and so love].

While there are three things on account of which people love, friend-

---

13 · Empedocles of Agrigentum (ca. 494–434) attempts the reconciliation of Eleatic and Heraclitean thought; according to Diogenes Laertius, the Sophist Gorgias was a student of Empedocles. This saying is preserved also by Athenaeus and Stobaeus.

14 · There is no direct or obvious discussion of this in the *Ethics*; Burnet refers the reader to Aristotle's *On Sense Perception and Perceptible Things*, chap. 6.

15 · Or, "what elicits friendly feeling" (*to philētos*), an adjective (here used substantively) derived from the word for "friend" or "dear one," *philos*. We will always translate the verb *philein* as "to love" (or "to be loved," in the passive voice), while noting Aristotle's use of other verbs closely associated with *love*: *eran* (to love [in the erotic sense]), *stergein* (to feel affection for), and *agapein* (to be fond of).

ship is not spoken of when it comes to loving inanimate objects, since in that case there is no reciprocated love or wish for the good of the inanimate thing: it is perhaps laughable to wish for good things for the wine,

30   but, if anything, one wishes that it be preserved so that one may have it. But people assert that a friend ought to wish for good things for his friend for that friend's sake. Yet people speak of those who do wish for the good things in this way as having "goodwill" if the other person involved does not return that same wish, for they say that goodwill in those who reciprocate it is friendship. Or perhaps we must set down in addition "good-

35   will that does not go unnoticed," for many people have goodwill toward those they have not seen but whom they assume to be decent or useful,

1156a and one of the latter might feel this same thing toward the former. These people, then, appear to have goodwill toward each other—but how could one say that they are friends when they are unaware that they each have this feeling for the other? Friends must, therefore, have goodwill toward each other and not go unnoticed in their wishing for the good things for

5   the other, on account of some one of the [lovable] things mentioned.

CHAPTER THREE

These things differ in form from one another; so, therefore, do both the kinds of friendly love and the friendships that result. The forms of friendship, then, are three, equal in number to the things that are lovable; in accord with each is a reciprocal love that does not go unnoticed, and those who love each other wish for the good things for each other in that respect in which they love each other.

10   Those who love each other on account of utility, then, do not love each other in themselves, but only insofar as they come to have something good from the other. Similar too is the case of those who love on account of pleasure, for people are fond of[16] those who are witty, not because they are of a certain sort, but because they are pleasant to them. Therefore,

15   those who love on account of utility feel affection[17] for the sake of their own good, just as those who love on account of pleasure feel affection for

16 · Aristotle uses *agapein* rather than *philein* here (from which *philia* comes). According to LSJ, the former, as distinguished from the latter, implies regard rather than affection. In the Christian tradition, the noun *agapē* is typically used to denote the love of God for humankind, as well as the kind of selfless love of one person for another that is without sexual implications.

17 · *Stergein*, typically used to describe familial love.

the sake of their own pleasure. He who is loved in each case is not loved for himself but only insofar as he is useful or pleasant. And these, then, are friendships incidentally; for it is not for being what he is that the person loved is loved, but only insofar as he provides (in the one case) something good or (in the other) pleasure.

These sorts of friendships, then, are easily dissolved when the people involved do not remain the same as they were. For if they are no longer 20 pleasant or useful, those who love them will cease to do so. And what is useful does not remain constant but is different at different times. When that on the basis of which they were friends is nullified, then so too the friendship is dissolved, since the friendship exists with a view to the thing in question. This sort of friendship seems to arise especially among the 25 old (for those of such an age pursue not what is pleasant but what is beneficial to them) as well as among all those in their prime, or the young, who pursue what is advantageous. And such people do not frequently live with each other either, for sometimes they are not even pleasant to each other. They therefore have no additional need of this sort of association if they supply no benefit to the other, for they are pleasant to each other 30 only insofar as they foster hopes of obtaining something good from the other. It is also among these sorts of friendships that people place the kind connected with foreigners.[18]

But the friendship of the young seems to be based on pleasure, for they live according to passion and most of all pursue what is pleasant to them and at hand. But since this time of life is prone to undergoing change, the pleasures too come to be different. Hence the young swiftly become friends and cease being so: the friendship changes together with 35 what they find pleasant, and change in this sort of pleasure is swift. The 1156b young are given to erotic love as well.[19] For the greater part of erotic love is bound up with passion and is based on pleasure, which is why they love[20] and swiftly cease loving, often changing in the course of the same day. But the young do wish to pass their days together and live together, for in this 5 way they attain what friendship for them involves.

18 · *Xenikos* (from *xenia*), that is, the friendship between host and guest, an important relationship in ancient Greece, which carried obligations of hospitality and the protection of Zeus. It also had a political dimension, in the hosting of and giving gifts to foreign guests or ambassadors.

19 · *Erōtikoi*, derived from *erōs*, sexual love, the fourth term for "love" in the discussion of friendship.

20 · Here *philein*, "to love" in the sense of friendship.

But complete[21] friendship is the friendship of those who are good and alike in point of virtue. For such people wish in similar fashion for the good things for each other insofar as they are good, and they are good in themselves. But those who wish for the good things for their friends, for their friends' sake, are friends most of all, since they are disposed in this way in themselves and not incidentally. Their friendship continues, then, while they are good, and virtue is a stable thing. Each person involved is good simply and for the friend, since good people are good simply and beneficial to one another. So too are they pleasant, for the good are both pleasant simply and pleasant to one another. To each person, his own actions and those like them accord with his pleasure, and the actions of those who are good are the same or similar.

It is with good reason that this sort of friendship is stable, since it combines in itself all those things that ought to belong to friends. For every friendship exists on account of a good or pleasure, either simply or for the person who loves, and in accord with the likeness involved.[22] And in this complete friendship, all that has been spoken of is present in the friends themselves, since in this respect the friends are alike and the remaining [reasons for forming friendship] are present as well—both the good simply and the pleasant simply[23]—and these things are lovable most of all. So it is among these people that both loving and friendship are especially prevalent and best.

Yet friendships of this sort are likely to be rare, since people of this sort are few. Further, there is also need of the passage of time and the habits formed by living together;[24] for as the adage has it, it is not possible for people to know each other until they have eaten together the

---

21 · Or, "perfect" (teleia).

22 · There is disagreement among commentators concerning the meaning of this last clause: does the "likeness" refer to the likeness of the friends, or does it indicate that friendships based on a good or pleasure relative to the one who loves are friendships only in their likeness to complete friendship?

23 · With Burnet, we accept the reading of the best MS and Aspasius, against Bywater and others, who read: "for the remaining [kinds of friendships] are alike to this one, and what is good simply is also pleasant simply." If one accepts the former reading, it would seem to support the argument that the "likeness" Aristotle refers to in the previous line is the likeness of the friends.

24 · The phrase "the habits formed by living together" translates a single word (sunē-theia) that suggests both living or dwelling together and the habits or customs acquired thereby. We will sometimes translate the term more simply as "living together" or "the habit of living together."

proverbial salt, nor is it possible, before this occurs, for them to accept each other and to be friends until each appears to each as lovable and is trusted. Those who swiftly make proofs of friendship to each other wish   30
to be friends but are not such unless they are also lovable and know this about each other. For a wish for friendship arises swiftly, but friendship itself does not.

CHAPTER FOUR

This friendship, then, is complete, in regard to both time and the remaining considerations [namely, the good and pleasure]; and in every respect each friend comes to possess from the other the same or similar things, which is just what ought to be the case with friends. Friendship based on   35
what is pleasant bears a resemblance to this one, for in fact the good are   1157a
pleasant to one another as well. Similar too is the case of friendship based on utility, for the good are also useful to one another. But among those who seek pleasure or utility, friendships endure especially whenever each attains the same thing from the other—for example, pleasure—and not   5
only this but whenever it comes from the same type, as in, for example, those who are witty, and not as in the case of lover and beloved.[25] For lover and beloved are not pleased by the same things; rather, the lover is pleased by seeing the beloved, the beloved by being attended to by his lover. And sometimes when the bloom of youth fades, so too the friendship fades (since for the lover, the sight of the other is not pleasant, and for the beloved, the attention of the lover is no more). Many in turn do   10
remain friends, however, whenever, as a result of their living together, they feel affection for their characters, if they are of the same character. But in the case of lovers whose mutual exchange is not for pleasure but utility, they are and remain friends to a lesser degree. And those who are friends on account of utility dissolve the friendship at the same time as   15
the advantage ceases, for they were friends not to each other but to the profit involved.

In the case of pleasure and utility, then, it is possible even for the base to be friends with one another and for the decent to be friends with the base, as well as for those who are neither [base nor decent] to be friends with any sort whatever. Yet it is clear that only the good can be friends on account of who they themselves are. For those who are bad do not delight

---

25 · The terms for "lover" and "beloved" here are based on *erōs*: *erastēs* and *erōmenos*.

20   in one another,[26] unless some benefit should accrue to them. Moreover,
only the friendship of the good is secure against slander, for it is not easy
to trust anyone when it comes to slander about someone who has been
tested by oneself over a long time; and in the case of these people, one
finds such statements as "I trust him," "he would never commit injustice,"
and all those other things deemed worthy of true friendship. In the case of
25   the other sorts of friendships, there is nothing to prevent such bad things
from arising.

Now, since human beings call friends both those who are friendly
on account of the utility involved (as in the case of cities, for alliances
struck by cities seem to be for the sake of what is advantageous), and those
who feel affection for one another on account of pleasure (as in the case
of children), perhaps we too ought to say that these sorts of people are
30   friends, but that there is more than one form of friendship; and that the
friendship of good human beings, insofar as they are good, is friendship
in the primary and authoritative sense, the remaining friendships being
such only by way of a resemblance. For insofar as there is some good involved and some likeness,[27] they are friends. And in fact what is pleasant
is a good for the lovers of pleasure. But these kinds of friendship do not
often go together, and those who become friends on account of utility
35   are not the same as those who do so on account of pleasure, for incidental
things are not often yoked together.

1157b   Given that these are the forms into which friendship has been divided,
base people will be friends on account of what is pleasant or useful to
them, since it is in this respect that they are alike, whereas the good will
be friends on account of who they themselves are, in that they are good.
The latter, then, are friends simply, whereas the former are friends incidentally and only by resembling the latter.

CHAPTER FIVE

5   Just as in the virtues, so too in friendship: some people are spoken of
as good in reference to the characteristic they possess, others as good
in reference to the activity they engage in. For those who live together

26 · Or, perhaps, "in themselves."
27 · Here and in what immediately follows, commentators again disagree about the nature of the "likeness": is the likeness to one another, in the respect in which they love,
or is it to complete friendship, that is, insofar as these friendships are like the friendship of the good?

delight in and provide good things to one another, whereas those who are asleep or separated by location are not active, though they are so disposed as to be active as a friend. For location dissolves not friendship in the unqualified sense but rather its activity. Yet if the absence lasts a long time, it seems to make even the friendship forgotten, which is why it has been said that "indeed, many friendships the lack of contact dissolves."[28]

But neither the old nor the sour types appear disposed to form friendships, for there is little that is pleasant in them, and no one is able to pass the day together with someone who causes him pain or who is not pleasant: nature appears to avoid most of all what is painful and to aim at what is pleasant. But those who approve of one another without living together are more like those with goodwill than like friends. For nothing so much belongs to friends as living together (those in need long to be benefited, and even the blessed long to spend their days together with others, since it belongs to them least of all to be solitary). But it is not possible to go through life with one another when people are not pleasant or do not delight in the same things, which is in fact what seems to characterize the friendship between comrades.

The friendship of those who are good, then, is friendship most of all, just as has been said many times. For what is good or pleasant in an unqualified sense seems to be lovable and choiceworthy, whereas what is good or pleasant to each individual seems to be such only to that person. But a good person is lovable and choiceworthy to a good person on both accounts.

Friendly affection is also like a passion, whereas friendship is like a characteristic: friendly affection exists no less toward inanimate things, whereas people reciprocate love as a matter of choice, and choice stems from one's characteristic. People also wish for good things for those who are loved, for the sake of the loved ones themselves, not in reference to a passion but in accord with a characteristic. And in loving their friend, they love what is good for themselves, since the good person who becomes a friend becomes a good for the person to whom he is a friend. Each one, then, both loves what is good for himself and repays in equal measure what they wish for the other and what is pleasant.[29] For it is said,

28 · The source of this saying is unknown, and this is the only known instance of the word for "lack of contact" (*aprosēgoria*) in the extant Greek literature.
29 · Some MSS read "in form" instead of "what is pleasant," that is, those who are good repay either the same or proportional things.

"friendship is equality," and these things belong most of all to the friendship of those who are good.

CHAPTER SIX

1158a   Friendship arises less among those who are sour or old, inasmuch as they
are surlier than others and delight less in their associations. For being
without surliness and delighting in one's associations seem especially to
5   be marks of friendship and productive of friendship. Hence the young
become friends swiftly, but the old do not, since people do not become
friends with those in whom they do not delight, and neither, similarly,
do those who are sour. But such people do have goodwill toward one
another, for they wish for good things for one another and meet one another's needs. Yet they are still not quite friends, because they do not pass
10   their days together or delight in one another, the very things that especially seem to be marks of friendship.

It is also not possible to be a friend to many, at least not when it comes
to complete friendship, just as it is not possible to be in love[30] with many
at the same time either (since such love is akin to an excess, and such a
thing naturally arises in relation to one person). It is also not easy for
many people to be very pleasing to the same person at the same time or,
perhaps, for many to be good. Also, one must acquire experience of the
15   other person and be in the habit of living together, which is altogether difficult. But when it comes to what is useful or pleasant, it is possible to be
pleasing to many, since people of that sort are many and their services are
rendered in a short time.

Of these friendships, the one based on what is pleasant is more like
friendship properly speaking, whenever the same things come from both
20   parties and they delight in each other or in the same things; such are the
friendships of the young, since they have more of what is liberal[31] in them.
But friendship based on utility belongs to those who frequent the marketplace. And although the blessed have no need of useful people, they
do of pleasant ones: they wish to live with certain people, and although
they might bear what is painful for a short time, no one could endure

30 · Here *eran*, to love in the erotic sense.
31 · The adjective (*eleutherios*) refers most generally to the quality or qualities that
distinguish a "free man" (*eleutheros*)—above all, in the *Ethics*, the freedom from any
undue or slavish attachment to money; hence the virtue of "liberality" (*eleutheriotēs*).

it continuously—not even the good itself, should it be painful to him. 25
Hence they seek out friends who are pleasant. Yet perhaps they ought to
seek out the sorts of people who are good as well, and, further, good for
them themselves: in this way all that ought to belong to friends will be
theirs.

But people in positions of authority appear to make use of friends who
are divided into two groups: some are useful to them and others pleasant, though the same people are not often both. For those in authority
seek out neither those who are pleasant and have virtue, nor those who 30
are useful with a view to noble things. Rather, they seek out the witty,
when they aim at pleasure, and the clever to do their bidding, and these
qualities do not frequently arise in the same person. It has been said that
the serious person is at once pleasant and useful; yet such a person does
not become a friend to someone who exceeds him [in power], unless [the
person in power] is also exceeded [by the serious person] in virtue. But 35
if this does not occur, [the serious person] is not rendered equal [to the
person of greater power], since he is exceeded in the relevant proportion.
Yet [those in positions of authority] are not much accustomed to becoming these sorts [of friends to the virtuous].[32]

The friendships that have been spoken of, then, involve equality. For 1158b
the same things come from both people involved, and they wish for the
same things for each other, or they exchange one thing for another—for
example, pleasure in exchange for a benefit. That these latter are friendships to a lesser degree and endure less has also been stated. Yet on account of their likeness and unlikeness to the same thing, they seem both 5
to be and not to be friendships: given their likeness to the friendship that
accords with virtue, they appear to be friendships (for they involve either
pleasure or utility, and these belong also to the friendship that accords
with virtue); but insofar as the friendship of the virtuous is secure against
slander and is stable, whereas these friendships change quickly and differ 10
in many other ways, they appear not to be friendships, given their unlikeness to this friendship.

32 · We follow Aspasius's generally accepted interpretation of this passage, but the
Greek is obscure, and more recent commentators suggest the following: "such a person does not become a friend to one who exceeds him [in power], unless he is exceeded
[by the powerful] also in virtue. But failing that, [the serious person] is not equalized
by being exceeded in proportion. Yet [those in positions of authority] are not much accustomed to becoming such [i.e., virtuous]."

CHAPTER SEVEN

A different form of friendship is that which is based on a superiority—for example, the friendship of a father for a son, and, in general, an older man for a younger, a husband for a wife, and every ruler for one who is ruled. These friendships differ from one another as well: the friend-
15 ship of parents for their children is not the same as that of rulers for the ruled. Yet the friendship of a father for a son is not even the same as that of the son for the father, nor is that of a husband for a wife the same as that of a wife for a husband. For in each case there is a different virtue and work involved, and different too are the reasons why they love each other. Both the feelings of friendly affection and the friendships, then, are different.
20   Each person, therefore, does not come to possess the same things from the other, nor ought each to seek the same things. But whenever children render to their parents what they owe to those who have begotten them, and parents [to their sons][33] what they owe to their children, the friend-ship of such people will be stable and equitable. And in all friendships based on a superiority, the feelings of friendly affection too ought to be
25 proportional—for example, the better person ought to be loved more than he loves, and so also with the more beneficial person, and similarly with each of the others. For whenever the friendly affection accords with merit, at that point equality somehow arises, which of course is held to belong to friendship.
        But what is equal in matters of justice does not appear to hold simi-
30 larly in the case of friendship. For in matters of justice, what is equal is, first, what accords with merit, and, second, what accords with a certain quantity; in the case of friendship, however, what accords with a certain quantity is first, what accords with merit second. And this is clear when-ever a great difference arises between the friends in point of virtue, vice, resources, or some other thing; for not only are the parties involved no
35 longer friends, but they do not even deem themselves worthy to be. This is most apparent in the case of the gods, for they exceed [human beings] in all good things to the greatest degree. But it is clear too in the case of
1159a kings. For those who are much inferior to kings do not deem themselves worthy to be friends with them, and neither do those who are worthy of nothing, with the best or the wisest.

33 · A phrase that is omitted in the best MS.

In these sorts of cases, then, there is no precise definition regarding the point up to which friends remain friends. For although many things may be taken away, the friendship still endures; but when someone is separated from the other to a great degree, as is the god, then the friendship 5 no longer endures. This is also why the perplexity arises as to whether friends perhaps never wish for the greatest goods for their friends—for example, for them to be gods—since then they will no longer be friends to them, and neither will they therefore be goods, for friends are goods. So if it has been nobly said that a friend wishes for the good things for the friend for his friend's sake, the friend would need to remain as whatever 10 sort he is. For the one friend will wish for the greatest goods for the other *as a human being*—and perhaps not all such goods, since each wishes for the good things for himself most of all.

CHAPTER EIGHT

But the many seem, on account of their love of honor,[34] to wish to be loved more than to love. Hence the many are lovers of flattery. For the 15 flatterer is a friend who is inferior, or at any rate he pretends to be inferior and to love more than he is loved. Moreover, being loved seems to be close to being honored, which is indeed what the many aim at. But they seem to choose honor not on its own account but only incidentally. For the many delight in being honored by those in positions of authority, on 20 account of the hope thus fostered (for they suppose that they will obtain what they need from them; they delight in honor, therefore, as a sign of their faring well).

But those who long for honor from people who are decent and who know them aim at confirming their own opinion of themselves. They delight in honor, therefore, since they trust that they are good as a result of the judgment of those who say so. But they delight in being loved in it- 25 self. Hence being loved would seem to be better than being honored, and friendship would seem to be choiceworthy in itself. But friendship seems to consist more in loving than in being loved. And a sign of this is mothers who delight in loving their children: some mothers give away their own children to be raised, and though they love them just because they know who they are, they do not seek to be loved in return if both are not 30 possible. Rather, it seems to be enough for mothers if they see their chil-

---

34 · *Philotimia*, the term translated as "ambition" in 4.4.

dren doing well; and they love them even if their children, in ignorance of who their mothers are, may render to them nothing of what is proper to a mother.

Since friendship consists more in loving than in being loved and those who love their friends are praised, loving seems to be a virtue of friends. As a result, those in whom this arises in accord with merit are stable friends, as is their friendship. It is in this way especially that even those who are unequal might be friends, since they could be rendered equal [by a difference in the love offered on each side]. Equality and likeness constitute friendly affection, and especially the likeness of those who are alike in point of virtue: since they are stable in themselves, they remain the same also in relation to each other, and they neither need base things nor offer aid of this sort; rather, they even obstruct it, so to speak, for it belongs to good people neither to err themselves nor to permit their friends to do so. Those who are corrupt are without steadiness, however, for they do not remain alike even to themselves; yet for a short time they do become friends, when they delight in each other's corruption. But those who are useful and pleasant remain friends for a longer time, for however long they provide pleasures or benefits to each other.

It seems that friendship based on utility arises especially from opposites—for example, the friendship of a poor person with a wealthy one, that of an ignorant person with a knower: because the one aims at what he happens to need, he gives something else in return for it. Someone might bring in here both lover and beloved, or the beautiful and the ugly. Hence lovers in fact appear laughable sometimes, when they deem themselves worthy to be loved as they themselves love.[35] Perhaps those who are similarly lovable ought to be deemed worthy of such reciprocal love, but if they are nothing of the sort, it is laughable.

Yet perhaps one opposite does not aim at the other opposite in itself, except incidentally. Rather, the longing involved is for the middle term, since this is good—for example, what is good for the dry is not to become wet but to come to the middle condition, and similarly in the case of heat and the rest. Now, then, let us leave aside these considerations, for indeed they are rather foreign to our purpose.

35 · Although Aristotle is speaking of the lover and the beloved in the erotic sense here, *erastēs* and *erōmenos*, the verbs he uses are the passive and active of *philein*.

CHAPTER NINE

But it seems, as was said in the beginning, that both friendship and the   25
just are concerned with the same matters and are present among the
same persons. For in *every* community, something just seems to exist, and
friendship as well. At any rate, people address their shipmates and fellow soldiers as friends, just as those in other communities do. And to the   30
extent that people share in community, there is friendship, since to this
extent there is also what is just. The proverb "the things of friends are in
common" is correct, since friendship resides in community—for brothers and comrades, all things are in common, whereas for others, only certain definite things are in common, to a greater or lesser degree. In the
case of friendships as well, there is greater and lesser community.

The just things too differ, since these are not the same for parents in re-   35
lation to children and for brothers in relation to one another, or for com-   1160a
rades and for citizens, and similarly in the other friendships. The unjust
things also differ in relation to each of them, and they increase the more
they concern friends—for example, it is more terrible to steal money   5
from a comrade than from a fellow citizen, not to aid a brother than not
to aid a stranger, and to strike a father than to strike anyone else. It is natural for what is just to increase together with friendship,[36] on the grounds
that justice and friendship are present among the same persons and are
coextensive.

But all communities are like parts of the political community, for
people come together for a certain advantage, namely, to provide some of   10
the things conducive to life. And the political community seems to come
together from the outset, and to continue to exist, for the sake of what
is advantageous; lawgivers aim at this and claim that the advantage held
in common is what is just. The other communities, then, aim at a partial
advantage—for example, sailors aim at the advantage of making money   15
from sailing or some such thing; soldiers at the advantage bound up with
war, since they long for either money, victory, or a city; and similarly too
in the case of members of the same tribe or district.

But some communities seem to arise on account of pleasure—like
communities of Bacchic revelers and members of a dinner club, for these   20
exist for the sake of performing a sacrifice and of getting together with

36 · One MS reads, "what is just *appears to* increase together with friendship ..."

others. But all these seem to fall under the political community; for the political community aims not at the present advantage but at that pertaining to life as a whole, [since those engaged in political life] perform sacrifices and host gatherings concerning them, thereby distributing honors to the gods and providing a pleasant rest for themselves.[37] For the ancient sacrifices and gatherings appear to take place after the harvest—for example, the "first fruits"—because people used to have leisure especially in these seasons. All communities, therefore, appear to be parts of the political community, and the sorts of friendships will correspond with the different sorts of communities.

CHAPTER TEN

There are three forms of regime and an equal number of deviations that are like corruptions of the former three. The regimes are kingship, aristocracy, and a third that is based on property assessments [*timēma*], which it appears proper to speak of as "timocracy," though most people are accustomed to calling it "polity."[38] And the best of these is kingship; the worst, timocracy.

The deviation from kingship is tyranny, for while both are monarchical, they differ the most because the tyrant looks to what is advantageous for himself and the king to what is advantageous for the ruled. A king is not someone lacking in self-sufficiency or superiority in any goods; he is, rather, the sort of person who is in need of nothing. He would look to what is beneficial, then, not for himself, but for the ruled. Were he not of this sort, he would be a kind of king appointed merely by lot. But tyranny is in this respect the opposite, for the tyrant pursues the good for himself; and it is quite manifest in this case that tyranny is the most inferior regime, since the opposite of the best is the worst.

The change from kingship is to tyranny, for tyranny is the base form of a monarchy, and the corrupt king becomes a tyrant. From aristocracy the change is to oligarchy as a consequence of the vice of the rulers, who dis-

37 · The text appears to be corrupt. Bywater brackets and some editors consider an interpolation the lines "But some communities ... getting together with others," since a version of this claim is restated a few lines later. The textual difficulty is tied to an interpretive question: is it the city as a whole, as opposed to a partial community, that attends to the gods and the proper sacrifices?

38 · The Greek is the same as the general term for "regime," *politeia*. It is the name that Aristotle gives to the third of the good regimes in his *Politics* (see, e.g., 1279a22).

tribute what belongs to the city contrary to merit—that is, they distribute all or most of the goods to themselves and the political offices always   15
to the same people, since they make being wealthy their greatest concern.
A few corrupt people rule, therefore, instead of the most decent. From
timocracy the change is to democracy, for they share a defining feature:
timocracy too wishes to be [rule] of the multitude, and all those who
meet the property assessment are considered equal. Democracy is the   20
least corrupt, for it deviates only slightly from the form of "polity." The
regimes change especially in this way, then, since in this way they change
least and hence most easily.

One could find likenesses and, as it were, models of the regimes in
households too. For the community of a father in relation to his sons
bears a resemblance to kingship, since the father cares for his children.   25
And this is why Homer too addresses Zeus as "Father,"[39] since kingship
tends to be paternal rule. But among the Persians, the rule of the father
is tyrannical, for he uses his sons as slaves. Tyrannical too is the rule of a
master over slaves, since it is the advantage of the master that is achieved   30
in it. This latter kind of rule, then, appears to be correct, the Persian in
error; for over those who differ, the kinds of rule differ.

The community of husband and wife appears to be aristocratic: the man
rules in accord with merit regarding the things over which a man ought to
rule, whereas all things suited to a woman, he hands over to her. The man
who takes control of *all* things turns his rule into oligarchy, for he does this 35
contrary to merit and not inasmuch as he is better. Sometimes women rule,   1161a
when they are heiresses. Their rule, therefore, arises not in accord with virtue but on account of their wealth and power, as in oligarchies.

The community of brothers is like timocracy, since they are equals, except insofar as they differ in their ages, which is exactly why the friendship   5
is no longer brotherly if there is a great difference in age. But democracy
is found especially in households where there is no master (since in these
households all are on an equal footing) and in those where the ruler is
weak and each person has license to act as he likes.

CHAPTER ELEVEN

Friendship appears in each of the regimes to the extent that what is just   10
does as well. In a king in relation to those over whom he is king, friend-

---

39 · See, e.g., Homer, *Iliad* 1.503.

ship consists in superiority in granting benefactions, for he benefits those over whom he is king—if in fact, being good, he cares for them so that they fare well, just as does a shepherd for his sheep. So it is that Homer too spoke of Agamemnon as the "shepherd of the people."[40] But a paternal friendship is also of this sort, though it differs in the magnitude of its benefactions; for a father is the cause of one's very being, which is held to be the greatest thing, as well as of one's rearing and education; ancestors too are credited with these things. For the rule of a father over his sons is by nature, as is that of ancestors over their descendants and that of a king over those whom he rules as king. These friendships involve superiority; hence parents are also honored. And what is just in these cases, therefore, is not the same for both, but it does accord with merit, since the friendship does as well.

The friendship of a husband for a wife is the same as that in aristocracy, for it accords with virtue, and to the better person goes more of the good and to each what is suited to each. So also in the case of what is just. The friendship of brothers is like that of comrades, for they are equals and similar in age, and such people for the most part have the same feelings and habits. Also resembling this friendship is the friendship pertaining to timocracy, for the citizens wish to be equals and equitable[41]—to rule in turn, therefore, and on an equal basis. Such too, therefore, is the corresponding friendship.

In the case of the deviations, in the same way as what is just exists there to a small degree, so too does friendship, and it exists least of all in the worst one: in tyranny, there is little or no friendship. For where there is nothing in common for ruler and ruled, there is no friendship either, since what is just does not even exist, as in the cases of an artisan in relation to his tool, the soul in relation to the body, and the master in relation to his slave. For all these are benefited by those who use them, but there is no friendship for inanimate things and nothing just pertaining to them. But neither is there friendship for a horse or an ox, nor for a slave insofar as he is a slave: there is nothing in common, since a slave is an animate tool, and a tool an inanimate slave. Insofar as he is a slave, then, there is no friendship in relation to him, but only insofar as he is a human being, since there seems to be something just for every human being in relation to everyone able to share in law and compact. There is friendship, then,

40 · See, e.g., ibid. 2.243.
41 · Or, "decent" (epieikeis).

insofar as the slave is a human being. So to a small degree, friendships and what is just exist even in tyrannies; but in democracies, they exist to a greater degree, since those who are equal have many things in common.   10

CHAPTER TWELVE

Every friendship, then, involves community, as has been said. But one might separate out both the friendship of kinfolk and that of comrades. For the friendships of fellow citizens, tribesmen, sailors, and all of that sort seem more like communities [than friendships], since they appear   15 to be based on a certain agreement among the parties—and with these sorts of friendships one might also assign the friendship connected with foreigners.[42]

But the friendship of kinfolk appears to have many forms, though every one of them appears to depend on the paternal sort: parents feel affection for their children on the grounds that they are something of their own, whereas children feel affection for their parents on the grounds that they themselves are something that comes from them. But parents know   20 what issues from them to a greater degree than their offspring know that they issue from their parents; and the begetter feels more united in kinship to its offspring than does the offspring to its maker, for what comes from the begetter itself is its own—for example, a tooth, a hair, or anything whatsoever in relation to its possessor—but the begetter is not at all the offspring's own, or is such only to a lesser degree. The length of time involved also makes a difference, for parents immediately feel affection   25 for those who are born, whereas offspring feel affection for their parents after a period of time, once they acquire comprehension or perception. From these considerations too it is clear why mothers are more loving [than fathers].

Parents, then, love children as they love themselves (for those who come from them are like other selves separately existing), whereas children love their parents on the grounds that they are born from them, and brothers love each other because they were born from the same parents.   30 Their sameness in relation to these parents constitutes the sameness brothers share with each other, which is why people claim to be of the same blood, the same root, and such things. They are in some way the same thing, therefore, even though this same thing resides in separate

42 · See n. 18 above.

persons. But it is a great matter, when it comes to friendship, for both to have been brought up together and to be of similar age: "like age [glad-
35   dens] like age,"[43] and those who live together are comrades. Hence too the friendship of brothers is like that of comrades. First cousins and the other
1162a   descendants are also bound by ties of kinship as a result of these things, since they come from the same persons. Some are closer in kinship, while others are more foreign by dint of being nearer to or farther from the family founder.

5   The friendship of children for their parents, and that of human beings for gods, is a friendship with what is good and superior. For they have produced the greatest benefits: they are the causes of a child's being and his rearing, and of the education of those born. And this sort of friendship affords both what is pleasant and what is useful to a greater degree than does that between unrelated[44] persons, inasmuch as their lives have
10   more in common. There are qualities of the friendship of brothers that are found also in the friendship of comrades. These qualities are present even more among those brothers who are decent and generally alike, insofar as there is a closer kinship among them and they begin having affection for one another from birth, and insofar as they share more of the same habits, coming as they do from the same parents and having been reared and educated together. Also, their testing of one another over time
15   is greatest and most certain. And what conduces to friendship is present in proportion also among the rest of those who are kin.

The friendship between a husband and a wife seems to be in accord with nature. For a human being is by nature more a coupling being than a political one, inasmuch as a household is earlier and more necessary than a city and the begetting of children is more common to animals. Among
20   the other animals, then, community exists to that extent; but human beings live together not only for the sake of begetting children but also for the sake of the things that contribute to life, for the tasks involved are divided immediately, those of the husband being different from those of the wife. They assist each other, then, by putting their own things in the service of what is in common. For these reasons, both what is useful and
25   what is pleasant seem to be found in this friendship, though there would be such a friendship also on account of their virtue, should they be decent. For there is a virtue belonging to each, and they would delight in a

43 · A proverb that is quoted in its full form in the *Eudemian Ethics* (1238a33) and *Rhetoric* (1371b15) as well as in Plato, *Phaedrus* 240c1–2.
44 · Literally, "strangers" or "foreigners," but here opposed most directly to "kin."

person of a comparable sort. Children too seem to be a common bond; hence childless couples break up more readily, since children are a good common to both parents, and what is common holds things together.

How a husband must live in relation to his wife, and, in general, a   30
friend in relation to a friend, appears no different a thing to inquire into than how it is just to do so, for the just does not appear to be the same thing for a friend in relation to a friend as it is in relation to a foreigner, a comrade, or a schoolmate.

CHAPTER THIRTEEN

Now, friendships are threefold, as was said in the beginning; and in each   35
case, there are friendships consisting in an equality, others based on a superiority. For those who are similarly good become friends, or a good   1162b
person befriends a worse one; and those who are pleasant and those who are useful become friends in like manner, whether they are equal in the benefits they confer or different. Those who are equal ought to love each other equally, in accord with the relevant equality, whereas those who are unequal ought to render to each what is proportional given the relevant superiorities.

But accusations and blame arise in the friendship based on utility, ei-   5
ther in it alone or in it especially, and with good reason. For those who are friends on account of their virtue are eager to benefit each other (for this belongs to virtue and to friendship); and since they compete with a view to this, there are no accusations or fights: no one is annoyed by   10
someone who loves and benefits him, but if he is refined, he retaliates by doing some good to his friend. And since he who surpasses in doing good obtains what he aims at, he would not level an accusation against his friend, for each longs for the good. There are also not many accusations in the friendships based on pleasure either, since both parties come to possess simultaneously what they long for, if they delight in going through life together. In fact, he who would accuse the other of not pleasing him   15
would appear laughable, since it is possible for him not to spend his days together with him. But friendship based on utility is prone to accusa-
tions. For those who use each other with a view to some benefit always want more and suppose they obtain less than what is proper. And so they blame the other because they do not obtain as much as they want and think they merit, and those who perform the benefactions are not able to   20
supply as much as the recipients want.

It seems that, just as there is a twofold distinction in what is just— what is unwritten and what accords with law—so also in the friendship based on utility, there is the moral[45] friendship and the legal one. Accusations arise, then, especially when people do not dissolve the friendship on the same basis on which they entered into it. And the legal type of this friendship depends on stated terms: one kind belongs wholly to marketplace transactions that happen immediately; another is more liberal as regards the time to pay but depends on an agreement that one thing is exchanged for another. The debt is clear and undisputed in this latter case, but it bears the mark of friendship because of the deferral of the payment to the seller. For this very reason, there are no legal arbitrations of these agreements in some places, but people suppose instead that those who entered into agreements on trust ought to feel affection for each other.

The moral type of this friendship, on the other hand, does not depend on stated terms. Instead, a gift (or whatever else) is given as to a friend; but the giver thinks he deserves to receive what is equal, or more than that, in return, on the grounds that he has not given anything but lent it. Yet if someone dissolves the friendship in a way different from that in which he entered into the agreement, the other friend will level an accusation. This happens because all or most people wish for noble things but choose the beneficial ones instead. It is a noble thing to perform a benefit without expecting it to be requited, but it is of course beneficial to receive a benefaction.

He who is able, therefore, must give in return the worth of what he received, and do so voluntarily[46]—for he must not make a friend of someone who is not voluntarily one. On the grounds that he erred completely in the beginning and was done a good deed by someone by whom he ought not to have been done one—for it was not done by a friend or by someone doing this for its own sake—he must therefore dissolve the relation, just as if he had received a benefaction on stated terms. And a person

45 · This is the same adjective, *ēthikē*, that Aristotle uses to speak of "moral virtue." The "moral" type of friendship Aristotle goes on to discuss is a category within friendship based on utility and is not to be confused with friendship based on character simply.

46 · Bywater brackets "and do so voluntarily," with some manuscript support. Moreover, commentators dispute whether the phrase refers to the person who is returning the benefit—that he must do so "voluntarily"—or to the one who is receiving it—that he must accept it "voluntarily."

ought to agree to repay whatever he is able to,[47] whereas if he should be unable to repay something, not even the giver would expect him to do so. As a result, he must repay it if he can; yet at the outset, he must consider the person from whom he receives a benefaction and on what terms, so that he may submit to these terms or not.

There is also a dispute regarding whether one ought to measure the benefit to the recipient and make repayment with a view to this, or to measure the good deed of the person who performed it. For the recipients assert that they received from those giving the benefaction such things as were small to the givers and which it was possible to receive from others, thus depreciating what they received. Conversely, the givers assert that the recipients received their greatest things, that it was not possible to get them from others, and that they gave them amid dangers or comparable situations of need. Since the friendship is based on utility, then, is the relevant measure the benefit to the recipient? For the recipient is the one in need, and the other aids him on the grounds that he will get back what is equal to the aid. The amount of aid, then, is as much as the recipient has been benefited; and so he must repay as much as he has partaken of, or even more, since doing the latter is nobler.

But in friendships that accord with virtue, there are no accusations; and the choice made by the person performing the benefaction is like a measure, for what is authoritative in matters of virtue and character resides in the choice involved.

CHAPTER FOURTEEN

But differences arise also in friendships based on a superiority, since each thinks he is worthy of having more; and when this happens, the friendship is dissolved. For he who is better supposes that it is proper that he have more, since it is proper to distribute more to a person who is good. Similar too is the case of the greater benefactor. For people assert that someone who is useless ought not to have what is equal: the relation becomes a matter of charitable service and not a friendship if what comes from the friendship will not accord with the worth of the friend's deeds. For people suppose that just as in a financial partnership, those who con-

---

47 · Bywater and others suggest the following emendation: "he must repay what he would have agreed to repay if he was able."

tribute more receive more, so it ought to be in friendship too. But he who is in need and is the inferior asserts the converse—that it belongs to a good friend to aid those in need; for, they assert, what advantage is there
35   in being a friend of a serious or powerful person if there is no benefit to be enjoyed from the friendship?

1163b   It seems, then, that each partner correctly deems himself worthy of something—that is, that one ought to distribute more to each of them from the friendship, but not more of the same thing. Rather, to the person who is superior, one ought to distribute honor, and to the one in need, gain. Honor is the reward of virtue and of benefaction, whereas aid is the gain appropriate to need.

5   It appears to be this way also in the regimes. For he who provides nothing good to the community[48] is not honored, since what is held in common is given to the person who benefits the community, and honor is held in common. For it is not possible to make money from the common affairs and at the same time to be honored [by the community]. No one puts up with having the lesser share in all things, and so people distribute
10   honor to the person who [, in performing a benefaction,] suffers a monetary loss, and they give money to the person who accepts gifts.[49] For what accords with merit equalizes and preserves friendship, as has been said. It is in this way too, therefore, that one must associate with those who are unequal; and someone who is benefited in money or virtue must give
15   honor in return, thus giving back what he can. For friendship seeks what is possible, not what accords with the merit [of the giver]. In fact, it is not even possible in every case to do so, as in the honors directed toward the gods and parents; for no one could ever repay what they merit, though he who does service to them to the extent of his capacity is held to be decent.

Hence too it would seem impossible for a son to renounce his father,
20   but possible for a father to renounce his son. For the son must repay the debt, but nothing he may do is worthy of what was done for him, with the result that he is always in debt. But those who are owed have the capacity to discharge the debt, and certainly the father does. At the same time, perhaps, it seems that no father would ever cut off a son who was not of exceeding corruption. For even apart from their natural friendship, it is

48 · The Greek here and in the following line is *to koinon*, literally "the common."
49 · The term (*dōrodokos*) often has the negative connotation of one who accepts not just gifts but bribes.

characteristically human not to reject aid. Yet for the son who is corrupt, aiding his father is something he avoids or does not eagerly pursue. For 25 the many wish to be done a good turn, but they avoid doing one on the grounds that that is unprofitable.

Let what concerns these matters, then, be spoken of to this extent.

Book 9

CHAPTER ONE

In all heterogeneous[1] friendships, what is proportional equalizes and preserves the friendship, as has been said—for example, in a political [friendship], the shoemaker is given in exchange for his sandals what accords with their worth, just as is the weaver and the rest. Here, then, a legal currency has been brought in as a common measure, and so everything is referred to this and measured by it.

But in erotic [love or friendship], the lover sometimes levels the accusation that although he loves[2] beyond measure, he is not loved in return, though it may so happen that he possesses nothing lovable; the beloved, on the other hand, often levels the accusation that his lover is not now fulfilling anything of all that he had earlier promised. Such accusations arise when the lover loves the beloved for the pleasure involved, the beloved his lover for his usefulness to him, and when both parties do not have what each wants. For the friendship based on these concerns is dissolved when that for the sake of which they loved each other is not attained. The affection they felt was not for what each in himself was, but for the things each supplied, which are not stable; hence the friendships too are not stable. But the friendship based on character, being for its own sake, endures, as has been said.

But people are at odds whenever they come to have something other than what they long for. For whenever somebody fails to obtain what he aims at, it is akin to his attaining nothing. For example, a person promises

1 · *Anomoioeidēs*, that is, friendships in which the two parties seek different kinds of objects; for example, one seeks pleasure, the other something useful. This is the first and only time Aristotle uses this term to describe these sorts of friendships.

2 · Although Aristotle is speaking about erotic love or friendship and a "lover" (*erastēs*), here and in what follows he uses *philein* (and related terms) rather than *eran*.

a cithara player that the better he should play, the more pay he would get; but at dawn, when the player demanded the fulfillment of what he had been promised, the other said that the player had been given pleasure in return for pleasure. If, then, this had been the wish of each party, it would have sufficed; but if the one person had wished for enjoyment and the other gain, and the former had received his wish whereas the latter had not, the terms of the partnership would not have been nobly carried out. For what a person happens to need, he is also intent on, and for the sake of the satisfaction of this need, at any rate, he will give what he does.

But to which of the two parties does it belong to assess the worth of what is given: to the person who takes the initiative in giving, or to the one who is first in receiving? For he who takes the initiative in giving appears to entrust this assessment to the receiver, which is in fact what they assert Protagoras used to do. For when he would teach anything whatever, he used to bid the learner to estimate how much he held these things to be worth knowing, and that is the amount he used to take.[3] Yet in such circumstances, some people are content with the "[fixed] wage for a man."[4] But as for those who take money in advance and then do nothing of what they claimed, because their promises were excessive, they appropriately become subject to accusations because they do not fulfill what they agreed to. The Sophists are compelled to do this, perhaps, because no one would pay money for what they know.

Those who fail to do what they took a wage for, then, are appropriately subject to accusations. But in the circumstances in which there is no agreement about the service, it was said that those who take the initiative in giving, for their partner's sake, do not give cause for accusation (the friendship that accords with virtue is of this sort); and one must make the repayment accord with the choice [involved in the giving] (for this is the choice that is the mark of a friend and of virtue). So too in the case of those who share in philosophy. For the worth involved is not measured in monetary terms, and honor could not be evenly balanced with it. But perhaps whatever it is possible to repay would be sufficient, just as it is with

20

25

30

35

1164b

5

---

3 · A version of this story is told in Plato, *Protagoras* 328b1–c2.

4 · The saying, given in part here, comes from Hesiod, *Works and Days* 368. The context is:

> Let a wage that has been stated for a man who is a friend be fixed,
> And even with your brother, while laughing, set things down before a witness,
> For, mark you, trust and mistrust alike destroy men.

gods and parents. Yet when the giving is not of this sort, but is done on some condition, then perhaps especially in this case the repayment ought to be what accords with the worth of what is given in the opinion of both parties. But if this should not happen, it would seem not only necessary

10 but also just that he who was the first to receive assess it. For if the giver receives as much as the recipient is benefited (or however much in return the recipient would have given in choosing the pleasure involved), the giver will have received what was merited from the recipient in question.

In fact, this is what manifestly happens when it comes to goods bought and sold. In some places there are laws to the effect that voluntary transactions are not subject to legal adjudication, on the grounds that it is fit-

15 ting, with someone one has trusted, to dissolve the transaction [or partnership] on the same terms on which one entered into it. The supposition is that it is more just that the person to whom something was entrusted assess its worth than that the one who entrusted it to him do so. For many things are not valued equally by those who possess them and by those who wish to receive them, since what is one's own and what one gives appears to everyone to be worth a great deal. Nevertheless, repayment is determined with a view to the amount that the recipients assess, though per-

20 haps one ought not to value what something's worth appears to be when the recipient possesses it, but how much he valued it before possessing it.

CHAPTER TWO

But there is perplexity too regarding such questions as whether one ought to render everything to one's father and obey him in everything, or whether, when a person is sick, he ought rather to trust a doctor, or again

25 whether one ought to elect as general someone with military skill. Similarly, there is also perplexity as to whether one must serve a friend more than a serious man, and whether one must repay a favor to a benefactor rather than give away something to a comrade, if both are not possible. Is defining all such matters precisely, then, no easy thing? For there are many and various differences at issue, connected with whether what is involved is great or petty, noble or necessary.

30 That someone ought not to give back everything to the same person is not unclear; nor is it unclear that, for the most part, he must repay good deeds more than gratify his comrades, just as a person must pay back a loan to someone he owes, more than he must give away something to a comrade. But perhaps not even this is always so. For example, must a per-

son who has been ransomed from pirates pay in return the ransom of his
ransomer, regardless of the sort of fellow he may be, or, if the ransomer   35
has not been kidnapped, must he pay him back anyway if the fellow de-   1165a
mands repayment? Or must he ransom his father [first, even if he owes
his ransomer money]? For it would seem that a person should ransom his
father even in preference to himself.

Just as has been said, then, a person must in general pay back a debt.
But if an act of giving outstrips in its nobility or necessity the repayment
of a debt, one must incline toward these noble or necessary acts. For
sometimes the repaying of a previous service is not even equal [or fair]—   5
when someone benefits a person he knows to be serious, but the repayment is to one whom the serious person supposes to be corrupt. And in
fact sometimes a person should not make a loan even to someone who
has given him a loan, for the original lender, supposing that he would recover the money, made the loan to a decent person, whereas now the decent person has no hope of recovering it from his original lender, who is   10
base. Accordingly, if the original lender is base in truth, then his claim to
worthiness to receive a loan is not equal [or fair]; or, if he is not of this
character, but people suppose him to be, they would not think it strange
to refuse him. So it has been frequently stated, then, that arguments concerning passions and actions possess the same definiteness as those things
with which they deal.

It is not unclear, then, that one should not give back the same things
to all people or all things even to one's father, just as one does not offer   15
all sacrifices even to Zeus. But since different things go to parents, brothers, comrades, and benefactors, one must distribute to each what is properly his and fitting. People appear to do this in fact: they invite their relatives to weddings because the family line is something they share in common, as are the actions pertaining to their family. People also suppose   20
that relatives ought to gather especially at funerals for the same reason.
It would seem as well that one ought to provide sustenance especially to
parents, on the grounds that we are in their debt and that it is nobler thus
to provide for those who are the causes of our being than to provide for
ourselves. Honor too we owe to parents, just as to the gods—though not
every honor. For we do not owe the same honor to a father as to a mother;   25
nor, in turn, do we owe them the honor proper to a wise man or general;
rather, we owe them the honor due a father and a mother respectively. To
every old man is due the honor that accords with age, in rising and giving him a seat at the table and such things. To comrades, in turn, and to

30   brothers is due frankness and the sharing of all things in common. And to
relatives, fellow tribesmen, citizens, and all the rest, one must always try
to distribute to them what is properly theirs and to compare what belongs
to each, given their nearness in kinship and their virtue or usefulness.
Now, such a comparison involving members of the same family is easier,
whereas that involving people of different ones is more of a task. Nev-

35   ertheless, one must not, on this account, give up the attempt but rather
make the relevant distinctions, to the extent possible.

CHAPTER THREE

But there is perplexity also concerning whether or not to dissolve friend-
1165b   ships with those who do not remain the same as they were. Since people
are friends with a view to what is either useful or pleasant, is it nothing
strange to dissolve the friendship when these no longer exist? For they
used to be friends of these things; when they lose them, it is with good
reason that they no longer love each other. But someone could level an

5   accusation if another who was fond of him on account of utility or pleasure was pretending to be fond of him on account of his character. For as
we said in the beginning, most differences arise among friends when the
sort of friends they suppose themselves to be is not the same as the sort of
friends they actually are. When someone is deceived, then, and assumes
that he is loved on account of his character, even though the other person

10   does no such thing, he should blame himself. But when he is deceived by
the other who is pretending, it is just to accuse the deceiver, and more
so than to accuse those who are counterfeiting currency, insofar as the
wrongdoing concerns a more honorable thing.

But if someone accepts another person as good, and that other becomes corrupt or seems so, must he still love him? Or is it not possible, if

15   indeed not everything is lovable but only the good? For what is base is neither lovable nor ought to be loved, since one must not be a lover of what
is base or make oneself like a base person; and it has been said that "like is
friend to like." Must one, then, immediately dissolve the friendship? Or
should one not do this in every case, but only in the case of those whose
corruption is incurable? And as for those who can be set aright, one must
come to their aid, more as regards their character than their property,[5]

20   insofar as doing the former is better and belongs more to friendship.

5 · *Ousia*, one's "substance" or (in other contexts) "being."

But he who dissolves the friendship in such a circumstance would not be held to be doing anything strange, for he was not originally a friend to a person of this sort. When it is not possible to rehabilitate someone who has changed, he keeps his distance.

But if one person in the friendship should remain the same, while the other becomes more decent and in fact greatly surpasses him in virtue, ought the latter to treat the former as a friend? Or is this impossible? And where the difference is great, this impossibility becomes especially 25 clear—for example, in childhood friendships. For if the one person remains a child in his understanding, whereas the other should be a most excellent man in this very respect, how could they be friends if they neither are pleased by the same things nor delight in and are pained by the same things? For they will also not find these things in each other; but without such shared pleasures and pains, they would not be friends, since 30 it would be impossible for them to live together. But what concerns these matters was spoken of.

Must one, then, behave no differently toward the fellow than if he had never been a friend? One ought rather to remember the life lived together with him; and just as we suppose that a person ought to gratify friends more than foreigners, so too he must, on account of their prior friend- 35 ship, render something to those who were once friends, when its dissolution was not due to excessive corruption.

CHAPTER FOUR

But the marks of friendship in relation to those around us,[6] and by which 1166a friendships are defined, seem to have arisen from things pertaining to oneself. For people set down as a friend someone who wishes for and does things that are (or appear to be) good, for the other person's sake, or as someone who wishes for his friend, for the friend's own sake, to ex- 5 ist and to live. This is just what mothers feel toward their children, as do even those who have quarreled with their friends. Some also set down as a friend someone who goes through life together with another and who chooses the same things as he does, or who shares in sufferings and joys with his friend. This too happens especially in the case of mothers. It is by certain of these criteria that in fact people define friendship. 10

But each of these criteria is present in the decent person in relation to

6 · We follow the reading of one MS, though several MSS read: "in relation to friends."

himself (and in the rest insofar as they understand themselves to be decent; and it appears, just as has been said, that virtue and the serious person are the measure in each case). For this decent person is of like mind with himself and longs for the same things with his whole soul. Indeed,

15 he both wishes for the good things for himself, that is, the things that appear such to him, and he does them (since it belongs to a good person to work at what is good); and he does them for his own sake, since he acts for the sake of the thinking part of himself, which is in fact what each person seems to be. He also wishes that he himself live and be preserved, and especially that [part of himself] with which he is prudent. For existence is a

20 good to the serious person, and each wishes for the good things for himself. Yet no one chooses to possess every good by becoming another[7]— for even now,[8] the god possesses the good—but rather by being whatever sort he is;[9] and it would seem that it is the thinking part that each person is or is most of all. Such a person also wishes to go through life with himself, since he does so pleasantly: the memories of what he has done are

25 delightful, his hopes for the future are good, and such things are pleasant. His thought is also well supplied with objects of contemplation. He shares pains as well as pleasures with himself above all, since what is painful as well as pleasant is always the same for him and not different at different times. Hence he is without regret, so to speak. And so, because each

30 of these belongs to the decent person in relation to himself, and because he stands in relation to a friend as he does to himself—for the friend is another self—friendship too seems to be a certain one of these qualities and friends, those to whom these belong.

As to whether or not there is friendship in relation to oneself, let us

35 set this question aside for the present, though it would seem that there is friendship in this way insofar as [each person is] two or more, on the

7 · We follow here several modern editors and commentators, who bracket a difficult phrase in the Greek that would give the following translation: "no one chooses, by becoming another, that this one who has come into being possess every good."

8 · The phrase (*kai nun*) may be translated as "even now" in the sense of "now and always" or as "as it is," to indicate that what is wished for already exists (if not necessarily for the person who is wishing for it).

9 · Some commentators punctuate this last line differently to suggest that the remark regarding the god is not parenthetical and that what follows applies to the god. The line would then read: "for even now, the god possesses the good, but by being whatever sort he is ..."

basis of the points stated, and that the peak of friendship is like friend-   1166b
ship toward oneself.[10] Yet the qualities spoken of appear to belong also
to the many, even to those who are base. Insofar, then, as they are pleasing to themselves and assume themselves to be decent, do they share in
these qualities? For these certainly do not belong to any who are thor-   5
oughly base or act impiously; nor do they even appear to. They scarcely
belong even to base people, for they differ with themselves and desire
some things but wish for others—as do those who lack self-restraint, for
instead of what seems to be good to them, those lacking self-restraint
choose harmful pleasures. Others, in turn, through cowardice and idle-   10
ness, avoid doing what they otherwise suppose to be best for themselves.
And those who have done many terrible things and who hate themselves
on account of their corruption, even flee living and do away with themselves. Corrupt people seek to pass their days with others, but they flee
themselves because, when by themselves, they are reminded of many odi-   15
ous things and anticipate still others. When they are with others, however, they forget. And since they possess nothing lovable, they feel in no
way friendly toward themselves. Such people certainly do not share in either joys or sufferings with themselves, since their soul is torn by faction:
one part, on account of its corruption, feels pain when abstaining from   20
certain things, while another part feels pleasure; one part drags them here
and the other drags them there, as if tearing them asunder. And if it is not
possible for someone to feel pain and pleasure simultaneously, the base
person can, after a little while at least, be pained because he felt pleasure,
and he would wish that he had not gotten pleasure from those things. For
base people teem with regret.   25

The base person, therefore, does not appear to be disposed in a friendly
way even toward himself, because he possesses nothing lovable. If, therefore, to be thus disposed is to be extremely miserable, a person must flee

---

10 · The Greek term for the "peak" of friendship is *huperbolē*, which we elsewhere render as "excess"; in this context it can mean the extreme of friendship in its perfection
or preeminence, the "best and noblest friendship" (LSJ). It is not clear what "two or
more" refers to, and some commentators think that the sentence is an interpolation, in
which case the phrase may refer to the soul's having two or more parts. Other commentators, who reject the idea that the sentence is an interpolation, argue that the phrase
refers to the conditions of friendship that have just been discussed. It may mean simply
that any given person is "two or more," particularly in light of what follows concerning
those who are corrupt.

corruption with the utmost effort and attempt to be decent, since in this way he would both be disposed toward himself in a friendly way and become a friend to another.

CHAPTER FIVE

30   Goodwill resembles something friendly, but it is surely not friendship. For goodwill arises even in relation to those whom one does not know and without their being aware of it, whereas friendship does not. (These points too have been spoken of earlier.) But goodwill is not even friendly affection, because it is without intensity or longing, things that accompany friendly affection. And friendly affection goes together with the
35   habit of living together, whereas goodwill arises suddenly—for example,
1167a it even arises for competitors, since people come to have goodwill for competitors and share their intent, though they would do nothing to assist them. For, just as we said, people feel goodwill suddenly and so feel only superficial affection.

Goodwill seems, therefore, to be the beginning of friendship, just as the pleasure stemming from sight is the beginning of erotic love. For
5   no one falls in love who is not first pleased by someone's appearance—though a person who delights in another's looks does not for all that fall in love,[11] except whenever he also yearns for the person who is absent and desires his presence. In this way, therefore, it is not possible for those without goodwill to become friends, but those who have goodwill do not for all that feel friendly affection.[12] They merely wish for the good things
10   for those they feel goodwill toward but would do nothing actively to assist them, nor would they even be troubled over them. Hence by way of a metaphor, someone might claim that goodwill is friendship that lies idle; but if that goodwill is prolonged over time and carries over into the habit of living together, it becomes friendship—though not a friendship based on what is useful or pleasant, for goodwill does not arise in these cases.
15   For he who has received a benefaction renders goodwill in return for what he has received, thereby doing what is just. And he who wishes that another fare well because he hopes to be well taken care of by this person does not seem to have goodwill toward him but rather toward himself—

11 · The term for "falls in love" is *eran*, rather than *philein*. Aristotle also uses here the terms *idea* and *eidos* to designate outward "appearance" and "looks," terms that also have a technical meaning in the philosophy of Plato; see, e.g., 1.6.

12 · Here the verb is not *eran*, to love in the erotic sense, but *philein*, to love as a friend.

just as he is also not a friend if he attends to that other person because that person is of some utility to him. On the whole, goodwill arises on account of virtue and a certain decency, whenever someone appears to another as noble or courageous or some such thing, just as we said in the case of com-   20 petitors as well.

CHAPTER SIX

Like-mindedness[13] too appears to be a mark of friendship. Hence it is not merely likeness of opinion, since this could belong even to those who do not know one another. But people do not claim that those who are of like mind concerning just anything whatever are like-minded—for example,   25 those who are of like mind concerning the things in the heavens (for it is not a mark of friendship to be like-minded about these). Rather, they claim that cities are like-minded whenever people are of the same judgment concerning what is advantageous, choose the same things, and do what has been resolved in common.[14] It is about matters of action, therefore, that people agree, and in particular about what is of great import and admits of belonging to both parties or to all involved. For example,   30 cities are like-minded whenever it is resolved by all to make the political offices elective, or to conclude an alliance with the Lacedaimonians, or to have Pittacus rule when he too was willing to do so.[15] But when each person wishes that he himself rule, as do those in *The Phoenician Women*,[16] there is civil faction. For to be like-minded is not for each to have the same thing in mind, whatever it may be, but to have it in mind in the same   35 way—for example, when both the *demos* and the decent have it in mind   1167b for the best persons to rule—since in this way what they aim at comes to pass for everyone.

Like-mindedness, therefore, appears to be political friendship, just as it is also said to be, for it concerns advantageous things and those that

---

13 · Or, "oneness of mind" (*homonoia*); see also 8.1.

14 · Here and below, we translate the verb *dokein* in its political sense, "it is resolved," which was the form in which Athenian laws were given: "It is resolved by the people that …"

15 · Pittacus (ca. 640–569), considered one of the Seven Sages of Greece, was elected dictator of the Mytilineans during a period of civil strife. He governed for ten years, after which he voluntarily stepped down. Aristotle refers to the "elected" dictatorship or tyranny of Pittacus also at *Politics* 1285a35.

16 · Aristotle here refers to the brothers Eteocles and Polyneices in Euripides's play.

relate to life [or livelihood]. But this sort of like-mindedness is present
among the decent, since they are like-minded both with themselves and
with one another, being on the same page, so to speak (for with these
sorts of people the objects of their wishing remain constant and do not
ebb and flow like a violent strait); they also wish for what is just and what
is advantageous, and they aim at these also in common. But it is impossible for base people to be like-minded, except to a small degree, just as
it is impossible for them to be friends: their aim is to grasp for more of
what is beneficial to them; but when it comes to performing labors and
public services, they are deficient. While wishing for these beneficial
things for himself, each of them scrutinizes his neighbor and obstructs
him [from pursuing his wishes]. For when people do not keep watch over
the commons, it is destroyed. It results, then, that they fall into civil faction, compelling one another by force and not wishing to do what is just
themselves.

CHAPTER SEVEN

Those who perform a benefit seem to love those who receive this benefit
more than those who are the recipients of the benefit love those who perform it, and this is investigated on the supposition that it occurs contrary
to reason. So, to most people, it appears that one party owes a debt and
the other is owed. Just as in the case of loans, then, where debtors wish
that those whom they owe did not exist, whereas lenders even care for the
preservation of their debtors, so also those who perform a benefit wish for
the existence of those who receive it, on the grounds that they will, out of
gratitude, do favors for them in turn, whereas the recipients are not anx-
ious to repay the debt.

Now, perhaps Epicharmus[17] would assert that those who say these
things take a base view, though it seems characteristically human. For
most people are forgetful [of favors done them] and aim more at being
done some good than at doing it. The cause would seem to have more to
do with nature and is not at all similar to the case of lenders: lenders feel
no friendly affection toward their debtors but only wish that they be pre-

17 · A Greek comic poet from Megara, of the sixth and fifth centuries. The context of
the saying is lost, and thus it is not entirely clear whether the "base view" is a result of
external obstacles, such as being in a bad seat in the theater, or the result of base character.

served so they may recover the debt. Those who have done others some good, on the other hand, love and are fond of those who are the recipients of it, even if these recipients are not useful to them and might not be such later. This in fact happens with artisans, for every one of them is fond of his own work more than he would be loved by that work, should it come to have a soul; and this happens especially, perhaps, with poets, since they are exceedingly fond of their own poems and feel affection for them just as if they were their children. The case of those who perform a benefit is like this too, for what has received the benefit is their own work. Therefore, they are fond of this more than the work is of its maker. A cause of this is that to exist is for all people something choiceworthy and lovable, and we exist by means of activity (for this consists in living and acting). And in his activity, the maker of something somehow *is* the work; he therefore feels affection for the work because he feels affection also for his own existence. This is natural, for what he is in his capacity [or potential], the work reveals in his activity.[18] But at the same time too, what pertains to the action involved is noble for the benefactor, so that he delights in the person who is its object. For the recipient, however, there is nothing noble in the person doing it,[19] but, if anything, something advantageous, and this is less pleasant and lovable. What is pleasant is the activity of the present moment, the hope of what is to come, and the memory of what has been. Most pleasant, and lovable too, is what pertains to the activity. For him who has produced it, then, the work endures (for what is noble is long lasting), whereas for the recipient, its usefulness passes away. And the memory of noble things is pleasant, but that of useful ones is not at all or less so, though the reverse seems to be the case with anticipation.

Friendly affection also resembles an active "making," whereas being loved resembles a passive "undergoing," and loving and the qualities of friendship attend those who excel in the action [rather than those who undergo it]. And further, all feel more affection for what arises through painful labor, just as those who have themselves acquired their money feel more affection for it than do those who have inherited it, for example. Being done some good seems to be without toil, whereas doing someone some good is troublesome. For these reasons too, mothers love their chil-

35
1168a
5
10
15
20
25

18 · Aristotle uses terms here, for "capacity" (*dunamis*) and "activity" (*energeia*), that have a technical meaning in his *Metaphysics* (consider *Metaphysics* 1050a7), and are often translated as "potential" (or "potentiality") and "actuality."
19 · Or, perhaps, "there is nothing noble in the deed done."

dren more than do fathers, for giving birth is of greater pain to them, and they know to a greater degree that their children are their own. And this would seem to be the case also with those who are benefactors.

CHAPTER EIGHT

But there is perplexity too as to whether one ought to love oneself most or someone else. For people censure those who are fondest of themselves, and on the grounds that these sorts of people are in disgrace, they stigmatize them as "self-lovers." The base person is held to do everything for his own sake, and the more corrupt he is, the more he does this: people accuse him of doing nothing apart from what concerns his own [good].[20] The decent person, by contrast, acts on account of what is noble; and the better a person he is, the more he acts on account of what is noble and for the sake of a friend, while disregarding himself.

Yet the deeds are discordant with these arguments, and not unreasonably. For people assert that one ought to love one's best friend most and that one's best friend is someone who, when he wishes for good things for a person, does so for that person's sake, even if no one will know about it.[21] But these are qualities present especially in the person in relation to himself, and indeed so are all the other things by which a friend is defined, for it was said that all that characterizes friendship stems from oneself and extends toward others. Moreover, all the proverbs are of the same judgment, such as "one soul," "the things of friends are in common," "friendship [is] equality," and "the knee is closer to the shin."[22] For all these things would belong to the person in relation to himself most of all: he is most a friend to himself, and so one ought to love oneself most. Therefore, there is understandably perplexity as to which view it is right to follow, since both have credibility.

Perhaps, then, one ought to take apart such arguments and determine the extent to which, or in what respect, each is true. If, therefore,

20 · Burnet suggests that the meaning of this line is that the self-lover "does nothing of himself," that is, he does nothing that does not concern himself.

21 · There is an alternate reading: "one's best friend is someone who wishes for or someone for whom is wished the good things for that person's sake."

22 · For the first of these proverbs, see Euripides, *Orestes* 1045–46. The last is given in inverse form, "the knee is farther off from the shin," in Theocritus, *Idylls* 16.18. Aristotle has referred to the two other proverbs earlier: "the things of friends are in common" at 8.9 (1159b31) and "friendship is equality" at 8.5 (1157b36).

we should grasp how each side is speaking of the self-lover, perhaps the matter would become clear. Now, then, those who bring self-love into reproach call "self-lovers" those people who allot to themselves the greater share of money, honors, and bodily pleasures, for the many long for these things and are serious about them on the grounds that they are what is best; hence too such things are fought over. Those who grasp for more of these things gratify their desires and, in general, their passions and the nonrational part of their soul. Such is the character of the many. Hence too this familiar term of reproach has arisen from the case that mostly prevails, which is indeed base. Those who are self-lovers in this way, therefore, are justly reproached.

It is not unclear that the many are accustomed to saying that those who allot such things to themselves are self-lovers. For if someone should always take seriously that he himself do what is just, or moderate, or whatever else accords with the virtues, and, in general, if he should secure what is noble for himself, no one would say that he is a "self-lover" or even blame him. But this sort of person would seem to be *more* of a self-lover; at any rate, he allots to himself the noblest things and the greatest goods, he gratifies the most authoritative part of himself, and in all things he obeys this part. Just as a city and every other whole composed of parts seem to be their most authoritative part above all, so too does a human being.

A self-lover, therefore, is especially that person who is fond of and gratifies this authoritative part; and he is said to be either self-restrained or lacking in self-restraint depending on whether or not his intellect is in control,[23] on the grounds that this part *is* the person himself. And those deeds that are accompanied by reason seem above all to be the ones done by people themselves, and done voluntarily. It is not unclear, then, that each person is this [rational] part, or is this above all, and that the decent person is fond of this especially. Hence he especially would be a self-lover, but in reference to a different form of it than the one subject to reproach. In fact it differs as much from this latter form as living in accord with reason differs from living in accord with passion, as much as longing for what is noble differs from longing for what is held to be advantageous.

Now, all approve of and praise those who are preeminently serious about noble actions. And if all compete with a view to what is noble and

---

23 · Elsewhere translated as "overpowers," the verb Aristotle here uses (*kratein*) is linked to "self-restraint" (*enkrateia*).

exert themselves to the utmost to do what is noblest, then in common
10   there would be all the necessities and for each individually the greatest
goods, if in fact virtue is of such a character. As a result, the good person
ought to be a self-lover—he will both profit himself and benefit others
by doing noble things—but the corrupt person ought not to be—he will
harm both himself and his neighbors, since he follows his base passions.
15   In the case of the corrupt person, then, what he ought to do and what
he actually does are in discord, whereas the decent person does what he
ought to do. Every intellect chooses what is best for itself, and the decent person obeys the rule of his intellect. It is true, in the case of the serious person, that he does many things for the sake of both his friends and
20   his fatherland, and even dies for them if need be: he will give up money,
honors, and, in general, the goods that are fought over, thereby secur-
ing for himself what is noble. He would choose to feel pleasure intensely
for a short time over feeling it mildly for a long one, to live nobly for one
year over living in a haphazard way for many years, and to do one great
25   and noble action over many small ones. This is perhaps what happens to
those who die for others; they thus choose some great noble thing for
themselves. They would also give away money on the condition that their
friends will receive more of it, for while his friend gains money, he gains
what is noble. He assigns to himself, therefore, the greater good. And the
30   same holds regarding honors and political offices: he will give up all these
things to his friend, for doing so is noble for him and praiseworthy. Understandably, therefore, he is held to be serious, since instead of all the
things mentioned, he chooses what is noble. But it is possible too that he
forgo, in favor of his friend, the performance of certain [noble] actions,
and that it is nobler for him thus to become the cause of his friend's actions than to perform those actions himself. In all praiseworthy things,
35   therefore, the serious man manifestly allots more of the noble to himself.
1169b   In this way, then, one should be a self-lover, as has been said; but in the
way that the many are, one must not be.

CHAPTER NINE

There is a dispute too regarding the happy person, namely, whether or
not he will need friends. For people assert that those who are blessed and
5   self-sufficient have no need of friends, since the good things are theirs already; and that, since the happy are self-sufficient, they have no need of

anyone in addition, whereas a friend, since he is another [or different] self, provides only what someone is unable to provide on his own—hence the saying, "when a *daimon* gives well, what need of friends?"[24]

Yet it seems strange to allot all that is good to the happy person, but not to give him friends, which are held to be the greatest of the external goods. If it belongs more to a friend to do some good than to be done it; if it is also a mark of a good man and of virtue to be a benefactor; and if it is nobler to do good to friends than to strangers, then the serious person will need those who may be done some good. Hence too it is a matter for investigation whether one needs friends more in good fortunes than in bad, on the grounds that in bad fortunes a person needs those who will benefit him, in good fortunes those to whom he may do some good. It is perhaps strange also to make the blessed person solitary: no one would choose to have all good things by himself, since a human being is political and is disposed by nature to live with others. So this too belongs to the happy man, for he possesses the things good by nature, and it is clear that it is better to pass the days together with friends and decent people than with strangers and people at random. For the happy man, accordingly, there is need of friends.

What, then, are the first set of people speaking of, and in what respect are they stating what is true? Or is it that the many suppose those who are useful to them to be their friends? The blessed person, then, will have no need of these sorts of friends, since the good things belong to him. Nor, indeed, will he have need of those who are friends on account of what is pleasant, or he will only to a small degree: since his life is inherently pleasant, he has no need of pleasure from without. Yet because he has no need of these sorts of friends, he is held not to need friends at all. But this is perhaps not true. For it was said in the beginning that happiness is a certain activity, and an activity is clearly something that comes into being and not something that belongs to us like a sort of possession. But if being happy consists in living and being active; if the activity of a good person is serious and pleasant in itself, as was said in the beginning; if what is his own also falls among the pleasant things; and if we are better able to contemplate those near us than us ourselves, and their actions better than our own, then the actions of serious men who are friends are pleas-

24 · Euripides, *Orestes* 667. A daimon was, at least in Plato, a sort of divine being inhabiting the realm between human beings and gods; the Greek word for "happiness" (*eudaimonia*) suggests the condition of having a good daimon on one's side.

1170a   ant to those who are good (for both have things pleasant by nature).[25] So
the blessed person will need these sorts of friends, if indeed he chooses to
contemplate actions that are decent and his own, and such are the actions
of a good man who is a friend.

   People also suppose that the happy person ought to live pleasantly. For
5   a solitary person, then, life is hard, since it is not easy to be active continuously by oneself, whereas it is easier with others and in relation to others.
The activity of the happy person, then, will be more continuous, since it
is pleasant in itself, which it ought to be in the case of the blessed person.
The serious person, insofar as he is serious, delights in actions that accord
10   with virtue and is disgusted by those that stem from vice, just as the musical person is pleased by beautiful melodies and pained by bad ones. And a
certain training in virtue would arise from living with those who are
good, just as Theognis too asserts.[26]

   But to those examining this in a manner more bound up with nature,
the serious friend seems to be choiceworthy by nature to a serious man,
15   for what is good by nature was said to be good and pleasant in itself to
the serious person. They define living in the case of animals as a capacity
for perception, and in the case of human beings as a capacity for perception or thought.[27] But a capacity is traced back to its activity, and what
is authoritative resides in the activity. So it seems that living is, in the authoritative sense, perceiving or thinking. And living is among the things
20   in themselves good and pleasant: it is determinate, and the determinate
is a part of the nature of the good. What is good by nature is also good for
the decent person, on account of which it seems to all to be pleasant. But
one ought not to take the case of a corrupt and ruined life, or a life lived
25   in pain, for this sort of life is indeterminate, as are its attributes. (In the
remarks that follow, what concerns pains will be more apparent.)

   But if living is itself good and pleasant—as it seems to be also from the
fact that all people, and especially the decent and blessed, long for it, since

---

25 · Commentators debate the meaning of *both* in this sentence, some arguing that it
refers to the serious man and his friend, others (e.g., Aquinas) that it refers to the good
and the lovable, still others (e.g., Grant) that it refers to actions that are both decent
and one's own.

26 · Theognis of Megara was a poet of the latter half of the sixth century who wrote di-
dactic poems. At the end of the discussion of friendship (1172a13–14), Aristotle quotes
a line from the verse to which he here refers; see also 1179b6.

27 · Some commentators (e.g., Aquinas and Gauthier and Jolif) prefer "capacity for
perception *and* thought," but there is no basis in the extant MSS for this reading.

to such people life is most choiceworthy and their life is most blessed; and if he who sees perceives that he sees, he who hears that he hears, he who walks that he walks (and similarly in the other cases), then there is something that perceives that we are active. The result is that if we are perceiving something, we also perceive that we are perceiving; and if we are thinking, that we are thinking. And to perceive that we are perceiving or thinking is to perceive that we exist—for to exist is to perceive or to think. Moreover, perceiving that one lives belongs among the things pleasant in themselves, for life is by nature a good thing, and to perceive the good present in oneself is pleasant; and living is a choiceworthy thing, especially to those who are good, because existing is good for them and pleasant, for in simultaneously perceiving what is good in itself, they feel pleasure. And if as the serious man stands in relation to himself, so he stands also in relation to a friend (for a friend is another [or different] self)—then, just as one's own existence is choiceworthy to each, so also is the existence of a friend, or nearly so. Existing is, as we saw, a choiceworthy thing because of a person's perception that he is good, and this sort of perception is pleasant on its own account.

Accordingly, one ought to share in the friend's perception that he exists, and this would come to pass by living together and sharing in a community of speeches and thought—for this is what living together would seem to mean in the case of human beings, and not as with cattle, merely feeding in the same place. So if, for a blessed person, existing is something choiceworthy in itself, since it is good by nature and pleasant, and nearly so too is the existence of a friend, then the friend would be among the choiceworthy things. But that which is choiceworthy for him ought to be his, or else in this respect he will be in need. Accordingly, he who will be happy will need serious friends.

CHAPTER TEN

Must one, then, make as many friends as possible? Or—just as it seems to have been said appropriately concerning hospitality,[28] "be a host neither to many guests nor to none"[29]—will it be fitting in the case of friendship too, neither to be without a friend nor in turn to have excessively many friends? In the case of those who are friends with a view to their useful-

28 · See book 8, n. 18 on *xenia*.
29 · Hesiod, *Works and Days* 715.

ness, the point stated would seem very fitting indeed. For it is laborious
25   to serve many in return, and in fact a lifetime is not sufficient for doing
so. Having more friends than is sufficient for one's own life, accordingly,
is superfluous and an impediment to living nobly. There is then no need
of them. And with a view to pleasure too, a few friends are enough, just
as with seasoning in food.

But ought one to make friends with the greatest number of serious
30   human beings, or is there some measure here too of the quantity conducive to friendship, just as there is in a city? For a city could not come
into being from ten human beings, yet when there are ten times ten thousand, it is no longer a city either. The quantity in question is perhaps not
some single number but anything between certain limits. Accordingly,
1171a   the number of friends too is limited and is perhaps the greatest number
someone would be able to live together with (for living together seemed
to be most conducive to friendship). That it is impossible to live together
with many people and to distribute oneself among them is not unclear.
5   Further, one's friends ought to be friends with one another, if all are going to spend their days with one another, but it is a task for this to happen
among numerous people. It is also difficult for many to share intimately
in both joys and sufferings, for it is likely to happen that one shares simultaneously the pleasure of one person and the grief of another.

Perhaps, then, it is good not to seek to have as many friends as pos-
10   sible but only as many as are sufficient with a view to living together, for it
would seem that it is not even possible to have an intense friendship with
many. Hence in fact it is also not possible to be passionately in love with[30]
more than one person, since this love tends to be a certain extreme[31] of
friendship and is directed at one person. Intense friendship, accordingly,
is only with a few people. This also seems to be what is actually done:
many do not become friends in the manner of close comrades, and friend-
15   ships of that sort, celebrated in hymns, are spoken of in terms of pairs. But
those who have many friends and who fall in with everyone as familiars
seem to be friends with no one—except as fellow citizens—and people
in fact call these types "obsequious." Now, as fellow citizens, it is possible
to be a friend to many without being obsequious but as a truly decent person. Yet it is not possible to be a friend to many if the friendship is based

30 · That is, to love erotically (*eran*).
31 · Or, "peak": see also n. 10 above.

on virtue and on what the people involved are in themselves, and it is de- 20
sirable enough to find even a few people of this sort.

CHAPTER ELEVEN

Does one need friends more in good fortune than in misfortune? For
people seek them out in both cases: those who are unfortunate need aid,
and those who are fortunate need to live together with those whom they
will benefit, for they wish to do some good. This is more necessary, of
course, in misfortunes; and so, in these cases, a person needs those who 25
are useful to him. But friendship is nobler in good fortunes, and so it is
that people also seek out those who are decent: it is more choiceworthy
to benefit the decent and to pass through life with them. For the mere
presence of friends is pleasant in both good fortunes and misfortunes,
the pain of those who are suffering being alleviated when their friends 30
share it with them. Hence too someone might be perplexed as to whether
people share in the friend's suffering as though taking up a load, or, rather,
whether the presence of friends, which is pleasant, and the thought of
their sharing in the suffering lessen the pain. But whether it is for these
reasons, then, that those who suffer are relieved, or something else, let us
leave aside, though the point mentioned does appear to happen.

But the presence of friends seems to be some mixture of these consid- 35
erations. For seeing friends is itself pleasant, especially for someone suf- 1171b
fering misfortune, and is some aid in not feeling pain: both the sight of
a friend and his speech are apt to console one, if he is tactful, since he
knows his friend's character and in what ways he is pleased and pained.
Yet to perceive a friend's being pained by one's own misfortunes is itself 5
a painful thing, for all avoid being a cause of pain to their friends. Hence
those who are manly by nature are cautious of making friends share their
grief, and unless such a person is excessively insensitive to pain,[32] he does
not tolerate becoming a source of pain to them; on the whole, he does not
allow them to mourn with him, since he himself is not given to lament- 10

32 · The reading and translation of this phrase have occasioned much dispute among
commentators. We adopt the suggestion of Stewart that Aristotle refers here to the potentially callous side of a manly nature, but other suggestions include those of Burnet,
"even if he is not exceptionally resistant to pain," and Grant, "unless there be a great
balance of relief." Gauthier and Jolif accept an emendation, which would produce the
translation "unless he does not exceed in misfortune."

ing. But women, and men of such a sort, delight in laments, and they love their friends as friends who share in their suffering. But it is clear that one ought to imitate the better person in everything.

But the presence of friends in good fortunes involves both the pleasant conduct of one's life and the thought that they are pleased by the good things that are one's own. Hence it would seem that a person ought eagerly to invite friends to share his good fortunes (for it is a noble thing to be beneficent), but to hesitate to invite them to share his misfortunes, since one ought to share the bad things as little as possible. Hence the saying, "that I suffer misfortune is enough."[33] But a person must summon friends especially whenever they will be put to little trouble and yet will greatly benefit him. Conversely, it is perhaps fitting to go to a friend without having to be summoned, and indeed to go eagerly to those who are unfortunate. For it belongs to a friend to do some good, especially for those in need who do not expect it: for both parties, this is nobler and more pleasant. It is fitting also to cooperate eagerly in the friend's good fortunes—for even in these there is need of friends—but to be slow to request being done some good, since it is not noble to be eager to be benefited. Yet in refusing aid, one perhaps must beware of a reputation for unpleasantness, for sometimes this happens. The presence of friends, therefore, appears choiceworthy in all cases.

CHAPTER TWELVE

Just as, then, lovers are fondest of seeing [the beloved] and choose this sense perception more than the rest on the grounds that love exists and arises especially in reference to sight, so is it similarly the case for friends that living together is most choiceworthy? For friendship is a community, and as someone is disposed toward himself, so he is disposed also toward a friend. The perception a person has about himself—namely, that he exists—is choiceworthy, just as is the comparable perception about the friend as well. The activity of this perception arises in living together, and the friends understandably aim at this as a result. Whatever existing is for each, or whatever the goal is for the sake of which they choose living—it is while being engaged in this that they wish to conduct their lives with their friends. So it is that some drink together, others play at dice, still others exercise and hunt together or philosophize together, all and

33 · The source of this saying is unknown.

each passing their days together in whatever they are fondest of in life. For since they wish to live with their friends, they pursue and share in those things in which they suppose living together consists.[34]

Now, the friendship of base people is corrupt: they share in base things and, being unsteady, they come to be corrupt by becoming like one another. But the friendship of decent people is decent and is increased by their associating with one another. They also seem to become better by engaging in activity together and by correcting one another, for they take an imprint from one another of the qualities they find pleasing. Hence the saying "noble things from noble people."[35]

Let what concerns friendship, then, be stated up to this point. Following next in order would be to go through what concerns pleasure.

34 · There is some dispute among commentators about the final phrase, "in which they suppose living together consists," which Gauthier and Jolif argue is a pleonasm. Burnet, for example, argues for the reading of one MS: "they do these things and share in them as they are able." Gauthier and Jolif suggest: "they do these things and share in those in which they suppose life consists"; Bekker: "they do these things and share in those in which they suppose living well consists."

35 · Theognis, v. 35, referred to by Aristotle also in 9.9. The term translated as "noble" here is not *kalos* but *esthlos*, which can also mean (morally) "good."

Book 10

CHAPTER ONE

Perhaps it follows next, after these matters, to go through what concerns pleasure. For pleasure especially seems to be closely bound up with the genus [of human beings]—hence people educate the young by steering them by means of pleasure and pain. And with a view to the virtue of character, the greatest consideration seems to be delighting in what one ought and hating what one ought, since these extend throughout life as a whole, having a weight and capacity that bear on virtue as well as the happy life. For people choose the pleasant things but avoid the painful.

It would seem that what concerns such matters ought least of all to be passed by, especially since they admit of much dispute. For some say that pleasure is the good, others that pleasure is, to the contrary, an altogether base thing—some of these latter perhaps because they have been persuaded that pleasure is such in fact, others because they suppose it to be better with a view to our life to declare that pleasure is among the base things, even if it is not. For the many, they suppose, tend toward it and are in fact enslaved to pleasure. Hence one ought to lead them toward its contrary, since in this way they might arrive at the middle.

But this may not be nobly stated. For arguments concerning matters of passions and actions carry less conviction than do the relevant deeds. Whenever, then, such arguments are discordant with what is perceived, they are treated with contempt and undermine the truth. Should someone who blames pleasure ever be seen aiming at it, he is held to incline toward it, because he holds *every* pleasure to be good. For the drawing of precise distinctions does not belong to the many. It is the true arguments, then, that seem most useful, not only with a view to knowledge but also with a view to life. For since true arguments are in harmony with the deeds, they carry conviction; hence they prompt those who understand them to live in accord with them.

But enough about such things. Let us proceed to what has been said about pleasure.

CHAPTER TWO

Now, Eudoxus[1] thought that the good was pleasure, because he saw that all things aim at it—things both rational and nonrational—and that, in all cases, what is choiceworthy is what is fitting,[2] and what is especially choiceworthy, most excellent. So the fact that all are borne toward the same thing reveals, he thought, that this is what is best for all (for each discovers what is good for itself, just as it does also its nourishment); and what is good for all and what all things aim at is the good.

His arguments carried conviction more because of the virtue of his character than on their own account, for he seemed to be moderate to a distinguished degree. Indeed, he seemed to say these things, not because he was a friend of pleasure, but rather because he thought that such was the case in truth.

He also thought the matter no less apparent from the contrary consideration: pain by itself is something that all avoid, as indeed its contrary is similarly choiceworthy. What is especially choiceworthy is that which we choose neither on account of nor for the sake of something else, and pleasure is agreed to be of this character. For, on the grounds that pleasure is by itself choiceworthy, nobody asks for the sake of what someone feels pleasure. Moreover, adding pleasure to any good whatever—for example, to acting justly and being moderate—makes that good thing more choiceworthy, whereas the good is increased only by itself.

This latter argument, at any rate, does seem to affirm that pleasure is among the good things—but not that it is so more than any other good. For every good thing, when accompanied by another good, is more choiceworthy than when taken on its own. Indeed, by this sort of argument, Plato too establishes, by way of refutation, that the good is not pleasure: the pleasant life is more choiceworthy with prudence than without it; and if the mixture of prudence and pleasure is superior to plea-

1 · Eudoxus was a philosopher from Cnidos (ca. 390–340), best known for his studies in geometry and astronomy.
2 · *To epieikes*, elsewhere translated as "decency," "equity" or "the equitable."

sure alone, pleasure is not the good, for the good does not become more choiceworthy through the addition of anything to it.[3] And it is clear that anything that does become more choiceworthy, when accompanied by one of the things good in themselves, would not be the good either. What thing, then, is of this sort, a thing in which we too may share? For it is some such thing that is being sought.

Those who hold the opposed view, that a good is not what all things aim at, make no sense. For what is held by all to be the case is what we assert to be so, and one who denies this conviction will hardly speak in a manner apt to produce greater conviction. For if it is only beings devoid of intelligence that strive for pleasures, what they say would make some sense; but if intelligent ones do too, how would they make any sense? And perhaps even in the base [animals], there is something naturally good that is superior to[4] them and that aims at the good proper to them.

As for what concerns the contrary of pleasure, it does not seem to be stated nobly either. For they deny that if pain is bad, pleasure is therefore good: one bad thing, they say, can be opposed to another bad thing, and both can be opposed to something that is neither good nor bad. In these respects they do not speak badly—and yet they do not grasp the truth, at least not in the cases mentioned. For if both pleasure and pain were bad, we ought also to avoid both; if both were neither good nor bad, we ought to avoid neither, or avoid each alike.[5] But as things stand, people[6] manifestly avoid pain, on the grounds that it is bad, and choose pleasure, on the grounds that it is good; and so in this way each is in fact opposed to the other.

CHAPTER THREE

And again, if pleasure is not a quality, it does not on this account fail to be among the good things. For virtuous activities are not qualities either, nor is happiness [, and yet they are clearly good].

3 · Consider Plato, *Philebus* 20e–22e, 60a and following.

4 · Or, perhaps, "stronger than" (*kreitton*).

5 · The last clause attempts to translate a single adverb (*homoiōs*); it might also mean: "or avoid and choose them both alike."

6 · Literally, "they": Aristotle may still have in mind the critics of Eudoxus, though he frequently uses verbs in the third person plural to speak of people in general.

People also say that the good is limited[7] but pleasure unlimited,[8] because it admits of degrees, the more and the less. Now, if they make this
judgment as a result of their experience of feeling pleasure, the same will
hold also for justice and the other virtues, with reference to which people
plainly assert that some are of such-and-such a quality and act[9] in accord   20
with the virtues to a greater or lesser degree: there are those who are more
just and courageous than others, and it is possible both to act justly and to
be moderate to a greater or lesser degree. But if they make this judgment
by recourse to the pleasures, they may fail to state the cause of this—if
some pleasures are unmixed, others mixed.[10] And what prevents the case
of pleasure from being like that of health, which, although it is limited,
admits of degrees, the more and the less? For the proportion that consti-   25
tutes health is not the same in all people, nor is some one proportion always present in the same person. Rather, even when it slackens, the proportion remains present up to a certain point and varies in degree, more
and less. What concerns pleasure also admits of being of such a kind.

In positing that the good is also complete,[11] whereas motions and processes of coming-into-being are incomplete, they attempt to affirm that
pleasure is a motion and a process of coming-into-being. But even their   30
statement that pleasure is a motion does not seem a noble one; for quickness
and slowness seem to be properties of every motion—if not of motion in
itself (for example, the motion of the cosmos), then relative to something

7 · Or, "defined," "definite," "determinate" (*hōristhai*), here and throughout this section.
8 · Or, "undefined," "indefinite," "indeterminate" (*aoriston*), here and throughout this
section.
9 · The verb *act* does not appear in the MSS but is a modern emendation, accepted by
Bywater; the whole phrase "and act in accord with the virtues" may be an extraneous
gloss meant to explain the phrase translated as "with reference to which."
10 · In addition to having a variant reading, the text here is quite compressed, even for
Aristotle, and admits of different interpretations. For example, some scholars maintain
that the final clause of the sentence states Aristotle's own account of the possible cause
of the unlimited or indefinite character of (some) pleasures (Apostle); others, that it
expresses a reason why the would-be critics of pleasure fail to state the cause of the supposed unlimitedness of pleasure—because they fail to take into account the distinction between mixed and unmixed pleasures (Irwin); still others, that the clause repeats
a premise held by the critics themselves, one that further complicates their own position (e.g., Aquinas, Stewart, Gauthier and Jolif).
11 · Or, "perfect" (*teleion*).

else. But neither quickness nor slowness belongs to pleasure. For it is possible to enter quickly into the state of feeling pleasure, just as it is possible
1173b   to become angry quickly; but it is not possible to feel a given pleasure
quickly, not even in relation to another person, as is the case with walking and growing and all things of that sort. It is possible, then, to undergo
a change in one's pleasure either quickly or slowly, but it is not possible
to undergo the activity pertaining to it quickly—I mean feeling the pleasure itself.

And how would pleasure be a process of coming-into-being? For, it
5   seems, not any chance thing comes into being out of any chance thing,
but rather that out of which a thing comes into being is that into which
it is dissolved—and pain should be the destruction of that thing whose
coming-into-being is pleasure.

They also say that pain is a deficiency in one's natural condition and
that pleasure is a replenishment [or restoration] of it. But these are things
experienced by the body. So if pleasure is a replenishment of our natural
10   condition, then that in which the replenishment occurs would also feel
the pleasure. This would therefore be the body. Yet this seems not to be
the case. And neither is the replenishment pleasure, therefore, although
someone would feel pleasure when the replenishment is taking place and
would be pained when being cut.[12] This opinion seems to have arisen
from the pains and pleasures associated with nourishment, for as people
15   become depleted and feel pain in anticipation, they feel pleasure at the
replenishment. But this does not happen in the case of all pleasures. For
the pleasures associated with learning are free of pain, and among the
pleasures related to sense perception, those of smell are free of pain too,
in addition to many sounds, sights, memories, and hopes. Of what, then,
20   will these be the coming-into-being? For no depletion has arisen of which
there could then be a replenishment.

And against those who adduce the most disgraceful of the pleasures

---

12 · Editors have questioned the reading of the MSS here and suggested different interpretations of and indeed alternatives to it. Some hold that Aristotle is referring to the
undergoing of a surgical operation, as the word (*temnomenos*) can mean (e.g., Burnet);
Gauthier and Jolif suggest that he means simply a cut resulting from a grievous accident
(referring also to Plato, *Timaeus* 64d and 65b). The point would be this: although the
body undergoes the replenishment or the cutting, it is not or not simply the body that
feels the resulting pleasure or pain but rather the person as a whole, body and soul. Still
other editors suggest emendations that would read in translation: "when he is undergoing emptying [depletion]."

[to prove that pleasure is not good], someone might say that these are not pleasures. For if they are pleasant to people in a bad condition, one should not suppose that they are in fact pleasant, except to such people, just as one should not suppose either that things that are healthful or sweet or bitter to sickly people—or again, things that appear white to   25 those with diseased eyes—are such in fact. Or someone might speak in this way: the pleasures are choiceworthy, but not when they arise from *those* things, at any rate—just as being wealthy is choiceworthy, but not by betraying someone, and so is being healthy, but not by eating just anything whatever. Or [someone might say]: the pleasures differ in form.[13] For the pleasures arising from noble things are different from those arising from what is shameful; and it is not possible to feel the pleasure as-   30 sociated with what is just for someone who is not just or to feel the pleasure of what is musical for someone unmusical, and similarly with the rest as well.

Moreover, that the friend is different from the flatterer seems to make it apparent that pleasure is not good or that it differs in form from what is good. For the friend seems to keep our company with a view to what is good, the flatterer with a view to pleasure; and as the latter is blamed, so people praise the former, on the grounds that each is keeping company   1174a with a view to different things. And nobody would choose to live out his life with the intelligence of a child, even if he should take pleasure to the greatest possible extent in things that children enjoy; nor would anyone choose to delight in doing something utterly shameful, even if he should   5 never feel any pain thereby. We would also take seriously many things, even if they should bring us no pleasure—for example, seeing, remembering, knowing, possessing the virtues. And if pleasures necessarily follow from these, that makes no difference at all: we would choose them even if we were to receive no pleasure from them.

That pleasure is not the good,[14] then, and not every pleasure choiceworthy, seems to be clear, as is also that there are some pleasures choice-   10 worthy in themselves that differ from others in form or in the things that give rise to them.

Let this be an adequate statement, then, of what is said about pleasure and pain.

13 · *Eidos*: see the glossary.
14 · Gauthier and Jolif argue for the deletion of the article accompanying the word *good*, a reading supported by some MSS: "That pleasure is (a) good, then, and not every pleasure ..."

CHAPTER FOUR

But what or what sort of a thing pleasure is would become more manifest to those who take it up from the beginning.

15   For the act of seeing seems to be complete at any given moment: seeing is not deficient in anything that could subsequently come into being so as to complete its form. And pleasure too seems to be a thing of this sort, for it is something whole; no one could at a given moment experience a pleasure whose form will be completed, provided the pleasure lasts longer. Hence pleasure is not a motion either. For every motion occurs
20   in time and is bound up with some end—for example, the building of a house[15]—and is complete when it accomplishes what it is aiming at, either in the whole of the time in question or at that moment [of completion]. But all motions, considered in their parts and at any moment, are incomplete and differ in form from the whole and from one another: the putting together of the stones is different from the fluting of the pillar,
25   and these are different from the construction of the temple. In fact, the construction of the temple is complete (for it lacks nothing with a view to the task proposed), but the construction of the foundation and of the triglyph[16] are incomplete, for each is but a part. They differ, then, in form, and it is not possible to find a motion that is complete in its form at any given moment, but, if ever, only in the whole time involved.

    Similar is the case of walking and the rest of the motions. For if loco-
30   motion is motion from somewhere to somewhere, there are differences in point of form belonging to locomotion too: flying, walking, jumping, and things of that sort. And not only is this the case, but there are differences in point of form even in walking itself: the places one starts from and heads toward are not the same in the case of the whole racecourse and one of its parts, or in this or that part of it, nor is traversing this line here
1174b   the same as traversing that one there. For not only does one cross over a line, but a line that is also in a given place, this line being in a different

15 · We read, with Burnet and against the MSS, "the building of a house" (*oikodomia*) rather than "the art of house-building" (*oikodomikē*), on the grounds that "the MS. reading ... is due to the following *kai* ['and'] which has disappeared from all the MSS. but [one]. We do not want the art here, but the process" (Burnet).

16 · A term from Doric architecture, the triglyph was a "three-grooved tablet placed at equal distances along the frieze" (LSJ, s.v.)—a decorative detail, in short, that would presumably be among the last stages of construction, as distinguished from the foundation.

place from that one. What concerns motion has been spoken of precisely elsewhere,[17] but it does seem that it is not complete at any given moment; rather, there are many incomplete motions that also differ in form, if in fact the points from which and toward which one moves constitute the form of the motion. But of pleasure the form is complete at any given moment. It is clear, then, that pleasure and motion would be different from each other, pleasure being something that is both a whole and complete.

This would seem to be the case also from the fact that it is not possible to be in motion except over time, whereas it is possible so to feel pleasure, for what resides in the "right now" in the case of pleasure is something whole. And from these considerations, it is clear too that when people say that pleasure is motion or a process of coming-into-being, they do not speak nobly. For these motions or processes are not spoken of in the case of all things, but only in the case of things that are parts and not wholes: there is no coming-into-being of the act of seeing, of a mathematical point, or of a numerical unit, and of none of these is there any motion or coming-into-being. So neither is there in the case of pleasure, for it is something whole.

Every sense perception is active in relation to the thing perceived, and it is active in a complete way when it is in a good condition with a view to the noblest of the things subject to sense perception (for such especially seems to be complete activity; and let it make no difference whether one says that the perception itself is active or that in which it resides is so). In each particular case,[18] then, that activity is best that belongs to what is in the best condition with a view to the most excellent of the things falling under its purview; and this would be what is most complete and most pleasant. For in the case of every sense perception (and similarly also with thinking and contemplation), there exists a corresponding pleasure; but the most complete perception is most pleasant, and the most complete perception is the one belonging to what is in a good condition and directed toward what is most serious among the things in its purview.

Pleasure also completes the relevant activity. But pleasure does not complete it in the same manner as do the thing perceived and sense per-

17 · See, e.g., *Physics*, book 3.

18 · The reading of the MSS, defended by Gauthier and Jolif. Most modern editors follow a reading—erroneously attributed to pseudo-Alexander of Aphrodisias, according to Gauthier and Jolif—that would read in translation: "As regards each sense perception, then..."

ception when they are of serious worth, just as health and the physician are
not in similar ways the cause of one's being healthy either. But that pleasure arises in the case of each sense perception is clear (for we assert that
things seen and things heard are pleasant); it is clear too that this is especially so whenever the perception is most excellent and is active in relation
to something of the same sort. When both the thing perceived and that
which perceives are of this most excellent sort, there will always be pleasure—when, that is, something that will act as well as something that will
be acted on are present. And pleasure completes the activity, not in the
manner of a characteristic that is already inherent in it, but as a certain end
that supervenes on it—as, for example, the bloom of youth supervenes on
those in the prime of life. For so long, then, as both the intelligible or perceptible thing and that which forms a judgment or contemplates are such
as they ought to be, there will be pleasure in the activity. For when both
that which is acted on and that which acts remain what they are and have
the same relation to each other, the same thing naturally arises.

How is it, then, that no one feels pleasure continuously? Or does one
grow weary? For nothing characteristically human has the capacity to
engage in continuous activity. Pleasure too, then, does not arise continuously, since it follows the activity. And some things, because they are
novel, do give delight, but later on they do not do so as much, and for the
same reason. For at first our thinking is roused and active to the utmost
degree regarding them—as is the case with sight, when people stare at
something—but subsequently the activity involved is not of such intensity but has instead become relaxed. Hence the pleasure involved too is
dimmed.

But someone might suppose that all strive for pleasure, because all also
aim at being alive. Living is a certain activity, and each engages in an activity concerned with and by means of those things he is especially fond
of—the musical person, for example, engages, by means of hearing, in an
activity concerned with melodies; the lover of learning engages, by means
of thinking, in an activity concerned with the objects of contemplation;
and so on with each of the rest. Pleasure also completes the activities, as
indeed it does in being alive, which people long for. It is reasonable, then,
that they aim also at pleasure, since it completes for each what it is to be
alive, which is a choiceworthy thing.

As to whether we choose to live on account of the pleasure involved or
choose the pleasure on account of our being alive, let that be dismissed at
present. For these things appear to be yoked together and not to admit

of separation: without activity, pleasure does not arise, and pleasure completes every activity.

CHAPTER FIVE

So it is that pleasures seem to differ in form from one another as well. For we suppose that things different in form are completed by different things: so it appears with natural things and those made by art—for example, animals, trees, a drawing, a statue, a house, and a utensil. In a similar way too, activities different in form are completed by things different in form: the activities bound up with thinking differ from those related to sense perceptions, and they themselves differ from one another in point of form. So too, then, do the pleasures that complete them.

    This would be apparent also from the fact that each pleasure is closely bound up with the activity that it completes, for the pleasure proper to the activity helps increase it: those who engage in an activity with pleasure judge each particular better and are more precise about it. For example, those who delight in practicing geometry become skilled geometers and grasp each particular better, and in the same way, lovers of music, lovers of house building, and each of the rest advance their respective work because they delight in it. The pleasures help increase the activities, and things that help increase something are proper to it; but when things differ in form, what is proper to them also differs in form.

    This would be still more apparent from the fact that given activities are impeded by the pleasures arising from other activities: those who love the aulos are incapable of paying attention to speeches if they overhear someone playing the aulos, because they take greater delight in the art of aulos playing than they do in the activity before them. The pleasure deriving from the art of aulos playing, then, spoils the activity concerned with speech. A similar thing happens also in other cases, whenever someone is simultaneously engaged in two activities. For the more pleasant activity dislodges the less pleasant one; and if it differs greatly in point of pleasure, it does this all the more, such that one ceases to be engaged in the other activity at all. Hence when we take intense delight in anything whatever, we hardly do anything else; and when the satisfaction we receive from some things is mild, we turn to other things—for example, those who eat sweets in the theaters do so especially when the actors are poor. But since the pleasure proper to the activities adds precision to them and makes them longer lasting and better, whereas alien pleasures ruin them, it is clear that there is a great difference between the two kinds of pleasure. For the alien pleasures pretty much do what in fact the pains belonging to the activities do: the pains belonging to the activities spoil the activities. For example, if writing is unpleasant and indeed painful to someone, or doing calculations, then he does not write or do calculations because the activity is painful. As regards a given activity, then, the contrary thing results from the pleasures or pains proper to it; and those are proper to it that arise from the activity itself, whereas the alien pleasures, as has been said, accomplish something comparable to the relevant pain: they spoil the activity, albeit not in the same way.

Moreover, since the activities differ in point of decency and baseness, and some are choiceworthy, others to be avoided, and still others are neither the one nor the other, the pleasures involved too are similar. For in the case of each activity, there is a pleasure proper to it: the pleasure proper to a serious activity, then, is decent; that to a base one, corrupt. For desires too are praised when they are for noble things, but when for shameful things, they are blamed. But the pleasures residing in the activities themselves are to a greater degree proper to them than are the longings [from which the activities in question arise]; for the longings involved are distinct from the activities both in time and by nature, whereas the pleasures are closely akin to the activities and are in fact so indistinct from them that there is a dispute whether the activity and the pleasure are one and the same. And yet it does not seem, at any rate, that pleasure is thinking or sense perception—that would be strange—but because they are not separate, they appear to some people to be the same. Just as there are different activities, then, so too are there different pleasures. Sight differs from[19] touch in point of purity, and hearing and smell from taste. So the pleasures involved too differ in a similar way, the pleasures of thinking differing from those of the senses—in fact, each of these latter differs from one another as well.

It seems too that there is a pleasure proper to each animal, as there is also a work, for the pleasure accords with the activity. This too would be apparent to someone who contemplates each case: the pleasures belonging to a horse, a dog, and a human being are each different, just as Heraclitus[20] asserts that donkeys would choose rubbish over gold, for to don-

19 · The verb (*diapherein*) can also mean "is superior to."

20 · Heraclitus of Ephesus was among the most prominent of the pre-Socratic philosophers, perhaps best known for his doctrine of the *logos* at work in the cosmos. The line here quoted or paraphrased appears as B9 in Diels-Kranz, *Die Fragmente der Vorsokratiker*.

keys nourishment is more pleasant than gold. The pleasures, then, that belong to things differing in form, themselves differ in form, and it is reasonable that the pleasures belonging to the same things do not differ. But the pleasures do vary to no small degree in the case of human beings, at any rate: the same things cause delight to some and pain to others, and things painful to and hated by some are pleasant to and loved by others. This happens even in the case of sweets: the same things are not held to be sweet by the feverish person and by the healthy one, nor is the same thing held to be warm by a sickly person and by one in good condition, as happens similarly also in other cases. But in *all* such circumstances, what appears to a serious person seems to be the case in fact; and if this is nobly stated, as indeed it seems to be, and [if] virtue and the good human being, insofar as he is good, are the measure of each thing, then the pleasures that appear to him would be pleasures in fact, and the pleasant things would be those in which he delights. But if what is disagreeable to him appears pleasant to someone else, that is nothing to be wondered at. For there are many things that cause the ruin and maiming of human beings; and although these are not pleasant in fact, they are pleasant to such people when they are in such a condition. As for the pleasures agreed to be shameful, then, it is clear that one ought not to assert that they are pleasures, except to those who have been ruined.

And as for those pleasures held to be decent, which ones, or ones of what sort, ought to be said to belong to a human being? Or is this clear on the basis of the activities? For it is these that the pleasures follow. Whether, then, the activities belonging to a complete and blessed man are one or more than one, the pleasures that complete these activities could be said to be, in an authoritative sense, the pleasures belonging to a human being, the remaining pleasures being such only in a secondary or much lesser sense, as are also the respective activities.

CHAPTER SIX

Since what pertains to the virtues has been stated, as well as what pertains to friendships and pleasures, it remains to go through in outline what concerns happiness, since we posit it as the end of human concerns.

Now, for those who take up again the points stated previously, the argument would be briefer. We said, then, that happiness is not a characteristic, for in that case it could be present even to someone asleep throughout his life, living the life of plants, and to someone undergoing the

1176b   greatest misfortunes. So if these consequences are not satisfactory, and
one must instead posit happiness as residing in a certain activity, just as
was said in what came before, and [if] some activities are necessary and
choiceworthy for the sake of other things, whereas other activities are
choiceworthy in themselves, then it is clear that one must posit happiness
5   as being among the activities that are choiceworthy in themselves and not
for the sake of something else. For happiness is in need of nothing but is
self-sufficient. And the activities choiceworthy in themselves are those
from which nothing beyond the activity itself is sought; the actions that
accord with virtue are held to be of this sort, for the doing of noble and
serious things is held to be among the things choiceworthy for their own
sake.

But so too are the pleasures of play. For people do not choose these
10   pleasures for the sake of other things: people are more harmed than benefited by them, when they neglect their bodies and property in pursuit of
them. And the majority²¹ of those deemed to be happy seek refuge in such
ways of conducting one's life.²² Thus those who have a certain charming
dexterity in these ways are well regarded by tyrants, for they make them-
15   selves pleasant in the very things the tyrants are after, and such are the
sort of people tyrants need. These pleasures, then, seem apt to produce
happiness, because those in positions of authority devote their leisure to
them. But perhaps people of that sort are not proof of anything. For neither virtue nor intellect, from which the serious activities arise, consists
20   in the exercise of authority. And if they, who have not tasted pure and lib-
eral²³ pleasure, seek refuge in the bodily pleasures, one should not on this
account suppose that such pleasures are the more choiceworthy ones. For
children too suppose that what is honored among themselves is most excellent. So it is reasonable that, just as different things appear honorable
to children and to men, so also do they to base human beings and to the
25   decent. As has been said many times, then, what is honorable and pleas-

---

21 · Literally "the many" (*hoi polloi*), with its negative connotation.

22 · This phrase attempts to capture the meaning of a single Greek word, *diagōgē* (here
in the plural). Its most literal meaning is "carrying through," and it can have the extended sense of the conduct of one's life, its way or course, hence also a manner of passing time. We decline to use the traditional translation "pastime," chiefly because this
term suggests slight or trivial activities, whereas Aristotle proves to have in mind quite
weighty, and perhaps the weightiest, activities for a human being. See also 4.8 n. 36.

23 · That is, a pleasure marked by freedom or belonging to a free human being
(*eleuththerios*).

ant to the serious person is such in fact; for each person, the most choice-worthy activity is the one that accords with the characteristic proper to him, and for the serious person, of course, that activity is the one that accords with virtue.

Happiness, therefore, does not consist in play. For it would be strange if our end were play, and if we exert ourselves and suffer bad things through the *whole* of life for the sake of playing. For we choose *everything*, so to speak, for the sake of something else—except happiness, for it is an end. And it appears that to be serious and to labor for the sake of play is foolish and excessively childish.[24]

But to play so that one may be serious, as Anacharsis[25] has it, seems to be correct. For play resembles relaxation, and because people are incapable of laboring continuously, they need relaxation. Relaxation, then, is not an end: it arises for the sake of activity. The happy life also seems to accord with virtue, and this is the life that seems to be accompanied by seriousness but not to consist in play. We also say that serious things are better than those that prompt laughter and are accompanied by play, and that the activity of the better part or better human being is always the more serious one. The activity of what is better, moreover, is superior and so more apt to produce happiness. And any chance person whatever, even a slave, might enjoy the bodily pleasures no less than the best person enjoys them; but nobody attributes to a slave a share in happiness if he does not attribute to him a share even in [his own] life. For happiness does not consist in such ways of conducting one's life, but rather in the activities that accord with virtue, just as was said previously as well.

CHAPTER SEVEN

If happiness is an activity in accord with virtue, it is reasonable that it would accord with the most excellent virtue, and this would be the virtue belonging to what is best. So whether this is the intellect or something else that seems naturally to rule, to command, and to possess intelligence concerning what is noble and divine, whether it itself is in fact divine or the most divine of the things in us—the activity of this, in accord with

---

24 · The adjective *childish* (*paidikon*) is closely related to the word for "play" (*paidia*); both have as their root the word for "child" (*pais*).

25 · Among the traditional Seven Wise Men of Greece, Anacharsis was a Scythian royal prince of the sixth century who made his way to Athens and there befriended Solon; see Herodotus 4.76–77, as well as Diogenes Laertius 1.101–2.

the virtue proper to it, would be complete happiness. And that this activity is contemplative has been said.

This would also seem to be in agreement both with the points made before and with the truth. For this activity is the most excellent[26] one: the intellect is the most excellent of the things in us, and the things with which the intellect is concerned are the most excellent of the things that can be known. Further, this activity is most continuous, for we are more able to contemplate continuously than we are to do anything else whatever. We also suppose that pleasure must be mixed into happiness, and the most pleasant of the activities in accord with virtue is agreed to be the one that pertains to wisdom. At any rate, philosophy seems to have pleasures that are wondrous in purity and stability, and it is reasonable that those who are knowers conduct their lives[27] with greater pleasure than do those who are seeking knowledge.

The self-sufficiency spoken of would pertain especially to the contemplative life. For a wise person, a just person, and all the others are in need of the necessities of life. But when these necessities have been supplied sufficiently, the just person needs others toward whom and with whom he will act justly, and similarly with the moderate person, the courageous, and each of the rest. The wise person, by contrast, is capable of contemplating even when by himself, and the wiser he is, the more capable of doing so he will be. And though it is perhaps better to have those with whom he may work, nonetheless he is most self-sufficient. In addition, contemplation alone would seem to be cherished for its own sake, for nothing comes into being from it apart from the contemplating itself; but from matters bound up with action, we gain something, to a greater or lesser degree, apart from the action itself.

Happiness, moreover, is held to reside in leisure;[28] for we are occupied or are without leisure[29] so that we may be at leisure, and we wage war so that we may be at peace. The activity of the virtues bound up with action, then, consists in matters of either politics or war, and the actions concerned with these seem to be without leisure. This is altogether the case with warlike actions. For nobody chooses to wage war, or even prepares

---

26 · Or, perhaps, "strongest," "most powerful" (*kratistē*).

27 · *Diagōgē*: see n. 22 above.

28 · So we consistently translate the Greek term *scholē*, from which is derived the term *school*—where one goes when free of the necessity of work.

29 · This phrase translates a single verb whose root, *ascholia*, is the contrary of *scholē* (leisure: see the preceding note).

for war, for the sake of waging war: a person would seem to be altogether   10
bloodthirsty if he should make enemies of his friends so that battles and
slaughter might arise. But the activity of the politician too is without leisure: quite apart from the politician's engaging as a fellow citizen in political life, his activity looks to gain positions of authority and political
office, or at any rate to gain the happiness of the politician himself and
of his fellow citizens, which is something other than the political activity   15
and which we clearly seek out on the grounds that this happiness is something other than that activity.

So, if, among the virtuous actions, the political and warlike ones are
preeminent in nobility and greatness, they are nonetheless without leisure and aim at some end—that is, they are not choiceworthy for their
own sake—whereas the activity of the intellect, because it is contempla-   20
tive, seems to be superior[30] in seriousness, to aim at no end apart from itself, and to have a pleasure proper to it (and this pleasure helps increase
the activity), such that what is self-sufficient, characterized by leisure, and
not subject to weariness to the extent possible for a human being, and all
else that falls to the lot of the blessed person, manifestly accord with this
contemplative activity—if all this is so, then this activity would constitute the complete happiness of a human being. Provided, that is, that it   25
goes together with a complete span of life, for there is nothing incomplete
in what belongs to happiness.

But a life of this sort would exceed what is human. For it is not insofar as he is a human being that a person will live in this way, but insofar as
there is something divine present in him. And this divine thing is as far
superior to the composite thing as its activity is superior to the activity
that accords with the other virtue.[31] So if the intellect is something di-   30
vine in comparison to the human being, the life in accord with this intellect would also be divine in comparison to the human life. But one ought
not—as some recommend—to think only about human things because
one is a human being, nor only about mortal things because one is mortal, but rather to make oneself immortal, insofar as that is possible, and to
do all that bears on living in accord with what is the most excellent of the
things in oneself. For although that most excellent thing is small in bulk,   1178a
in point of its capacity and the honor due it, it prevails by far over everything. And it would seem that each person even *is* this thing, if in fact it

30 · Or, "to differ" (see n. 19 above).
31 · That is, moral virtue. The phrase appears again in the first sentence of 10.8.

is what is authoritative and better in him. It would be strange, then, if a
person should not choose the life that is his own but rather that of something else. What was said before fits well now too, for what is proper to
each is by nature most excellent and most pleasant for each. And so for a
human being, this is the life that accords with the intellect, if in fact this
especially *is* a human being. This life, therefore, is also the happiest.

CHAPTER EIGHT

But the life that accords with the other virtue is happy in a secondary way.
For the activities that accord with such virtue are characteristically human
ones: it is in relation to one another that we do what is just, courageous,
and whatever else accords with the virtues, by observing closely what is
fitting for each person in contracts, necessary services, and all manner
of actions, as well as in matters involving the passions; and all these concerns appear to be characteristically human. Some of them seem even to
result from the body, and the virtue of one's character seems in many respects to be closely bound up with the passions. Prudence too is yoked to
the virtue of one's character, and it to prudence, if in fact the principles of
prudence are in accord with the moral virtues and what is correct in the
moral virtues accords with prudence. These virtues, moreover, in being
knit together with the passions, would be concerned with what is composite in us, and the virtues of this composite thing are characteristically
human. Such too, then, would be both the life and the happiness that accord with these virtues. But the happiness belonging to the intellect is
separate. Let this much be said about it. For to be very precise about it is
a greater task than what has been proposed.

Contemplative virtue would also seem to need little in the way of external equipment, or less than does moral virtue. Let the need of both for
the necessities even be equal (though in fact the politician labors more
over what concerns the body and other things of that sort); in this respect
there might be only a small difference between them, but when it comes
to the activities, [moral and contemplative,] there will be a great difference. For the liberal person will need money with a view to doing what
is liberal; the just person too will need money, for making repayments
(a person's wishes are immanifest, and even the unjust pretend that they
wish to act justly); the courageous person will need power, if in fact he
will bring to completion anything that accords with his virtue; and the

moderate person will need license [to act immoderately]. For how else will he, or any of the others, be manifest?

It is also disputed whether the more authoritative thing in virtue is the choice or the actions involved, on the grounds that virtue is found in both things—indeed it is clear that the complete thing would be found in both. But with a view to actions, much is needed; and the greater and nobler the actions are, the more things would be needed. But for the person who contemplates, there is no need of any of these sorts of things, at least not with a view to the activity itself; rather, such things are even impediments, as it were, when it comes to contemplation. But insofar as he is a human being and lives together with a number of others, he chooses to do what accords with virtue. He will need such things, then, with a view to living as a human being.[32]

But that complete happiness is a certain contemplative activity would appear also from this: we have supposed that the gods especially are blessed and happy—but what sort of actions ought we to assign to them? Just acts? Or will they appear laughable as they make contracts, return deposits, and do anything else of that sort? But what about courageous acts?[33] Do the gods endure frightening things and run risks, because doing so is noble? Or liberal acts? But to whom will they give? And it is strange if they too will have legal currency or something of that sort. And what would their moderate acts be? Or is the praise, "they do not have base desires," a crude one? All that pertains to actions would appear, to those who go through it, petty and unworthy of gods.

Yet all people have supposed that the gods are alive, at least, and therefore active; for surely one does not suppose that they are asleep, like Endymion.[34] So for one who is living, when his acting is taken away, and, still more, his making something, what remains except contemplation? As a result, the activity of the god, because it is superior in blessedness, would be contemplative. And so in the case of the human activities, the one that is most akin to this would be most characterized by happiness. A sign of this is also that the rest of the animals do not share in happiness,

---

32 · This phrase translates a rare verb (*anthrōpeuesthai*), which may suggest living as a *mere* human being (as distinguished from a god or divine being, for example).

33 · Many editors posit a lacuna in the text here and have proposed various emendations or suggestions. We translate the reading of the MSS.

34 · A handsome king beloved by the Moon, Endymion is said to have slept everlastingly, perhaps as a result of Zeus's gift.

25 because they are completely deprived of such an activity. For to the gods, life as a whole is blessed; but to human beings, it is blessed to the extent that something resembling such an activity is available. But none of the other animals are happy, since they in no way share in contemplation. 30 Happiness, then, is also coextensive with contemplation; and the more contemplation is possible for some, the happier they are—not accidentally but in reference to the contemplation. For it is in itself honorable. As a result, happiness would be a certain contemplation.

But for one who is a human being, external prosperity will also be needed. For human nature is not self-sufficient with a view to contem-35 plating, but the body must be healthy as well, and nourishment and other 1179a such kinds of care must be available. Yet one ought not to suppose, at least, that he who will be happy will need many or great things, just because it is not possible to be blessed in the absence of external goods. For self-sufficiency does not consist in excess, and neither does action, it being possible even for someone who does not rule land and sea to do 5 noble things. In fact, someone would be able to act in accord with virtue even from measured means. (It is possible to see this plainly, since private persons seem to act decently no less than those in positions of power—rather, they seem to do so even more.) And having this much available is sufficient, for the happy life will belong to someone who is active in accord with virtue.

10 Solon too, in like fashion, nobly affirmed who the happy are, when he said that they are those with a measured amount of external equipment who have done the noblest things, as he supposed,[35] and lived moderately: it is possible for those who possess a measured amount of equipment to do what they ought. It also seems that Anaxagoras too did not suppose the happy person to be rich or politically powerful, when he said 15 that it would be nothing to wonder at if such a person [who is neither rich nor powerful] should appear strange to the many. For they judge by external things, because they perceive only these. So the opinions of the wise seem to be in agreement with the arguments adduced.

Such considerations, then, foster a certain conviction, but the truth in matters of action is judged from deeds and from life, for it is in these 20 that the authoritative criterion resides. One ought, then, to examine what has been stated previously by applying it to deeds and to life; and should

---

35 · The phrase translated "as he supposed" is questioned by some editors but is present in the MSS. For Solon's sentiment, consider Herodotus 1.30.

what has been said be in harmony with the deeds, one ought to accept it, but should it be discordant, one ought to take the remarks to be mere speeches.

But the person who is active in accord with the intellect, who cares for this and is in the best condition regarding it, also seems to be dearest to the gods.[36] For if there is a certain care for human things on the part of gods, as in fact there is held to be, it would also be reasonable for gods to delight in what is best and most akin to them—this would be the intellect—and to benefit in return those who cherish this above all and honor it, on the grounds that these latter are caring for what is dear to gods as well as acting correctly and nobly. And that all these things are available to the wise person especially is not unclear. He is dearest to the gods, therefore, and it is likely that this same person is also happiest. As a result, in this way too, the wise person would be especially happy.[37]

CHAPTER NINE

If, then, what concerns these matters, as well as the virtues and, further, what concerns friendship and pleasure, have been sufficiently stated in outline, ought one to suppose that the task chosen has reached its end? Or, just as is said to be the case, is the end in matters of action not contemplating each thing in turn and understanding it, but rather doing them? And so is knowing about virtue not sufficient either, but is it necessary instead to try to possess the virtues and make use of them, unless we become good in some other way?

Now, if speeches were sufficient by themselves to make people decent, they would justly fetch "much pay and great," as Theognis has it, and one ought to pay it. But as things stand, speeches appear to have the capacity to exhort and to incite those youths who are free,[38] and to make someone who has a wellborn character and is truly a lover of what is noble receptive to virtue. Yet speeches are incapable of exhorting the many to nobility and goodness.[39] For the many are not naturally obedient to the gover-

25

30

35

1179b

5

10

36 · The phrase "dearest to the gods" translates a single Greek word (*theophilestatos*), one that leaves it unclear whether there is one or more than one god in question. "Dearest to the divine" is another possible translation.
37 · Or, perhaps, "in this way too, the wise person especially would be happy."
38 · Or, "liberal" (*eleutherious*).
39 · Or, "to gentlemanliness" (*kalokagathia*).

nance supplied by a sense of shame[40] but rather to that supplied by fear, and they do not naturally abstain from base things because of the shamefulness involved but do so rather because of the vengeance that may be exacted. For since they live by passion, they pursue the pleasures that are theirs, together with what gives rise to those pleasures, and they avoid the opposing pains. As for what is noble and truly pleasant, they do not have even a conception of it, never having tasted it. So what speech might reform people of this sort? For it is not possible, or not easy, to alter by means of speech what has long been enforced by their characters.[41] But perhaps it is a desirable enough thing if, when everything through which we are held to become decent is present, we might have some share in virtue.

Some suppose that people become good by nature, others that we do so by habit, still others that it is through teaching. Now, as for what comes from nature, it is clear that it is not present due to us; rather, it is present through certain divine causes for those who are truly fortunate. And speech and teaching never prevail in *all* cases, but the soul of the student[42] must be prepared beforehand by means of habits so as to feel delight and hatred in a noble way, just as must land that will nourish the seed. For someone who lives according to passion would not listen to a speech meant to deter him, nor in turn would he even comprehend it. And how is it possible to change a person of that sort by means of persuasion? In general, passion seems to yield not to speech but to force. So there must first be an underlying character that is somehow appropriate for virtue, one that feels affection for the noble and disgust at the shameful.

To obtain from childhood a correct upbringing with a view to virtue is difficult for someone not reared under laws of the requisite sort. For living in a moderate and controlled way is not pleasant to the many, especially the young. Hence by means of laws, the rearing and the regular practices involved must have already been put into the proper order, for once these become habitual, they will not be painful. And, in like manner, it is not sufficient if people when they are young attain the correct rearing and care; rather, once they have reached adulthood, they must also make

40 · The word here is *aidōs* (reverence, awe, respect) rather than *to aischron* (the shameful, ugly), which appears in the next clause.

41 · Another reading, based on an ancient translation, is possible: "enforced by their habits" (*ethesi* rather than *ēthesi* of the MSS).

42 · Literally, "the listener" or "auditor."

a practice of these things and be thus habituated. And for these matters—
indeed, for life as a whole more generally—we would need laws. For the
many obey the governance of necessity more than of speech [*logos*], and   5
of punishments more than of what is noble. Hence some suppose that
legislators ought to encourage people in the direction of virtue and exhort them to act for the sake of what is noble, on the grounds that those
who have been decently guided beforehand by means of habits will be
obedient, whereas for those who are disobedient and too deficient in nature, they suppose the legislators ought to inflict on them various chas-
tisements as well as acts of vengeance; the wholly incurable, they ought
to banish. For, they suppose, someone who lives decently, with a view   10
to what is noble, will be obedient to the governance of speech [*logos*],
whereas someone who strives for pleasure in a base manner must be chastised by means of pain, like a beast of burden. Hence they also assert that
there ought to be such pains as are especially opposed to the pleasures a
person is fond of. If, then, as was said, the person who will be good must   15
be reared and habituated in a noble manner, and subsequently live his life
in this way, with decent regular practices, and do nothing base, whether
involuntary or voluntary, then these things will come to pass for those
people who live in accord with a certain intellect and a correct ordering,
provided such an ordering has strength behind it.

Now, the command characteristic of a father does not have such
strength or compulsion behind it, nor indeed does the command of one   20
man in general, unless he is a king or something of that sort. But the law
does have a compulsory power, it being speech [*logos*] that proceeds from
a certain prudence and intellect. And though people hate those other human beings who oppose their impulses, even if the latter are correct to
do so, the law is not invidious when it orders what is equitable.[43] Only in
the city of the Lacedaimonians[44] (or it together with a few others) is the   25
legislator held to have taken care for the rearing and the regular practices
of the citizens. But in most cities, what concerns such things has been utterly neglected, and each lives as he wishes, "laying down the sacred law
for children and wife" in the manner of the Cyclops.[45] The most excellent

43 · Or, "decent" or "fitting" (*to epieikes*).
44 · That is, the Spartans. For Aristotle's harsh assessment of the Spartan rearing and
education, consider *Politics* 2.9.
45 · See Homer, *Odyssey* 9.112–15, as well as Aristotle, *Politics* 1252b22–23. The root
of the participle used here is *themis*, not the usual *nomos*, and can suggest divine or
sacred law.

30   thing, then, is for the public[46] care to be correct.[47] But when cities utterly
      neglect the public care, it would seem appropriate for each individual to
      contribute to the virtue of his own offspring and friends, or at least to
      make the choice to do so.[48]

      Yet, on the basis of what has been said, it would seem that a person is
      more able to do this by becoming a skilled legislator. For it is clear that the
35   public care comes into being through laws, and decent care through seri-
1180b ous laws. But whether these laws are written or unwritten would seem to
      make no difference, nor whether, through them, one person or many will
      be educated, just as it does not matter either in the case of music or gym-
      nastic and the other practices. For just as it is the laws and customs[49] that
5   hold sway in cities, so also it is the speeches and habits of the father that do
      so in households—and these latter to a greater degree, on account of the
      kinship and the benefactions involved, for from the outset household
      members feel affection for one another and are readily obedient by nature.

      Further, individual educations also differ from public ones, just as the
      case of medicine suggests. For rest and fasting are generally advantageous
10   to someone with a fever but perhaps are not to a given person. And the
      skilled boxer, in like manner, does not prescribe to all the same kind of
      fighting. So it might seem that what pertains to each person would be
      more precise when there is a private care involved, for in that case each at-
      tains what is suitable to a greater degree. But a doctor, gymnastic trainer,
      and anyone else would best exercise care in the individual case by know-
15   ing what applies to all and what applies to this or that sort of person (for
      the sciences are said to be, and are, concerned with what is common or
      universal). Of course, nothing prevents someone—even someone with-
      out scientific knowledge—from exercising a noble care for a certain in-
      dividual, provided that he has, through experience, contemplated in a
      precise way the results for each, just as even some people seem to be their
      own best doctors but are unable to aid another at all.
20   Yet it might seem to be no less necessary, at least for someone who

---

46 · Or, "common" (koinē).

47 · The MSS have at this point a phrase that would produce the translation: "and capable of doing this," but most editors, following Bywater, delete it and move it to the
place indicated in n. 48 below.

48 · Bywater suggests moving the phrase indicated in the preceding note such that the
latter half of the present sentence would read: "to the virtue of his own children and
friends, and to be capable of doing this, or at least to make the choice to do so."

49 · Or, "characters" (ēthē), as elsewhere. See the glossary as well as book 1, n.14.

wishes to become skilled in a given art or in contemplation, to proceed to the universal and become acquainted also with this to the extent possible. For it was said that it is with the universal that the sciences are concerned. And perhaps it is necessary also for someone who wishes to make others better through his care, whether these be many or few, to attempt to become a skilled legislator, if it should be through laws that we become   25 good. For it does not belong to just any chance person to inculcate a noble disposition in whoever happens to be set before him; rather, if this belongs to anyone, it would be to a knower, just as with medicine and whatever else has a certain care and prudence associated with it.

Is it necessary, then, after this, to examine from what source, or how, someone might become a skilled legislator? Or is it (just as in other cases)   30 from those who are skilled politicians? For this legislative skill seemed to be a part of the political art.[50] Or does the same thing appear not to pertain in the case of the political art as in that of the other sciences and capacities? For in those others, it is manifestly the same people who both transmit the capacities in question and are engaged in the corresponding activities—for example, doctors and painters. But as for matters of   35 politics, the Sophists profess to teach them, but none of them undertake   1181a political actions. It is rather those who are engaged in political life who would seem to do this by dint of a certain capacity and experience rather than by means of thought. For they manifestly neither write nor speak about such things (though perhaps this would be nobler than making speeches for courtrooms and popular assemblies), nor in turn have they   5 made their own sons or any of their friends into skilled politicians. But this would be a reasonable thing to do, if they were so able. For there is nothing better they could have bequeathed to the cities, nor is there anything they would have chosen to possess for themselves—or indeed for those dearest to them—other than a capacity of this kind. Yet experience   10 does seem to make no small contribution, for otherwise people would not have become skilled politicians through living together with others in a political community.[51] Hence those who aim at knowing about the political art seem to need experience in addition.

50 · The reference would seem to be to 1141b24–26 and context.
51 · The final phrase here includes a word (*sunētheia*) that can mean living (or herding) together, or the habits formed from such communal living. The same word appears also at a crucial place in Plato's *Meno* (76d8), a dialogue that bears directly on Aristotle's argument here concerning the special—if limited—skill of the politician: consider Plato, *Meno* 96d and following.

But those Sophists who profess to teach the political art appear to be very far indeed from doing so. For in general they do not even know what sort of a thing it is or with what sorts of things it is concerned: otherwise they would not have posited it as being the same thing as rhetoric—or even inferior to it—nor would they have supposed that legislating is an easy thing, by simply putting together a collection of the well-regarded laws. For, they suppose, it is easy to pick out the best laws—as if the selection were not a part of the comprehension involved and as if the correct judging of them were not the greatest thing, just as it is in music. For those with the relevant experience in each thing judge the works involved correctly, and they comprehend through what or how the works are brought to completion and what sorts of things are in harmony with what. For the inexperienced, it is desirable enough if it does not entirely escape their notice whether the work has been done well or badly, as in the art of painting. But laws are like works [or products] of the political art. How, then, would someone become a skilled legislator as a result of those collections of well-regarded laws or judge the best laws? For physicians too do not appear to come into being as a result of reading treatises, although such treatises attempt, at least, to state not only the treatments but also, by distinguishing the various characteristics of each patient, how physicians might cure each of them, and how they ought to treat them. These treatises do seem profitable to those with experience, but they are useless to those without the requisite knowledge. Perhaps, then, collections of both laws and regimes would be of good use to those who are capable of contemplating and judging what is noble (or its contrary) and what sorts of things accord with which circumstances. As for those without this characteristic who go through such collections, it would not fall to them to judge nobly (unless they should happen to do so accidentally), though they might perhaps thereby gain greater comprehension of these matters.

Now, since those prior to us have left undiscovered what pertains to legislation, it is perhaps better for us to investigate it ourselves—and indeed what concerns the regime in general—so that, to the extent of our capacity, the philosophy concerning human affairs might be completed. First, then, let us attempt to go over whatever partial point has been nobly stated by our predecessors; and then, on the basis of the regimes collected together, let us attempt to contemplate what sorts of things preserve and destroy cities, what sorts of things do so for each of the regimes, and through what causes some regimes are governed nobly, others contrary way. For once these matters have been contemplated, we 1 perhaps understand better also what sort of regime is best, and how regime has been ordered, and by making use of what laws and customs.

With this as our beginning, then, let us speak.

INTERPRETIVE ESSAY

Of the great many texts devoted to identifying the best way of life for a human being, the *Nicomachean Ethics* of Aristotle is surely the most famous and influential—if we exclude those writings that, looking beyond what unaided human reason can discover, claim to offer divinely inspired or revealed knowledge: "He has told you, O mortal, what is good; and what does the Lord require of you but to do justice, and to love kindness, and to walk humbly with your God?" (Micah 6:8). Aristotle never heard this injunction, of course, but had he done so, he could not have agreed with it, let alone simply deferred to it. For Aristotle raises as a question central to his "philosophy of human affairs" (1181b15) what the highest human good is, and in so doing he declines to rely on the authoritative answer given him by gods and human beings living together—that is, by the political community (consider 1145a10–11, 1094a24–28). Similarly, he fails to include humility (or sense of shame) as one of the eleven moral virtues (4.9), to say nothing now of his exclusion from that list of piety itself. As for justice and kindness, these certainly do find counterparts in Aristotle's account of the good life (consider books 5 and 4.5–6). But because he finally ranks contemplative virtue above every moral virtue, justice and kindness cannot occupy, in the life that Aristotle argues is best, the place they hold in the life commanded by the Hebrew Bible, by the God of Abraham.

Still, this disagreement between Aristotle and the Bible is unlikely to constitute an insurmountable obstacle in our time to taking the *Nicomachean Ethics* seriously. A greater problem, perhaps, is posed by the lasting effects of the victory of a new "philosophy of human affairs" that began with a vigorous assault on precisely Aristotle: "scarce anything can be more absurdly said in natural Philosophy, than that which now is called

Aristotle's *Metaphysics*, nor more repugnant to Government, than much of that he hath said in his *Politics*; nor more ignorantly, than a great part of his *Ethics*" (Thomas Hobbes, *Leviathan*, chap. 46). For, contrary to Aristotle, Hobbes argues that we are not by nature political animals; that there is no justice grounded in nature; and that there is no highest human good accessible to human reason, on the grounds that the very words "good, evil, and contemptible are ever used with relation to the person that useth them, there being nothing simply and absolutely so, nor any common rule of good and evil to be taken from the nature of the objects themselves" (ibid., chap. 6). And yet the new approach to political philosophy that Hobbes helped inaugurate has recently lost much of its appeal and all of its evident, not to say self-evident, character. We are witnesses to the collapse of confidence in human reason, the very tool intended by Hobbes and his great successors to enlighten the world and so to liberate us from both the rule of "unpleasing priests" and the darkness of "vain philosophy." This collapse is surely disorienting. But it also permits us to raise as a serious question—as a question whose answer cannot be known in advance—whether the modern assault on premodern philosophy was in every respect justified or whether it remains possible for human reason to discover, in the manner indicated by Aristotle, the good or indeed best way of life.

In support of this possibility, we offer the following remarks on Aristotle's *Nicomachean Ethics*. Our intention is not to provide a comprehensive commentary but to clarify some of the central arguments of this work and our interpretive approach to them. To this end, we begin with a fairly close exploration of book 1 and, in particular, of Aristotle's manner of writing—a discussion that is fundamental to our understanding of how to read his *Ethics*. We then take up the other books with a view to outlining key themes or questions: the problem of happiness; the relation to happiness of moral virtue, and especially the two "complete" virtues, greatness of soul and justice; the status of prudence; the role of friendship in the good life; the possibility that pleasure is the human good; and the final ranking of moral and contemplative virtue.

ON HAPPINESS AND THE HUMAN GOOD (BOOK I)

The first book of the *Nicomachean Ethics* demands our attention in part because it serves as the proper introduction to Aristotle's "philosophy of human affairs" as a whole, which he sets forth in the *Ethics* and *Politics* taken together. But book 1 is of crucial importance above all on account of its analysis of our longing for happiness or of what precisely we mean when we give voice to our deepest hope for happiness, together with the remarkable way in which it sketches the serious alternatives available to us.

Book 1 is noteworthy also for the great caution Aristotle exercises there in accomplishing these tasks, a caution born of the sensitivity or delicacy characteristic of anyone who sees the significance of the difficulties at hand. Aristotle offers in book 1 an "official" and profoundly attractive solution to the problem of happiness—but a solution that is, as he knew it to be, finally inadequate to meet the challenge as he himself sets it out. This admittedly strange procedure can be defended on the following grounds: by offering an alluring but ultimately unsatisfactory answer to what proves to be *the* human problem, Aristotle at once satisfies those who accept this answer and encourages the unsatisfied to think through for themselves the difficulty in all its gravity. He thereby encourages these latter also to consider the principal alternatives to resolving the problem of happiness, alternatives that, however attractive, each have their shortcomings or costs.

Aristotle's Manner of Writing as Exemplified in Book 1

Our thesis implies that Aristotle's manner of writing is unusually complex and subtle. That Aristotle's procedure is marked by peculiarities, including everything from apparently needless repetition and digression to outright self-contradiction, is clear even from a glance at the text of book 1. On three occasions, for example, and at some length, Aristotle reminds us of the necessary limits to the precision to be demanded of the arguments in question (1094b11–27, 1095a30–1095b14, 1098a20–1098b8); he twice sketches the argument that all our actions and choices necessarily aim at some good, going so far as to indicate that he is repeating himself (1097a24 and context; consider also 1098a26 and context, which refers to 1094b11–25); and in little more than twenty pages, Aristotle offers three explicit digressions that stray apparently quite far from his stated purpose (consider 1095a14, 1095b14, 1097a15 and contexts). He also contradicts himself by stating, in 1.4, for example, that it is certain of "the many" (*hoi polloi*) who hold honor to be the human good we seek, only to maintain, in the next chapter, that it is "the refined" who do so (compare 1095a20–23 with 1095b22–23); he identifies as "strange" the idea that the dead can be happy, but subsequently accepts that very idea and adds to it that nothing can overturn their happiness (compare 1100a11–14 with, e.g., 1101b5–9); and, finally, he both asserts and denies that knowledge (*gnōsis*) of the good is essential to our lives, a matter of obviously great importance to his argument as a whole (compare 1094a22–24 with 1095a5–6).

These peculiarities could perhaps be dismissed as either textual glitches or even inadvertent lapses, were they not traceable to a cause or causes demanding their use—to a cause or causes justifying the manner of arguing they amount to. The most obvious cause in question is the authority of the political community. Immediately after sketching the necessity of there being some good in which all our strivings culminate and which thereby justifies them—as the bridle produced by the lowly art of bridle making is ultimately for the sake of victory in war, under the guidance of the general's art—Aristotle suggests that such a good "might be held" to belong to the "most authoritative and especially architectonic" science or power. And what "appears," at least, to be such a thing, to make clear to us *the* good, that is, "the human good," is the political art (*politikē*: 1094a18–28): even the general's expertise is subordinate to the art of politics. The political community, one might say, tries to answer with finality the question of the good life for a human being and hence of the best human type. Every community not on the verge of collapse teaches or habituates its members to accept the ordering of goods it holds to and embodies (consider, e.g., 1099b30–32).

Aristotle cannot specify "the human good" in question because the conception of it varies from community to community, a fact already indicative of a grave difficulty with every community's claim to have identified correctly *the* good. The most that Aristotle can do, and what he does do ostentatiously, is bow to the supreme authority of politics by repeating and so appearing to accept the premise on which all communities agree: to secure and preserve the good of the nation or city is "nobler and more divine" than to do so for the individual (1094b7–10; consider also 1097b8–11). The political community regards and wishes to have regarded as settled not only the specific character of the good life for its citizens—be it the life of commerce, piety, or martial courage, for example—but also the superiority of the good of the community to that of any private good.

In the present context, Aristotle stresses the extraordinary influence exercised by politics on knowledge or science (*epistēmē*): it is politics or the political art that "ordains what sciences there must be in cities and what kinds each person in turn must learn and up to what point.... Because [the political art] makes use of the remaining sciences and, further, because it legislates what one ought to do and what to abstain from, its end would encompass those of the others, with the result that this would be the human good" (1094a28–1094b7). And yet, since Aristotle's own inquiry into the human good is a necessary one, he in fact refuses to accept what the community wishes to be a definitive identification of "the human good"; his own inquiry too is "a sort of political" inquiry (1094b11), which is to say that it is in competition with the comparable efforts of the political community (consider also 1152b1–3). For example, Aristotle will later raise as an open question whether the virtue of the good citizen is ever the same as that of the good human being, and his answer to it—that the two coincide only in the case of one who shares in ruling in the best regime—implies that the virtue of the citizen in every existing regime falls short of human virtue simply (1130b26–29; *Politics* 1276b16–1277b32, 1278a40–1278b5 and context). Because of the awesome power of the political community, which he here both describes and defers to, Aristotle is compelled to exercise great caution in exploring the question of the human good, a caution that is most in evidence at the beginning of his inquiry.

It is not surprising, then, that the first of Aristotle's three accounts of the apparently necessary limits attending his inquiry immediately follows his declaration of the political character of that inquiry. These limits are largely (though not entirely) self-imposed (consider 1097a14 and 1101a21): each of the three accounts follows the raising of a "sensitive" issue and amounts to a retreat from it; the subject matter in question admits of greater clarity than Aristotle here chooses to admit. In the present context, Aristotle discourages his audience from pressing for precise arguments, on the grounds that "the noble things and the just things," which politics examines, admit of much dispute and variability such that they are held by some to exist by convention (*nomos*) alone rather than by nature; indeed, even the good things are strikingly variable: wealth and courage are sometimes good, sometimes ruinous. In the same spirit, Aristotle states that "the end is not knowledge but action" (1095a5–6), and although this might seem from the context to apply only to the young or immature, he will subsequently state in his own name that "we are conducting an examination, not so that we may know what virtue is, but so that we may become good" (1103b27–28): not knowledge but noble action is our goal, and since the means to inculcate the characteristic needed so to act is habituation rather than teaching, it seems possible that, to be good, we need little or no knowledge in the strict sense (consider also 1105b2–3).

These arguments are striking for several reasons. For example, in order to parry any expectation of precision in the present argument, Aristotle stresses the variability of things noble and just—a quality they share even with the good things—and alludes to the controversy concerning whether what is noble and just—as distinguished from what is good—exists merely by convention. But this very allusion can serve to remind us that the just things, at least, do admit of more precision than the merely conventional may allow: there is according to Aristotle the just by nature (5.7). What is more, Aristotle had indicated, earlier in book 1, the very great *importance* of knowledge of the good in order to live well: "with a view to our life, then, is not the knowledge of this good of great weight, and would we not, like archers possessing a target, better hit on what is needed?" (1094a22–24; consider also 1095a10–11). And when Aristotle turns in 1.7 to "repeat," for the third time, his argument concerning the limits imposed on him by his subject matter, he adds a wholly new consideration, according to which it is (also) the purpose of the inquiry—not, or not only, the subject matter—that determines the precision to be expected: the geometer and carpenter are equally concerned with a right angle, but given their different purposes, only the geometer need avail himself of precise knowledge of it. In principle, then, such knowledge is possible in mathematics. Are the matters dealt with in Aristotle's political philosophy too susceptible of such knowledge, if only for the equivalent of the "geometer" as distinguished from the "carpenter"?

Here the question of the character of Aristotle's primary audience arises, for as we have just seen, it bears directly on the precision that Aristotle will permit himself in the inquiry. He makes clear that that audience is made up of those who are no longer immature in character, because they have been subject to and hence shaped by the habituation needed to effect good rearing. In the second and therefore central of his statements concerning the limits of his inquiry, Aristotle indicates that such people will "listen" to things noble and just, or to political matters in general, "in an adequate manner," that is, they will accept the goodness of justice and nobility as self-evident, or they accept the "that" without needing the "why" in addition (1095b4–8). At the end of book 1, Aristotle indicates that this capacity to listen and obey—to one's father, for example (1103a3)—is rational only in a very loose sense; strictly speaking, it is a function of the irrational part of the soul that is characterized by desire and appetite. To put the point in more general terms, Aristotle's primary audience is made up of *spoudaioi*, of "serious" human beings, who as such accept as their starting point or principle the supreme goodness of moral virtue and hence of noble action. For them it is enough to yield to the habituation they have been subject to from early childhood and so to accept this principle. They need not inquire into the path to that principle but instead proceed from it as a given: to paraphrase Aristotle, the principle or principles of moral action are "known to them," but not "known simply," which amounts to saying that they do not, strictly speaking, know the *archai* at all (1095a30–1095b4). Since moral virtue is the product of habituation and not of teaching, the morally virtuous do not know in the strict sense the principles or starting points of moral virtue.

In this important respect, then, Aristotle's insistence on the imprecise character of his inquiry is fully justified, for he cannot make precise what is not known, to those by whom it is not known, without at the same time transforming their understanding of their principles and hence of themselves. And this means, in turn, that Aristotle must to some extent defer in his inquiry not only to the power of the political community but also to the consequences of that power, for the community instills in us deeply held opinions about the human good that we cannot rationally explain or defend because we do not know the matters with which they deal.

As this implies, Aristotle differs from his primary audience in at least one respect: he understands, as they do not, both the fact and the cause— the "that" and the "why"—of the limits attending their "knowledge." Hence he is able not only to make precise the necessity dictating a certain imprecision but even to go further. He occasionally indicates in book 1 the possibility of proceeding in the manner of a geometer, that is, as an observer ("contemplator") of the truth (1098a31–32): deference to the authority of others is indeed good, but "altogether best" is he who "himself understands all things" (1095b10–13, quoting Hesiod, *Works and Days* 293, 295–97). For the right kind of person, at least, "knowing about these things would be of great profit" (1095a10–11). It follows, then, that Aristotle's primary audience is not necessarily his sole audience, and his subsequent analyses must be read also in the light of this fact.

The Problem of Happiness

Aristotle's analysis of the problem of happiness unfolds gradually. He begins, in 1.4–5, with a survey of opinions concerning the chief of the goods bound up with action, the good aimed at by politics or the political art: even if most people agree that this good is "happiness," nonetheless there is a variety of views as to what might constitute it. More precisely, Aristotle speaks of three things, the possession of which could secure or constitute our happiness, namely, pleasure, wealth, and honor. To this he adds a list of three possible ways of life whose connection to the three goods indicated is not entirely clear: the life of pleasure, the political life, and the contemplative life. As for the life devoted to pleasure, Aristotle is extraordinarily harsh toward it: it is a life suitable only for fatted cattle. The harshness of this dismissal is indicative not only of the character of his primary audience, for whom a life led in pursuit of pleasure is beneath contempt because it obviously conflicts with what is noble and good (consider again 1095b4–6), but also of the preliminary character of this discussion. Even in book 1, Aristotle will to some extent rehabilitate pleasure—it is a necessary accompaniment of the life of one who loves moral virtue (1099a7–21)—and in books 7 and 10, he will subject pleasure to a subtle and lengthy analysis, in the course of which it is not always clear that he denies it pride of place (consider, e.g., 1153b25–26 and context).

By taking up honor next, Aristotle violates the order in which he had originally listed it but thereby makes it central (compare 1095a23 with 1095b22–1096a4 and context). The change is reasonable. For although honor seems to be the core of the political life, those who are serious about honor in fact want to be honored for their virtue; and in this way Aristotle is first permitted or compelled to discuss virtue, the subject of the great bulk of the *Nicomachean Ethics*. Most striking here is the firmness with which Aristotle denies that virtue can be *the* goal of our striving and hence equivalent to happiness: it is "incomplete," since one can possess virtue while asleep or inactive or while suffering the greatest misfortunes, and "no one would deem happy somebody living in this way, unless he were defending a thesis" (1095b30–1096a2). Although Aristotle now abruptly cuts off the discussion of virtue, he has made it clear enough that the practice of virtue in no way guarantees the happiness of the virtuous. And finally, having declined to speak at present about the contemplative or theoretical life, he briefly but powerfully dismisses the only life remaining, that of moneymaking, by arguing that money is always for the sake of something else and hence cannot be the end we seek.

By the end of 1.4–5, then, we reach a dead end. All the most popular opinions about happiness, however refined, lead nowhere; and if "the contemplative life" holds the key to happiness, Aristotle refuses to tell us as much. It might well seem, it is true, that he takes at least a step in this direction in the immediately following chapter (1.6), where he considers at length the view of certain unnamed friends—presumably the Platonists, if perhaps not Plato himself—according to which the (true) good, the *idea* of the good, is not "in" any one thing but separate from the several good things here and now and responsible for their goodness. In fact, the exploration of this sophisticated view has less to do with the contemplative life than it does with Aristotle's observation, made in 1.4, that when "the many" become aware of their own ignorance, they wonder at or admire those who speak over their heads in lofty terms: awareness of the elusive character of happiness renders us susceptible to fantastic doctrines like that of the Platonic ideas, which holds out the promise of our participating in a separate or "transcendent" and eternal world that is as such free of the limits marring this one. To say the least, in his critique of the *idea* of the good here, Aristotle throws cold water on any hope of this kind. He even adopts, in 1.6, the point of view that may be said to be the contrary of the one that probably guides "the many" in their attraction to the *idea* of the good: an eternal good would be no more good than a good lasting a day (1096b3–5).

Hence Aristotle begins again in 1.7. To do so, he explicitly repeats a line of argument from 1.1–2, according to which all arts aim at some good. But rather than state immediately, as a given, that "happiness" is the greatest good aimed at, Aristotle instead speaks of happiness only at the conclusion of a fairly lengthy, two-part argument (compare 1095a18 and context with 1097a15–1097b21, especially 1097a34 and 1097b15–16). The "repetition" of the earlier argument marks an advance over it inasmuch as Aristotle now explores the idea of happiness itself. He does so first by making explicit our guiding hope or supposition concerning it. "We say" that what is pursued for its own sake is more complete or perfect than what is pursued for the sake of something else, and, following out the logic of this, the most complete (or perfect) such good "is held" to be happiness above all. Moreover, "we suppose" that happiness is a state of self-sufficiency, a self-sufficiency so great that it "*by itself* renders life choiceworthy and in need of *nothing*" (1097b14–15, emphasis added). "So happiness appears to be something complete and self-sufficient, it being an end of our actions" (1097b20–21). Aristotle here makes explicit what we are content to leave mostly implicit or unstated but which guides our lives in fact: we suppose that by acting in certain ways, we can come to possess for ourselves a good that will truly complete us and so render us in need of "nothing" else. "Happiness," then, appears to be a kind of perfect self-sufficiency, for oneself and of course one's immediate family. The expression of this deepest hope or wish is a turning point in Aristotle's argument, and the rest of book 1 is a cautious exploration of this hope for happiness so understood.

In the immediate sequel, Aristotle further refines the idea of happiness by asking what the "work" proper to a human being must be, the completion of which will presumably be equivalent to happiness. And although the argument that follows culminates in the famous definition that the "work" of a human being is "an activity of soul in accord with virtue," Aristotle fails to identify precisely either the activity in question (consider 1099a30) or—the character of the virtue being dependent on the nature of the activity—the relevant virtue (consider 1098a17–18). This line of argument, then, is not as revealing as it is sometimes taken to be. Moreover, he adds immediately a demand or qualification that he will wrestle with for the remainder of book 1: a happy life must be also "a complete life. For one swallow does not make a spring, nor does one day. And in this way, one day or a short time does not make someone blessed and happy either" (1098a18–20). As becomes clear when he returns to this same criterion (1100a4–9), Aristotle here alludes to the problem of fortune or chance. Although he had spoken of chance in his account, in 1.5, of the impotence of virtue to secure our happiness in the face of "the greatest misfortunes," he now seems to have particularly in mind a premature death or the uncertain timing of the mortality attending us. The introduction of this problem prompts him to state his third account of the limits he will adhere to in his inquiry, in the manner of a carpenter (1098a20 and following).

The section 1.1–7 is devoted above all to fleshing out our convictions concerning happiness. The idea of happiness proves surprisingly hard to pin down, for almost everyone can agree that it is this that we most want, but no one seems able to state precisely what it might consist in. Aristotle's identification of the leading contenders in that respect (pleasure, honor, virtue, money), and his methodical rejection of each in turn (1.4–5), makes clear that none of these goods is sufficient by itself to be *the* good that we conceive of with the mind's eye, however vaguely, and hope to attain. The first five chapters of book 1 at once capture the experience of the elusiveness of happiness and begin, at least, to explain it. From 1.7, however, it appears that we have taken the meaning of "happiness" too much for granted, and Aristotle there equates happiness with a complete good that would render our lives self-sufficient and hence "in need of nothing."

The most promising path to such happiness now appears to be a certain "work" of the soul "in accord with virtue." In this way Aristotle reintroduces the connection between virtue and happiness, which he had apparently left behind after his blunt statement of the insufficiency of virtue in 1.5. That our dedication to virtue will form the core of the rest of book 1 is indication enough of the inadequacy of Aristotle's earlier account of virtue. And by introducing our desire for "a complete life," immediately after he has put virtue back on the table, Aristotle prompts us to consider the possibility that the dedication to virtue is connected with that desire. In fact, in the next section, Aristotle will confirm this possibility in the strongest terms: the dedication to virtue will be shown to hold out the promise of our attaining precisely "a complete life"; and "a complete life," in turn, proves to require not only a bulwark against chance but the overcoming of death itself. At all events, the movement of the argument in 1.1–7 as a whole suggests that an adequate analysis of happiness must begin from the concern for virtue—and not, for example, from the identification of happiness with pleasure, a view whose dismissal in 1.4–5 Aristotle saw to immediately.

Still, as important as the analysis of our hope for happiness and the continuing relevance of virtue surely are, Aristotle declines, as we have seen, to identify the virtuous "activity of soul" peculiar to human beings. What is more, his indication of the obstacles to fulfilling the promise held out by virtuous activity cannot be dismissed or forgotten: the virtuous too may be made wretched by misfortune, and they too are exposed to a premature death. How, then, can we secure for ourselves, not merely an ephemeral contentedness, but a happiness that is lasting and secure and complete—a happiness, in short, deserving of the name? In the next section, Aristotle will offer a solution to these difficulties.

The Problem of Happiness Solved?

The next four chapters (1.8–11) form a unit meant to treat the problem of happiness in general and that of chance or misfortune in particular. Aristotle first defends his official *logos* (happiness is "an activity of soul in accord with virtue") on the grounds that it is sanctioned by a range of august opinions linking happiness with (among other things) some sort of virtue. Moreover, happiness, which is attainable by engaging in "the best activities," will be best and most pleasant and noblest, and the active life of virtue will not fall short even in point of pleasure, to say nothing of its goodness and nobility (1099a7–21).

But none of this deals with the problem of chance, as Aristotle makes perfectly clear (consider 1099a31–1099b8). Accordingly, he turns, in 1.9, to consider how happiness may be acquired, including the extreme possibility that it is due finally to chance. Aristotle contends, to the contrary, that happiness is either a god-given thing or at least among the most divine things. He thus introduces, for the first time, the question of the existence of gods and their concern for our happiness, and he leaves open the possibility that happiness is not due to chance, because it is due to the intercession of gods. For now, Aristotle is content to argue on his own authority that happiness is, in addition to being available to many or most (1099b18–20), not at all due to chance, for "[t]o entrust the greatest and noblest thing to chance would be excessively discordant" (1099b24–25).

Yet Aristotle concludes 1.9 by repeating and even strengthening the demand that happiness include "a complete life" (1100a4–5; compare 1098a18), this time referring to the legendary sorrows of virtuous Priam. In this way he indicates that nothing he has said thus far deals adequately with the shadow cast on our happiness by chance. The deepest purpose of the immediately following discussion, in 1.10, as to whether one can reasonably call a man happy only after he has died, is to make clear *the* means to solve this problem of chance: one must have recourse to a doctrine of the afterlife, according to which the deceased continues to enjoy at least some awareness (of the lives of his descendants, for example). Aristotle insists, however, that only one's own virtuous activities determine happiness; that is, the happiness of a virtuous person cannot be affected, even if some of his descendants receive in life a lot contrary to what they deserve. Indeed, in the midst of his own troubles while alive, the virtuous person will bear up "altogether nobly and suitably in every way," and it will be in just such circumstances that his "nobility shines through." It seems that nothing is so solid or lasting as the virtue and therefore the happiness of the virtuous.

As powerful and attractive as this view is, however, Aristotle immediately backs away from it in one respect, for he now (1.11) characterizes as "excessively opposed to what is held dear" (*aphilon*) and "contrary to the opinions held" (1101a22–24) the view that how the living descendants fare in no way affects the deceased. Aristotle therefore revises his position one last time: "The friends' faring well, then, appears to make some contribution to the condition of those who have passed away, as does, similarly, their faring ill—but a contribution of such a kind and degree as not to make the happy unhappy or anything else of that sort." By the end of 1.11, Aristotle has adopted a tone quite different from that seen in 1.6, where he had treated the concern for eternity unsympathetically, not to say scornfully.

Here, then, is Aristotle's official answer in book 1 of the *Nicomachean Ethics* to the problem of happiness: if we engage in the requisite activity of soul that accords with (the best) virtue, we will secure for ourselves here and now a life that is at once best, noblest, and most pleasant, and we will enjoy this life most continuously. We will also enjoy an afterlife in which nothing, not even the awareness we will have of the fate of our descendants, good or bad, can fundamentally disturb the happiness we will enjoy there. Of the two responses to the problem of happiness that Aristotle had sketched at the end of 1.8, then—to hold either that happiness is (merely) good fortune, or that it is equivalent to virtue (1099b7–8)— he here rejects the former, because he holds to the latter. Happiness is not due to chance, because it is evidently governed by the practice of virtue.

"Blessed Human Beings"

The tension at the heart of Aristotle's argument in book 1 is now clear. On the one hand, virtue cannot guarantee the happiness of the virtuous because it cannot protect them from grave misfortune—witness Priam (1100a8, 1101a8)—and, on the other hand, precisely virtue bestows on those who practice it, probably in this life and certainly in the next, a happiness that can never be transformed into its contrary.

To resolve this tension, we might be tempted to suppose that the first position indicated is merely a preliminary one, a statement of the *problem*, and that the latter position, which is after all set forth at far greater length, is Aristotle's final *answer* to it. And yet, attractive though it may be, this suggestion cannot stand. It is crucial to see, to begin with, that Aristotle himself vouches for almost none of the positions he offers in 1.8–11 in response to the problem of happiness. For example, the whole of the argument is begun by his turn away from "premises" and "conclusions"—from arguments, properly speaking—to "the things said about [happiness]," that is, to opinions (1098b9–11). The opinions that are permitted to exercise most influence there belong to "the ancients" and those of "high repute," in contrast to "those who philosophize" (compare 1098b12–22 with 1098b22–31, where "the few of high repute" take the place of the philosophers). And since Aristotle does not fail to report a contrary opinion conveyed by no less than an inscription at Delos (1099a27–28), perhaps from the very temple of Leto, he must select from among the august but contradictory opinions available to him. He does so on the basis of the hunch that "it is reasonable that neither of these two groups [the ancients and the few of high repute] be wholly in error, but rather that they be correct in some one respect, at least, or even in most respects" (1098b28–29). Similarly, he rejects the view that happiness is due to chance, on the basis of two conditional clauses (1099b20–23) and the thought that to hold otherwise would be "excessively discordant" (1099b24–25). In the same way, he accepts that the dead must be aware of the lives of their surviving descendants (and hence must themselves be alive after death), on the grounds that to deny this would be "excessively opposed to what is dear" and "contrary to the opinions"—as if we could be certain that the most important truths accord with our opinions and preserve the things dear to us, subphilosophic considerations if ever there were any.

Aristotle's striking deference to these opinions, and to the hopes they reveal, is evidence enough of their great power; no adequate account of happiness could proceed without acknowledging the existence of these opinions, the denial of which is indeed harsh. It is not only the political community's great power and its consequences, then, that guide Aristotle in his exposition, but also our hopes or suppositions regarding happiness. If the political community habituates us to accept the view that the preservation of its good is "nobler and more divine" than the attainment of our own, it must be said that we are creatures peculiarly open to such habituation; we are by nature "political animals," in part because we can be deeply moved by considerations of what is noble and divine.

Once we strip 1.8–11 of the assertions that are, if not groundless, then grounded in something other than rational argument, we are permitted to see with greater clarity Aristotle's occasional frankness here. For example, he raises as a rhetorical question whether it is not altogether "strange" to hold that the dead can be happy, especially for those who maintain that happiness is dependent on activity: the dead as such cannot be active, still less happy (1100a12–14). Even in the course of sketching the apparent solution to every problem attending happiness, Aristotle insists on repeating those problems and in effect strengthening the force of them. For example, the problem of chance includes that of our necessary dependence on "external goods" or "equipment," under which heading he now discusses the premature death of friends and children (1.8: 1099a31–1099b7); and he repeats, as we have seen, the requirement of a "complete life" (1.9: 1100a4–9). Finally, in his impressive struggle with the fact of our exposedness to chance, Aristotle resorts to a non sequitur: we may grant that those who are "'foursquare, without blame'" will bear fortunes "most nobly"—they deal with all fortunes "in a becoming way and always [do] what is noblest given the circumstances" (1.10: 1100b30–31, 1101a1–3)—but we need to know that such human beings will also be, not merely not wretched (1100b34, 1101a6), but *happy* as a result of their superlative nobility or virtue (compare 1100b9–10 with 20–22, for example). This Aristotle declines to affirm (1101a6–8). Aristotle himself, then, does not equate happiness with virtue—a position that is, after all, most extreme in denying to chance any empire whatever.

But what of someone who is active in accord with complete virtue and who is adequately equipped with external goods in the course of a complete life—someone, that is, who combines virtue with remarkably good fortune (1101a14–16)? Such a combination is surely conceivable. Aristotle's response to this question is as graceful as it is brief: "we will say that those among the living who have and will have available to them the things stated are blessed—but blessed human beings" (1101a19–21). To understand this all-important qualification, we must begin from the fact that Aristotle reminds us of, namely, that "the future is immanifest to us" (1101a18). The difficulty is not only that our ignorance of the future helps render things generally good of uncertain goodness in fact or in the event (recall 1094b16–19). The difficulty is also, and more, that we can never be certain of enjoying (genuine) goods tomorrow: awareness of our exposedness to chance *must* cast a shadow on any possible happiness here and now. One might even say that it makes happiness, as distinguished from a kind of contentedness, impossible. Not just the calamity, but the knowledge of its possibility; not just the loss of loved ones, but the knowledge of its possibility; not just, above all, the uncertainty of one's own death but the knowledge of its eventual certainty—all these contribute to rendering our hope for happiness unrealizable. We can hope to be blessed—but always and merely "blessed human beings," with the necessary limits attending us as mortals.

It now becomes necessary to revisit a premise guiding book 1, according to which the greatest good, "the human good," is happiness understood as some complete good that as such conveys to its possessor a thorough self-sufficiency or freedom from need. In his first formulation of this premise, Aristotle notes that in fact only "most" agree to it: it is clearly joined in by "the many" (*hoi polloi*) and "the refined," but not so clearly by the wise (compare 1095a18–20 with 21). (The apparently sharp line Aristotle draws between "the many" and "the refined" vanishes when either is compared to "the wise": the view that honor is the greatest good, characteristic of the refined, is really a view of the many, if not the most vulgar of them [compare 1095b16 and 22–23 with 1095a22–23, where the point of comparison is the wise].) And, as we have seen, "those who philosophize" are not among the ancients and the reputable who hold various opinions about what happiness consists in (compare again 1098b12–22 with 1098b22–31). Finally, it may make sense to say of the gods that they are happy and blessed, but even the "most divine" of human beings cannot properly be said to be happy (consider 1101b23–25, with the reading of the MSS). At the close of book 1 of the *Ethics*, the view that seems most fundamental if least explicit is that "the human good" is not indeed happiness, if that term is understood as it ought to be. The good that we cannot help but seek must be one in which we can have some share (1172b34–35).

THE FINAL SECTIONS OF BOOK I

The last chapter of book 1 that deals with virtue in its relation to happiness (1.12) is a curious appendix not obviously related to what has preceded it. Aristotle raises the question of whether happiness belongs among the things praised or among the things honored. The distinction amounts to this: everything praised is inferior to the "good and serious" thing to which our praise refers, whereas everything honored is honored because it is complete. Accordingly, happiness, the complete good, must be among the things honored. But this means that moral virtue in general, and justice in particular, is to be praised—merely praised—and not honored. The moral virtues, in short, are inferior to happiness. They are praiseworthy only insofar as they contribute to happiness. In these terms, it is very hard to see why anyone would take moral virtue as seriously as we typically do—or as seriously as Aristotle soon will. For once he makes the transition, effected in 1.13, to moral virtue, the theme of the next four books of the *Ethics*, he more or less consistently adopts the view that a truly virtuous act will be undertaken only "for the sake of the noble" or that virtuous acts are done "for their own sakes" and not because they contribute to a good greater than moral virtue itself—to one's own happiness, for example (compare 1097b1–4). He will for the most part speak, that is, as though moral virtue falls among the things honored.

The reasons to take virtue very seriously evidently persist at the close of book 1. In book 1, Aristotle explains what "happiness" is and clearly indicates the obstacles to achieving it. He also, of course, indicates a path around them. Those satisfied with Aristotle's account will be all the more eager to learn of the specific demands of moral virtue, for meeting them takes on a new urgency given the risks to which our happiness is exposed and, above all, given the reward that evidently awaits us. But even those dissatisfied with this solution (for which dissatisfaction there is, we have suggested, ample justification) cannot be assumed also to have uprooted their hope for happiness in the precise sense. They will therefore remain open to dedicating themselves to virtue, in whatever form such virtue may ultimately take.

MORAL VIRTUE AND THE VIRTUES UP TO JUSTICE (BOOKS 2–4)

As we have noted, Aristotle effects the transition from the analysis of happiness to that of virtue in the final chapter of book 1. He does so chiefly on the basis of what he admits is a provisional sketch of the human soul: in addition to the nonrational part responsible for nutrition and growth, there is clearly also a part of the soul possessing reason or speech (*logos*), the rational part "in the authoritative sense." And the completion or perfection of this part would be an aspect of human virtue, namely, intellectual virtue. Less clear is the precise character of that part of the nonrational soul that is obedient to reason and yet itself not quite rational, the operation of which one can discern in the successful struggle of self-restrained persons with their desires or appetites. Aristotle here even entertains the possibility that this part of the soul, because it is or can be "obedient" to reason, properly belongs in the rational soul—but only in the sense that it renders one apt to listen to the commands of one's father. And it is this part of the soul, rational or not, whose excellence is moral virtue, the virtue of character.

Tentative though this argument is, it has a certain plausibility, which

makes it all the easier to miss Aristotle's "failure" here to identify clearly
the peak human activity that alone could determine the specific characteristics or qualities of soul to be praised as virtuous. Aristotle has done
no more, by the end of book 1, than equate the happiness we seek with
"an activity of soul" (1102a16–17) or with "a certain activity of soul in accord with complete virtue" (1102a5–6), thereby declining to specify the
activity (or the virtue) in question. It is tempting to assume even at this
point that the peak activity must be the contemplative one, the peak virtue therefore contemplative — but Aristotle has limited himself thus far
to an explicit postponement of the consideration of the contemplative
life or activity, to which he does not return until book 10 (1096a4–5,
1177a12–18 and following). The next four books of the *Ethics*, books 2
through 5, focus on moral virtue, in general and in particular, and Aristotle begins these books also from an explicit postponement of the question that would determine the ground or the definition of the virtues: the
question of "correct reason" and "how it relates to the virtues" (1103b31–
34). Our concern at present, he insists, is not theoretical — "not for the
sake of contemplation" — but practical: "we are conducting an examination, not so that we may know what virtue is, but so that we may become
good" (1103b26–29).

Accordingly, in what follows, Aristotle takes up the question of "how
one ought to perform" matters of action (1103b29–30). Yet since such
matters are very much related to what is opportune in the circumstances,
they vary with those circumstances. Consequently, it is necessary to speak
merely "in outline"; the argument concerned with particulars "does not
fall under an art or any set of precepts" (1103b34–1104a10). In seeking to
be of general assistance, then, Aristotle first lays out not only the manner
in which the virtues are acquired — how habituation works through repeated action and the proper application of pleasure and pain — but also
the manner in which they are exercised. Here it further becomes clear
that morally virtuous actions depend less on knowledge in any strict
sense than on a person's character: the "knowing" and the "choosing" involved in these actions stem from the possession and activity of the correct characteristics or virtues. Indeed, Aristotle concludes his account of
these matters by rebuking "the many," who, in failing to practice the virtues, "[seek] refuge in argument" and thus suppose that "they are philosophizing and that they will in this way be serious" (1105b12–18). What is
needed, rather, is repeated action that instills in us the requisite "steady
and unwavering state" (1105a32–33). Only such training shapes the desir-

ing part of the soul—the part of the soul from which action issues—so as to dispose it to make the correct choice.

The necessity to speak "in outline" affects also how Aristotle proceeds to define virtue in book 2 and his difficult, at times dark, account of voluntary action, choice, deliberation, wish, and responsibility in the first five chapters of book 3. In his definition of virtue, Aristotle articulates his famous doctrine of the mean: virtue is a "characteristic" that brings that which possesses it into good condition and makes it able to perform its work well; and it is a "mean" that is relative both to us and to two extremes, an excess and a deficiency that constitute its associated vices. The mean is relative to us not because the good characteristic varies from individual to individual but because the passions do: some people are more fearful than others, for example, others more given to the bodily appetites; hence people require different degrees and types of training to be brought to the mean. But as the precise "middle point" in relation to excess and deficiency, the mean, or the proper state of soul that mean represents, is "defined by reason and as the prudent person would define it" (1106b36–1107a2). The "mean," therefore, is not an independent standard for virtue but in each case remains dependent on a "definition" or a determination of reason or prudence. Yet this is precisely the difficulty Aristotle set aside at the beginning of his account of moral virtue in postponing the question of "correct reason."

In postponing this question, Aristotle mirrors the manner in which the virtues are acquired: not by argument or reasoning strictly speaking, as we have seen, but by habituation in accord with the prudence of another, be it a parent or teacher. Hence the question of how the prudent person determines the virtuous action, simply and in each circumstance, overshadows Aristotle's investigation of choice, deliberation, wish, and responsibility in book 3: choice and deliberation prove to be directed not at the end but at what conduces to the end, and in light of the role of habituation in forming character, it is difficult to see how one can be made responsible for that which is, as Aristotle has emphasized, the source or ground of action, namely, one's characteristics. Finally, the postponement of the inquiry into correct reason means that Aristotle's delineation of the particular moral virtues—the starting points or principles of action—remains untethered not only to any precise account of *the* human activity or "work" that would fix both their character and rank but also to any precise account of the correct reason that determines the virtues and virtuous action. Perhaps the most that one can say is that our hope for happiness, sketched so powerfully in book 1, is permitted to exercise its influence on the subsequent account of the moral virtues. The principal task of the following outline is to discern the goal or goals guiding Aristotle's account of the eleven moral virtues he selects.

The Ascent to Greatness of Soul: Courage through Magnificence

Aristotle opens his account of the virtues with a discussion of courage, the proper disposition with respect to the passions of fear and confidence. Yet since courage pertains more to fear than to confidence, he seeks first to identify the object of fear with which it is concerned, naming five possibilities: disrepute, poverty, illness, friendlessness, and death. After eliminating the first four, he establishes that courage is the virtue that pertains to the fear of death, reasoning that the courageous human being is concerned with the greatest of the frightening things—"for no one more steadfastly endures terrible things"—and that the greatest of the frightening things is death, "for it is a limit [or end], and there seems to be nothing else for the dead, nothing either good or bad" (1115a25–27).

That death is so unambiguously terrible, and thus the greatest evil, is not obvious if we recall the view to which Aristotle acceded in book 1, when he allowed that to some extent good and bad really exist for the dead (1100a18–19). By here taking the strictest view of the matter, however, he disallows the possibility that courageous action may be taken with the hope of a reward extrinsic to the act and for the sake of which one might risk death. Yet one who acts courageously does not do so simply without hope, for courage is a mean with respect to both fear and confidence. Aristotle establishes how courage pertains to confidence by observing that the courageous man does not appear to be concerned with death in every circumstance but only with the "noblest" kinds of death, and these occur in war because war contains the "greatest and noblest danger" (1115a28–30). By next referring to the honors paid to courageous men by cities and monarchs (1115a31–32), Aristotle indicates the perspective from which he speaks. In war, the welfare of the entire community is at risk, and this welfare is a good that Aristotle had called "nobler and more divine" than the good of any single individual (1094b7–10).

It is in the discussion of courage that Aristotle explicitly establishes that the end (telos) of virtue is "the noble" (1115b11–13). Since courage involves an action in which an individual places his life at risk in behalf of his city or nation, it would seem to be the apparent selflessness of this action that Aristotle intends to point to when he identifies the noble as the end of virtue. Thus it would also seem that it is the noble selflessness of death in war that arouses the confidence proper to courage.

Yet to leave the matter here would be unsatisfactory. For the confidence proper to courage is aroused not by the prospect of selfless sacrifice but by the opportunity that action in war affords: the courageous man may perform some noble action of his own by showing himself to be a real man (*andrizesthai*), either by demonstrating his great prowess or, if it is noble to die, then by facing death in the proper way. Lacking such an opportunity, a courageous man may well endure death with steadfastness but also with a certain despair. Thus one who acts out of courage—with the proper disposition toward fear and confidence—also seeks to achieve something for himself: he acts also for his own sake. On the one hand, this corrects what might understandably be our impression, our mistaken impression, that courage consists in the selfless sacrifice of one's life for the greater good of the city. On the other hand, it raises the question of how Aristotle can continue to maintain that the courageous man acts "for the sake of the noble" while at the same time suggesting that he acts for his own sake.

Aristotle resolves this problem through recourse to the principle that virtue is an end in itself that is chosen for its own sake (1105a28–33). He observes that "the end of every activity is that which accords with the characteristic" and, further, that "to the courageous man, courage is noble. Such too, therefore, is the end, for each thing is defined by its end" (1115b20–21). The nobility of the truly courageous human being, then, is constituted by his dedication, not to something outside himself, but to his own virtue: although his action benefits the "nobler and more divine" good of the city or nation (as the honors paid to it testify), it is also its own end, which the courageous man seeks to perform for his own sake. This would appear to resolve, at least on one level, the difficulty of how his action is both noble and for his own sake. To speak more generally, the virtuous or serious human being views virtuous actions as noble and good (1099a22–23). Indeed, the argument of book 1 is but a step away: it is through the activity of virtue that a good person finds his happiness (1098a7–18, 1099a24–31).

Yet, to speak now more explicitly than Aristotle does, there is a difficulty, particularly vivid in the case of courage, with maintaining that the same action is both noble and good. At the end of his account of courage, Aristotle quietly points to the problematic relation between courage and happiness. He does this in the context of addressing what might seem to be, from the virtuous person's point of view, a somewhat lesser difficulty: that courageous action is not pleasant. As he observes, "the more [the courageous man] possesses complete virtue and the happier he is, the more he will be pained at the prospect of death. For to this sort of person, living is especially worthwhile, and he is deprived of the greatest goods knowingly—and this is a painful thing" (1117b11–13). That life is worth living especially for the virtuous human being is the claim made on behalf of virtue itself, the claim that it is our true good, such that the more we live in accord with virtue, the happier our life will be. Yet the choice in battle reflects precisely the courageous man's virtue, "for he chooses what is noble in war instead of these [greatest goods]" (1117b13–15). Given what courageous action requires, then, we are left with a certain circularity: he who acts courageously must forsake his true or greatest good, his virtuous and happy life, and choose instead to do what is noblest in war; but it is in choosing to do this very noble deed that the courageous human being seeks his true or greatest good. In the same action in which the courageous man seeks his own good, therefore, he nobly suffers pain or death and therewith the cessation of his own good.

Thus, although it is a part of virtue's claim that virtuous action is choiceworthy for its own sake—it is good for the person who so acts—in the case of courage, the same act that promises our good also requires us to endure nobly its loss. This difficulty, inherent as it is in courageous action, cannot be resolved within the sphere of courage. That it remains a difficulty is suggested by Aristotle's strange concluding admission that courageous men, who have been identified as possessing the virtue connected with war and battle, are perhaps not the best soldiers. The best soldiers, rather, are those unfortunate souls who, having no other good in life, are willing to exchange their lives "for small gain" (1117b17–20).

Aristotle leaves no doubt that courage is noble, and in this respect a virtue, but the problematic character of its goodness raises the question whether there is a kind of noble action more consistent with our good. The concern for our self-preservation and well-being comes so much to the fore in the next virtue, moderation, that "the noble" as an end almost recedes from view. As the virtue pertaining to the bodily pleasures, moderation involves the restraint of the desires with a view to our own health or good condition. Moreover, if the desires are not restrained, they will constantly clamor for satisfaction and, if indulged, grow to such proportions as to "drive out calculation" (1119b6–7, 9–10). Just as in courage, the aim in moderation is the virtue itself; but since moderation is largely identified with one's good condition, it leads to our bodily well-being and preservation rather than our harm or destruction. The dedication to such well-being and preservation seems scarcely noble, but it is otherwise sensible.

The unambiguous connection of moderation with one's own good and its more tenuous connection with nobility is reflected in the fact that Aristotle refers only twice to the noble, the stated end of virtue, in the account of moderation (1119a16–18, b16; compare, e.g., 1115a29–35, b11–24, 1116a10–15). Indeed, the contrast between courage and moderation raises one of the most fundamental questions for virtue: is it possible to reconcile that aspect of nobility represented most clearly by courageous action with a concern for one's own good, without having "the noble" as the aim of virtue disappear? The movement of Aristotle's discussion through the next virtues—liberality, magnificence, and greatness of soul—indicates a response to this question from within the moral perspective.

Moderation, which has no action of its own, proves instrumental to the virtue that follows "next in order," liberality: the liberal human being is best able to use his own wealth well, and this use consists in giving (1119b22–26). This noble act of giving is made possible in part through the restraint with respect to pleasure provided by moderation; and the liberal person not only benefits those whom he ought but, in giving of his own things, displays a noble lack of concern for his own good—in particular for his economic welfare. Indeed, "it very much belongs to the liberal person also to exceed in giving, such that there is little left for himself, for it is typical of a liberal person not to look out for himself" (1120b4–6).

In the discussion of liberality, Aristotle begins again to emphasize the connection of virtue with nobility. It is this connection of liberal action to nobility that appears to inform his decision to discuss liberality after moderation instead of another virtue connected with money, justice. In making his initial point that liberality pertains to money, he departs from his usual procedure by noting also what liberality does not pertain to, namely, matters of war, the concerns of the moderate human being, and legal adjudications (1119b23–25). He thus distinguishes liberality not only from the two preceding virtues but also from justice, for justice too will prove to be concerned with money (1130b1–2), though more with respect to acts of "taking" or acquisition than with acts of giving, the province of liberality. Since central to justice are judgments about what is fair or equal, about what share of the good is due to different parties, the movement here to liberality instead of to justice allows Aristotle to give the fullest possible expression to moral virtue's connection with noble deeds. As he observes, "it belongs to virtue more to act well than to fare well and more to do what is noble than not to do what is shameful"; and giving, as opposed to taking, is more closely connected with acting well and doing noble deeds.

The nobility of liberal action, like that of courageous action, involves incurring the loss of a good—in this case, money. But the loss suffered by the liberal man is neither fatal nor, it turns out, of great significance to him. He is so easygoing in this respect as to be vulnerable to and even unconcerned about suffering injustice; and in making expenditures, he is pained more if he fails to buy something fitting than if he loses money on something useless. Although those who are liberal need money if they are to give to others, unlike "the many," they are not "lovers of money" (1121b12–16). Stinginess (*aneleutheria*, literally "illiberality"), the vice connected with this particular "greediness for gain," is in fact the extreme most opposed to liberality, though its pervasiveness would appear to be behind Aristotle's persistent condemnations of it and to make all the more remarkable the liberal person's choice to suffer the loss entailed by his action.

Like liberality, the next virtue, magnificence, pertains to money but specifically to making a "fitting expenditure on a great thing" (1122a18–24). The difference between liberality and magnificence is one of scale. Both the liberal and the magnificent man act for the sake of the noble, action that is "common to the virtues" (1122b6–7), but the latter surpasses the former not simply with respect to expenditure but also in his aim: the magnificent man seeks to produce a great and noble work (or product: *ergon*), and "even from an equal expenditure the magnificent person will produce the more magnificent work" (1122b13–14). In this way, magnificence is also the virtue of the work itself; and in his effort to achieve the greatest and noblest such work, which will produce wonder or admiration, the magnificent man, free from the love of money Aristotle so vigorously condemned, spares no expense and feels no twinge of pain over the cost. Because magnificence pertains to expenditures on a great scale, it is out of the reach of those who are without the requisite resources. The man who is magnificent is especially concerned to do what is fitting with regard to the "greatest and most honored" expenditures: public expenditures, including most notably "those that concern the gods—votive offerings, [sacred] buildings, and sacrifices—and similarly too those that concern the entire divine realm" (1122b19–23).

This is the sole explicit statement, in the account of the virtues, of the virtuous person's attitude toward the gods and the divine; it serves to alert us to the omission of piety from the list of the virtues (compare 1123b18–20). Moreover, Aristotle chooses this context to remind us that the person who exhibits magnificence does what is fitting not only to the object of his expenditure but also to himself, that is, to his own great wealth, reputation, and nobility. Thus his magnificent expenditures—his works—must be understood as reflections of his own greatness. This suggestion and the omission of piety indicate the character of his self-understanding and action: his aspiration to do what is fitting to the gods and the divine is commingled with his sense of his own greatness. Even as Aristotle notes in his discussion of private expenditures that "the same thing is not suitable for gods and human beings, or in the case of a temple and that of a burial tomb," he observes that the magnificent man prefers to adorn his home especially with works that will endure, "for these are noblest" (1123a6–10). In the permanence of these works, the magnificent man seeks for himself and as fitting to himself a permanence akin to, if not as resplendent as, the immortality of the gods.

In the longing for the noble, there is a natural directedness toward great acts that the movement from liberality to magnificence captures: to benefit one person is good, to be sure, but to be the "cause of the greatest good" by benefiting the city as a whole is nobler and even divine (*Nicomachean Ethics* 1094b7–10; *Politics* 1253a30–31). The peak of this movement is reached in the next virtue, greatness of soul, the first complete virtue in Aristotle's list: the great-souled man not only is capable of the greatest actions but also claims for himself the greatest of the external goods, namely, honor. As Aristotle will suggest, greatness of soul is a peak in that it comprises all the virtues and serves as their "crown" or "ornament" (1124a1–2).

Greatness of Soul

Aristotle's transition to his account of greatness of soul is seamless: there is no obvious conclusion to the discussion of magnificence because greatness of soul, like magnificence, is concerned with great things. Aristotle describes the great-souled man as one who both is worthy of great things and deems himself worthy of them. His self-regard arises from the fact that he possesses all the virtues and each of them to the greatest degree. Because of his great virtue, he rightly regards himself as worthy of the external good considered the greatest, "that which we assign to the gods, that at which people of worth aim, and that which is the prize conferred on the noblest people" (1123b18–20). This good is honor.

Greatness of soul requires both that the great-souled person possess "what is great in each virtue" and that he have the correct regard for his virtue; the honor he pays to himself is the natural complement of the magnificent man's attitude toward his works. Yet even though the great-souled man considers honor his just due, the regard he has for his own virtue has a paradoxical effect: it makes him ambivalent toward this greatest external good. Precisely as a result of his self-awareness, the great-souled man disdains all external goods, including honor, as paltry, because nothing is commensurate in his eyes with perfect virtue, and virtue is the only end to which he is devoted. The perspective of the great-souled man thus represents the explicit fulfillment of a most fundamental principle of virtue: that it be chosen as an end in itself. Greatness of soul accordingly constitutes the peak of an ascent of the virtues from courage. Aristotle calls it the "crown" (*kosmos*) of the virtues, an adornment of them by which they are magnified.

Since the great-souled man acts only in a manner appropriate to his virtue, he can be expected to reflect his greatness in all his attitudes and actions. For example, he accepts only great honors or those bestowed by serious men, he is equanimous in both good and bad fortune, he seeks to benefit others but disdains requesting or receiving aid because it is a sign of inferiority, he is not fearful of the opinion of others, and he never descends to partaking in personal conversation about himself or others or to being concerned with petty evils or revenge. In the course of enumerating the great-souled man's impressive qualities, Aristotle notes also that he will undertake few actions, and then only great actions and risks, since these alone are appropriate to his great virtue. Yet whenever he takes risks, "he throws away his life on the grounds that living is not at all worthwhile" (1124b8–9). The dedication to virtue that issues in the great-souled man's contempt for external goods—the same contempt that gives him his dignified equanimity in the face of good and bad fortune—appears also to influence his view of life itself. Just as external goods pale in comparison to virtue, so even life itself takes on a certain insignificance—Aristotle says three times of the great-souled man that "nothing is great" to him.

By recalling one of Aristotle's most poignant observations concerning the courageous man, we see that a certain transformation has been involved in the movement from courage to greatness of soul: whereas the courageous man will lay down his life for the sake of the noble but feels pain in doing so, because he knows that he is forsaking his greatest goods, the great-souled man, because he cares only for virtue and identifies it fully with his own good, is willing to throw away his life for the sake of one great and noble act. The progression from courage to greatness of soul thus refines our understanding of nobility: it consists not in the forsaking of one's greatest goods, but in "greatness." At the peak of this progression that is greatness of soul, we have arrived at the most complete and explicit identification of virtue as that end which is both noble and good—in other words, as the highest end of human action.

Yet a difficulty threatens to obtrude. In book 1 Aristotle had insisted that although virtue is an end in itself, it is also subordinate to the end that is truly most final for human beings: happiness (1097b1–5). Book 1 suggested that rigorous attention to the question of the highest good entails an express admission of the subordination of virtue to happiness. This admission, however, is in tension with the principle that virtue must have itself as an end; and these two ends, and their apparent ranking, may well color even a serious human being's dedication to virtue. For this reason, Aristotle deflects attention from the subordination of virtue to happiness when he moves to the account of moral virtue: whereas in book 1, he had maintained that the prize and end of virtue is happiness, in his account of courage he identifies the end of virtue as nobility and, in the discussion of greatness of soul, as honor.

Nevertheless, the problem of the relation between virtue and happiness remains present, even or precisely at the peak of the virtues. This difficulty is revealed also in seemingly small contradictions in the views of the great-souled man. Despite his apparently singular dedication to virtue, for example, he wishes that it be rewarded with a good other than itself, even an inferior good such as he thinks honor to be. Further, although in his dedication to virtue he seeks to be fully self-sufficient and impervious to reverses of fortunes, he is in fact quite dependent on fortune: his greatness of soul depends on a certain wealth, position, and good birth, and the exercise of his great virtue requires the opportunity for great actions. Indeed, as a result of his wish to undertake only great and renowned actions, he is largely idle. Yet happiness requires the activity of virtue. Finally, the great-souled man's concern for happiness or the good life in a broad sense is evidenced by his willingness to accommodate a friend; he thus seeks friends, who are indispensable to our happiness and are held to be our greatest external good, as Aristotle observes in book 9.

By pressing the question of happiness here, we may bring to the account of the virtues an indelicate explicitness with regard to the problematic relation of virtue and happiness, as Aristotle's own efforts to mute the question suggest. Such indelicacy, however, alerts us to an important feature of the discussion to follow: in the movement away from the peak that is greatness of soul, Aristotle will identify virtue less with the doing of noble and great deeds and more with those qualities that contribute to the good life broadly speaking. Most significantly, he emphasizes virtues that contribute to good relations in our associations with others. This movement culminates in his account of the altogether political virtue, justice, which constitutes the use of all the virtues "in relation to another" (1129b26–7).

In thus identifying a second complete virtue, Aristotle invites the comparison between justice and greatness of soul. It is in fact less indelicate, and closer to the surface of Aristotle's discussion, to note that greatness of soul sometimes falls short when it comes to this other complete virtue. For although greatness of soul is said to constitute the possession of each and every virtue, the great-souled man is deficient from the point of view of justice: he does not like to recall his debts, he overlooks evils, and he acts not out of a sense of justice but out of a sense of his superiority. The first step in the correction of the defects inherent in greatness of soul, in light of the requirements of justice, is taken in Aristotle's account of ambition. As he proceeds on this path to the second complete virtue, moreover, he takes up virtues—gentleness, friendliness, truthfulness, and wittiness—that point to the good or goods of associations that are not political and that pertain to the speeches and actions of these associations and to a "living together" that is for the sake of pleasure or play.

The Turn to Justice and Friendship: Ambition and Gentleness

Described first as the virtue that pertains to lesser honors, ambition (literally "love of honor": *philotimia*) represents in one respect a descent from the heights of greatness of soul. Given the small imperfections in this crown of the virtues, however, the discussion of ambition also represents an advance in pointing to the need for a standard by which the proper measure of the love of honor can be established. If we take our bearings from the perspective of the great-souled man, the question of this standard has been rendered moot inasmuch as he rejects honor as an end for its own sake: from this very high point of view, the love of honor so characteristic of the few who favor the political life is not properly classified as a virtue. Yet, as Aristotle now insists, we generally praise the man who loves honor "more than the many do" and call him "manly and a lover of what is noble" (1125b11–17). Moreover, honor is indeed an object of longing and a good for which human beings vie, as is evidenced by the opinion of those who strive for it, including even the great-souled man himself. But while the account of ambition points to the need for a standard by which the competition for this good can be mediated, Aristotle concludes the discussion without establishing any such standard, saying only that the relevant mean is nameless and that consequently "the extremes seem to dispute over it as if it were unclaimed" (1125b17–18).

In the discussion of justice, honor is one of the common goods that is apportioned in accord with the distributive principle of merit, and the great-souled man's claim that virtue is the true ground of merit in this regard proves to be but one among others: in the dispute about what constitutes merit, democrats say that it is freedom; oligarchs, wealth; others, noble birth; and aristocrats, virtue. The great-souled man's claim for honor must accordingly establish its worthiness not only to the satisfaction of his own, albeit high, point of view but also against these other claims (compare *Politics* 1281a11 and following). Hence, although the discussion of ambition may represent a descent from greatness of soul, this movement takes account of the political character of human existence and a new peak in justice, the virtue that attends to the demand that each individual be assigned his just share of the good.

Aristotle begins his ascent to this new peak by turning next to the characteristic pertaining to anger. Acknowledging that, like ambition, this virtue has no name, Aristotle chooses to call it "gentleness," a name that actually suggests the virtue's similarly nameless deficiency. But one who is correctly disposed with respect to anger in fact tends toward its deficiency or lack: the gentle person is distinguished as one who "wishes to be calm and not led by his passion, but rather as reason may command," and he is consequently more disposed to forgive than to be moved by the common desire for revenge and punishment. This disposition toward forgiveness sometimes makes the gentle person an object of blame rather than praise: he is thought to be a fool and slavish, for he appears to endure foul abuse and to overlook his own affairs. Strictly speaking, in fact, the person who has the correct disposition with regard to anger becomes angry "at the things and with whom he ought … and, further, in the way, when, and for as much time as he ought" (1125b31–32). Indeed, in certain circumstances, not gentleness but harshness, the extreme of anger identified as most opposed to the mean, is praised: harsh human beings are sometimes praised as manly on the grounds that they are able to rule.

In the account of gentleness, we begin to see a divergence of ends within moral virtue itself, a divergence indicated by the fact that gentleness is not always praised. That harshness is sometimes praised, gentleness sometimes censured, points to the tension between the punitive justice necessary to political rule and the forgiveness toward which reason by itself tends. Aristotle's account of gentleness thus suggests that moral virtue points to at least two different ends: one that tends toward politics or rule, one that tends away from it. This latter possibility is suggested by Aristotle's observation that gentleness contributes to good relations among friends and associates. It is explored in the subsequent account of three virtues that pertain to the virtues bound up with our associations that are not strictly political: friendliness, truthfulness, and wittiness.

The "Social" Virtues: Friendliness, Truthfulness, and Wittiness

In taking up the virtues that pertain to these associations, Aristotle changes the order from his original list in 2.7. There he had listed "friendliness" after truthfulness and wittiness and had unqualifiedly identified it as friendship, implying that he meant nothing less than the full scope of associations he discusses in books 8 and 9 (1108a26–30). By now changing the order of the three virtues and omitting friendship for the time being, Aristotle indicates that an account of our shared life or associations demands the fuller treatment provided in the two books on friendship; the discussion of the moral virtues cannot be the last word on the question of the best life. Indeed, in naming these largely nameless virtues that pertain to pleasure and truth in our speeches and actions, including our playful amusements, Aristotle also points to a good or goods that, not being wholly within the ordinary moral horizon, need to be identified and defined. Consequently, his discussion of these apparently minor virtues expands the perspective of the *spoudaios* and would seem perhaps even to cross "conventional" boundaries of moral virtue.

Aristotle here paints a portrait of refinement that illuminates the significance of the virtues in our associations: the civility of well-mannered friendliness, for example, against obsequious fawning and peevish quarrelsomeness, the refreshing truthfulness of a "plain dealer" in contrast to a tedious boaster, and the elevated humor of tactful wittiness against coarse buffoonery or dour boorishness. As he proceeds, moreover, two issues arise: first, a question that had not before been in doubt, whether the virtues are means or whether they can be defined in terms of the particular end they serve; and second, whether there is an end that may reflect or support the life of moral virtue without being wholly encompassed within it. These issues are most pointed in his accounts of truthfulness and wittiness.

Aristotle restricts truthfulness and its associated vices to what a person claims to be or to possess, as distinguished from anything related to justice and injustice. The truthful person claims to be nothing more or less than he is. He is flanked on the one extreme by the boaster, who pretends to be greater than he is, and on the other by the person who pretends to be less than he is, whom Aristotle chooses to call "ironic." Because both extremes involve lying or dissembling, they prove blameworthy when held up against the noble dedication to truthfulness. Yet their blameworthiness becomes less apparent when Aristotle proceeds to observe that those who boast for monetary gain—who pretend, for example, to be a prophet, a wise man, or a doctor with a view to their own profit— are worse than those who boast because they desire a good reputation or honor. Thus, although each type of boaster manifests the same vice, blameworthiness is assessed largely on the basis of the particular end each chooses; it is this choice, Aristotle now says, that makes each a boaster.

Just as the blameworthiness of boasting proves to be more complicated than we might expect, so too does the blameworthiness of the other extreme, irony. Although Aristotle insistently maintains that the truthful person acts and speaks truthfully, because this is "the sort of person he is" (1127a27–28, b1–3), the hierarchy of boasters here suggests that this person's virtue is also connected with a preference for truth over money or repute. In a word, he is what Aristotle calls a "lover of truth" (*philalēthēs*), and his love of truth is appropriate to his virtue since falsehood is wretched and blameworthy, truth noble and praiseworthy. Yet Aristotle makes clear that, in certain circumstances, truthfulness, the mean, is not praiseworthy: even the truthful person sometimes prefers irony as the more graceful manner of speech. Those who employ irony appear refined in character, for they seem to speak not with a view to gain

but to avoid bombast. Offering a rare example of one who possesses a specific characteristic, Aristotle maintains that this is what "Socrates used to
do" (1127b22–26).

To present Socrates as the exemplar of irony, however, does not illus-
trate the immediate point. Rather, it serves to blur what is in fact a sharp
line between gentlemanly or moral virtue and Socratic or philosophic virtue. For though a lover of truth, the gentleman is not yet a philosopher:
a gentleman sometimes speaks ironically because it is graceful or noble
to do so, whereas Socrates's irony was a part of his quest for wisdom, a
quest often in tension with conventional convictions and authorities. The
essential difference between a gentleman and a philosopher can be expressed also as a distinction between the ends to which each is dedicated:
to moral virtue, on the one hand, and to wisdom, on the other (compare
1095b17–19). The implication of these different ends sheds light on Aristotle's willingness in this latter half of his account, and precisely at the beginning of his account of truthfulness, to raise the question of whether
the virtues really are means.

After praising irony for a second time and reproaching by comparison
the other extreme, boasting, Aristotle turns to wittiness. Though he earlier classified wittiness as pertaining to pleasure in play, he now broadens
it as pertaining to rest, one part of life, and specifically to passing the time
(*diagōgē*) in play, a part of rest. Rest and play, he observes, are "necessary
in life" (1128b3–4). He will later make clear that we play for the sake of
further activity, noting on the authority of Anacharsis that we do not play
for its own sake but in order to be serious (1176b33–1177a1). The serious
activity of life to which play is ancillary is, for the gentleman, clearly political activity, and the discussion of wittiness thus provides a fitting prelude
to that of the next virtue, justice. Yet the discussion of wittiness points
also in another direction, toward a possibility Aristotle will fully consider
only in book 10.

With respect to play too there is a graceful way of conducting oneself, and Aristotle praises gentlemanly wit as a mean between the crude
jesting of buffoons, who always strive after a laugh and spare no one, not
even themselves, from pain or embarrassment, and the dour humorless-
ness of boors, who will not abide any kind of fun, either of their own or
of others' making. Those who "play gracefully" are both nimble-witted
and tactful; as they engage in their amusements, they do not say or listen to anything that would cause another distress or be inappropriate for
a liberal and decent human being—a refinement that marks the superi-

ority of free and educated people over the slavish and of the graceful innuendo of new comedy over the coarseness and crudeness of the old.
Nevertheless, however graceful gentlemanly wit may be, it has its dangers. In the midst of his praise of wittiness, Aristotle issues a warning: just
as lawgivers forbid slandering certain things, so perhaps they need also to
prohibit joking about some things. The need for such legal prohibition
is grounded in the power of comedy to effect a kind of liberation; for to
mock something, and thus to slander it, is to liberate oneself from it. It
is precisely this power that prompts Aristotle, in his account of the best
regime, to prohibit the young from seeing lampoons and comedic spec-
tacles (*Politics* 1336b27–35).

It is curious that Aristotle should choose to distinguish wittiness as the
virtue pertaining to rest, especially since he never refers to it in his discussion of rest and leisure in the *Politics* and mentions comedy only to com-
ment on its deleterious effect on the young. Yet if laughter and comedy
have the liberating power he suggests, then the gentleman, in the very operation of his wit, possesses the capacity to achieve a certain distance and
even liberation from law and the regime to which he is otherwise dedicated. Indeed, wittiness may even be the gentlemanly version of Socratic
irony, since both appear to follow a law of their own but employ a kind
of understatement out of deference to convention and the authority of
the lawgiver. The gentleman's graceful play thus shows itself, if not to be
ancillary to philosophy, then to share in some of the character of the lei-
sured activity that in book 10 Aristotle will praise as best. It is accordingly
fitting that Aristotle should choose to single out wittiness as the virtue
pertaining to play and should use the discussion of this apparently minor virtue to praise the virtuous person as being "like a law unto himself"
(1128a31–32).

But if, by dint of its quasi-independence from convention and the regime, the wittiness of the gentleman is the closest he comes to philosophic
enlightenment, this amounts to saying that he does not fully achieve it:
there are still things he will never say, and some he will not abide even
hearing. Thus Aristotle includes tact as a part of the mean, because it belongs to the gentleman to heed convention and the lawgiver's prohibi-
tions, a suggestion Aristotle strikingly reiterates in the brief account of
the passion of shame preceding the discussion of justice. Shame is not
strictly speaking a virtue, because the decent (or equitable: *epieikes*) person will not do shameful things, and whether such things are shameful in
truth or only by opinion does not matter. To put this suggestion in its best

light: while the gentleman is "like a law unto himself," he is never lawless, which is appropriate to his virtue, and especially to his justice.

But for Aristotle's efforts, the grandeur of greatness of soul and the nobility or brilliance of other virtues such as courage and magnificence might cause us to overlook the otherwise nameless and apparently minor virtues he includes in his list. The consideration of these very characteristics, however, has proved to be an integral part of his investigation of the good life in a complete sense. The particular virtues are never simply incompatible with one another, as Aristotle's insistence that the virtues are all parts of a whole suggests; but the status of each within that constellation differs, as is clearly indicated by the fact that there are two "complete" virtues: greatness of soul, or virtue in relation to oneself, and justice, or virtue in relation to another. The investigation of the moral virtues thus moves from the three virtues that refine our various associations with one another to culminate in Aristotle's lengthy account of justice, the comprehensive virtue that looks to the happiness of the political community as a whole.

ON JUSTICE (BOOK 5)

Aristotle begins his inquiry into this final moral virtue by emphasizing that justice is like the other virtues in constituting a characteristic that disposes us to act well, namely, to do just things, act justly, and wish for just things. His first task, then, is to examine justice as a virtue that constitutes our perfection. The immediate complication is that justice has two similar but not identical meanings: the lawbreaker is thought to be unjust, but so too is "he who grasps for more [*pleonektēs*] and is unequal [or "unfair": *anisos*]" (1129a32–34). In short, justice may mean either "lawfulness" or "fairness," alternatives that Aristotle classifies under the respective headings of general and particular justice. Accordingly, there are two different, though related, characteristics in the case of justice: general justice as lawfulness is complete virtue, understood as the sum of all the virtues directed toward the good of another; and particular justice, understood as equality or fairness, is the proper disposition concerning the goods— security, money, and honor—in which all who belong to the political community must share.

In exploring the full range of justice as a virtue, Aristotle addresses the question raised by its relation to greatness of soul: whether the devotion to the common good can be reconciled in the best case with the dedication to one's perfection in virtue simply. The potential limits of justice in this regard first become apparent in the discussion of particular justice. In brief, the requirements of particular justice prove to be grounded in a standard other than the one that Aristotle himself establishes as that by which an individual ought to choose the good things, namely, one's true benefit, which, in the best case, is the possession and activity of the virtues that pertain to the good things simply. Yet, in contrast to the other virtues, justice as a mean is defined not in relation to our perfection in this respect, but in terms of a principle of equality that grounds the "regime" (*politeia*) and determines the distribution of common goods. For this reason, Aristotle will clarify the character of justice as a virtue only after he has investigated the "proportional reciprocity" at the origin of the political community. After setting forth Aristotle's accounts of general and particular justice as perfections, then, we will turn to his discussion of reciprocity for the light it sheds on the limits of justice.

Justice as the Lawful

General justice is complete virtue in being all the virtues "summed up" in one and "directed toward another," and central here is its connection with the law. As Aristotle observes, "all lawful things are somehow just," not only because they have been "defined by the legislative art," but also because they have a comprehensive scope and end: the laws "pronounce on *all* things" and seek the common advantage, which may be understood, given the variety of regimes, as "either [the advantage] for all persons or for the best or for those who have authority, either in accord with virtue or in some other such way" (1129b14–17). Complete virtue is justice, then, because as the lawful, it both commands the deeds of virtue and forbids those of vice in order to "produce and preserve happiness and its parts for the political community" (1129b17–19). With this end in view, for example, the law commands courage in requiring that soldiers not break ranks in battle; moderation, in prohibiting adultery or outrage; and gentleness, in forbidding assault or slander. The law thus strives to instill all the virtues, or "general justice," in every citizen.

The orientation of general justice toward the common good constitutes its unique power — "justice *alone* of the virtues is held to be another's good" (1130a3–5, emphasis added) — and as a result of this, justice attracts very high praise as "the greatest of the virtues" (1129b27–29). Indeed, the case for justice as the greatest virtue is the one Aristotle offers here in opposition to the attack on justice to which he alludes. For whereas Thrasymachus, in Plato's *Republic* (338c–339a), decries as dupes precisely those who are just and law-abiding because they do nothing more than serve the advantage of the rulers who are "stronger," Aristotle here recalls Bias's saying that "office will show the man" (1130a1–2)—a man, that is, who is "a guardian of the just" and not, as Thrasymachus would have it, a tyrant. Indeed, far from condemning justice as the advantage of another, Aristotle distinguishes between the best and worst human beings in a manner heavily weighted on the side of justice: "Worst, then, is he who treats both himself and his friends in a corrupt way, but best is he who makes use of virtue not in relation to himself but in relation to another. For this is a difficult task" (1130a5–8). By identifying the best actions with definitively just acts, at the same time as he singles out the difficulty of such acts, Aristotle captures a side of justice that Thrasymachus's attack obscures. Justice does indeed require us to act with a view to another's good, and this is exactly why it is and should be admired.

Insofar as it is citizens who carry out virtuous actions, all such actions have a dual aspect: they can be understood from the point of view of either one's own perfection or another's benefit. Justice would appear to be the most complete of the virtues because, in obvious contrast to the pride and self-sufficiency of greatness of soul, it comprises both the sum of the virtues and the "use" of this perfection for another's good. General justice, by this account, constitutes both another's good and our true perfection, a conclusion Aristotle encourages by saying that virtue and justice are the same, though "in their being" they differ: "in the respect in which [the characteristic] bears a relation to another, it is justice; in the respect in which it is simply a characteristic of this sort, it is virtue" (1130a10–13).

Having bestowed such praise on general justice, Aristotle turns to particular justice, which he tells us is the true focus of our investigation. Like the other virtues, particular justice is a part of the law and so of general justice: it is therefore not only its own perfection as a virtue but also a part of that complete virtue commanded by the law with a view to the common advantage. Like general justice, however, particular justice is also distinguished from the other virtues in being defined by its orientation "toward another," and the investigation of particular justice begins to illuminate the problematic consequence of this orientation for justice as a mean and a virtue.

Justice as Fairness or Equality

Most commentators who treat particular justice in the *Nicomachean Ethics* tend to focus on its technical terms, that is, the proportional equalities of its two forms, distributive and corrective justice. "Distributive" justice is concerned with equality in the distribution of the goods common to those who share in the regime, and it assigns those goods in accord with a principle that "all" agree with, which is merit or desert. "Corrective" justice pertains to contracts or transactions, "voluntary and involuntary," and because it is blind to the differences in merit of those involved in the transaction, it employs an arithmetical proportion to restore the parties involved in an unjust transaction to the correct equality by compensating the plaintiff and inflicting a loss on the wrongdoer.

Aristotle's own first order of business in the discussion of particular justice, however, is to prove that it is in fact like the other virtues in being a characteristic and a specific perfection. Yet his very efforts in this direction suggest room for doubt. He argues that although some bad actions may appear to issue from a vice other than injustice, they actually stem from the desire "to grasp for more" than is one's share. The person who acts from cowardice may flee danger, for example, or a stingy person may begrudge a loan, but neither acts with a view to profit or gain strictly speaking; indeed, they may even suffer a loss as a result of their specific vices. By contrast, in wanting more of the good things without consideration for others, the one who acts out of injustice would perform these same deeds simply from the desire for gain. Particular justice is thus distinguished both from the other virtues and from complete justice as the perfection that pertains specifically to gain: the just human being in this sense is disposed to take only his own fair or equal portion of the goods that are shared. The crucial question for particular justice, then, is this: how ought one to define the "equality" in accord with which one must choose those goods? For it is in connection with this question that the crucial difference between justice and the other virtues begins to emerge.

This difference comes to sight as Aristotle links the assignment of "the equal" in particular justice with the definition of justice as a mean and virtue. For the just mean represents not our good condition with respect to two extremes, deficiency and excess, but the principle of equality established by law, in relation to which the excess and the deficiency—taking more and receiving less than this equality—are then defined. In its distributive form, particular justice is the object of a dispute that points ulti-

mately to the problematic significance of the regime in defining justice as
a mean and a virtue. For the regime and its principle of merit determine
the distribution of ruling offices and the end for the sake of which that
rule is exercised; the regime thus constitutes the fundamental "equality"
in accord with which one is deemed just in any given community (*Politics*
1278b10–15, 1279a25–1279b10). Aristotle acknowledges, however, that
there are deep divisions concerning what constitutes merit in the distribution of the common goods: "democrats say it is freedom; oligarchs,
wealth; others, good birth; aristocrats, virtue" (1131a27–29). The "fights
and accusations" that break out when there is a perceived inequality extend not only to the distribution of security, money, and honor, then, but
also to the regime itself as the defining distributive principle of the political community.

Aristotle leaves the full resolution of the dispute connected with ruling offices to his *Politics* (1280a7 and following), but his discussion of
"reciprocity" points to the necessary and problematic role of the regime
in establishing justice as a mean and a virtue. As Aristotle's final step in
clarifying the limits of justice, this discussion also begins to illuminate a
tension within moral virtue between the two ends that demand our devotion as morally serious human beings: the common good, on the one
hand, and our perfection in virtue as an end in itself, on the other.

Reciprocity and the Regime

Aristotle's discussion of reciprocity presents itself largely as an analysis of
the conditions for economic exchange necessary for the common life of
individuals seeking the good. Yet this analysis also raises the more fundamental question concerning the very foundation of political rule. While
rejecting the view of the "Pythagoreans" that justice is simple reciprocity (or "retaliation," *antipeponthos*)—suffering what one has done to another—Aristotle insists that a certain proportionate reciprocity is necessary if human beings are to come together in a political association.
There is the necessity of "exchange" in the case of both evils and goods;
for if people cannot requite evil for evil, they are regarded as slaves, and
without an exchange of goods, there is no community. Accordingly, reciprocity in the form of an original equality among individuals must exist
if a community is to exist. Indeed, this equality, however it is finally elaborated, is the ground of law, since law is natural only among those "for
whom there is equality in ruling and being ruled" (1134b14–15).

Now, in the case of economic exchange, the natural standard by which goods are valued is "need," and the "measure"—the term which represents need, makes the value of goods comparable, and acts as a guarantee of future exchange—is, by general agreement or convention, money. By equalizing goods in this manner, money makes possible a relation of exchange that holds the community together. But every political association must agree also on the distribution of political goods, the most fundamental of which are the ruling offices. The arrangement of these offices is determined, as we have seen, by the distributive principle everyone agrees with: to each in accord with merit. Not need but merit, then, establishes commensurability, and honor, not money, is the currency when it comes to the distribution of political offices (compare *Politics* 1278b8–17, 1279a22–32, 1280a7–21, 1281a28–39).

In determining what or who is to be honored in the matter of ruling, however, we are thrown back on the dispute over what constitutes merit: is it freedom, wealth, noble birth, or virtue? The "fights and accusations" that erupt over the distribution of offices in particular are the most pressing issue for justice, as an important example brings home. For if, Aristotle observes, a ruler strikes one who is ruled, the ruler should not be struck in return; if the reverse were to happen, however, then the one who is ruled should not only be struck in return but also be punished in addition. As this example pointedly recalls, justice must preserve rule and justify the compulsion or punishment necessary for ensuring the obedience to law. In acknowledging the necessity for such coercion, in fact, Aristotle draws our attention to his general reticence to speak of force and punishment throughout his account of justice. In this regard, we note that his treatment of justice, and of moral virtue generally, is intended to temper moral indignation, which Aristotle classifies not as a virtue but as a passion. His "mathematical" treatment of distributive and commutative justice not only downplays the dispute over rule but also virtually ignores the role of anger and retribution in the punishment of harms. Even as he acknowledges the need to "reciprocate harm for harm" in his analysis of proportionate reciprocity, he focuses on the exchange of goods and thereby on the more voluntary pursuits that bring human beings together in community. Nevertheless, the role of reciprocity at the origin of the political community reminds us that justice involves an agreement concerning the most fundamental question of rule, and even Aristotle's studied avoidance of the issue of force cannot fully cover over the partly compulsory character of this "agreement" and so of the defining principle of the political community, the regime, in accord with which justice is a mean and a virtue.

Once he has clarified the origin of the political community in proportionate reciprocity, Aristotle acknowledges that justice is not a mean with respect to two vices. Rather, in hewing to the mean or middle term, the just person "is said to be disposed to act according to his choice of what is just, and to distribute things to himself in relation to another (and to another person in relation to a third), *not* in such a way as to distribute more of what is choiceworthy to himself and less to his neighbor, and of harm the reverse, *but rather to distribute what is equal in accord with the proportion*" (1134a1–6, emphasis added). As a characteristic and a part of general justice, therefore, particular justice disposes a person to abide by the mean established in law, and the law itself accords with the equality consistent with the common advantage of those who "share in the regime" (compare 1130b30–32).

Justice and the Dual Ends of Moral Virtue

In light of the conclusion that the just choice accords with the mean established in law and, more fundamentally, the regime, we are now in a position to consider the status of justice with respect to the other standard for choice pointed to by Aristotle. This standard, to repeat, was the good—in the best case, the individual's possession and activity of virtue. Aristotle's analysis of justice as a virtue has raised the question whether, even in the best case, the law can reconcile the two ends to which it demands our devotion as morally serious human beings: the common good, on the one hand, and our perfection in virtue as an end in itself, on the other.

Aristotle proposed a preliminary answer to this difficult question in his discussion of particular justice as a characteristic: justice is the specific perfection that pertains to the desire for gain. To choose in accord with justice and the law, by this account, is to act in accord with the virtue with respect to gain. But in the course of providing evidence that there is a characteristic we identify with particular justice, Aristotle reminded us that there are other characteristics pertaining to gain: liberality, for example, in the case of wealth, as well as courage and greatness of soul in their relation to security and honor, the other goods associated with particular justice. How, then, can it be said that particular justice constitutes the proper perfection pertaining to gain? Aristotle suggests an answer by making particular justice a part of complete justice: particular justice constitutes the proper mean pertaining to gain in relation to the common good. But this answer, we can now see, merely begs the question. For justice's status as a virtue is on the table precisely because the mean in the case of justice is established not simply by reference to our good condition regarding gain but by the proportion established by law concerning parties who contend for the good things. If in its connection with the common good, particular justice is not a mean with respect to two vices, then by this very fact, it is also not like the other virtues in being an "extreme" in accord with "what is best and the doing of something well" (1107a6–8). Just action accords with what is held by the regime to be fair or equal, and not with the good judged by any other standard.

We are confronted by the difficulty, then, that particular justice as a mean is necessarily defined by a standard other than the good condition of the individual with respect to moral virtue. For in determining the distribution of goods among equals, justice must guard the good of the community as a whole, and even in the best case—the regime in which merit is defined by virtue—not only are there competing claims of merit, but the goods human beings generally pursue are limited and must be shared. Indeed, by definition, the "equal" as a measure for particular justice exists to adjudicate competing claims with regard to the good, and the very "nature of justice" is to be this principle of equality by which limited goods are distributed. It is for this reason also that justice can never be wholly separated from compulsion.

The problem presented in the case of particular justice mirrors the problem for justice generally. In being oriented toward the general advantage of the community, the virtues understood as general justice must take their bearings from an end other than themselves. The difficulty for the virtuous individual is most striking in the situations in which the community's good and the activity of moral virtue are most at odds: for example, when the common good requires ignominious surrender rather than noble action in battle; when a generous or magnificent act would mean robbing from one to give to another; when the defense of the country calls for deception or fraud, or even the betrayal of a friend; when justice demands punishments at which reason balks. In seeking to handle this difficulty, and to preserve the law's full moral authority and goodness, one might be tempted to redefine virtue solely in terms of the common good: if surrender is necessary for the preservation of the community, then surrender is the truly courageous or noble act. Yet Aristotle's own investigation of moral virtue indicates that this temptation should be resisted. For, in addition to his insistence that each virtue has its own precise definition and is an end in its own right, he shows that the law also looks to more than the requirements of the political community in defining our perfection, and that the morally serious person understands this perfection not simply in terms of the common good, but in terms of his own nobility. Even in the case of a community as intimate and grounded in affection as the family, Aristotle suggests, if a base act should be required for the "noble end" of its preservation, the act itself does not cease to be base, and the action of a virtuous person in such a situation is therefore "chosen" under compulsion. Although the law and a decent human being may bow to the necessity of actions that preserve the common good, then, neither would wish to redefine as virtue such deception, fraud, or betrayal that the common good may require but moral virtue abhors.

The deepest difficulty that Aristotle points to in his account of particular justice is the tension between moral virtue's orientation toward the common good and its requirements and activity as an end independent of that good. Accordingly, when he cautions early in his discussion of justice that the education of the citizen (the education with a view to the community or common good [*to koinon*]) may not be the same as the education of the good man simply (1130b25–29), he is pointing in the first place not to a tension between moral virtue and some other possibility, but to a tension *within* moral virtue. He thus clarifies the problem at the heart of civic education: the two ends that necessarily demand our devotion as morally serious human beings cannot be fully reconciled. In this way, Aristotle's account of the virtues both describes the political community's noblest pedagogic aim and, on the basis of this community's own aim, establishes its limits.

Natural Justice, Equity, and "Correct Reason"

Having completed his investigation of justice as a virtue, Aristotle indicates that he has sufficiently treated the "nature of each [justice and injustice]" and "the just and unjust in the general sense" (1134a14–16), but his discussion does not end here. He proceeds with accounts of political and natural justice; just and unjust action in their relation to choice; equity; and a final statement on the connection between law and correct reason. In his discussion of political justice, Aristotle recalls the primacy of justice and the political community. For law, and so political justice, "exists among those who share a life in common with a view to being self-sufficient, who are free and equal, either in accord with a proportion or arithmetically" (1134a26–31). The political community is thus constituted not only by "equality in ruling and being ruled" (1134b14–15; compare *Politics* 1287a8–18), but also by a common life that aims at "self-sufficiency"—at living well (*Politics* 1252b27–1253b1). The political community's primacy in this regard—its constitution of the good life in common—underlies the moral authority of the law, the greatness of justice as a virtue, and the nobility, not to say divinity, of the city's claim on its citizens.

Yet, to raise only one serious question that may ultimately bear on the political community's claim in this regard, we note a controversy that has long divided commentators on Aristotle's astonishingly brief account of natural justice: whether we can infer from this account the existence of immutable principles of action. The immediate problem is that Aristotle classifies natural justice as a part of political justice. Yet political justice itself is derived, not from nature, which is always the same, whether here or in Persia, but from particular regimes, which vary. Nevertheless, against those who would argue that *all* the just things exist solely by law or convention, Aristotle unambiguously insists that there are indeed just things by nature. In his most puzzling statement, he acknowledges that "what is by nature is unchangeable and has the same capacity everywhere," only then to assert that "among us [human beings], there is in fact something that is [just] by nature, though it is altogether changeable" and that the just by nature and the just by convention "are similarly changeable" (1134b24–32). If the fundamental question raised by justice is the identity of the true good of human beings, then among the puzzles that Aristotle's discussion of natural justice presents is the one with which he concludes: "the just things that are not natural but human are not everywhere the same, since the regimes are not either; but everywhere there is only one regime that is in accord with nature, the best regime" (1135a3–5). Aristotle seems to take his bearings here by the good rather than the just: the naturally *best* is not always and everywhere just.

It is not surprising, given all this, that Aristotle underscores how difficult it is to act justly or to know what is just, since, we now learn, laws "are not the just things, except incidentally" (1137a9–12). Indeed, his next important subject, equity, points to the same conclusion. Equity is a "correction of the legally just," which is necessary because, given the law's generality, it can speak accurately to the infinite variety of particular circumstances only "for the most part." Still, Aristotle maintains, the law itself is not "ignorant of the error" involved, which is "not in the law or in the lawgiver but in the nature of the matter at hand. For such is simply the stuff of which actions are made" (1137b8–19). In seeking to rectify the error caused by the law's necessary generality, then, we look to "what the lawgiver himself would have said if he had been present and, if he had known of this case, what he would have legislated" (1137b22–24). Aristotle calls this correction of the law "the nature of the equitable" (1137b26). Equity in this sense would appear to be a reasonable solution to the problem of the generality of the law. But it also covers over the more fundamental problem: what does the lawgiver himself look to in establishing the laws?

The extraordinary precision of Aristotle's account of justice in book 5 has the unexpected effect of highlighting the instances in which he is ambiguous or opaque: the changeable character of natural justice and hence the obscurity of its precise dictates, the uncertain status of law as what is just, and the somewhat perplexing character of equity. In light of these difficulties, Aristotle's return to the subject of "correct reason" (1138a10) as he concludes the account of justice is understandable. For the law is not and cannot be our guide simply—it is not absolute in determining action—and the specific direction we might hope to gain from the fact of the existence of natural justice is undercut, to say the least, by its inherent changeability. By recalling the subject of correct reason, Aristotle prepares us for the discussion of intellectual virtue, with the problem of the law and the tension within the ends of moral virtue still in play.

AFTER MORAL VIRTUE: PRUDENCE AND SELF-RESTRAINT (BOOKS 6–7.1–10)

With the taxonomy of the eleven moral virtues now complete, we must return to Aristotle's statement in book 2 that his whole inquiry into virtue is being conducted, "not so that we may know what virtue is, but so that we may become good" (1103b26–28). Accordingly, he insisted there that what pertains to actions—how one ought to carry out one's serious deeds—must be investigated as well. For although it is certainly instructive to say that courage, for example, is a mean between two extremes with regard to confidence and fear and that courageous actions aim at what is noble, above all in war, none of this yet helps us determine in this or that concrete circumstance precisely what action would be truly courageous and so neither cowardly nor reckless: sometimes standing one's ground might well be courageous, sometimes merely reckless, sometimes even cowardly. It is important but also insufficient to answer the question "what is courage?," for we need to know also what specific action will, in the circumstances before us, meet the general definition of courage. How, in other words, can the courageous person *know* that a given action must be undertaken in order to hit on the mean, the "target," and so to avoid the vicious extremes?

In book 2, Aristotle had limited himself to the following remark: "Now, 'acting in accord with correct reason' is commonly granted, and let it be posited for now—what pertains to it will be spoken of later, both what 'correct reason' is and how it relates to the virtues" (1103b31–34). Only at the beginning of book 6 does he return to explore "correct reason," and he states there with perfect clarity the inadequacy of saying only that the virtuous act is the one that accords with "correct reason" and so hits the mean:

> But speaking in this way is, though truthful, not at all clear. For in all the other concerns too about which a science exists, it is true to say that one ought not to strain or slacken either too much or too little, but as accords with the mean and as correct reason states. Yet if somebody should possess this alone, he would be no further ahead in his knowledge—for example, he would not know what sorts of things ought to be applied to the body if somebody should say, "so many things as the art of medicine commands and as he who possesses that art commands." Hence in the case of the characteristics of the soul too, not only ought this to be stated truly, but what correct reason is must also be defined, that is, what its defining boundary is.

Now, book 6 contains many fascinating arguments concerning (among other things) the nature of the human soul, the five ways in which it can attain the truth—art, science, prudence, wisdom, and intellect (*nous*)—and the similarities and differences between them. But it has to be said that by the end of the book, Aristotle leaves the precise operation of "correct reason," in the form of what he calls "prudence" (1144b27–28), obscure: it is the problem, not the solution to the problem, that he chooses to state with perfect clarity. We limit ourselves to a brief account of Aristotle's remarks concerning the status of the knowledge bound up with moral action and of its problematic character.

The Problem of Prudence

Aristotle begins by repeating that just as the whole soul is divided into rational and nonrational—that is, into a part possessing *logos* and a part without it—so there must be virtues related to each, the excellence of the rational soul being the virtue "of thinking," or contemplative virtue, that of the nonrational soul the virtue "of character," or moral virtue. But because Aristotle has completed his treatment of the moral virtues, he is especially concerned now to indicate that the rational soul too admits of division: one part is that by which we contemplate all those sorts of beings whose principles do not admit of being otherwise, the other part that by which we contemplate all those things that do admit of being otherwise. The former is bound up with science, with knowledge in the strictest sense, the latter with calculation or deliberation and therewith prudence. Science, one might say, is the grasp of the necessity governing such beings as exist of necessity and hence (Aristotle here notes) eternally. Prudence, by contrast, is concerned not only with things that do admit of being other than they are, but also, as a subset of that category, with actions performed rather than artifacts made, the latter falling within the province of art (6.4). Further, the prudent person is marked by excellence in deliberation, and we deliberate only about things that can be both otherwise and acted on by us: we cannot deliberate about past events, for example, or about things that happen of necessity, such as solstices and sunrises (3.3). Moreover, the subject of concern to the prudent human being is not some partial good or advantage, like health, but rather the sorts of things conducive to living well in general: Pericles and his like are held to be supremely prudent, because they—as distinguished from the wise but imprudent Anaxagoras or Thales—understand what is good for themselves and for human beings generally, both as members of a political community and as individuals.

Now, Aristotle contends that prudence must be possessed of or accompanied by a *logos*. Yet it must also be distinguished from science as well as from wisdom, the most precise of the sciences (1141a16–17), and hence also from the kind of *logos* characteristic of them. By what kind of *logos*, then, is prudence characterized? For *logos* is an ambiguous term. It may mean a fully rational argument, on the one hand, or, on the other, a mere speech or account. Here we note that prudence, or correct reason, is or permits the proper choice of means to an end that has been given and that is therefore not itself the subject of deliberation: good deliberation in the unqualified sense, which is the mark of a prudent person, "accords with what is advantageous in relation to the end, about which end prudence is a true conviction" (1142b29–33). The operation of prudence, then, is limited to the selection of means and is therefore dependent on some prior positing of the correct end. It is for just this reason that one's moral character must be such as to shape correctly the appetites involved in choice (1139a31–b5) and that prudence in general is tied inextricably to moral virtue, to the excellence of character: "virtue makes the target correct, prudence the things conducive to that target" (1144a7–9, 1145a5–6, also 1178a16–19). It is for this reason too that moral virtue arises through habituation, as distinguished from teaching.

All of this amounts to saying that prudence is not and does not supply knowledge of the ends of action, the very knowledge we most need; it is but a "conviction" of a kind; it is the virtue of that part of the soul "involved in the formation of opinions" (1140b25–28). The entire discussion of prudence may be said to culminate, if that is the right word, in Aristotle's recommendation that one "pay attention to the undemonstrated assertions and opinions of experienced and older people, or of the prudent, no less than to demonstrations, for because they have an experienced eye, they see correctly" (1143b11–14). Awareness of the end or ends of moral action is not knowledge but a conviction or opinion, instilled in us by habituation at the hands of our community—by obedience to one's father (recall 1102b32 and 1103a3), for example, and to the law (consider 1138a10). Only when attempting to define prudence, in contrast to the other ways of attaining the truth, does Aristotle take his bearings by those who are said to be prudent and by what opinion holds about them: prudence is fundamentally tied to opinion, to opinions expressed in speech.

Impressive as the prudent person's ability is to choose correctly among the means available to him, he cannot be said strictly speaking to know why he acts. And this is of a piece with the fact that Aristotle's primary audience in the *Ethics* is said to understand the "that" as distinguished from the "why" concerning things noble and just, and concerning the political things generally. Prudence is less an intellectual virtue than the completion or necessary accompaniment of the moral virtues.

Self-Restraint

At the beginning of book 7, Aristotle indicates clearly that although he remains concerned with what pertains to "character," he is making a new beginning. The principal subject of the first ten chapters of book 7 proves to be what "we call" self-restraint and its contrary, the lack of self-restraint. The precise nature of these qualities, as well as their place within the *Ethics* as a whole, is somewhat puzzling.

That self-restraint is not a moral virtue is manifest: Aristotle has concluded his treatment of the moral virtues at the end of book 5, and he here explicitly contrasts self-restraint and the lack of it with moral virtue and vice. Indeed, we now see that just as there are two things apart from moral vice that must be avoided—brutishness and lack of self-restraint—so also there are two choiceworthy things apart from moral virtue—self-restraint and a certain superlative virtue that is "heroic and divine." Moreover, as brutishness in human beings is worse than vice (consider 1150a1–3), so divine virtue is superior to moral virtue (1145a26). Neither moral virtue nor vice, then, marks the boundaries of the extremes of which human beings are capable.

Yet self-restraint *is* akin to the moral virtue of moderation, lack of self-restraint to the vice of licentiousness, because all prove to be concerned with those bodily pleasures that, while connected with the necessities of food, drink, and sex, readily admit of excess. The self-restrained person in the unqualified sense is capable of resisting the attractive pull of these excessive pleasures, which he knows one ought to resist, whereas the moderate person simply does not feel their pull at all and so has nothing to resist. The person lacking self-restraint, by contrast, is unable to withstand the temptation of the (excessive) bodily pleasures that he knows one ought to resist, whereas the licentious person chooses actively to pursue them on the grounds that they are good. Moderation, then, seems better than self-restraint, licentiousness worse than lack of self-restraint.

Aristotle also treats in book 7 the qualities of steadfastness and softness—that is, the capacity and incapacity respectively to withstand the pains a person knows one ought to withstand, those stemming from unsatisfied desire, for example—that bear some similarity to the virtue of courage and the vice of cowardice. We can now see that the uniting theme of book 7 is pleasure and pain, for the first ten of its chapters are devoted to the various capacities to withstand them, the last four to pleasure understood as the human good. But, we suggest, these will be taken up only partly from the point of view of moral virtue: self-restraint and lack of self-restraint will be considered also from the point of view of what transcends moral virtue (compare, e.g., 1148a22–24 with 1146a9–16). In accord with this, Aristotle proceeds by first sticking closely to "received opinions" (*endoxa*) about self-restraint and the lack of it, about steadfastness and softness; he begins with a survey of what is praised and what is blamed, in the element of opinion. Yet it quickly becomes clear that among the relevant opinions there number certain difficulties raised by unnamed Sophists as well as by Socrates—who appears both more frequently here than elsewhere in the *Ethics* and in the company of Empedocles, Heraclitus, and "those who study nature" (1147b8–9). The discussion of self-restraint will therefore include, but also go well beyond, ordinary opinion.

As for Socrates, he denied that anyone can really lack self-restraint, on the grounds that "nobody acts contrary to what is best while supposing that he is so acting; he acts instead through ignorance" (1145b25–27). Aristotle notes immediately that Socrates's argument flies in the face of common sense, for who could deny the experience of failing to stick to one's better knowledge in the face of certain pleasures, of "giving in to temptation"? It is as a result surprising to discover that Aristotle will shortly vindicate the core of the Socratic position: "what Socrates was seeking turns out to be the case" (1147b14–15). Socrates was correct to maintain that we cannot act against the knowledge (of what is good) in us: in all that we do we necessarily seek out what we hold to be good. The prospect of enjoying powerful pleasures can, in the case of those who lack self-restraint, somehow alter the knowledge in them such that it is ineffective in guiding their action. Aristotle takes up several explanations for this change in the status of one's knowledge—the operation of the particular or ultimate premise as distinguished from the general or universal one, for example; the differing ways in which one can be said to "have" knowledge, just as reason is possessed and yet temporarily suspended in those who are asleep, mad, or drunk; and the effect of the union of opinion and desire in prompting action. Aristotle asserts that there is such a thing as lack of self-restraint, then, against the letter of Socrates's position, but agrees with its spirit in that he too contends that knowledge (of the good) cannot be "drag[ged] around as if it were a slave" but is, in those who lack self-restraint, either temporarily altered or rendered impotent by the prospect of intense pleasure. Self-restraint, then, is the impressive, if also somewhat mysterious, ability to stick to one's knowledge—or for that matter to one's firm opinion (consider 1146b24–26 and following)—of what is good in the face of competing pleasures, just as the lack of self-restraint is the susceptibility of one's convictions concerning what is good to alteration in the presence of certain pleasures.

Aristotle spends much more time discussing the defects that are the lack of self-restraint, softness, and brutishness than he does their impressive contraries—indeed, after having mentioned it once, Aristotle never again speaks of the "heroic and divine" virtue. This emphasis is perhaps due to the fact that lack of self-restraint and softness (and brutishness) are more common than their corresponding strengths (consider 1150a15–16). Here Aristotle repeatedly takes his bearings by what "the many" (the majority) are capable of, and it is in the context of discussing lack of self-restraint that he has recourse to "correct reason" once again. The reappearance of "correct reason" suggests a connection to book 6 and hence to the thought that the "knowledge" with which the human being lacking self-restraint struggles is bound up with moral opinion as instilled by habituation. In contrast, then, to the sharp distinction between lack of self-restraint and moral vice that Aristotle draws at the outset, and elsewhere, he sometimes blurs that distinction (consider 1149b20, 1151a6). What is more, and stranger, Aristotle also indicates that there is a kind of unrestraint that is brutish, one that goes beyond what is (typically) found in human beings. If there is a sort of unrestraint that is or is very close to moral vice, on the one hand, and a sort that is brutish, on the other, what then of their contraries? That is, if there is a self-restraint that takes its bearings by "correct reason" and hence by the ends of moral action as given by habituation, might there also be another, extraordinary self-restraint, the contrary of the brutish lack of self-restraint, that looks to some goal other and indeed higher than morally virtuous action?

One can arrive at the same possibility by asking—as Aristotle does at the beginning of 7.9—precisely what sort of *logos* it is that the truly self-restrained person will abide by. What, in other words, might this remarkable capacity be *for*? Aristotle there replies that the self-restrained person in the unqualified sense will abide by his true opinion, as distinguished from a false opinion or, we suggest, a merely "correct" one. For there are those who remain in full command of their great capacities precisely because they know or desire to know the demonstrations and verses of Empedocles, for example; there may be a kind of self-restraint characteristic of those whose desires are both strong and not base (compare 1146a9–16). The case of Socrates himself suggests as much (consider Xenophon,

Memorabilia 1.5). Might this extraordinary self-restraint even be the otherwise missing account of "heroic and divine virtue" as that phrase was understood, not of course by the Spartans (1145a28), but by Aristotle?

ON FRIENDSHIP (BOOKS 8–9)

The two books that examine friendship stand between Aristotle's discussions of pleasure in books 7 and 10 and form a bridge between his account of moral virtue in books 2 through 5 and his final discussion of happiness in book 10. In the discussion of moral virtue, as we have seen, the question of happiness as our end all but disappears or is subsumed by an emphasis on the noble. But happiness reenters the scene in the books on friendship, and Aristotle's account offers an extended reflection on what we can now see are two of our deepest concerns: to possess the greatest good for ourselves, or to be happy, and to dedicate ourselves nobly and wholeheartedly to virtue, not least to the virtue embodied by a true friend. Friendship in the best case may offer both.

The singular importance of friendship in Aristotle's investigation of virtue and the human good is made clear by its length: the discussion of friendship covers two books, whereas that of justice, the "greatest" of the moral virtues, covers but one. As Aristotle insists at the outset, friendship is necessary to living well, so much so that, without friends, no one would wish to live, even if he possessed all the other goods. Aristotle underscores here the broad scope of its activity and actions: the young, the old, and those in their prime all need friends, as do the wealthy and the poor, the fortunate and the unfortunate, the powerful and the weak. Moreover, friendship naturally inheres in parents and offspring, and it holds together political communities in concord (or "like-mindedness": *homonoia*); indeed, lawgivers are more serious about such friendship than about justice. Friendship thus encompasses both necessary and noble things, and it will prove inextricably linked to sharing in the activity or activities, and so the accompanying pleasure, that each person associates with happiness.

At the start, however, Aristotle directs our attention to friendship as a "virtue" or at any rate as something "accompanied by virtue" (1155a3–4). And he asks first what elicits friendship or is "lovable" (*philētos*). The lovable in this sense "seems to be what is good, pleasant, or useful," or, more precisely, what is good or pleasant, since something is useful if it should achieve either of these two. Strikingly absent here is what is "noble," the

very thing he had insisted is *the* end of virtue. Aristotle is franker here
than before about the final end of human action: it is the case not only
that "most people wish for noble things but choose the beneficial ones,"
but also that even when a virtuous person chooses a noble action, he
chooses it as the greater or greatest good; indeed, Aristotle will say, "each
wishes for the good things for himself most of all" (1159a10–12).

Because friendship is a reciprocal relation, however, it is not sufficient
simply to identify the things on account of which people love one another. For friendship as "reciprocated love" requires "goodwill," such that
each friend wishes for the good things for the other and for that other's
sake. This goodwill, moreover, must not go unnoticed if the friendship
is to be active; "goodwill," Aristotle will later say, is like friendship that is
idle. There are three forms of friendship, then, in accord with the three
things that are said to be lovable—the good, the useful, and the pleasant—and each form involves a reciprocal love that does not go unnoticed.

In the case of friendships grounded in the useful and the pleasant,
however, the parties "do not love each other in themselves, but only insofar as they come to have something good from the other" (1156a10–
12). On this basis, Aristotle makes a key distinction between "complete"
(or "perfect": *teleia*) friendship—the "friendship of those who are good
and alike in point of virtue" (1156b7–8)—and the other two forms. This
distinction is key, because such complete friendship is "the friendship of
good human beings, insofar as they are good," and is indeed "friendship
in the primary and authoritative sense" (1157a30–31).

Complete friendship, then, is based on virtue—on the good character
of the friends—and it is for this reason best. The two other forms bear
a resemblance to the complete form, but they are more clearly grounded
in the reciprocity that obtains when, for instance, "each attains the same
thing from the other" (1157a4). Because mutual exchange is also consti-
tutive of friendship, the question of this reciprocity occupies a substan-
tial part of the discussion of friendship, particularly in book 8 and the
first chapters of book 9. Mutual exchange must be equal or made equal
in friendships in which each party obtains the same thing from the other,
whether pleasure or something beneficial, or in which each obtains something different in kind, as in "heterogenous" friendships (1163b30–35),
or in which one party is superior to another in some respect—for instance, in virtue or money, as with a father and a son or a wealthy and
a poor person. Hence, despite Aristotle's introductory insistence that

"[w]hen people are friends, they have no need of justice at all" (1155a26–27), it turns out that, given its connection with reciprocity, friendship necessarily involves considerations of just exchange—of equality, commensurability of goods, and merit. As he later notes even in regard to familial associations, "[h]ow a husband must live in relation to his wife, and, in general, a friend in relation to a friend, appears no different a thing to inquire into than how it is just to do so" (1162a29–31).

Because "both friendship and the just are concerned with the same matters and are present among the same persons" (1159b25–26), Aristotle can speak of the concord that lawgivers seek to inculcate in their political communities, and he examines six regimes—kingship and tyranny, aristocracy and oligarchy, timocracy (or polity) and democracy—in terms of friendship. He can also investigate the "likenesses" of these regimes in the household, even though "a human being is by nature more a coupling being than a political one." Hence familial relations are more natural to human beings than are political ones, and the household is "earlier and more necessary than a city" (1160b22–24, 1162a17–19). In short, questions of justice arise even in the family, since in living together in a household, human beings seek not only to procreate but also to obtain in common the "things that contribute to life," and husband and wife "assist each other … by putting their own things in service of what is in common" (1162a19–24). As Aristotle notes in introducing his analysis of the regimes, "all communities are like parts of the political community, for people come together for a certain advantage," and so "the sorts of friendships will correspond with the different sorts of communities" (1160a8–10, 29–30).

Yet this correspondence of the political community and friendship cannot be sustained, especially in the best case: the best regime here—kingship—does not correspond to the best kind of friendship, which is not paternal friendship but that which obtains between equals in point of virtue. Nevertheless, or for that very reason, Aristotle's treatment of the regimes shows that the investigation of friendship too must confront the problem of the common good that is central to justice. On the one hand, in every community, justice and friendship may be said to exist insofar as each member of the community achieves his individual advantage as a member of that community. Accordingly, in light of the connection of friendship to individual advantage, a significant part of Aristotle's account is occupied with questions of exchange, debt, and repayment, as well as the accusations and blame that arise in such matters and the dissolution of friendships when the relevant advantage ceases. On the other hand, justice and friendship are said to exist also to the extent to which each member seeks not or not only his own advantage but also the advantage of the community as a whole. And complete friendship holds out the possibility of a community in which each achieves his own good precisely by acting in accord with the good of another. In contrast with the political community and even with the family, then, complete friendship would seem to constitute most fully this kind of community, because it is grounded in virtue and because each friend wishes for the good things for the other for that other's sake. Moreover, such friendship can be said to achieve the good simply for each, since virtuous friends love each other on account of their good character or who they are themselves. For this reason, it can be said of two virtuous friends especially that there is "no need of justice" (1155a27), and in this sense, complete friendship as a community is potentially superior rather than subordinate to the political community.

Unlike friendships based on pleasure and usefulness, then, complete friendship is less concerned with questions of just exchange, is not subject to accusations or blame, and, since it is based on virtue, is stable and lasting. Consequently, Aristotle's treatment of complete friendship is occupied with how complete friendship achieves the good, a question that he pursues most fully in the latter chapters of book 9. We can provide only a sketch of this complex discussion and some of the important issues it raises with respect to the overarching question of the *Ethics*, that of the character of happiness or the human good.

As Aristotle observes in book 8, friendship is like virtue in being both a characteristic and an activity; in the absence of activity, there may be goodwill but no friendship properly speaking. Indeed, Aristotle insists, "nothing so much belongs to friends as living together" (1157b19). Both time and the "habits of living together" (*sunētheia*) are necessary if friendship is to arise at all, for people must live together over time if they are to come to know, trust, and love one another. More important, it is in living together that friends "delight in and provide good things to one another" (1157b7–8). Given our nature, even those who are "blessed" and who have no need of useful things still have need of pleasant ones and "seek out friends who are pleasant" (1158a25–26). Since that which is good simply is also pleasant simply, the living together of virtuous friends is both good for and pleasant to each. Furthermore, active friendship involves "feelings of friendly affection" (*philēsis*)—of loving and being loved—either equally so or in proportion to the relevant superiority; and Aristotle considers in this regard whether friendship consists more in loving, as it is held to do, or in being loved. The evidence he adduces for the common opinion is the love of a mother, who loves her children and seeks their good even when it is not possible that she receive love in return. But the common opinion regarding this matter is implicit also in the view that true friends wish for the good of their friend and do not love themselves more than they love their friend. In this respect, the love of mothers for their children—the only example in his discussion of what we might call selfless love—would seem to constitute a peak of friendship or be friendship simply.

Yet, as Aristotle's discussion has emphasized, people seek friends as a good. In a most striking example, he observes that one friend would never wish that the other become a god, since the distance between them would then be so great that he would no longer be a friend and therefore a good to his friend. Indeed, Aristotle concludes, even though someone may wish for the greatest goods for his friend as a human being, nevertheless "each wishes for the good things for himself most of all" (1159a10–12). Here, then, is the crucial difficulty bound up even in, or precisely in, complete friendship: a virtuous person loves his virtuous friend and wishes for good things for the friend for his sake, but he also loves his friend as a good for himself, and friends "are held to be the greatest of the external goods" (1169b9–10; compare 1123b21–22). Is it the case, then, that in complete friendship a common good is achievable in which each obtains the greatest goods, or does even (or especially) the virtuous friend love himself and his own good most? When Aristotle returns to the question of friendly affection or love in book 9, he investigates most directly the question of self-love and friendship. This investigation is the culmination of the account of friendship, and, acknowledging its complexity, we conclude simply by sketching how it leads to book 10 and his final discussion of happiness.

Aristotle takes up the question of self-love first by noting that the marks of friendship "seem to have arisen from things pertaining to oneself" (1166a1–2). The marks by which people define friendship are five: (1) a friend wishes for and does what appears good for the other person's sake; (2) a friend wishes for his friend to exist and live for the friend's sake; (3) friends go through life together; (4) they choose the same things; and (5) they share in sufferings and joys. But a serious or decent person is disposed in just these ways toward himself too, since he is "of like mind with himself and longs for the same things with his whole soul" (1166a13–14). Free from internal strife, then, he always acts in accord with and for the sake of his "thinking part"—the part "each person seems to be" and "with which he is prudent"—and he wishes that this part especially be preserved, delighting in it and sharing always in the same pains and pleasures. It is possible to speak of friendship toward oneself, then, if one speaks in terms of the best or most authoritative part of the soul, the thinking or prudent part.

Aristotle relies on this distinction to clarify the status of self-love in friendship, that is, "whether one ought to love oneself most or someone else" (1168a28–29). The obvious difficulty is that ordinarily we reproach self-lovers as base people who do everything for their own sakes alone, whereas a person who is decent acts "on account of what is noble," and the better a person he is, the more he does so and hence "disregard[s] himself" (1168a29–35). Yet both those who reproach self-love and those who defend it have credibility. For people justly reproach those self-lovers who gratify the "nonrational part of their soul" in allotting to themselves "the greater share of money, honors, and bodily pleasures"—the things people generally fight over (1168b15–21). But we do not call a self-lover, let alone blame as one, the person who seems to be *more* of a self-lover, namely, he who "allots to himself the noblest things and the greatest goods [and] gratifies the most authoritative part of himself," which he obeys in all things (1168b28–31). Aristotle now identifies the most authoritative part of the soul, earlier called the "thinking part" and the part that possesses prudence, as the "intellect" (1168b30–1169a1). We do not reproach such a self-lover because, in obeying the intellect, the decent person is "preeminently serious about noble actions" (1169a6–8). Even though this person "manifestly allots more of the noble to himself" and so "the greater good" (1169a35–b1, 1169a28–29), this kind of self-love is not reproached or reproachable since it also benefits others, particularly with respect to the lesser goods people typically fight over.

Aristotle thus claims that "if all compete with a view to what is noble and exert themselves to the utmost to do what is noblest, then in common there would be all the necessities and for each individually the greatest of goods, if in fact virtue is of such a character" (1169a8–11). Even though the serious man is a self-lover, his noble action contributes to the good of another and the common good. His preference for noble action over all other goods explains his extraordinary choice in certain circumstances even to forsake his life in behalf of his friends or city; it explains, as well, his preference "to feel pleasure intensely for a short time over feeling it mildly for a long one, to live nobly for one year over living in a haphazard way for many years, and to do one great and noble action over many small ones" (1169a22–25). His noble action thus makes him a good friend and citizen, even though he is a self-lover to the highest degree; Aristotle himself advises that one ought to be a self-lover in this way and not as the many are.

Having established the correct form of self-love, and so its correct relation to friendship, Aristotle proceeds to discuss what may seem to be practical matters, such as whether the happy person needs friends, how many friends one should have, and whether one needs friends more in good fortune than in bad. Accordingly, he would seem to have disposed of the difficulty whether in the best friendship—the friendship grounded in virtue—there can be a community in which each individually achieves the greatest goods for himself while not denying the greatest goods to his friend. Yet Aristotle's argument leaves at least one loose thread, since in the "competition" in which virtuous friends each undertake to act nobly in behalf of one another or their city, only one can obtain the greater good, either supplying his friend with a lesser good or denying him the opportunity for noble action in behalf of their city. One might resolve the problem, as Aristotle tries to do, by being "the cause" of a friend's noble action, but even in this case, he concedes, it is "nobler" to be such a cause (1169a29–1169b1). What is more, given the equality of the two friends in point of virtue, the problem may seem intractable: is friendship in the best sense really possible between two equally virtuous human beings?

In the face of this difficulty, Aristotle offers a complicated argument regarding the natural grounds and goodness of friendship when it obtains between virtuous people and when friends share in an activity in which each achieves his highest good. He suggests that those who perform benefits for others love these others as their own "work" (*ergon*: 1169a2–3). The cause of this experience "would seem to have more to do with nature" than does the love that people ordinarily attribute to lenders for their debtors, namely, the connection of activity with existing and living, which are choiceworthy and lovable: in activity, the maker himself "somehow *is* the work," for which work he feels affection because he loves his own existence (1167b28–30, 1168a5–9). Even mothers, who earlier seemed to be a peak of friendship insofar as they love their children and wish for their good without expectation of return, can now be seen as also loving their children as their own work, and "they are fond of this more than the work is of its maker" (1168a4–5).

Having broached this line of argument, Aristotle pursues it most fully only once he has brought out the connection between the serious man's preference for noble deeds and his self-love. What follows in the final chapters on friendship confirms the claim with which he began: no one would choose to live without friends, even if he had all the other goods. For friendship is so fundamentally tied to our existence—to our perception and love of that existence—that to rob human life of it would be to make it not worth living: friendship makes possible the noblest of actions and the most intense and continuous of pleasures; it allows the virtuous person to contemplate his own noble and choiceworthy actions in those of his friend; and, finally, it involves sharing in whatever activity—from drinking and playing at dice to hunting and philosophizing—that "existing is for each, or whatever the goal is for the sake of which they choose living" (1172a1–2). As Aristotle guides his readers through these arguments, he also prepares them for the return in book 10 of the consideration of pleasure and of the question of the activity or activities that, being best, may be said to constitute the human good or happiness.

ARISTOTLE ON PLEASURE (BOOKS 1, 7, 10)

Aristotle has three principal discussions of pleasure in the *Ethics*. As we have seen, the first occurs in his opening analysis, in book 1, of happiness, or the human good at which we all aim. He there raises the possibility that pleasure is the end we seek, only to dismiss it with contempt: to live for the sake of pleasure is to live a slavish life fit only for fatted cattle. But Aristotle rehabilitates pleasure even in book 1, since he argues that precisely those who act in morally virtuous ways, and for the right reason, will also take pleasure in doing so. Yet he takes up hedonism—the philosophic doctrine that pleasure is the human good—only after his treatment of moral virtue has come to an end: only in book 7, that is, following his discussion of self-restraint, does he take seriously pleasure as a, or rather the, good (7.11–14). The deepest reason for this becomes clear on reflection: Aristotle has already implied, and he will state perfectly clearly in book 10, that the life of moral virtue by itself cannot supply us with the happiness we seek. It therefore requires some supplement, and pleasure is a strong candidate to be that supplement.

Aristotle begins with a survey of the positions opposed to pleasure, ranging from the most to the least hostile to pleasure: pleasure is never good, or some pleasures are good, though pleasure is not *the* good. He then proceeds to criticize the critics of pleasure, a move which suggests that according to him, their arguments do not in fact refute the possibility that pleasure is the good. And although the criticisms of pleasure here include the strictly moral argument that pleasure, or some pleasures, are shameful, Aristotle himself is silent about shame: he takes his bearings by the "nature" of pleasure and its goodness. (This may explain too the highly theoretical character of his discussion: is pleasure a process of coming-into-being, a *genesis*, or not?) In fact, Aristotle offers an explanation as to why pleasures and especially the bodily pleasures—those that most attract the condemnation of the critics—are so compelling. For such pleasures drive away pains; the more intense they are the better they do this, at least for a time. And, as Aristotle notes in this context, our nature is such that we are subject to "destruction": we are mortal. Far from condemning those who pursue to excess the bodily pleasures, then, Aristotle helps us understand and even sympathize with them. They may be responding, in their desire for great pleasure, to a serious problem, to the pain of the awareness of our mortality.

Aristotle turns one last time to discuss pleasure, as a preface to his concluding discussion of happiness in book 10 (10.1–5). Here too he begins with a lengthy survey of opinions, but this time he includes also the advocates of pleasure, represented in this context by the thoroughly respectable philosopher Eudoxus (10.2): extra-moral hedonism can supply the foundation of a life that is indeed respectable. Aristotle notes as if in passing that some of those who argue against pleasure do so insincerely but for a good reason, namely, so that they may curb the tendency of a good many people to pursue pleasure incorrectly. In other words, their public opposition to hedonism is feigned, albeit for a good purpose. One has to say that Aristotle, at least in book 1 of the *Ethics*, falls into this category.

But what, then, *is* Aristotle's view of pleasure? If his highly moralistic opposition to hedonism in book 1 is rhetorical, and if he takes pains in book 7 to criticize the critics of pleasure, is he a hedonist? The question is harder to answer than one might think. For example, in book 10, Aristotle raises the crucial question, the question we are considering, only to decline to answer it: "As to whether we choose to live on account of the pleasure involved or choose the pleasure on account of our being alive, let that be dismissed at present. For these things appear to be yoked together and not to admit of separation: without activity, pleasure does not arise, and pleasure completes every activity" (1175a18–21). Do we choose activity for the sake of pleasure, or for its own sake, however pleasant it may be? Aristotle, to repeat, declines to decide the question here.

Still, we think, Aristotle is not finally a hedonist. On the one hand, he does argue that the happy life we seek must include pleasure, and that there are natural pleasures without which life would be impossible: the pleasures of food and drink, for example. There are also certain other natural pleasures that do not presuppose a prior emptying or depletion (like hunger) and that are good nonetheless or for that very reason: he speaks here of the pleasures of certain smells, sights, and sounds, as well as memories and hopes. Aristotle, then, is far from being an ascetic. But, on the other hand, he stresses the priority of activity to pleasure: happiness is a certain activity in accord with virtue, and this will necessarily give rise to pleasures that accompany, augment, and improve the activity. Yet the activity is prior; the pleasure attending it is but a sign of its goodness. In other words, Aristotle insists that the good will be (among other things) pleasant, not that pleasure is the good.

THE RETURN TO HAPPINESS (BOOK 10.6–9)

Aristotle turns for the last time to take up happiness in 10.6, referring explicitly to the discussion in book 1. In fact, he tells us four times here that he is repeating himself. Happiness must reside in an activity chosen for its own sake, and so it must be in that sense self-sufficient: "happiness is in need of nothing but is self-sufficient" (1176b5–6; consider 1097b15 and context). Above all, Aristotle repeats that since "the actions that accord with virtue" are chosen for their own sake, happiness must reside in action or activity in accord with virtue (1176a35–1176b9; consider 1098a16–18).

But which virtue? In book 10, of course, Aristotle will finally describe, and praise, intellectual or contemplative virtue. The first step in that direction consists of his surprisingly lengthy denial that the pleasures of play constitute happiness, though they do appear to be chosen for their own sake. Here, then, Aristotle begins his case for the centrality of "virtue"—still unmodified—by criticizing the trifling pleasures of play; and he does so by relying partly on the bad example of "the many," tyrants, and children, partly also on the good examples of decent or equitable men who are serious, and of a certain wise statesman (Anacharsis) who praised seriousness. The quite limited argument in 10.6, then, serves chiefly to return our attention, after three books, to "virtue." It hardly prepares us for the speed with which Aristotle now identifies, at the beginning of 10.7, the "virtue" in question: the activity of that which is most excellent in us would be "complete [perfect: *teleia*] happiness," and since this most excellent thing is the intellect "or something else that seems naturally to rule, to command, and to possess intelligence concerning what is noble and divine," the activity in question would be contemplative (1177a12–18). This too he claims to have said before—falsely, so it seems (consider, however, 1098a7–8). Chapters 7 and 8 together are devoted to establishing the supreme goodness of contemplation and for that reason can lay claim to being the peak of the *Ethics*.

Of the five arguments in praise of contemplation in 10.7, the last two are most important (and longest): the contemplative way of life is marked by the greatest self-sufficiency, understood now not as the perfect freedom from all need or want—Aristotle makes clear here that this is impossible—but as the relative freedom from reliance on other human beings above all, a freedom enjoyed by the wise when engaging in their characteristic activity as compared with the activities of the just, the moderate, and the courageous. For the first time, Aristotle's praise of contemplative virtue comes at the expense, not of mere play, but of moral virtue; from the point of view of the self-sufficiency now on the table, the wise man is superior to the man of justice, or moderation, or courage, which means of course that he is different from them. Here Aristotle goes so far as to affirm that contemplation "*alone* would seem to be cherished for its own sake" (1177b1–2, emphasis added): those who sought, in the life dedicated to the moral virtues, an end in itself, must now look to (or look up to) a fundamentally new kind of virtue and a fundamentally new way of life.

Aristotle's fifth and final argument here appeals to another standard admired by his audience: he appeals to "leisure," to the freedom from the necessity of work, which is after all connected with the needs of the body, even in the actions of great political men. Aristotle demonstrates that the activities of generals and statesmen at their peak are defective from the point of view of the political men themselves: peace and happiness are the goals of each activity respectively, but these goals are rightly understood to be distinct from and superior to the activities themselves. Only contemplation, then, is characterized by "leisure," because it is undertaken for its own sake and so is not in service of some higher goal.

Aristotle concludes his account of the superiority of contemplation in 10.7 as follows: "if all this is so, then this activity [of contemplation] would constitute the complete [perfect] happiness of a human being ..." (1177b24–25). Even if we cannot be fully self-sufficient and altogether at leisure, nonetheless "complete" happiness is possible for a human being. Or is it? For Aristotle adds, as if in passing, *the* difficulty we saw in book 1: "Provided, that is, that [such happiness] goes together with a complete span of life, for there is nothing incomplete in what belongs to happiness" (1177b24–26; recall 1098a18 and 1100a5). And he states immediately: "But a life of this sort would exceed what is human." Is "complete happiness" *impossible*, then, since our lives remain fundamentally exposed to chance? Aristotle's answer proves once again to praise the intellect or its activity: it is the practice of contemplative virtue, not "the other virtue," that is most godlike for a human being; not nobility of action but correctness of understanding constitutes assimilation to god. And such assimilation is most characterized by happiness. Mortals though we are, we should nonetheless strive to make ourselves immortal, to live as the immortals do.

In 10.8, Aristotle continues to demote the life and the happiness connected with moral virtue, on the grounds that these are "characteristically human"—*human* here being very close to a term of disparagement: the moral virtues are largely bound up with the body and its passions, as is, by extension, even prudence. To confirm the inferiority of moral to contemplative virtue, Aristotle discusses at length "external equipment" and finds contemplation to need far less of it than do the moral virtues. Money and the like are even impediments to contemplation; the two kinds of virtue are not only different, then, but in some tension. (The addition here of the liberal human being to the list of the morally virtuous has the effect of stressing their reliance on money, on lucre, and not just on other human beings: compare 1177a30–34 with 1178a28–34.) A measure, perhaps, of the advance in Aristotle's argument here is the more exalted character of his authorities, for he relies now not just on the view of a wise statesman (Solon), as he had done before, but also on that of a genuine philosopher (Anaxagoras) (1179a9–17; compare 1176b23–35). One who contemplates is of course a human being and so must live among human beings; for this utilitarian reason alone he will choose what accords with (moral) virtue, at least within the limits imposed by the self-sufficiency and leisure he enjoys.

As if to compensate for this remarkable bluntness, but in fact to compound it, Aristotle again defends the superiority of contemplation by recourse to the gods: we suppose that they are especially happy and blessed, and is it not ridiculous to think of them as acting morally? "[W]hat sort of actions ought we to assign to them? Just acts? Or will they appear laughable as they make contracts, return deposits, and do anything else of that sort? But what about courageous acts? Do the gods endure frightening things and run risks, because doing so is noble?" (1178b7–13; compare, e.g., 1115b11–13). Indeed, "[a]ll that pertains to actions would appear, to those who go through it, petty and unworthy of gods" (1178b17–18). If the gods do not act or (still less) make anything, and if, as all suppose, the gods are alive, then they can "do" nothing other than contemplate. In this way, Aristotle bestows on contemplative virtue something of the grandeur he has stripped from moral virtue. By imitating the only possible activity of gods, the philosopher exhibits a kind of austere piety that expresses itself in reasoned reflection but evidently not in worship or sacrifice or prayer.

Still, nothing Aristotle has said thus far quite addresses *the* problem he himself has raised, the problem of chance, of longevity of life. For to live as much as possible like an immortal is not yet to be one in fact (compare 1145a22–24). His long treatment of "external equipment" may be meant in part to lull us into supposing that this problem *has* been solved, or perhaps to divert our attention from it. Aristotle indicates the persistence of the problem of chance by the fact that, after having twice held out the possibility of our attaining "complete [perfect] happiness," he makes the much more limited conclusion that a contemplative life would be "happiest," in this way availing himself of the ambiguity of the superlative (1178a8; compare 1177a17 and 24; for exactly the same move, compare 1178b7 with 23 and 1179a31; consider also, e.g., the clear meaning of the superlative [*autarkestatos*] at 1177b1).

Even stranger, immediately after having affirmed in 10.7 that intellect is the most divine thing in us, Aristotle asserts that it is in fact the most *human* thing about us:

> it would seem that each person even *is* this thing [i.e., *nous*].... It would be strange, then, if a person should not choose the life that is his own but rather that of something else.... [W]hat is proper to each [*to oikeion*] is by nature most excellent and most pleasant for each. And so for a human being, this is the life that accords with the intellect, if in fact this especially *is* a human being. (1178a2–8)

Is the contemplative life choiceworthy, then, because it is the most fully human life or because it is the least (merely) human life?

The chief motive to conceive of oneself as striving to live the most divine life possible, or as being something other than a composite thing, body and soul, becomes clearer once Aristotle has completed his account of "external equipment." He then insists that all such arguments be tested against life itself, lest they prove to be mere speeches. Life itself, we suggest, may teach us that engaging in theoretical activity is not an inoculation against chance, though it does indeed confer great self-sufficiency and least of all serves any other end. Moreover, life surely teaches us that strive as we may or must, we are finally mortals. And so, in what is literally his last word on happiness, Aristotle proceeds to describe the affection and care of the gods for those who seek to perfect the intellect—a sort of divine providence (consider 1179a24). Such care pertains only to those who, bowing as little as possible to the demands of the all-too-human body, most fulfill the promise of the intellect and so are most deserving of the gods' love or friendship (1179a22–32; compare 1178b7–32, where the gods serve only as a model, as well as 1178b7–13). The precise function of such providential care is unclear. But only it could guarantee the benignity of the fortune to which our hopes for happiness are necessarily exposed: no conceivable technological or scientific innovation, for example, will ever be adequate to this task.

By carefully tracing out the most powerful opinions about happiness, and by giving full expression to our concern for virtue, the *Nicomachean Ethics* indicates that the core of our hope for happiness is a longing for a completion that renders us "in need of nothing," a longing that only a god could fulfill.

Yet Aristotle in the *Nicomachean Ethics* does not simply accept the view that "the god" or gods are finally responsible for our happiness, his willingness to repeat and hence promote it notwithstanding. He does not in fact assert in book 1 that our happiness is god-sent—this thought rests on the protasis of a conditional sentence that is compatible with the gods giving no gifts whatever to human beings (1099b11–13)—and he immediately entertains the view that happiness is *not* god-sent (1099b14–15). As we have seen, Aristotle raises the possibility, at least, that the idea of the dead enjoying happiness is "altogether strange." In addition, since he asserts the impossibility of our knowing the future, he must also deny the worth of those claims to special access to it, through divination and the like. As for his description in book 10 of the providence attending the wise, is this "solution" too not problematic? For even if we accept without question the utterly mysterious operation of this providence, which is introduced in a conditional clause, happiness would still be beyond the reach of almost everyone, because intellectual virtue is available to exceedingly few. And this is a harsh thought.

What goal or goals, then, govern Aristotle's manifestly complex manner of argument concerning happiness and the gods in the *Ethics*? It is generally held today that his most pious remarks, those pertaining to the afterlife, for example, cannot be taken to be sincere. We agree with this judgment. After all, Aristotle declines to include piety in the eleven moral virtues analyzed in the *Ethics*, and in the *Politics* he famously declares that the city comes into being "by nature" and not (as this already implies) by the workings of the gods, notwithstanding the claim of many ancient cities to be traceable to divine law (e.g., Plato, *Laws* 624a1–6). The first purpose of such pious statements, tentative as they are, seems to be to lessen the suspicion or ire of the most unphilosophic and censorious in Aristotle's audience—he who wished to give no cause to Athens to sin against philosophy a second time.

Yet Aristotle indicates a threefold division among human beings and so among his potential audience: the many, the refined, and the philosophic (or wise). We tentatively suggest that at least some of the refined, properly reared and so correctly dedicated to moral virtue, would nonetheless be among those who see through Aristotle's apparently pious remarks. While such readers would remain dedicated to virtue, they would look only half-heartedly, if indeed at all, to gods and to an afterlife to solve the shortcomings of this life; here one may think of Laches and Demosthenes, for example, as they are presented by Plato (in the *Laches*) and by Aristophanes (in the *Knights*)—together with a great many of Aristotle's readers today. Such readers would not blanch at Aristotle's omission of piety in the enumeration of the virtues belonging to a *kaloskagathos* and would be content to imitate, in the conduct of their own lives or the life of their community, the wholly inward-looking "activity" of "the god" to whom Aristotle appeals briefly in the *Politics*, a god who bears no resemblance to Zeus or, for that matter, to the God of Abraham (1323b21–29 and 1325b28–30). Might then an effect, an intended effect, of Aristotle's less-than-convincing remarks about the divine here also be to encourage, in just such readers, the conviction that the life of noble action brings with it a completeness or self-sufficiency that renders reliance on the divine unnecessary? Aristotle's manifest distance from simple orthodoxy and the obviously conditional character of his own assertions concerning the divine would strengthen this confidence in the sufficiency of moral virtue that characterizes his more refined readers.

At the same time, however, Aristotle also points to the ultimately ungrounded character of such confidence. He does so in part by insisting, in book 10, on the decisive superiority of theoretical to moral virtue, in part by drawing attention, in book 1, to the divine and the afterlife as involving *questions* that must at some point be confronted. The philosophically inclined in his audience, thus prompted to reflect on these questions, will be compelled to wonder whether recourse to the divine is not in fact necessary to the life of moral virtue, if it is to hope to attain the completeness it seeks.

◉   ◉   ◉

The study of the *Nicomachean Ethics* is useful today because it deals with a question—the nature of human happiness—whose relevance is obvious. Indeed, the vitality of the *Ethics* for contemporary readers testifies to the power of Aristotle's inquiry into happiness and of its promise that, by way of our own reason, we may come to have knowledge of the good that is of such "great weight" in our lives. Yet in the course of his inquiry, Aristotle also compels us to raise difficulties for ourselves that, far from being obvious today, are in danger of being forgotten. It is with a view to combating this danger and to clarifying the central difficulties that confront a rational account of the human good that the present introduction has attempted to explain, and hence been compelled at times to trample on, Aristotle's great delicacy or sensitivity in exploring our hope for happiness and the life of virtue that might realize that hope. Chief among these difficulties are, first, the true character of our hope for happiness and, ultimately, the necessity of there being a kind of divine care or providence if that hope is to be realized. Inasmuch as we still long for happiness, we must still undergo the pull of that necessity, however distant it may appear to us to be. In bringing out in this way our deepest longing, our longing for happiness, the study of the *Ethics* also prepares us to become serious students of Aristotle's "philosophy of human affairs" as a whole, which examines above all the possibility of philosophy as a way of life.

OVERVIEW OF THE MORAL VIRTUES AND VICES

The following is based on Aristotle's enumeration at 2.7, although the order in which he subsequently takes up the virtues and vices differs somewhat. Quotation marks indicate that the term in question is coined by Aristotle and is otherwise nameless.

VICE	VIRTUE	VICE
1. Recklessness* (*thrasutēs*)	Courage (*andreia*)	Cowardice (*deilia*)
2. Licentiousness (*akolasia*)	Moderation (*sōphrosunē*)	"Insensibility" (*anaisthēsia*)
3. Prodigality (*asōtia*)	Liberality (*eleutheriotēs*)	Stinginess (*aneleutheria*)
4. Vulgarity and Crassness (*apeirokalia* & *banausia*)	Magnificence (*megaloprepeia*)	Parsimony (*mikroprepeia*)
5. Vanity (*chaunotēs*)	Greatness of Soul (*megalopsuchia*)	Smallness of Soul (*mikropsuchia*)
6. Ambition (*philotimia*)	"Ambition" (*philotimia*)	Lack of Ambition (*aphilotimia*)
7. Irascibility** (*orgilotēs*)	"Gentleness" (*praotēs*)	"Unirascibility" (*aorgēsia*)

* Recklessness is excessive confidence; there is no name for the vice of excessive fearlessness.

** Aristotle speaks of various manifestations of anger, including those who are "choleric" (*akrocholos*), "harsh" (*chalepos*), and "bitter" (*pikros*).

VICE	VIRTUE	VICE
8. Boastfulness (*alazoneia*)	"Truthfulness" (*alētheia*)	Irony (*eirōneia*)
9. Buffoonery and Crudity (*bōmolochia* & *phortikotēs*)	Wittiness and Tact (*eutrapelia* & *epidexia*)	Boorishness and Dourness (*agroikia* & *sklērotēs*)
10. Obsequiousness or Flattery*** (*areskeia* or *kolakeia*)	"Friendliness" (*philia*)	Surliness and Quarrelsomeness (*duskolia* & *duseristia*)
11. ?	Justice (*dikaiosunē*)	?

*** Aristotle takes these up in book 4 in a different order: friendliness precedes truthfulness and wittiness. The Greek term *philia* is literally "friendship," though the virtue described in book 4 is not friendship in the full sense taken up in books 8 and 9, but a kind of friendliness.

GLOSSARY

Only the names of those moral virtues and vices requiring some explanation are included here; for a comprehensive list, consult the Overview of the Moral Virtues and Vices.

A

ACTION (*praxis*): Action issues from the part of the soul that desires and longs, the proper habituation of which part is the concern of the education to virtue. In the strict sense of the word, then, all action is moral; it involves deeds for which we may be praised or blamed—Aristotle denies that animals can "act" or engage in *praxis*.

ACTIVITY (*energeia*): A term that does not appear in the extant literature before Aristotle, at least not in its technical sense; it is constructed from *en*, "in" or "at," and *ergon*, "work" or "deed" and so means the state of being engaged in an act or the carrying out of a deed; see also WORK (*ergon*).

AMBITION (*philotimia*): Literally "love of honor."

ART (*technē*): Less "art" in the sense of "fine art" than any craft or body of "technical" knowledge used to produce an artifact: shoes, tables, a building and hence the art of shoemaking, of carpentry, and of architecture. In 6.4, Aristotle maintains that art, like prudence, pertains to the realm of things that admit of being otherwise but differs from prudence in that it is bound up with "making" (*poiēsis*) rather than with action (*praxis*); it therefore has an end other than its own activity.

AULOS: A double-reed wind instrument not unlike the modern oboe.

B

BASE (*phaulos*): That which is paltry or of poor quality, especially of poor moral character. Generally the contrary of virtue or the virtuous; see also VICE (*kakia*), WICKEDNESS (*ponēria*), and CORRUPTION (*mochthēria*).

BLESSED (*makaria, makarios*): Although often very close in meaning to "happy," the term may connote a lasting prosperity that outstrips happiness: Aristotle suggests that one could not say of a happy man who encountered the misfortunes of a Priam that he would be wretched—though he would not be "blessed" either (1101a7).

C

CAPACITY (*dunamis* or *dynamis*): Also "power." It refers to powers or capacities of various kinds—from powers of the body, such as sight and hearing, to political power—and, in a precise technical sense, it refers to the "power" or "potential" for "activity," *energeia* (see 9.7).

CARE (*epimeleia*): Also "concern" for a thing. Aristotle suggests at one point that the gods may exercise a kind of providential "care" for human beings.

CHANCE (*tuchē*): The notion of chance plays a crucial role in Aristotle's account of happiness, as does the idea of misfortunes (*dustuchiai*) or bad fortune (*atuchēma*). For Aristotle's extended account of it in relation to causation, see *Physics* 2.4–6.

CHARACTER (*ēthos*): As a plural adjective used substantively, it figures in the title of the *Nicomachean Ethics*: "ethics" are the things pertaining to one's character. See also HABIT (*ethos*).

CHARACTERISTIC (*hexis*): A central term and notoriously difficult to translate. It is related to the verb *echein*, meaning to have, hold, or (with an adverb) to be (of a certain character or in a certain state). The noun *hexis* is of fundamental importance to Aristotle's account of virtue: our *hexeis*, or characteristics, are our ordered and stable states of soul that mark us as the kind of persons we are and permit us to act as we characteristically do. Our characteristics, in this sense, display our character, the habits of body and mind that have been formed through habituation and that constitute a certain way of holding oneself toward the world, so to speak. Other possible translations are "condition," "active condition," "disposition," "state," and "habit," though no single English word can capture the full meaning of the Greek.

CHOICE (*proairesis*): The noun's component parts suggest the act of taking or selecting (*hairesis*) beforehand (*pro-*), i.e., before acting; Aristotle's account of choice is a crucial part of his complex argument concerning the voluntary and involuntary (see especially 3.2). Choice is the origin or starting point (*archē*) of action. It is defined in 6.2 as either intellect operating through longing (*orektikos nous*) or longing operating through thought (*orexis dianoetikē*).

CITHARA: A plucked wooden instrument akin to the lyre.

CITIZEN (*politēs*): A member of the *polis*, with the full complement of duties and rights characteristic of political life.

CITY (*polis*): The relatively small, politically independent unit typical of political life in ancient Greece. Although he knew of great empires, nations, and tribes, Aristotle argues (in the *Politics*) that a certain sort of *polis* is the best possible form of community, given the naturally political character of human nature.

CLASS (*genos*): The class, kind, or genus to which a thing belongs.

COMPLETE (*teleios*): That which marks a thing or state that has reached its natural end (*telos*); the word can also be translated as "perfect."

CONTEMPLATION (*theōria, theōrein*): Meaning in the first place simply to look upon or observe—our word *theater* is derived from it—the term in Aristotle (and Plato) comes to mean "contemplation," the act of looking upon something so as to understand it, an understanding that is sought as an end in itself and hence without regard to any subsequent doing or making.

CORRUPT, CORRUPTION (*mochthēros, mochthēria*): A strong term used to describe vicious human beings. Like the English term, the Greek has a range of meanings, from morally bad or wicked to perverse or depraved in one's longings and the like; it can also mean, in nonmoral contexts, simply "defective" or "bad condition." In the *Ethics*, *mochthēria* is sometimes used synonymously with the word for "vice" and so can serve as the contrary of "virtue"; see also VICE (*kakia*), BASE (*phaulos*), and WICKEDNESS (*ponēria*).

COURAGE (*andreia*): Related to the noun *anēr*, meaning a male human being, a man in the emphatic sense; *andreia* might also be translated as "manliness." See 3.6–9.

COWARDICE (*deilia*): One of the two vices opposed to courage, it is marked by excessive fear and/or insufficient confidence.

CUSTOM (*nomos*); see also LAW (*nomos*). The term suggests most generally the way things ought to be according to the authoritative element of a community and expressed in law, written or unwritten; the key alternative is the way things must be according to nature (*phusis* or *physis*). The crucial case in the *Ethics* is the dispute over whether justice exists by nature or (merely) by custom or law: 5.7.

D

DECENT (*epieikēs*): A general term referring to those who are upright or square-dealing; also translated as "equity" or "equitable" in the discussion of justice, as that which makes up for the deficiency inherent in the (necessarily general) law.

DECISION (*krisis*): Related to the verb (*krinein*) meaning to judge or determine; the moment of "crisis" is the one at which the crucial decision is made. "Judgment" is another possible translation, and the term can also apply to legal adjudications more narrowly.

DEFICIENCY (*elleipsis, to elleipon*; also *endeia*): A term that forms a crucial part of Aristotle's famous doctrine of moral virtue understood as a "mean" between two extremes: one marked by deficiency, the other by excess.

DEFINING BOUNDARY (*horos*): Meaning originally a stone or other marker indicating a property line or border, the term by extension indicates that which defines or limits a thing: "defining boundary" or simply "definition." The word also appears in Aristotle's logic and refers to the "term" of a proposition; see also SPEECH.

DELIBERATION (*boulē*): Closely related to choice and, in book 6, to calculation (*logismos*); the calculative part of the soul is the part that deliberates (see 6.1). Like choice, deliberation is directed at things that admit of being otherwise and that are up to us, and it is concerned not with the end (*telos*) but with what conduces to the end. Aristotle discusses deliberation most fully in 3.3 and 6.9.

DESIRE (*epithumia*): A species of *orexis* or the longing part of the soul and so the origin of action; see also LONGING.

DIVINE (*theios*): An adjective derived from the Greek word for "god" (*theos*). Aristotle speaks rather mysteriously of a certain "heroic and divine" virtue at the beginning of book 7.

E

END (*telos*): The goal or target of a thing, the attainment of which fulfills its nature. Hence the English term "teleological." It is related to the adjective *teleios*, translated as "complete" or "perfect," i.e., that which shares in the qualities of the end.

EQUITY (*epieikeia*): That which rectifies the necessary generality of the law; see also the more general sense of DECENT.

EXCESS (*huperbolē*): In relation to the "mean" (*mesotēs*), excess refers to one of the two ranges of extremes; see also DEFICIENCY (*elleipsis, to elleipon*).

EXPERIENCE (*empeiria*): The root of the English word *empirical*, *empeiria* suggests the acquaintance with or knowledge of something that stems from repeatedly dealing with it, perhaps without the knowledge of the principles involved (consider, e.g., Plato, *Laws* 857c8). It is sometimes closely allied with art or craft: for example, Aristotle, *Politics* 1282a1.

F

FLATTERY (*kolakeia*): Aristotle introduces this vice, which corresponds to the virtue of truthfulness, in close company with obsequiousness (*areskeia*).

FORM (*eidos*): Refers most simply to "that which is seen" and, in particular, the "form" or "shape" of a thing. Aristotle first uses the term in connection with the Platonic doctrine of the forms (see 1.6), but also more generally in the *Ethics*, he uses it to designate the "kind" of a thing or the class to which it belongs. See also IDEA (*idea*).

FRIENDLINESS, FRIENDSHIP (*philia*): Aristotle uses one and the same term to designate both the moral virtue of "friendliness" and friendship itself. The former is treated at 4.6, the latter in books 8–9.

G

GOD (*theos*): The term used in ordinary parlance to speak of the Olympian gods, for example, but Aristotle will speak more generally or vaguely of "the god" especially in his climactic discussion of (intellectual) virtue and happiness in book 10.

GOOD (*agathos*): When the term is accompanied by the definite article, it will usually be translated as "the good," suggesting *the* goal of all human striving and hence synonymous with happiness. Aristotle famously argues that all human beings do everything for the sake of what seems or is held to be good. The superlative, *to ariston*, is often translated by some as "the highest" or "chief" good, but we prefer to translate the term as "the best" to capture also its relative sense: it is perhaps the best of the goods available to us but not necessarily the best imaginable (as "highest" may suggest).

GRASPING FOR MORE (*pleonektēs*): The specific corruption that distinguishes the vice of injustice. The one who is *pleonektēs*—who is characterized by *pleonexia*—seeks to take more of the good (or less of the bad) than is his proper share.

GREATNESS OF SOUL (*megalopsychia*): An alternative translation is "magnanimity," although we have preferred the more literal rendering, which captures better the greatness of the sum of the virtues constituting this first "complete virtue"; see 4.3.

H

HABIT (*ethos*): Aristotle contends that habit is crucial in the formation of character—for it is by repeatedly doing courageous things or just things that we become courageous or just—and even suggests that the two are etymologically linked (see 2.1).

HAPPINESS (*eudaimonia*): Meaning literally the condition of having a good daimon, the term is in our judgment best rendered as "happiness," given Aristotle's description and analysis of it in book 1. See also our Introduction, p. x.

HELD TO BE (*dokein*): Also translated as "seems." Related to the noun translated as "opinion" (*doxa*). Aristotle's typical procedure in examining a controversial or puzzling point is to begin from what is "held to be" the case, i.e., from opinion.

HONOR (*timē*): One who is "ambitious" is more literally a "lover of honor," and the general term came reasonably enough to signify also political offices, on the one hand, and the price of something, on the other.

HUBRIS (*hubris*): A transliteration of the Greek term that in general implies a grievous lack of respect for that which demands respect, the gods not least, and so a kind of wanton arrogance or outrageous behavior. It is generally rendered as "hubris" (and related terms), though it appears, in the context of children who are so treated, as "wantonly abused" at 1148b30.

I

IDEA: A transliteration of the term made famous by Plato's Socrates in his doctrine of the Ideas; Aristotle treats the (Platonic) *ideas* in 1.6. Derived from the verb for "to see," the term *idea* means first or most simply the look of something, hence by extension the class to which all such things sharing the same look properly belong. See also FORM (*eidos*).

INDIGNATION (*nemesis*): Meaning most simply the distribution of what is due, the term has the sense of retribution or righteous anger aroused by injustice; *nemesis* is personified by Hesiod as a goddess who embodies these traits. Aristotle mentions it at 2.7 (together with sense of shame) as being something other than a moral virtue.

INDUCTION (*epagōgē*): A technical term in Aristotle's account in book 6 of how we come to know or learn, it means literally a bringing or leading of someone to something, or introducing him to it: "induction" occurs when one is brought to see a given universal from prior recognition of a set of particulars (consider also, e.g., *Posterior Analytics* 71a7–9).

INJUSTICE (*adikia*): The abstract noun closely related to "the unjust" (*to adikon*) or an "act of injustice" (*to adikēma*); see also JUSTICE.

INSENSIBILITY (*anaisthēsia*): Meaning literally a lack of (sense) perception, the term as Aristotle uses it refers to the (rare!) indifference to pleasure among human beings, a vice corresponding to the virtue of moderation.

INTELLECT (*nous*): According to Aristotle, *nous* is one of the three things in the soul that "exercise authoritative control over action and truth," together with sense perception and longing; it supplies the intellectual "grasp" of what something is, as a member of a given class, and so also of the class characteristics as such. See 6.2–3 and context. The term can also refer to the act of the intellect, its intellectual grasp of something.

INVOLUNTARY (*akōn*): Aristotle's complex and subtle account of what constitutes voluntary and involuntary action is found in 3.1–5. The translation unfortunately introduces the extraneous idea of the "will" (through the root of the word *voluntary*), but this seems unavoidable in English.

IRONY (*eirōneia*): One of the vices corresponding to the virtue of truthfulness. Aristotle's sole example of one who practiced this graceful vice of concealing one's knowledge is Socrates.

J

JUSTICE (*dikaiosunē*): The moral virtue of justice, treated at length in book 5. Aristotle also speaks frequently of "the just" (*to dikaion*) and a just act or deed (*dikaiōma*).

K

KNOWLEDGE (*gnōsis*): The noun is derived from the verb *gignoskein*, "to perceive, learn, come to know," and refers to knowledge or knowing in the general sense, of which there are particular forms; see book 6. In particular, we distinguish *gnōsis* from the term *epistēmē*, "science," or "scientific knowledge," i.e., knowledge in the strict sense.

L

LACK OF SELF-RESTRAINT (*akrasia*): Aristotle defines this defect, which is not strictly speaking a moral vice, as the inability to stick to one's knowledge or opinion of what is good when one is in the presence of certain strong pleasures. See SELF-RESTRAINT (*enkrateia*).

LAW (*nomos*); see CUSTOM (*nomos*).

LEARNING (*mathēsis*): Also "subject of learning" or "subject."

LIBERALITY (*eleutheriotēs*): Meaning in its broadest application the quality of soul characteristic of a free, as distinguished from an enslaved or slavish, human being. The term in the *Ethics* refers more narrowly to the freedom from undue attachment to money. The adjective *eleutherios* is also used to refer to the "free" man, meaning one who is both free in this broad sense and a citizen (*politēs*), with all the pertinent rights and privileges of citizenship.

LICENTIOUSNESS (*akolasia*): Meaning most literally a lack of chastisement and hence the likely results of such a lack, the term as Aristotle uses it comes to signify an undue attachment to (bad or shameful) pleasure.

LONGING (*orexis*): Related to the verb *oregein*, which means most literally "to reach out for" or "to stretch toward" and hence by extension "to strive for," "to yearn for," "to long for." *Orexis* is the general (technical) term for the appetency of the soul, of which *epithumia*, "desire," is one species, along with "wish" (*boulēsis*) and "spiritedness" (*thumos*); see 1102b30 as well as *De Anima* 414b2 and 433a13. The interplay between longing and reason is crucial in the formulation of choice: see 6.2. The related verb *oregein* will be translated as "to long for."

LOVE: Aristotle uses four verbs in the *Ethics* to speak of love: *philein* is the principal verb denoting the love (*philia*) friends feel for one another; *eran* suggests erotic or passionate love (*eros*); and *stergein* and *agapein* are both used to suggest nonsexual affection: we translate the former as "to feel affection for," the latter as "to be fond of."

M

MAGNIFICENCE (*megaloprepeia*): Literally "befitting greatness." Aristotle uses the term to refer to the proper spending of money on a grand scale.

MAKING (*poiēsis*): Or "production"; in book 6 Aristotle distinguishes it from "action" (*praxis*).

THE MANY (*hoi polloi*): Although the term can simply designate a numerical majority and is sometimes so translated ("most people"), it frequently designates the (uneducated) many, the vulgar, as indeed the Greek phrase has come to be used also in English.

MATTER OF ACTION (*pragma*; pl. *pragmata*): That which is of active concern to us; matter of concern; concerns.

MEAN (*mesotēs*): The key term in Aristotle's famous doctrine of the moral virtues as residing in the mean between two extremes; closely associated with MIDDLE or middle term.

MIDDLE (*to meson*): Also translated as "the middle term": see MEAN (*mesotes*).

MODERATION (*sōphrosunē*): Although the term in Plato is rather broad and suggests being knowledgeable or sensible, in Aristotle's *Ethics* the primary meaning of the term is the proper disposition toward the bodily desires and pleasures.

MONEY (*chrēmata*): The Greek can also mean simply "goods" or "property." In 4.1, Aristotle defines *chrēmata* as "all those things whose worth is measured in legal currency [*nomisma*]," another term which could be translated as "money," but which we generally translate as "legal currency" or "currency" to emphasize its conventional character and to distinguish it from the broader term *chrēmata*.

MORAL (*ēthikē*): Or "ethical"; the adjective of *ēthos*, "character," which appears as a plural adjective in the title and means literally "things pertaining to character." In 2.1, Aristotle offers an etymology that derives the term from *ethos*, the term for "habit," since character, and therefore the "ethical" action that issues from it, arises from habituation and is grounded in a characteristic (*hexis*) that constitutes a settled habit. We translate the word as "moral" in deference to tradition.

N

NATURE (*phusis* or *physis*): Related to the verb meaning in the first place "to grow," the noun *physis* presupposes the notion that the existence of some things is due, not to human production or opinion, but an internal necessity that governs how they grow and their characteristic way or character. Aristotle will occasionally refer to arguments from physics or natural science in the *Ethics*, and he distinguishes the existence of what is just by nature from that which is due to law or custom (5.7).

NOBLE (*kalos*): The Greek term requires at least three English words to capture its sense: that which is physically "beautiful," in the first place, that which is beautiful in a moral sense, i.e., "noble," and that which is in a more general sense "fine." We have opted to use "noble" wherever possible, since to say that courageous acts, for example, are done "for the sake of the beautiful" not only gives to the argument an oddly "aesthetic" character but also fails to capture the dimension of self-forgetting or self-sacrifice in courageous acts that, while not the whole of the virtuous act, contributes decisively to its being *kalos*, to its nobility.

O

OPINION (*doxa*): One's notion or judgment of something that does not, however, rise to the level of knowledge; hence the common rendering of the term *opinion*, which is often equivalent to mere conjecture. As noted in the discussion of the related verb, *dokein*, Aristotle's typical procedure in examining a controversial or puzzling point is to begin from what is "held to be" the case, i.e., from opinion. Aristotle's starting points in the *Ethics* are therefore the prevailing opinions, especially, though not always, the opinions held by decent or serious human beings. See also HELD TO BE (*dokein*).

OPPORTUNE MOMENT (*kairos*): The right or crucial moment; also translated as "opportunity."

P

PAIN (*algēdōn*; *lupē*): Aristotle's account of pain (and of course pleasure) is crucial not only to his analysis of the moral virtues and vices but also to his inquiry into the human good or happiness, for by the end of the *Ethics* we learn that hedonism is a doctrine worth taking seriously.

PASSIONS (*pathē*): That which one suffers or undergoes, including the passions in the English sense but also more generally whatever one experiences; sometimes translated as "experience" ("experiences").

PERCEPTION (*aisthēsis*): Also "sense perception."

PLEASURE (*hēdonē*): Together with PAIN, a crucial determinant of human action and hence crucial to Aristotle's account of moral virtue and vice. The noun supplies the root of the English term *hedonism*, that is, the philosophic doctrine according to which the good all human beings of necessity seek is (some kind of) pleasure.

POLITICAL ART (*politikē*): Literally "the political." Since Aristotle uses this adjective as a noun (as can easily be done in Greek) without always specifying the noun he has in mind, he avails himself of an important ambiguity: sometimes he clearly has in mind "political science" or "the political art"—but could he sometimes (e.g., 1094a27) have in mind "political power," whether or not it is guided by science or art?

POLITICIAN (*politikos*): That is, one who possesses the art or knowledge characteristic of life in and governance of the city, the *polis*. "Statesman" is another possible translation. Unfortunately, both "statesmen" and "politicians" carry connotations in English that are mostly foreign to the Greek term (but consider 1142a2 and context): a "statesman" is always good, a "politician" (almost) always bad.

PRINCIPLE (*archē*): The simple meaning of *archē* is the "beginning" or "starting point" of something—of a racecourse, for example—and we have sometimes so translated the term. But it also comes to mean more fundamentally the (first) principle of something, that which sets something in motion and therefore determines in part its character or course. It is derived from the verb *archein*, which means simply "to begin" but also (especially in political contexts) "to rule."

PRUDENT (*phronimos*): A term central to Aristotle's political philosophy, the prudent human being possesses the intellectual virtue of prudence (*phronēsis*) that permits him always to choose the correct action in a given circumstance and to perform it well and for the right reason. Prudence is inseparable, however, from moral virtue since, as Aristotle makes clear in book 6, "virtue makes the target correct, prudence the things conducive to that target."

R

REGIME (*politeia*): The kind or character of the governing body in any political community that as such determines not only the arrangement of offices but also the end—the way of life—of that community and its citizens. Aristotle will present an account of the various regimes in his discussion of friendship, which is elaborated on in the sequel to the *Ethics*, the *Politics*.

S

SCIENCE (*epistēmē*): Or "scientific knowledge," which is to say knowledge in the strict sense. It should go without saying that Aristotle's understanding of "science" has nothing to do with modern natural science, the modern scientific method, and so on. See especially 6.1, 3, 6–7.

SELF-RESTRAINT (*enkrateia*): Literally "inner strength" or "inner mastery." In the *Ethics*, *enkrateia* takes on a significance and precision that it does not have in other extant Greek literature. Most simply, it is the capacity, separate from the moral virtues, to withstand the attractive pull of especially those bodily pleasures that admit of excess and that one regards as bad. Aristotle's consideration of this capacity and its contrary, *akrasia*, takes up 7.1–10, a point in the book that he calls a "new beginning." There is no simply adequate English equivalent; some have rendered it "continence" or "self-control." Although there is no clear notion of the "self" in the Greek term, we prefer "self-restraint" inasmuch as it captures the inner struggle involved in *enkrateia* and avoids the unfortunate connotations of "continence" and especially "incontinence" in current usage.

SELF-SUFFICIENCY (*autarkeia*): One of the key terms in understanding what we mean by the term *happiness*, for, according to Aristotle, we all seek to possess for ourselves a good that is (among other things) "self-sufficient" and so renders us or our lives "in need of nothing."

SERIOUS (*spoudaios*): This term in the *Ethics* most often carries a sense of moral gravity or excellence when it is used in relation to a human being. But Aristotle will use the word also in relation to the virtue of other things—for example, the virtue of an eye makes both the eye and its work "serious," or one can be a "serious" cithara player only if one possesses the excellence or virtue that pertains to cithara playing. Hence the *spoudaios*, the serious person as such, is the possessor and model of moral virtue.

SHAME, SHAMEFUL, or UGLY (*aischros*) and SENSE OF SHAME (*aidōs*): The "ugly" or the "shameful" is the opposite of *to kalon*, the "beautiful" or the "noble," and the same word, *aischros*, can refer to the shame or disgrace that is felt as a result of a shameful deed. "Sense of shame" (*aidōs*) can refer to the same passion but also to "awe" or "reverence" due the gods and the divine things, for example. Aristotle argues that although a sense of shame is admirable in a young person who will as such err, in a mature person it is not a virtue, for the simple reason that someone with a good nature who has been properly reared will never commit those acts that arouse in their agent a sense of shame.

SMALLNESS OF SOUL (*mikropsychia*): One of the vices associated with the virtue of greatness of soul, which we translate literally; it can also be translated as "pettiness" or perhaps "small-mindedness."

SOUL (*psychē*): The seat of life in any living being. In the *Ethics*, Aristotle is mostly concerned to distinguish the two "parts" of the soul with and without reason respectively. He seeks only an "outline" (1.13) of the soul that is useful for the inquiry at hand, although he clearly indicates that a more precise account of the soul is possible, and his *De Anima* ("On the Soul") takes up the question at length.

SPEECH (*logos*): This complex term does not allow for a single English translation. Indicating most simply speech or the content of one's speech, the term comes to mean by extension an "account" of something and ultimately or in the best case a reasoned argument; hence the English term *logical*. We render it as "speech," "account," "reasoned account," "reason," "argument," "definition," and (in book 5) "ratio," depending on the context.

SPIRIT, SPIRITEDNESS (*thumos*): The seat of anger and of "natural courage"; it is also translated as "heart" in the quotation from Hesiod in book 1 (1095b13).

STINGINESS (*aneleutheria*): One of the vices related to the virtue of LIBERALITY; a more literal translation would be simply "illiberality."

STRANGE (*atopos*): Literally that which has no place (compare the English *utopia*) and so is out of place, strange, or odd.

T

TARGET (*skopos*): That at which correct reason aims and so hits on the mean between two opposed vices; the term appears most frequently in Aristotle's account of prudence in book 6.

U

"UNIRASCIBILITY" (*aorgēsia*): A term coined by Aristotle to indicate a vice associated with insufficient anger when anger is due.

UNIVERSAL (*kathalou*): Sometimes also translated as "general."

USEFUL (*chrēsimon*; *chrēsis*): The term appears frequently in Aristotle's discussion of those friendships that are limited to the usefulness of the parties involved.

V

VICE (*kakia*): Literally "badness," the root of the word being the contrary of "good" (*agathos*).

VIRTUE (*aretē*): The excellence of a specific type of thing, animate or inanimate, that marks the peak of that thing and permits it to perform its characteristic work or task well.

VOLUNTARY (*hekōn*); see also INVOLUNTARY (*akōn*). Aristotle's principal discussion of the voluntary and involuntary is found at 3.1–5.

W

WICKED, WICKEDNESS (*ponēros, ponēria*): Although the term may mean simply a "bad state" or "defective condition" of a thing or person (consider 7.14, end), in the *Ethics* it almost always amounts to a harsh moral condemnation. See also CORRUPT (*mochthēros*), VICE (*kakia*), BASE (*phaulos*).

WISDOM (*sophia*): That which the "philosopher," the "lover" of "wisdom," most seeks. For Aristotle's account of it in the *Ethics*, see especially 6.7.

WISE (*sophos*): The wise human being possesses knowledge or science of the highest objects of human understanding, including and especially those beings that exist of necessity or do not admit of being otherwise and are therefore (as Aristotle argues: 6.3) eternal.

WISH (*boulēsis*): A crucial element in Aristotle's account of what might be called moral responsibility (3.1–5, especially 4), in which he establishes that wish is directed at the end (*telos*), whereas choice and deliberation are directed at the things conducive to the end. The related verb (*boulesthai*) is translated as "to wish for."

WORK (*ergon*): Variously translated here as "work," "task," "product," or—in contrast to "speeches" (*logoi*)—"deeds."

WORTH (*axia*): Also translated as "worthy" and "merit," the term can mean both worthiness and fitness, as well as that which is rightly deserved; it is related to the verb *axioun*, "to deem oneself worthy": the one who possesses greatness of soul, for example, deems himself worthy, and is worthy, of great honor.

KEY GREEK TERMS

adikia: Injustice.
agapein: To be fond of.
agathos: Good.
agroikia: Boorishness.
aidōs: Sense of shame; awe or reverence.
aisthēsis: Perception, sense perception.
akolasia: Licentiousness.
akrasia: Lack of self-restraint.
alazoneia: Boastfulness.
alētheia: Truthfulness.
algēdōn: Pain.
anaisthēsia: "Insensibility."
andreia: Courage, manliness.
aneleutheria: Illiberality.
anēr: Man; husband.
anthrōpos: Human being.
aorgēsia: "Unirascibility."
apeirokalia: Vulgarity.
aphilotimia: Lack of ambition.
archē: Beginning, starting point, origin; principle.
areskeia: Obsequiousness.
aretē: Virtue.
asōtia: Prodigality.
atopos: Strange, odd.
autarkeia: Self-sufficiency.
axia: Worth, merit.

banausia: Crassness.
bōmolochia: Buffoonery.
boulēsis: Wish.

chaunotēs: Vanity.
chrēmata: Money; goods, property.
chrēsimon: Useful.

deilia: Cowardice.
dikaiosunē: Justice.
dokein: To be held (to be), to seem.
doxa: Opinion; repute.
dunamis (dynamis): Capacity, power.
duseristia: Quarrelsomeness.
duskolia: Surliness.

eidos: Form.
eirōneia: Irony.
eleutheriotēs: Liberality.
elleipsis: Deficiency.
empeiria: Experience.
endeia: Deficiency, need, lack.
energeia: Activity.
enkrateia: Self-restraint.
epagōgē: Induction.
epidexiotēs: Tact.
epieikeia: Equity; decency.
epimeleia: Care, concern for.
epistēmē: Science, scientific knowledge.
epithumia: Desire.
eran: To love (in a passionate or erotic sense).
ergon: Work, task; deed; product.
ēthikē: Moral (virtue).

ethos: Habit.
ēthos: Character.
eudaimonia: Happiness.
eutrapelia: Wittiness.

genos: Genus; class; kind.
gnōsis: Knowledge.

hēdonē: Pleasure.
hekōn: Voluntary.
hexis: Characteristic.
horos: Defining boundary; limit; definition.
hubris: Hubris, insolence, outrageous
treatment, wanton abuse.
huperbalē: Excess.

kairos: Opportune moment.
kakia: Vice.
kalos: Noble; beautiful; fine.
kathalou: Universal; general.
kolakeia: Flattery.
krisis: Decision; judgment; legal adjudication.

logos: Account, speech; argument; definition; ratio.
lupē: Pain.

makaria, makarios: Blessed.
mathēsis: Learning; subject of learning;
subject matter.
megaloprepeia: Magnificence.
megalopsuchia: Greatness of soul.
meson: The middle term, middle.
mesotēs: Mean.
mikroprepeia: Parsimony.
mikropsuchia: Smallness of soul.
mochthēros, mochthēria: Corrupt, corruption.

nemesis: Indignation.
nomisma: Legal currency; currency.

nomos: Law; custom.
nous: Intellect; intellectual grasp.

oregein: To long for.
orexis: Longing.
orgilotēs: Irascibility.

pathos (pl. *pathē*): Passion (passions); experience; that which one undergoes.
phaulos: Base; of poor quality.
philein: To love (as a friend).
philia: Friendliness, friendship.
philotimia: Ambition.
phronēsis: Prudence.
phronimos: Prudent (human being).
phusis (*physis*): Nature.
pistis: Trust or faith in something or
someone; hence also the sense of certainty that comes from such trust,
or that which prompts it: assurance,
guarantee.
pleonektēs, pleonexia: Grasping for
more.
poiēsis: Making; production; poetry,
poem.
polis: City.
politeia: Regime.
politēs: Citizen.
politikē: The political art, politics.
politikos: Politician.
ponēros, ponēria: Wicked, wickedness;
defective condition (in nonmoral contexts).
pragma (pl. *pragmata*): Matter, matter of
concern.
praotēs: Gentleness.
praxis: Action.
proairesis: Choice.
psuchē (*psychē*): Soul.

skopos: Target.
sophia: Wisdom.
sophos: Wise (human being).

sōphrosunē: Moderation.

spoudaios: Serious (human being).

stergein: To feel affection for.

technē: Art; skill.

teleios: Complete; perfect.

telos: End; goal.

theōria: Contemplation.

theos (theios): God (divine).

thrasutēs: Recklessness.

thumos (thymos): Spiritedness; spirit; heart.

timē: Honor; political office; price.

tuchē: Chance.

INDEX OF PROPER NAMES

The line numbers following the letters are keyed to the Greek text and therefore indicate only the approximate position in the translation.

GENERAL INDEX

References are to the standard Bekker page numbers in the margin of the translation. Since the line numbers following the letters are keyed to the Greek text, they indicate only the approximate position in the translation. Boldface numbers indicate books of the *Ethics*. Occasionally the demands of translation require that a word be repeated in English that does not appear in the Greek or, therefore, in the index. The number of times a given word appears in the line is indicated in parentheses.